BERNARD SHAW'S

SAINT JOAN
MAJOR BARBARA
ANDROCLES AND THE LION

BERNARD SHAW'S

Saint Joan

Major Barbara

Androcles and the Lion

THE MODERN LIBRARY · NEW YORK

CONTENTS

Saint Joan

A CHRONICLE PLAY IN SIX SCENES
AND AN EPILOGUE

PREFACE TO SAINT JOAN

JOAN THE ORIGINAL AND PRESUMPTUOUS

JOAN OF ARC, a village girl from the Vosges, was born about 1412; burnt for heresy, witchcraft, and sorcery in 1431; rehabilitated after a fashion in 1456; designated venerable in 1904; declared Blessed in 1908; and finally canonized in 1920. She is the most notable Warrior Saint in the Christian calendar, and the queerest fish among the eccentric worthies of the Middle Ages. Though a professed and most pious Catholic, and the projector of a Crusade against the Husites, she was in fact one of the first Protestant martyrs. She was also one of the first apostles of Nationalism, and the first French practitioner of Napoleonic realism in warfare as distinguished from the sporting ransom gambling chivalry of her time. She was the pioneer of rational dressing for women, and, like Queen Christina of Sweden two centuries later, to say nothing of Catalina de Erauso and innumerable obscure heroines who have disguised themselves as men to serve as soldiers and sailors, she refused to accept the specific woman's lot, and dressed and fought and lived as men did.

As she contrived to assert herself in all these ways with such force that she was famous throughout western Europe before she was out of her teens (indeed she never got out of them), it is hardly surprising that she was judicially burnt, ostensibly for a number of capital crimes which we no longer punish as such, but essentially for what we call unwomanly and insufferable presumption. At eighteen Joan's pretensions were beyond those of the proudest Pope or the haughtiest emperor. She claimed to be the ambassador and plenipotentiary of God, and to be, in effect, a member of the Church Triumphant whilst still in the flesh on earth. She patronized her own king, and summoned the

3

English king to repentance and obedience to her commands. She lectured, talked down, and overruled statesmen and prelates. She poohpoohed the plans of generals, leading their troops to victory on plans of her own. She had an unbounded and quite unconcealed contempt for official opinion, judgment, and authority, and for War Office tactics and strategy. Had she been a sage and monarch in whom the most venerable hierarchy and the most illustrious dynasty converged, her pretensions and proceedings would have been as trying to the official mind as the pretensions of Caesar were to Cassius. As her actual condition was pure upstart, there were only two opinions about her. One was that she was miraculous: the other that she was unbearable.

JOAN AND SOCRATES

If Joan had been malicious, selfish, cowardly or stupid, she would have been one of the most odious persons known to history instead of one of the most attractive. If she had been old enough to know the effect she was producing on the men whom she humiliated by being right when they were wrong, and had learned to flatter and manage them, she might have lived as long as Queen Elizabeth. But she was too young and rustical and inexperienced to have any such arts. When she was thwarted by men whom she thought fools, she made no secret of her opinion of them or her impatience with their folly; and she was naïve enough to expect them to be obliged to her for setting them right and keeping them out of mischief. Now it is always hard for superior wits to understand the fury roused by their exposures of the stupidities of comparative dullards. Even Socrates, for all his age and experience, did not defend himself at his trial like a man who understood the long accumulated fury that had burst on him, and was clamoring for his death. His accuser, if born 2300 years later, might have been picked out of any first class carriage on a suburban railway during the evening or morning rush from or to the City; for he had really nothing to say except that he and his like could not endure being shewn up as idiots every time Socrates opened his mouth. Socrates, unconscious of this, was paralyzed by his sense that somehow he was missing the point of the attack. He petered out after he had established the fact that he was an old soldier and a man of honorable life, and that his accuser was a silly snob. He had no suspicion of the extent to which his mental superiority had roused fear and hatred against him in the hearts of men towards whom he was conscious of nothing but good will and good service.

CONTRAST WITH NAPOLEON

If Socrates was as innocent as this at the age of seventy, it may be imagined how innocent Joan was at the age of seventeen. Now Socrates was a man of argument, operating slowly and peacefully on men's minds, whereas Joan was a woman of action, operating with impetuous violence on their bodies. That, no doubt, is why the contemporaries of Socrates endured him so long, and why Joan was destroyed before she was fully grown. But both of them combined terrifying ability with a frankness, personal modesty, and benevolence which made the furious dislike to which they fell victims absolutely unreasonable, and therefore inapprehensible by themselves. Napoleon, also possessed of terrifying ability, but neither frank nor disinterested, had no illusions as to the nature of his popularity. When he was asked how the world would take his death, he said it would give a gasp of relief. But it is not so easy for mental giants who neither hate nor intend to injure their fellows to realize that nevertheless their fellows hate mental giants and would like to destroy them, not only enviously because the juxtaposition of a superior wounds their vanity, but quite humbly and honestly because it frightens them. Fear will drive men to any extreme; and the fear inspired by a superior being is a mystery which cannot be reasoned away. Being immeasurable it is unbearable when there is no presumption or guarantee of its benevolence and moral responsibility: in other words, when it has no official status. The legal and conventional superiority of Herod and Pilate, and of Annas and Caiaphas, inspires fear; but the fear, being a reasonable fear of measurable and avoidable consequences which seem salutary and protective, is bearable; whilst the strange superiority of Christ and the fear it inspires elicit a shriek of Crucify Him from all who cannot divine its benevolence. Socrates has to drink the hemlock, Christ to hang on the cross, and Joan to burn at the stake, whilst Napoleon, though he ends in St Helena, at least dies in his bed there; and many terrifying but quite comprehensible official scoundrels die natural deaths in all the glory of the kingdoms of this world, proving that it is far more dangerous to be a saint than to be a conqueror. Those who have been both, like Mahomet and Joan, have found that it is the conqueror who must save the saint, and that defeat and capture mean martyrdom. Joan was burnt without a hand lifted on her own side to save her. The comrades she had led to victory and the enemies she had disgraced and defeated, the French king she had crowned and the English king whose crown she had kicked into the Loire, were equally glad to be rid of her.

WAS JOAN INNOCENT OR GUILTY?

As this result could have been produced by a crapulous inferiority as well as by a sublime superiority, the question which of the two was operative in Joan's case has to be faced. It was decided against her by her contemporaries after a very careful and conscientious trial; and the reversal of the verdict twenty-five years later, in form a rehabilitation of Joan, was really only a confirmation of the validity of the coronation of Charles VII. It is the more impressive reversal by a unanimous Posterity, culminating in her canonization, that has quashed the original proceedings, and put her judges on their trial, which, so far, has been much more unfair than their trial of her. Nevertheless the rehabilitation of 1456, corrupt job as it was, really did produce evidence enough to satisfy all reasonable critics that Joan was not a common termagant, not a harlot, not a witch, not a blasphemer, no more an idolater than the Pope himself, and not ill conducted in any sense apart from her soldiering, her wearing of men's clothes, and her audacity, but on the contrary goodhumored, an intact virgin, very pious, very temperate (we should call her meal of bread soaked in the common wine which is the drinking water of France ascetic), very kindly, and, though a brave and hardy soldier, unable to endure loose language or licentious conduct. She went to the stake without a stain on her character except the overweening presumption, the superbity as they called it, that led her thither. It would therefore be waste of time now to prove that the Joan of the first part of the Elizabethan chronicle play of Henry VI (supposed to have been tinkered by Shakespear) grossly libels her in its concluding scenes in deference to Jingo patriotism. The mud that was thrown at her has dropped off by this time so completely that there is no need for any modern writer to wash up after it. What is far more difficult to get rid of is the mud that is being thrown at her judges, and the whitewash which disfigures her beyond recognition. When Jingo scurrility had done its worst to her, sectarian scurrility (in this case Protestant scurrility) used her stake to beat the Roman Catholic Church and the Inquisition. The easiest way to make these institutions the villains of a melodrama was to make The Maid its heroine. That melodrama may be dismissed as rubbish. Joan got a far fairer trial from the Church and the Inquisition than any prisoner of her type and in her situation gets nowadays in any official secular court; and the decision was strictly according to law. And she was not a melodramatic heroine: that is, a physically beautiful lovelorn parasite on an equally beautiful hero, but a genius and a saint, about as completely the opposite of a melodramatic heroine as it is possible for a human being to be.

Let us be clear about the meaning of the terms. A genius is a person who, seeing farther and probing deeper than other people, has a different set of ethical valuations from theirs, and has

energy enough to give effect to this extra vision and its valuations in whatever manner best suits his or her specific talents.
A saint is one who having practised heroic virtues, and enjoyed
revelations or powers of the order which The Church classes
technically as supernatural, is eligible for canonization. If a historian is an Anti-Feminist, and does not believe women to be
capable of genius in the traditional masculine departments, he
will never make anything of Joan, whose genius was turned to
practical account mainly in soldiering and politics. If he is Rationalist enough to deny that saints exist, and to hold that new
ideas cannot come otherwise than by conscious ratiocination, he
will never catch Joan's likeness. Her ideal biographer must be
free from nineteenth century prejudices and biases; must understand the Middle Ages, the Roman Catholic Church, and the
Holy Roman Empire much more intimately than our Whig
historians have ever understood them; and must be capable of
throwing off sex partialities and their romance, and regarding
woman as the female of the human species, and not as a different kind of animal with specific charms and specific imbecilities.

JOAN'S GOOD LOOKS

To put the last point roughly, any book about Joan which
begins by describing her as a beauty may be at once classed as a
romance. Not one of Joan's comrades, in village, court, or camp,
even when they were straining themselves to please the king by
praising her, ever claimed that she was pretty. All the men who
alluded to the matter declared most emphatically that she was
unattractive sexually to a degree that seemed to them miraculous,
considering that she was in the bloom of youth, and neither
ugly, awkward, deformed, nor unpleasant in her person. The
evident truth is that like most women of her hardy managing
type she seemed neutral in the conflict of sex because men were
too much afraid of her to fall in love with her. She herself was
not sexless: in spite of the virginity she had vowed up to a point,
and preserved to her death, she never excluded the possibility of

marriage for herself. But marriage, with its preliminary of the attraction, pursuit, and capture of a husband, was not her business: she had something else to do. Byron's formula, "Man's love is of man's life a thing apart: 'tis woman's whole existence" did not apply to her any more than George Washington or any other masculine worker on the heroic scale. Had she lived in our time, picture postcards might have been sold of her as a general: they would not have been sold of her as a sultana. Nevertheless there is one reason for crediting her with a very remarkable face. A sculptor of her time in Orleans made a statue of a helmeted young woman with a face that is unique in art in point of being evidently not an ideal face but a portrait, and yet so uncommon as to be unlike any real woman one has ever seen. It is surmised that Joan served unconsciously as the sculptor's model. There is no proof of this; but those extraordinarily spaced eyes raise so powerfully the question "If this woman be not Joan, who is she?" that I dispense with further evidence, and challenge those who disagree with me to prove a negative. It is a wonderful face, but quite neutral from the point of view of the operatic beauty fancier.

Such a fancier may perhaps be finally chilled by the prosaic fact that Joan was the defendant in a suit for breach of promise of marriage, and that she conducted her own case and won it.

JOAN'S SOCIAL POSITION

By class Joan was the daughter of a working farmer who was one of the headmen of his village, and transacted its feudal business for it with the neighboring squires and their lawyers. When the castle in which the villagers were entitled to take refuge from raids became derelict, he organized a combination of half a dozen farmers to obtain possession of it so as to occupy it when there was any danger of invasion. As a child, Joan could please herself at times with being the young lady of this castle. Her mother and brothers were able to follow and share her fortune at court without making themselves notably ridicu-

lous. These facts leave us no excuse for the popular romance
that turns every heroine into either a princess or a beggarmaid.
In the somewhat similar case of Shakespear a whole inverted
pyramid of wasted research has been based on the assumption
that he was an illiterate laborer, in the face of the plainest evidence that his father was a man of business, and at one time a
very prosperous one, married to a woman of some social pretensions. There is the same tendency to drive Joan into the position of a hired shepherd girl, though a hired shepherd girl in
Domrémy would have deferred to her as the young lady of the
farm.

The difference between Joan's case and Shakespear's is that
Shakespear was not illiterate. He had been to school, and knew
as much Latin and Greek as most university passmen retain:
that is, for practical purposes, none at all. Joan was absolutely
illiterate. "I do not know A from B" she said. But many prin-
cesses at that time and for long after might have said the same.
Marie Antoinette, for instance, at Joan's age could not spell her
own name correctly. But this does not mean that Joan was an
ignorant person, or that she suffered from the diffidence and
sense of social disadvantage now felt by people who cannot read
or write. If she could not write letters, she could and did dictate
them and attach full and indeed excessive importance to them.
When she was called a shepherd lass to her face she very
warmly resented it, and challenged any woman to compete with
her in the household arts of the mistresses of well furnished
houses. She understood the political and military situation in
France much better than most of our newspaper fed university
women-graduates understand the corresponding situation of
their own country today. Her first convert was the neighboring
commandant at Vaucouleurs; and she converted him by telling
him about the defeat of the Dauphin's troops at the Battle of
Herrings so long before he had official news of it that he concluded she must have had a divine revelation. This knowledge
of and interest in public affairs was nothing extraordinary

among farmers in a war-swept countryside. Politicians came to the door too often sword in hand to be disregarded: Joan's people could not afford to be ignorant of what was going on in the feudal world. They were not rich; and Joan worked on the farm as her father did, driving the sheep to pasture and so forth; but there is no evidence or suggestion of sordid poverty, and no reason to believe that Joan had to work as a hired servant works, or indeed to work at all when she preferred to go to confession, or dawdle about waiting for visions and listening to the church bells to hear voices in them. In short, much more of a young lady, and even of an intellectual, than most of the daughters of our pretty bourgeoisie.

JOAN'S VOICES AND VISIONS

Joan's voices and visions have played many tricks with her reputation. They have been held to prove that she was mad, that she was a liar and impostor, that she was a sorceress (she was burned for this), and finally that she was a saint. They do not prove any of these things; but the variety of the conclusions reached shew how little our matter-of-fact historians know about other people's minds, or even about their own. There are people in the world whose imagination is so vivid that when they have an idea it comes to them as an audible voice, sometimes uttered by a visible figure. Criminal lunatic asylums are occupied largely by murderers who have obeyed voices. Thus a woman may hear voices telling her that she must cut her husband's throat and strangle her child as they lie asleep; and she may feel obliged to do what she is told. By a medico-legal superstition it is held in our courts that criminals whose temptations present themselves under these illusions are not responsible for their actions, and must be treated as insane. But the seers of visions and the hearers of revelations are not always criminals. The inspirations and intuitions and unconsciously reasoned conclusions of genius sometimes assume similar illusions. Socrates, Luther, Swedenborg, Blake saw visions and

heard voices just as Saint Francis and Saint Joan did. If Newton's imagination had been of the same vividly dramatic kind
he might have seen the ghost of Pythagoras walk into the or-
chard and explain why the apples were falling. Such an illusion
would have invalidated neither the theory of gravitation nor
Newton's general sanity. What is more, the visionary method
of making the discovery would not be a whit more miraculous
than the normal method. The test of sanity is not the normality
of the method but the reasonableness of the discovery. If Newton had been informed by Pythagoras that the moon was made
of green cheese, then Newton would have been locked up.
Gravitation, being a reasoned hypothesis which fitted remarkably well into the Copernican version of the observed physical
facts of the universe, established Newton's reputation for extraordinary intelligence, and would have done so no matter how
fantastically he had arrived at it. Yet his theory of gravitation is
not so impressive a mental feat as his astounding chronology,
which established him as the king of mental conjurors, but a
Bedlamite king whose authority no one now accepts. On the
subject of the eleventh horn of the beast seen by the prophet
Daniel he was more fantastic than Joan, because his imagination was not dramatic but mathematical and therefore extraordinarily susceptible to numbers: indeed if all his works were
lost except his chronology we should say that he was as mad as
a hatter. As it is, who dares diagnose Newton as a madman?

In the same way Joan must be judged a sane woman in spite
of her voices because they never gave her any advice that might
not have come to her from her mother wit exactly as gravitation
came to Newton. We can all see now, especially since the late
war threw so many of our women into military life, that Joan's
campaigning could not have been carried on in petticoats. This
was not only because she did a man's work, but because it was
morally necessary that sex should be left out of the question as
between her and her comrades-in-arms. She gave this reason
herself when she was pressed on the subject; and the fact that

this entirely reasonable necessity came to her imagination first as an order from God delivered through the mouth of Saint Catherine does not prove that she was mad. The soundness of the order proves that she was unusually sane; but its form proves that her dramatic imagination played tricks with her senses. Her policy was also quite sound: nobody disputes that the relief of Orleans, followed up by the coronation at Rheims of the Dauphin as a counterblow to the suspicions then current of his legitimacy and consequently of his title, were military and political masterstrokes that saved France. They might have been planned by Napoleon or any other illusionproof genius. They came to Joan as an instruction from her Counsel, as she called her visionary saints; but she was none the less an able leader of men for imagining her ideas in this way.

THE EVOLUTIONARY APPETITE

What then is the modern view of Joan's voices and visions and messages from God? The nineteenth century said that they were delusions, but that as she was a pretty girl, and had been abominably ill-treated and finally done to death by a superstitious rabble of medieval priests hounded on by a corrupt political bishop, it must be assumed that she was the innocent dupe of these delusions. The twentieth century finds this explanation too vapidly commonplace, and demands something more mystic. I think the twentieth century is right, because an explanation which amounts to Joan being mentally defective instead of, as she obviously was, mentally excessive, will not wash. I cannot believe, nor, if I could, could I expect all my readers to believe, as Joan did, that three ocularly visible well dressed persons, named respectively Saint Catherine, Saint Margaret, and Saint Michael, came down from heaven and gave her certain instructions with which they were charged by God for her. Not that such a belief would be more improbable or fantastic than some modern beliefs which we all swallow; but there are fashions and family habits in belief, and it happens that, my fashion being Victorian and my family habit Protestant, I find myself unable to attach any such objective validity to the form of Joan's visions.

But that there are forces at work which use individuals for purposes far transcending the purpose of keeping these individuals alive and prosperous and respectable and safe and happy in the middle station in life, which is all any good bourgeois can reasonably require, is established by the fact that men will, in the pursuit of knowledge and of social readjustments for which they will not be a penny the better, and are indeed often many pence the worse, face poverty, infamy, exile, imprisonment, dreadful hardship, and death. Even the selfish pursuit of personal power does not nerve men to the efforts and sacrifices which are eagerly made in pursuit of extensions of our power over nature, though these extensions may not touch the personal life of the seeker at any point. There is no more mystery about this appetite for knowledge and power than about the appetite for food: both are known as facts and as facts only, the difference between them being that the appetite for food is necessary to the life of the hungry man and is therefore a personal appetite, whereas the other is an appetite for evolution, and therefore a superpersonal need.

The diverse manners in which our imaginations dramatize the approach of the superpersonal forces is a problem for the psychologist, not for the historian. Only, the historian must understand that visionaries are neither impostors nor lunatics. It is one thing to say that the figure Joan recognized as St Catherine was not really St Catherine, but the dramatization by Joan's imagination of that pressure upon her of the driving force that is behind evolution which I have just called the evolutionary appetite. It is quite another to class her visions with the vision of two moons seen by a drunken person, or with Brocken spectres, echoes and the like. Saint Catherine's instructions were far too cogent for that; and the simplest French peasant who believes in apparitions of celestial personages to favored mortals is nearer to the scientific truth about Joan than the Rationalist and Materialist historians and essayists who feel obliged to set down a girl who saw saints and heard them talking to her as either crazy or mendacious. If Joan was mad, all Christendom was mad too; for people who believe devoutly in the existence of celestial personages are every whit as mad in that sense as the people who think they see them. Luther, when he threw his inkhorn at the devil, was no more mad than any other Augustinian monk: he had a more vivid imagination, and had perhaps eaten and slept less: that was all.

THE MERE ICONOGRAPHY DOES NOT MATTER

All the popular religions in the world are made apprehensible by an array of legendary personages, with an Almighty Father, and sometimes a mother and divine child, as the central figures. These are presented to the mind's eye in childhood; and the result is a hallucination which persists strongly throughout life when it has been well impressed. Thus all the thinking of the hallucinated adult about the fountain of inspiration which is continually flowing in the universe, or about the promptings of virtue and the revulsions of shame: in short, about aspiration and conscience, both of which forces are matters of fact more obvious than electro-magnetism, is thinking in terms of the celestial vision. And when in the case of exceptionally imaginative persons, especially those practising certain appropriate austerities, the hallucination extends from the mind's eye to the body's, the visionary sees Krishna or the Buddha or the Blessed Virgin or St Catherine as the case may be.

THE MODERN EDUCATION WHICH JOAN ESCAPED

It is important to everyone nowadays to understand this, because modern science is making short work of the hallucinations without regard to the vital importance of the things they symbolize. If Joan were reborn today she would be sent, first to a convent school in which she would be mildly taught to connect inspiration and conscience with St Catherine and St Michael exactly as she was in the fifteenth century, and then finished up with a very energetic training in the gospel of Saints Louis Pasteur and Paul Bert, who would tell her (possibly in visions but more probably in pamphlets) not to be a superstitious little fool, and to empty out St Catherine and the rest of the Catholic hagiology as an obsolete iconography of exploded myths. It would be rubbed into her that Galileo was a martyr, and his persecutors incorrigible ignoramuses, and that St Teresa's hormones had gone astray and left her incurably hyperpituitary or hyperadrenal or hysteroid or epileptoid or anything but asteroid. She would have been convinced by precept and experiment that baptism and receiving the body of her Lord were contemptible superstitions, and that vaccination and vivisection were enlightened practices. Behind her new Saints Louis and Paul there would be not only Science purifying Religion and being purified by it, but hypochondria, melancholia, cowardice, stupidity, cruelty, muckraking curiosity, knowledge without wisdom, and everything that the eternal soul in Nature loathes, instead of the virtues of which St Catherine was the figure head. As to the new rites, which would be the saner Joan? the one who carried little children to be baptized of water and the spirit, or the one who sent the police to force their parents to have the most villainous racial poison we know thrust into their veins? the one who told them the story of the angel and Mary, or the one who questioned them as to their experiences of the Edipus complex? the one to whom the consecrated wafer was the very body of the virtue that was her salvation, or the one who looked forward to a precise and convenient regulation of her health and her desires by a nicely calculated diet of thyroid extract, adrenalin, thymin, pituitrin, and insulin, with pick-me-ups of hormone stimulants, the blood being first carefully fortified with antibodies against all possible infections by inoculations of infected bacteria and serum from infected animals, and against old age by surgical extirpation of the reproductive ducts or weekly doses of monkey gland?

It is true that behind all these quackeries there is a certain body of genuine scientific physiology. But was there any the less a certain body of genuine psychology behind St Catherine and the Holy Ghost? And which is the healthier mind? the saintly mind or the monkey gland mind? Does not the present cry of Back to the Middle Ages, which has been incubating ever since the pre-Raphaelite movement began, mean that it is no longer our Academy pictures that are intolerable, but our credulities that have not the excuse of being superstitions, our cruelties that have not the excuse of barbarism, our persecutions that have not the excuse of religious faith, our shameless substitution of successful swindlers and scoundrels and quacks for saints as objects of worship, and our deafness and blindness to the calls and visions of the inexorable power that made us, and will destroy us if we disregard it? To Joan and her contemporaries we should appear as a drove of Gadarene swine, possessed by all the unclean spirits cast out by the faith and civilization of the Middle Ages, running violently down a steep place into a hell of high explosives. For us to set up our condition as a standard of sanity, and declare Joan mad because she never condescended to it, is to prove that we are not only lost but irredeemable. Let us then once for all drop all nonsense about Joan being cracked, and accept her as at least as sane as Florence Nightingale, who also combined a very simple iconography of religious belief with a mind so exceptionally powerful that it kept her in continual trouble with the medical and military panjandrums of her time.

FAILURES OF THE VOICES

That the voices and visions were illusory, and their wisdom all Joan's own, is shewn by the occasions on which they failed her, notably during her trial, when they assured her that she would be rescued. Here her hopes flattered her; but they were not unreasonable: her military colleague La Hire was in command of a considerable force not so very far off; and if the Armagnacs, as her party was called, had really wanted to rescue her, and had put anything like her own vigor into the enterprise, they could have attempted it with very fair chances of success. She did not understand that they were glad to be rid of her, nor that the rescue of a prisoner from the hands of the Church was a much more serious business for a medieval captain, or even a medieval king, than its mere physical difficulty as a military exploit suggested. According to her lights her expectation of a rescue was reasonable; therefore she heard Madame Saint Catherine assuring her it would happen, that being her way of finding out and making up her own mind. When it became evident that she had miscalculated: when she was led to the stake, and La Hire was not thundering at the gates of Rouen nor charging Warwick's men at arms, she threw over Saint Catherine at once, and recanted. Nothing could be more sane or practical. It was not until she discovered that she had gained nothing by her recantation but close imprisonment for life that she withdrew it, and deliberately and explicitly chose burning instead: a decision which shewed not only the extraordinary decision of her character, but also a Rationalism carried to its ultimate human test of suicide. Yet even in this the illusion persisted; and she announced her relapse as dictated to her by her voices.

JOAN A GALTONIC VISUALIZER

The most sceptical scientific reader may therefore accept as a flat fact, carrying no implication of unsoundness of mind, that Joan was what Francis Galton and other modern investigators of human faculty call a visualizer. She saw imaginary saints just as some other people see imaginary diagrams and landscapes with numbers dotted about them, and are thereby able to perform feats of memory and arithmetic impossible to non-visualizers. Visualizers will understand this at once. Non-visualizers who have never read Galton will be puzzled and incredulous. But a very little inquiry among their acquaintances will reveal to them that the mind's eye is more or less a magic lantern, and that the street is full of normally sane people who have hallucinations of all sorts which they believe to be part of the normal permanent equipment of all human beings.

JOAN'S MANLINESS AND MILITARISM

Joan's other abnormality, too common among uncommon things to be properly called a peculiarity, was her craze for soldiering and the masculine life. Her father tried to frighten her out of it by threatening to drown her if she ran away with the soldiers, and ordering her brothers to drown her if he were not on the spot. This extravagance was clearly not serious: it must have been addressed to a child young enough to imagine that he was in earnest. Joan must therefore as a child have wanted to run away and be a soldier. The awful prospect of being thrown into the Meuse and drowned by a terrible father and her big brothers kept her quiet until the father had lost his terrors and the brothers yielded to her natural leadership; and by that time she had sense enough to know that the masculine and military life was not a mere matter of running away from home. But the taste for it never left her, and was fundamental in determining her career.

If anyone doubts this, let him ask himself why a maid charged with a special mission from heaven to the Dauphin (this was how Joan saw her very able plan for retrieving the desperate situation of the uncrowned king) should not have simply gone to the court as a maid, in woman's dress, and urged her counsel upon him in a woman's way, as other women with similar missions had come to his mad father and his wise grandfather. Why did she insist on having a soldier's dress and arms and sword and horse and equipment, and on treating her escort of soldiers as comrades, sleeping side by side with them

on the floor at night as if there were no difference of sex between them? It may be answered that this was the safest way of
travelling through a country infested with hostile troops and
bands of marauding deserters from both sides. Such an answer
has no weight because it applies to all women who travelled in
France at that time, and who never dreamt of travelling otherwise than as women. But even if we accept it, how does it account for the fact that when the danger was over, and she could
present herself at court in feminine attire with perfect safety
and obviously with greater propriety, she presented herself in
her man's dress, and instead of urging Charles, like Queen Victoria urging the War Office to send Roberts to the Transvaal,
to send D'Alençon, De Rais, La Hire and the rest to the relief
of Dunois at Orleans, insisted that she must go herself and lead
the assault in person? Why did she give exhibitions of her dex-
terity in handling a lance, and of her seat as a rider? Why did
she accept presents of armor and chargers and masculine sur-
coats, and in every action repudiate the conventional character
of a woman? The simple answer to all these questions is that
she was the sort of woman that wants to lead a man's life. They
are to be found wherever there are armies on foot or navies on
the seas, serving in male disguise, eluding detection for aston-
ishingly long periods, and sometimes, no doubt, escaping it
entirely. When they are in a position to defy public opinion
they throw off all concealment. You have your Rosa Bonheur
painting in male blouse and trousers, and George Sand living a
man's life and almost compelling her Chopins and De Mussets
to live women's lives to amuse her. Had Joan not been one of
those "unwomanly women," she might have been canonized
much sooner.

But it is not necessary to wear trousers and smoke big cigars
to live a man's life any more than it is necessary to wear petticoats to live a woman's. There are plenty of gowned and bod-
iced women in ordinary civil life who manage their own affairs
and other people's, including those of their menfolk, and are

entirely masculine in their tastes and pursuits. There always were such women, even in the Victorian days when women had fewer legal rights than men, and our modern women magistrates, mayors, and members of Parliament were unknown. In reactionary Russia in our own century a woman soldier organized an effective regiment of amazons, which disappeared only because it was Aldershottian enough to be against the Revolution. The exemption of women from military service is founded, not on any natural inaptitude that men do not share, but on the fact that communities cannot reproduce themselves without plenty of women. Men are more largely dispensable, and are sacrificed accordingly.

WAS JOAN SUICIDAL?

These two abnormalities were the only ones that were irresistibly prepotent in Joan; and they brought her to the stake. Neither of them was peculiar to her. There was nothing peculiar about her except the vigor and scope of her mind and character, and the intensity of her vital energy. She was accused of a suicidal tendency; and it is a fact that when she attempted to escape from Beaurevoir Castle by jumping from a tower said to be sixty feet high, she took a risk beyond reason, though she recovered from the crash after a few days fasting. Her death was deliberately chosen as an alternative to life without liberty. In battle she challenged death as Wellington did at Waterloo, and as Nelson habitually did when he walked his quarter deck during his battles with all his decorations in full blaze. As neither Nelson nor Wellington nor any of those who have performed desperate feats, and preferred death to captivity, has been accused of suicidal mania, Joan need not be suspected of it. In the Beaurevoir affair there was more at stake than her freedom. She was distracted by the news that Compiègne was about to fall; and she was convinced that she could save it if only she could get free. Still, the leap was so perilous that her conscience was not quite easy about it; and she expressed this, as usual, by saying that Saint Catherine had forbidden her to do it, but forgave her afterwards for her disobedience.

JOAN SUMMED UP

We may accept and admire Joan, then, as a sane and shrewd country girl of extraordinary strength of mind and hardihood of body. Everything she did was thoroughly calculated; and though the process was so rapid that she was hardly conscious of it, and ascribed it all to her voices, she was a woman of policy and not of blind impulse. In war she was as much a realist as Napoleon: she had his eye for artillery and his knowledge of what it could do. She did not expect besieged cities to fall Jerichowise at the sound of her trumpet, but, like Wellington, adapted her methods of attack to the peculiarities of the defence; and she anticipated the Napoleonic calculation that if you only hold on long enough the other fellow will give in: for example, her final triumph at Orleans was achieved after her commander Dunois had sounded the retreat at the end of a day's fighting without a decision. She was never for a moment what so many romancers and playwrights have pretended: a romantic young lady. She was a thorough daughter of the soil in her peasantlike matter-of-factness and doggedness, and her acceptance of great lords and kings and prelates as such without idolatry or snobbery, seeing at a glance how much they were individually good for. She had the respectable countrywoman's sense of the value of public decency, and would not tolerate foul language and neglect of religious observances, nor allow disreputable women to hang about her soldiers. She had one pious ejaculation "En nom Dé!" and one meaningless oath "Par mon martin"; and this much swearing she allowed to the incorrigibly blasphemous La Hire equally with herself. The value of this prudery was so great in restoring the self-respect of the badly demoralized army that, like most of her policy, it justified itself as soundly calculated. She talked to and dealt with people of all classes, from laborers to kings, without embarrassment or affectation, and got them to do what she wanted when they were not afraid or corrupt. She could coax and she could hustle, her tongue having a soft side and a sharp edge. She was very capable: a born boss.

JOAN'S IMMATURITY AND IGNORANCE

All this, however, must be taken with one heavy qualification. She was only a girl in her teens. If we could think of her as a managing woman of fifty we should seize her type at once; for we have plenty of managing women among us of that age who illustrate perfectly the sort of person she would have become had she lived. But she, being only a lass when all is said, lacked their knowledge of men's vanities and of the weight and proportion of social forces. She knew nothing of iron hands in velvet gloves: she just used her fists. She thought political changes much easier than they are, and, like Mahomet in his innocence of any world but the tribal world, wrote letters to kings calling on them to make millennial rearrangements. Consequently it was only in the enterprises that were really simple and compassable by swift physical force, like the coronation and the Orleans campaign, that she was successful.

Her want of academic education disabled her when she had to deal with such elaborately artificial structures as the great ecclesiastical and social institutions of the Middle Ages. She had a horror of heretics without suspecting that she was herself a heresiarch, one of the precursors of a schism that rent Europe in two, and cost centuries of bloodshed that is not yet staunched. She objected to foreigners on the sensible ground that they were not in their proper place in France; but she had no notion of how this brought her into conflict with Catholicism and Feudalism, both essentially international. She worked by commonsense; and where scholarship was the only clue to institutions she was in the dark, and broke her shins against them, all the more rudely because of her enormous self-confidence, which made her the least cautious of human beings in civil affairs.

This combination of inept youth and academic ignorance with great natural capacity, push, courage, devotion, originality and oddity, fully accounts for all the facts in Joan's career, and makes her a credible historical and human phenomenon; but it clashes most discordantly both with the idolatrous romance that has grown up round her, and the belittling scepticism that reacts against that romance.

THE MAID IN LITERATURE

English readers would probably like to know how these idolizations and reactions have affected the books they are most familiar with about Joan. There is the first part of the Shakespearean, or pseudo-Shakespearean trilogy of Henry VI, in which Joan is one of the leading characters. This portrait of Joan is not more authentic than the descriptions in the London papers of George Washington in 1780, of Napoleon in 1803, of the German Crown Prince in 1915, or of Lenin in 1917. It ends in mere scurrility. The impression left by it is that the playwright, having begun by an attempt to make Joan a beautiful and romantic figure, was told by his scandalized company that English patriotism would never stand a sympathetic representation of a French conqueror of English troops, and that unless he at once introduced all the old charges against Joan of being a sorceress and a harlot, and assumed her to be guilty of all of them, his play could not be produced. As likely as not, this is what actually happened: indeed there is only one other apparent way of accounting for the sympathetic representation of Joan as a heroine culminating in her eloquent appeal to the Duke of Burgundy, followed by the blackguardly scurrility of the concluding scenes. That other way is to assume that the original play was wholly scurrilous, and that Shakespear touched up the earlier scenes. As the work belongs to a period at which he was only beginning his practice as a tinker of old works, before his own style was fully formed and hardened, it is impossible to verify this guess. His finger is not unmistakably evident in the play, which is poor and base in its moral tone; but he may have tried to redeem it from downright infamy by shedding a momentary glamor on the figure of The Maid.

When we jump over two centuries to Schiller, we find Die Jungfrau von Orleans drowned in a witch's caldron of raging romance. Schiller's Joan has not a single point of contact with the real Joan, nor indeed with any mortal woman that ever walked this earth. There is really nothing to be said of his play but that it is not about Joan at all, and can hardly be said to pretend to be; for he makes her die on the battlefield, finding her burning unbearable. Before Schiller came Voltaire, who burlesqued Homer in a mock epic called La Pucelle. It is the fashion to dismiss this with virtuous indignation as an obscene libel; and I certainly cannot defend it against the charge of extravagant indecorum. But its purpose was not to depict Joan, but to kill with ridicule everything that Voltaire righteously hated in the institutions and fashions of his own day. He made Joan ridiculous, but not contemptible nor (comparatively) unchaste; and as he also made Homer and St Peter and St Denis and the brave Dunois ridiculous, and the other heroines of the poem very unchaste indeed, he may be said to have let Joan off very easily. But indeed the personal adventures of the characters are so outrageous, and so Homerically free from any pretence at or even possibility of historical veracity, that those who affect to take them seriously only make themselves Pecksniffian. Samuel Butler believed The Iliad to be a burlesque of Greek Jingoism and Greek religion, written by a hostage or a slave; and La Pucelle makes Butler's theory almost convincing. Voltaire represents Agnes Sorel, the Dauphin's mistress, whom Joan never met, as a woman with a consuming passion for the chastest concubinal fidelity, whose fate it was to be continually falling into the hands of licentious foes and suffering the worst extremities of rapine. The combats in which Joan rides a flying donkey, or in which, taken unaware with no clothes on, she defends Agnes with her sword, and inflicts appropriate mutilations on her assailants, can be laughed at as they are intended to be without scruple; for no sane person could mistake them for sober history; and it may be that their ribald irreverence is more wholesome than the beglamored sentimentality of Schiller. Certainly Voltaire should not have asserted that Joan's father was a priest; but when he was out to *écraser l'infâme* (the French Church) he stuck at nothing.

So far, the literary representations of The Maid were legendary. But the publication by Quicherat in 1841 of the reports of her trial and rehabilitation placed the subject on a new footing. These entirely realistic documents created a living interest in Joan which Voltaire's mock Homerics and Schiller's romantic nonsense missed. Typical products of that interest in America and England are the histories of Joan by Mark Twain and Andrew Lang. Mark Twain was converted to downright worship of Joan directly by Quicherat. Later on, another man of genius, Anatole France, reacted against the Quicheratic wave of enthusiasm, and wrote a Life of Joan in which he attributed Joan's ideas to clerical prompting and her military success to an adroit use of her by Dunois as a *mascotte:* in short, he denied that she had any serious military or political ability. At this Andrew saw red, and went for Anatole's scalp in a rival Life of her which should be read as a corrective to the other. Lang had no difficulty in shewing that Joan's ability was not an unnatural fiction to be explained away as an illusion manufactured by priests and soldiers, but a straightforward fact.

It has been lightly pleaded in explanation that Anatole France is a Parisian of the art world, into whose scheme of things the able, hardheaded, hardhanded female, though she dominates provincial France and business Paris, does not enter; whereas Lang was a Scot, and every Scot knows that the grey mare is as likely as not to be the better horse. But this explanation does not convince me. I cannot believe that Anatole France does not know what everybody knows. I wish everybody knew all that he knows. One feels antipathies at work in his book. He

is not anti-Joan; but he is anti-clerical, anti-mystic, and fundamentally unable to believe that there ever was any such person
as the real Joan.

Mark Twain's Joan, skirted to the ground, and with as many
petticoats as Noah's wife in a toy ark, is an attempt to combine
Bayard with Esther Summerson from Bleak House into an un-
impeachable American school teacher in armor. Like Esther
Summerson she makes her creator ridiculous, and yet, being the
work of a man of genius, remains a credible human goodygoody
in spite of her creator's infatuation. It is the description rather
than the valuation that is wrong. Andrew Lang and Mark
Twain are equally determined to make Joan a beautiful and
most ladylike Victorian; but both of them recognize and insist
on her capacity for leadership, though the Scots scholar is less
romantic about it than the Mississippi pilot. But then Lang was,
by lifelong professional habit, a critic of biographies rather than
a biographer, whereas Mark Twain writes his biography frankly
in the form of a romance.

PROTESTANT MISUNDERSTANDINGS OF THE MIDDLE AGES

They had, however, one disability in common. To understand Joan's history it is not enough to understand her character:
you must understand her environment as well. Joan in a nine-
teenth-twentieth century environment is as incongruous a figure
as she would appear were she to walk down Piccadilly today in
her fifteenth century armor. To see her in her proper perspective
you must understand Christendom and the Catholic Church,
the Holy Roman Empire and the Feudal System, as they existed
and were understood in the Middle Ages. If you confuse the
Middle Ages with the Dark Ages, and are in the habit of ridiculing your aunt for wearing "medieval clothes," meaning those
in vogue in the eighteen-nineties, and are quite convinced that
the world has progressed enormously, both morally and mechan-
ically, since Joan's time, then you will never understand why

Joan was burnt, much less feel that you might have voted for
burning her yourself if you had been a member of the court
that tried her; and until you feel that you know nothing essential about her.

That the Mississippi pilot should have broken down on this
misunderstanding is natural enough. Mark Twain, the Innocent Abroad, who saw the lovely churches of the Middle Ages
without a throb of emotion, author of A Yankee at the Court
of King Arthur, in which the heroes and heroines of medieval
chivalry are guys seen through the eyes of a street arab, was
clearly out of court from the beginning. Andrew Lang was
better read; but, like Walter Scott, he enjoyed medieval history
as a string of Border romances rather than as the record of a high
European civilization based on a catholic faith. Both of them
were baptized as Protestants, and impressed by all their schooling and most of their reading with the belief that Catholic
bishops who burnt heretics were persecutors capable of any villainy; that all heretics were Albigensians or Husites or Jews or
Protestants of the highest character; and that the Inquisition was
a Chamber of Horrors invented expressly and exclusively for
such burnings. Accordingly we find them representing Peter
Cauchon, Bishop of Beauvais, the judge who sent Joan to the
stake, as an unconscionable scoundrel, and all the questions put
to her as "traps" to ensnare and destroy her. And they assume
unhesitatingly that the two or three score of canons and doctors
of law and divinity who sat with Cauchon as assessors, were
exact reproductions of him on slightly less elevated chairs and
with a different headdress.

COMPARATIVE FAIRNESS OF JOAN'S TRIAL

The truth is that Cauchon was threatened and insulted by
the English for being too considerate to Joan. A recent French
writer denies that Joan was burnt, and holds that Cauchon
spirited her away and burnt somebody or something else in her
place, and that the pretender who subsequently personated her

at Orleans and elsewhere was not a pretender but the real authentic Joan. He is able to cite Cauchon's pro-Joan partiality in
support of his view. As to the assessors, the objection to them is
not that they were a row of uniform rascals, but that they were
political partisans of Joan's enemies. This is a valid objection to
all such trials; but in the absence of neutral tribunals they are
unavoidable. A trial by Joan's French partisans would have been
as unfair as the trial by her French opponents; and an equally
mixed tribunal would have produced a deadlock. Such recent
trials as those of Edith Cavell by a German tribunal and Roger
Casement by an English one were open to the same objection;
but they went forward to the death nevertheless, because neutral tribunals were not available. Edith, like Joan, was an arch
heretic: in the middle of the war she declared before the world
that "Patriotism is not enough." She nursed enemies back to
health, and assisted their prisoners to escape, making it abundantly clear that she would help any fugitive or distressed person
without asking whose side he was on, and acknowledging no
distinction before Christ between Tommy and Jerry and Pitou
the *poilu*. Well might Edith have wished that she could bring
the Middle Ages back, and have fifty civilians, learned in the
law or vowed to the service of God, to support two skilled judges
in trying her case according to the Catholic law of Christendom,
and to argue it out with her at sitting after sitting for many
weeks. The modern military Inquisition was not so squeamish.
It shot her out of hand; and her countrymen, seeing in this a
good opportunity for lecturing the enemy on his intolerance,
put up a statue to her, but took particular care not to inscribe on
the pedestal "Patriotism is not enough," for which omission, and
the lie it implies, they will need Edith's intercession when they
are themselves brought to judgment, if any heavenly power
thinks such moral cowards capable of pleading to an intelligible
indictment.

The point need be no further labored. Joan was persecuted
essentially as she would be persecuted today. The change from

burning to hanging or shooting may strike us as a change for
the better. The change from careful trial under ordinary law to
recklessly summary military terrorism may strike us a change for
the worse. But as far as toleration is concerned the trial and
execution in Rouen in 1431 might have been an event of today;
and we may charge our consciences accordingly. If Joan had to
be dealt with by us in London she would be treated with no
more toleration than Miss Sylvia Pankhurst, or the Peculiar People, or the parents who keep their children from the elemen-
tary school, or any of the others who cross the line we have to
draw, rightly or wrongly, between the tolerable and the intolerable.

JOAN NOT TRIED AS A POLITICAL OFFENDER

Besides, Joan's trial was not, like Casement's, a national political trial. Ecclesiastical courts and the courts of the Inquisition
(Joan was tried by a combination of the two) were Courts
Christian: that is, international courts; and she was tried, not as
a traitress, but as a heretic, blasphemer, sorceress and idolater.
Her alleged offences were not political offences against England,
nor against the Burgundian faction in France, but against God
and against the common morality of Christendom. And although the idea we call Nationalism was so foreign to the medieval conception of Christian society that it might almost have
been directly charged against Joan as an additional heresy, yet
it was not so charged; and it is unreasonable to suppose that the
political bias of a body of Frenchmen like the assessors would
on this point have run strongly in favor of the English foreigners
(even if they had been making themselves particularly agreeable in France instead of just the contrary) against a French-
woman who had vanquished them.

The tragic part of the trial was that Joan, like most prisoners
tried for anything but the simplest breaches of the ten commandments, did not understand what they were accusing her of. She
was much more like Mark Twain than like Peter Cauchon

Her attachment to the Church was very different from the Bishop's, and does not, in fact, bear close examination from his point of view. She delighted in the solaces the Church offers to sensitive souls: to her, confession and communion were luxuries beside which the vulgar pleasures of the senses were trash. Her prayers were wonderful conversations with her three saints. Her piety seemed superhuman to the formally dutiful people whose religion was only a task to them. But when the Church was not offering her her favorite luxuries, but calling on her to accept its interpretation of God's will, and to sacrifice her own, she flatly refused, and made it clear that her notion of a Catholic Church was one in which the Pope was Pope Joan. How could the Church tolerate that, when it had just destroyed Hus, and had watched the career of Wycliffe with a growing anger that would have brought him, too, to the stake, had he not died a natural death before the wrath fell on him in his grave? Neither Hus nor Wycliffe was as bluntly defiant as Joan: both were reformers of the Church like Luther; whilst Joan, like Mrs Eddy, was quite prepared to supersede St Peter as the rock on which the Church was built, and, like Mahomet, was always ready with a private revelation from God to settle every question and fit every occasion.

The enormity of Joan's pretension was proved by her own unconsciousness of it, which we call her innocence, and her friends called her simplicity. Her solutions of the problems presented to her seemed, and indeed mostly were, the plainest commonsense, and their revelation to her by her Voices was to her a simple matter of fact. How could plain commonsense and simple fact seem to her to be that hideous thing, heresy? When rival prophetesses came into the field, she was down on them at once for liars and humbugs; but she never thought of them as heretics. She was in a state of invincible ignorance as to the Church's view; and the Church could not tolerate her pretensions without either waiving its authority or giving her a place beside the Trinity during her lifetime and in her teens, which was un-

thinkable. Thus an irresistible force met an immovable obstacle, and developed the heat that consumed poor Joan.

Mark and Andrew would have shared her innocence and
her fate had they been dealt with by the Inquisition: that is
why their accounts of the trial are as absurd as hers might have
been could she have written one. All that can be said for their
assumption that Cauchon was a vulgar villain, and that the
questions put to Joan were traps, is that it has the support of the
inquiry which rehabilitated her twentyfive years later. But this
rehabilitation was as corrupt as the contrary proceeding applied
to Cromwell by our Restoration reactionaries. Cauchon had
been dug up, and his body thrown into the common sewer.
Nothing was easier than to accuse him of cozenage, and declare
the whole trial void on that account. That was what everybody
wanted, from Charles the Victorious, whose credit was bound
up with The Maid's, to the patriotic Nationalist populace, who
idolized Joan's memory. The English were gone; and a verdict
in their favor would have been an outrage on the throne and
on the patriotism which Joan had set on foot.

We have none of these overwhelming motives of political
convenience and popularity to bias us. For us the first trial stands
valid and the rehabilitation would be negligible but for the
mass of sincere testimony it produced as to Joan's engaging personal character. The question then arises: how did The Church
get over the verdict at the first trial when it canonized Joan five
hundred years later?

THE CHURCH UNCOMPROMISED BY ITS AMENDS

Easily enough. In the Catholic Church, far more than in
law, there is no wrong without a remedy. It does not defer to
Joanesque private judgment as such, the supremacy of private
judgment for the individual being the quintessence of Protestantism; nevertheless it finds a place for private judgment *in
excelsis* by admitting that the highest wisdom may come as a

divine revelation to an individual. On sufficient evidence it will declare that individual a saint. Thus, as revelation may come by way of an enlightenment of the private judgment no less than by the words of a celestial personage appearing in a vision, a saint may be defined as a person of heroic virtue whose private judgment is privileged. Many innovating saints, notably Francis and Clare, have been in conflict with the Church during their lives, and have thus raised the question whether they were heretics or saints. Francis might have gone to the stake had he lived longer. It is therefore by no means impossible for a person to be excommunicated as a heretic, and on further consideration canonized as a saint. Excommunication by a provincial ecclesiastical court is not one of the acts for which the Church claims infallibility. Perhaps I had better inform my Protestant readers that the famous Dogma of Papal Infallibility is by far the most modest pretension of the kind in existence. Compared with our infallible democracies, our infallible medical councils, our infallible astronomers, our infallible judges, and our infallible parliaments, the Pope is on his knees in the dust confessing his ignorance before the throne of God, asking only that as to certain historical matters on which he has clearly more sources of information open to him than anyone else his decision shall be taken as final. The Church may, and perhaps some day will, canonize Galileo without compromising such infallibility as it claims for the Pope, if not without compromising the infallibility claimed for the Book of Joshua by simple souls whose rational faith in more important things has become bound up with a quite irrational faith in the chronicle of Joshua's campaigns as a treatise on physics. Therefore the Church will probably not canonize Galileo yet awhile, though it might do worse. But it has been able to canonize Joan without any compromise at all. She never doubted that the sun went round the earth: she had seen it do so too often.

Still, there was a great wrong done to Joan and to the conscience of the world by her burning. *Tout comprendre, c'est*

tout pardonner, which is the Devil's sentimentality, cannot excuse it. When we have admitted that the tribunal was not only
honest and legal, but exceptionally merciful in respect of sparing Joan the torture which was customary when she was obdurate as to taking the oath, and that Cauchon was far more
self-disciplined and conscientious both as priest and lawyer than
any English judge ever dreams of being in a political case in
which his party and class prejudices are involved, the human
fact remains that the burning of Joan of Arc was a horror, and
that a historian who would defend it would defend anything.
The final criticism of its physical side is implied in the refusal
of the Marquesas islanders to be persuaded that the English did
not eat Joan. Why, they ask, should anyone take the trouble to
roast a human being except with that object? They cannot conceive its being a pleasure. As we have no answer for them that
is not shameful to us, let us blush for our more complicated and
pretentious savagery before we proceed to unravel the business
further, and see what other lessons it contains for us.

CRUELTY, MODERN AND MEDIEVAL

First, let us get rid of the notion that the mere physical cruelty of the burning has any special significance. Joan was burnt
just as dozens of less interesting heretics were burnt in her time.
Christ, in being crucified, only shared the fate of thousands of
forgotten malefactors. They have no pre-eminence in mere
physical pain: much more horrible executions than theirs are on
record, to say nothing of the agonies of so-called natural death
as its worst.

Joan was burnt more than five hundred years ago. More than
three hundred years later: that is, only about a hundred years
before I was born, a woman was burnt on Stephen's Green in
my native city of Dublin for coining, which was held to be
treason. In my preface to the recent volume on English Prisons
under Local Government, by Sidney and Beatrice Webb, I
have mentioned that when I was already a grown man I saw

Richard Wagner conduct two concerts, and that when Richard
Wagner was a young man he saw and avoided a crowd of people hastening to see a soldier broken on the wheel by the more
cruel of the two ways of carrying out that hideous method of
execution. Also that the penalty of hanging, drawing, and quar-
tering, unmentionable in its details, was abolished so recently
that there are men living who have been sentenced to it. We
are still flogging criminals, and clamoring for more flogging. Not
even the most sensationally frightful of these atrocities inflicted
on its victim the misery, degradation, and conscious waste and
loss of life suffered in our modern prisons, especially the model
ones, without, as far as I can see, rousing any more compunction
than the burning of heretics did in the Middle Ages. We have
not even the excuse of getting some fun out of our prisons as
the Middle Ages did out of their stakes and wheels and gibbets.
Joan herself judged this matter when she had to choose between
imprisonment and the stake, and chose the stake. And thereby
she deprived The Church of the plea that it was guiltless of her
death, which was the work of the secular arm. The Church
should have confined itself to excommunicating her. There it
was within its rights: she had refused to accept its authority or
comply with its conditions; and it could say with truth "You
are not one of us: go forth and find the religion that suits you,
or found one for yourself." It had no right to say "You may return to us now that you have recanted; but you shall stay in a
dungeon all the rest of your life." Unfortunately, The Church
did not believe that there was any genuine soul saving religion
outside itself; and it was deeply corrupted, as all the Churches
were and still are, by primitive Calibanism (in Browning's
sense), or the propitiation of a dreaded deity by suffering and
sacrifice. Its method was not cruelty for cruelty's sake, but cruelty for the salvation of Joan's soul. Joan, however, believed that
the saving of her soul was her own business, and not that of *les
gens d'église*. By using that term as she did, mistrustfully and
contemptuously, she announced herself as, in germ, an anti-

Clerical as thoroughgoing as Voltaire or Anatole France. Had she said in so many words "To the dustbin with the Church Militant and its blackcoated officials: I recognize only the Church Triumphant in heaven," she would hardly have put her view more plainly.

CATHOLIC ANTI-CLERICALISM

I must not leave it to be inferred here that one cannot be an anti-Clerical and a good Catholic too. All the reforming Popes have been vehement anti-Clericals, veritable scourges of the clergy. All the great Orders arose from dissatisfaction with the priests: that of the Franciscans with priestly snobbery, that of the Dominicans with priestly laziness and Laodiceanism, that of the Jesuits with priestly apathy and ignorance and indiscipline. The most bigoted Ulster Orangeman or Leicester Low Church bourgeois (as described by Mr Henry Nevinson) is a mere Gallio compared to Machiavelli, who, though no Protestant, was a fierce anti-Clerical. Any Catholic may, and many Catholics do, denounce any priest or body of priests, as lazy, drunken, idle, dissolute, and unworthy of their great Church and their function as the pastors of their flocks of human souls. But to say that the souls of the people are no business of the Churchmen is to go a step further, a step across the Rubicon. Joan virtually took that step.

CATHOLICISM NOT YET CATHOLIC
ENOUGH

And so, if we admit, as we must, that the burning of Joan was a mistake, we must broaden Catholicism sufficiently to include her in its charter. Our Churches must admit that no official organization of mortal men whose vocation does not carry with it extraordinary mental powers (and this is all that any Church Militant can in the face of fact and history pretend to be), can keep pace with the private judgment of persons of genius except when, by a very rare accident, the genius happens to be Pope, and not even then unless he is an exceedingly overbearing Pope. The Churches must learn humility as well as teach it. The Apostolic Succession cannot be secured or confined by the laying on of hands: the tongues of fire have descended on heathens and outcasts too often for that, leaving anointed Churchmen to scandalize History as worldly rascals. When the Church Militant behaves as if it were already the Church Triumphant, it makes these appalling blunders about Joan and Bruno and Galileo and the rest which make it so difficult for a Freethinker to join it; and a Church which has no place for Freethinkers: nay, which does not inculcate and encourage freethinking with a complete belief that thought, when really free, must by its own law take the path that leads to The Church's bosom, not only has no future in modern culture, but obviously has no faith in the valid science of its own tenets, and is guilty of the heresy that theology and science are two different and opposite impulses, rivals for human allegiance.

I have before me the letter of a Catholic priest. "In your play," he writes, "I see the dramatic presentation of the conflict of the Regal, sacerdotal, and Prophetical powers, in which Joan was crushed. To me it is not the victory of any one of them over the others that will bring peace and the Reign of the Saints in the Kingdom of God, but their fruitful interaction in a costly but noble state of tension." The Pope himself could not put it better; nor can I. We must accept the tension, and maintain it nobly without letting ourselves be tempted to relieve it by burning the thread. This is Joan's lesson to The Church; and its formulation by the hand of a priest emboldens me to claim that her canonization was a magnificently Catholic gesture as the canonization of a Protestant saint by the Church of Rome. But its special value and virtue cannot be apparent until it is known and understood as such. If any simple priest for whom this is too hard a saying tells me that it was not so intended, I shall remind him that the Church is in the hands of God, and not, as simple priests imagine, God in the hands of the Church; so if he answers too confidently for God's intentions he may be asked "Hast thou entered into the springs of the sea? or hast thou walked in the recesses of the deep?" And Joan's own answer is also the answer of old: "Though He slay me, yet will I trust in Him; *but I will maintain my own ways before Him.*"

THE LAW OF CHANGE IS
THE LAW OF GOD

When Joan maintained her own ways she claimed, like Job, that there was not only God and the Church to be considered, but the Word made Flesh: that is, the unaveraged individual, representing life possibly at its highest actual human evolution and possibly at its lowest, but never at its merely mathematical average. Now there is no deification of the democratic average in the theory of the Church: it is an avowed hierarchy in which the members are sifted until at the end of the process an individual stands supreme as the Vicar of Christ. But when the process is examined it appears that its successive steps of selection and election are of the superior by the inferior (the cardinal vice of democracy), with the result that great popes are as rare and accidental as great kings, and that it has sometimes been safer for an aspirant to the Chair and the Keys to pass as a moribund dotard than as an energetic saint. At best very few popes have been canonized, or could be without letting down the standard of sanctity set by the self-elected saints.

No other result could have been reasonably expected; for it is not possible that an official organization of the spiritual needs of millions of men and women, mostly poor and ignorant, should compete successfully in the selection of its principals with the direct choice of the Holy Ghost as it flashes with unerring aim upon the individual. Nor can any College of Cardinals pray effectively that its choice may be inspired. The conscious prayer of the inferior may be that his choice may light on a greater than himself; but the sub-conscious intention of his self-preserving individuality must be to find a trustworthy servant for his own purposes. The saints and prophets, though they may be accidentally in this or that official position or rank, are always really self-selected, like Joan. And since neither Church nor State, by the secular necessities of its constitution, can guarantee even the recognition of such self-chosen missions, there is nothing for us but to make it a point of honour to privilege heresy to the last bearable degree on the simple ground that all evolution in thought and conduct must at first appear as heresy and misconduct. In short, though all society is founded on intolerance, all improvement is founded on tolerance, or the recognition of the fact that the law of evolution is Ibsen's law of change. And as the law of God in any sense of the word which can now command a faith proof against science is a law of evolution, it follows that the law of God is a law of change, and that when the Churches set themselves against change as such, they are setting themselves against the law of God.

CREDULITY, MODERN AND MEDIEVAL

When Abernethy, the famous doctor, was asked why he indulged himself with all the habits he warned his patients against as unhealthy, he replied that his business was that of a direction post, which points out the way to a place, but does not go thither itself. He might have added that neither does it compel the traveller to go thither, nor prevent him from seeking some other way. Unfortunately our clerical direction posts always do coerce the traveller when they have the political power to do so. When the Church was a temporal as well as a spiritual power, and for long after to the full extent to which it could control or influence the temporal power, it enforced conformity by persecutions that were all the more ruthless because their intention was so excellent. Today, when the doctor has succeeded to the priest, and can do practically what he likes with parliament and the press through the blind faith in him which has succeeded to the far more critical faith in the parson, legal compulsion to take the doctor's prescription however poisonous, is carried to an extent that would have horrified the Inquisition and staggered Archbishop Laud. Our credulity is grosser than that of the Middle Ages, because the priest had no such direct pecuniary interest in our sins as the doctor has in our diseases: he did not starve when all was well with his flock, nor prosper when they were perishing, as our private commercial doctors must. Also the medieval cleric believed that something extremely unpleasant would happen to him after death if he was unscrupulous, a belief now practically extinct among persons receiving a dogmatically materialist education. Our professional corporations are Trade Unions without souls to be damned; and they will soon drive us to remind them that they have bodies to be kicked. The Vatican was never soulless: at worst it was a political conspiracy to make the Church supreme temporally as well as spiritually. Therefore the question raised by Joan's burning is a burning question still, though the penalties involved are not so sensational. That is why I am probing it. If it were only an historical curiosity I would not waste my readers' time and my own on it for five minutes.

TOLERATION, MODERN AND MEDIEVAL

The more closely we grapple with it the more difficult it becomes. At first sight we are disposed to repeat that Joan should have been excommunicated and then left to go her own way, though she would have protested vehemently against so cruel a deprivation of her spiritual food; for confession, absolution, and the body of her Lord were first necessaries of life to her. Such a spirit as Joan's might have got over that difficulty as the Church of England got over the Bulls of Pope Leo, by making a Church of her own, and affirming it to be the temple of the true and original faith from which her persecutors had strayed. But as such a proceeding was, in the eyes of both Church and State at that time, a spreading of damnation and anarchy, its toleration involved a greater strain on faith in freedom than political and ecclesiastical human nature could bear. It is easy to

say that the Church should have waited for the alleged evil results instead of assuming that they would occur, and what they
would be. That sounds simple enough; but if a modern Public
Health Authority were to leave people entirely to their own
devices in the matter of sanitation, saying, "We have nothing to
do with drainage or your views about drainage; but if you catch
smallpox or typhus we will prosecute you and have you punished very severely like the authorities in Butler's Erewhon," it
would either be removed to the County Asylum or reminded
that A's neglect of sanitation may kill the child of B two miles
off, or start an epidemic in which the most conscientious sanitarians may perish.

We must face the fact that society is founded on intolerance.
There are glaring cases of the abuse of intolerance; but they are
quite as characteristic of our own age as of the Middle Ages. The
typical modern example and contrast is compulsory inoculation
replacing what was virtually compulsory baptism. But compulsion to inoculate is objected to as a crudely unscientific and mischievous anti-sanitary quackery, not in the least because we
think it wrong to compel people to protect their children
from disease. Its opponents would make it a crime, and will
probably succeed in doing so; and that will be just as intolerant
as making it compulsory. Neither the Pasteurians nor their opponents the Sanitarians would leave parents free to bring up
their children naked, though that course also has some plausible
advocates. We may prate of toleration as we will; but society
must always draw a line somewhere between allowable conduct
and insanity or crime, in spite of the risk of mistaking sages for
lunatics and saviors for blasphemers. We must persecute, even to
the death; and all we can do to mitigate the danger of persecution is, first, to be very careful what we persecute, and second,
to bear in mind that unless there is a large liberty to shock conventional people, and a well informed sense of the value of
originality, individuality, and eccentricity, the result will be
apparent stagnation covering a repression of evolutionary forces

which will eventually explode with extravagant and probably destructive violence.

VARIABILITY OF TOLERATION

The degree of tolerance attainable at any moment depends on the strain under which society is maintaining its cohesion. In war, for instance, we suppress the gospels and put Quakers in prison, muzzle the newspapers, and make it a serious offence to shew a light at night. Under the strain of invasion the French Government in 1792 struck off 4000 heads, mostly on grounds that would not in time of settled peace have provoked any Government to chloroform a dog; and in 1920 the British Government slaughtered and burnt in Ireland to persecute the advocates of a constitutional change which it had presently to effect itself. Later on the Fascisti in Italy did everything that the Black and Tans did in Ireland, with some grotesquely ferocious variations, under the strain of an unskilled attempt at industrial revolution by Socialists who understood Socialism even less than Capitalists understand Capitalism. In the United States an incredibly savage persecution of Russians took place during the scare spread by the Russian Bolshevik revolution after 1917. These instances could easily be multiplied; but they are enough to shew that between a maximum of indulgent toleration and a ruthlessly intolerant Terrorism there is a scale through which toleration is continually rising or falling, and that there was not the smallest ground for the self-complacent conviction of the nineteenth century that it was more tolerant than the fifteenth, or that such an event as the execution of Joan could not possibly occur in what we call our own more enlightened times. Thousands of women, each of them a thousand times less dangerous and terrifying to our Governments than Joan was to the Government of her day, have within the last ten years been slaughtered, starved to death, burnt out of house and home, and what not that Persecution and Terror could do to them, in the course of Crusades far more tyrannically pretentious than the medieval Crusades which proposed nothing more hyperbolical than the rescue of the Holy Sepulchre from the Saracens. The Inquisition, with its English equivalent the Star Chamber, are gone in the sense that their names are now disused; but can any of the modern substitutes for the Inquisition, the Special Tribunals and Commissions, the punitive expeditions, the suspensions of the Habeas Corpus Act, the proclamations of martial law and of minor states of siege, and the rest of them, claim that their victims have as fair a trial, as well considered a body of law to govern their cases, or as conscientious a judge to insist on strict legality of procedure as Joan had from the Inquisition and from the spirit of the Middle Ages even when her country was under the heaviest strain of civil and foreign war? From us she would have had no trial and no law except a Defence of The Realm Act suspending all law; and for judge she would have had, at best, a bothered major, and at worst a promoted advocate in ermine and scarlet to whom the scruples of a trained ecclesiastic like Cauchon would seem ridiculous and ungentlemanly.

THE CONFLICT BETWEEN GENIUS AND DISCIPLINE

Having thus brought the matter home to ourselves, we may now consider the special feature of Joan's mental constitution which made her so unmanageable. What is to be done on the one hand with rulers who will not give any reason for their orders, and on the other with people who cannot understand the reasons when they are given? The government of the world, political, industrial, and domestic, has to be carried on mostly by the giving and obeying of orders under just these conditions. "Dont argue: do as you are told" has to be said not only to children and soldiers, but practically to everybody. Fortunately most people do not want to argue: they are only too glad to be saved the trouble of thinking for themselves. And the ablest and most independent thinkers are content to understand their own

special department. In other departments they will unhesitatingly ask for and accept the instructions of a policeman or the
advice of a tailor without demanding or desiring explanations.

Nevertheless, there must be some ground for attaching authority to an order. A child will obey its parents, a soldier his
officer, a philosopher a railway porter, and a workman a foreman, all without question, because it is generally accepted that
those who give the orders understand what they are about,
and are duly authorized and even obliged to give them, and
because, in the practical emergencies of daily life, there is no
time for lessons and explanations, or for arguments as to their
validity. Such obediences are as necesary to the continuous operation of our social system as the revolutions of the earth are
to the succession of night and day. But they are not so sponta-
neous as they seem: they have to be very carefully arranged and
maintained. A bishop will defer to and obey a king; but let a
curate venture to give him an order, however necessary and sensible, and the bishop will forget his cloth and damn the curate's
impudence. The more obedient a man is to accredited authority the more jealous he is of allowing any unauthorized person
to order him about.

With all this in mind, consider the career of Joan. She was a
village girl, in authority over sheep and pigs, dogs and chickens,
and to some extent over her father's hired laborers when he
hired any, but over no one else on earth. Outside the farm she
had no authority, no prestige, no claim to the smallest deference.
Yet she ordered everybody about, from her uncle to the king,
the archbishop, and the military General Staff. Her uncle
obeyed her like a sheep, and took her to the castle of the local
commander, who, on being ordered about, tried to assert himself, but soon collapsed and obeyed. And so on up to the king,
as we have seen. This would have been unbearably irritating
even if her orders had been offered as rational solutions of the
desperate difficulties in which her social superiors found them-

selves just then. But they were not so offered. Nor were they offered as the expression of Joan's arbitrary will. It was never "I say so," but always "God says so."

JOAN AS THEOCRAT

Leaders who take that line have no trouble with some people, and no end of trouble with others. They need never fear a lukewarm reception. Either they are messengers of God, or they are blasphemous impostors. In the Middle Ages the general belief in witchcraft greatly intensified this contrast, because when an apparent miracle happened (as in the case of the wind changing at Orleans) it proved the divine mission to the credulous, and proved a contract with the devil to the sceptical. All through, Joan had to depend on those who accepted her as an incarnate angel against those who added to an intense resentment of her presumption a bigoted abhorrence of her as a witch. To this abhorrence we must add the extreme irritation of those who did not believe in the voices, and regarded her as a liar and impostor. It is hard to conceive anything more infuriating to a statesman or a military commander, or to a court favorite, than to be overruled at every turn, or to be robbed of the ear of the reigning sovereign, by an impudent young upstart practising on the credulity of the populace and the vanity and silliness of an immature prince by exploiting a few of those lucky coincidences which pass as miracles with uncritical people. Not only were the envy, snobbery, and competitive ambition of the baser natures exacerbated by Joan's success, but among the friendly ones that were clever enough to be critical a quite reasonable scepticism and mistrust of her ability, founded on a fair observation of her obvious ignorance and temerity, were at work against her. And as she met all remonstrances and all criticisms, not with arguments or persuasion, but with a flat appeal to the authority of God and a claim to be in God's special confidence, she must have seemed, to all who were not infatuated by her, so insufferable that nothing but an unbroken chain of overwhelming successes in the military and political field could have saved her from the wrath that finally destroyed her.

UNBROKEN SUCCESS ESSENTIAL IN THEOCRACY

To forge such a chain she needed to be the King, the Archbishop of Rheims, the Bastard of Orleans, and herself into the bargain; and that was impossible. From the moment when she failed to stimulate Charles to follow up his coronation with a swoop on Paris she was lost. The fact that she insisted on this whilst the king and the rest timidly and foolishly thought they could square the Duke of Burgundy, and effect a combination with him against the English, made her a terrifying nuisance to them; and from that time onward she could do nothing but prowl about the battlefields waiting for some lucky chance to sweep the captains into a big move. But it was to the enemy that the chance came: she was taken prisoner by the Burgundians fighting before Compiègne, and at once discovered that she had not a friend in the political world. Had she escaped she would probably have fought on until the English were gone, and then had to shake the dust of the court off her feet, and retire to Domrémy as Garibaldi had to retire to Caprera.

MODERN DISTORTIONS OF JOAN'S HISTORY

This, I think, is all that we can now pretend to say about the prose of Joan's career. The romance of her rise, the tragedy of her execution, and the comedy of the attempts of posterity to make amends for that execution, belong to my play and not to my preface, which must be confined to a sober essay on the facts. That such an essay is badly needed can be ascertained by examining any of our standard works of reference. They give accurately enough the facts about the visit to Vaucouleurs, the annunciation to Charles at Chinon, the raising of the siege of

Orleans and the subsequent battles, the coronation at Rheims, the capture at Compiègne, and the trial and execution at Rouen, with their dates and the names of the people concerned; but they all break down on the melodramatic legend of the wicked bishop and the entrapped maiden and the rest of it. It would be far less misleading if they were wrong as to the facts, and right in their view of the facts. As it is, they illustrate the too little considered truth that the fashion in which we think changes like the fashion of our clothes, and that it is difficult, if not impossible, for most people to think otherwise than in the fashion of their own period.

HISTORY ALWAYS OUT OF DATE

This, by the way, is why children are never taught contemporary history. Their history books deal with periods of which the thinking has passed out of fashion, and the circumstances no longer apply to active life. For example, they are taught history about Washington, and told lies about Lenin. In Washington's time they were told lies (the same lies) about Washington, and taught history about Cromwell. In the fifteenth and sixteenth centuries they were told lies about Joan, and by this time might very well be told the truth about her. Unfortunately the lies did not cease when the political circumstances became obsolete. The Reformation, which Joan had unconsciously anticipated, kept the questions which arose in her case burning up to our own day (you can see plenty of the burnt houses still in Ireland), with the result that Joan has remained the subject of anti-Clerical lies, of specifically Protestant lies, and of Roman Catholic evasions of her unconscious Protestantism. The truth sticks in our throats with all the sauces it is served with: it will never go down until we take it without any sauce at all.

THE REAL JOAN NOT MARVELLOUS ENOUGH FOR US

But even in its simplicity, the faith demanded by Joan is one which the anti-metaphysical temper of nineteenth century civilization, which remains powerful in England and America, and is tyrannical in France, contemptuously refuses her. We do not, like her contemporaries, rush to the opposite extreme in a recoil from her as from a witch self-sold to the devil, because we do not believe in the devil nor in the possibility of commercial contracts with him. Our credulity, though enormous, is not boundless; and our stock of it is quite used up by our mediums, clairvoyants, hand readers, slate writers, Christian Scientists, psychoanalysts, electronic vibration diviners, therapeutists of all schools registered and unregistered, astrologers, astronomers who tell us that the sun is nearly a hundred million miles away and that Betelgeuse is ten times as big as the whole universe, physicists who balance Betelgeuse by describing the incredible smallness of the atom, and a host of other marvel mongers whose credulity would have dissolved the Middle Ages in a roar of sceptical merriment. In the Middle Ages people believed that the earth was flat, for which they had at least the evidence of their senses: we believe it to be round, not because as many as one per cent of us could give the physical reasons for so quaint a belief, but because modern science has convinced us that nothing that is obvious is true, and that everything that is magical, improbable, extraordinary, gigantic, microscopic, heartless, or outrageous is scientific.

I must not, by the way, be taken as implying that the earth is flat, or that all or any of our amazing credulities are delusions or impostures. I am only defending my own age against the charge of being less imaginative than the Middle Ages. I affirm that the nineteenth century, and still more the twentieth, can knock the fifteenth into a cocked hat in point of susceptibility to marvels and miracles and saints and prophets and magicians and monsters and fairy tales of all kinds. The proportion of marvel to immediately credible statement in the latest edition of the Encyclopædia Britannica is enormously greater than in the Bible. The medieval doctors of divinity who did not pretend to settle how many angels could dance on the point of a needle cut a very poor figure as far as romantic credulity is concerned beside the modern physicists who have settled to the billionth of a millimetre every movement and position in the dance of the electrons. Not for worlds would I question the precise accuracy of these calculations or the existence of electrons (whatever they may be). The fate of Joan is a warning to me against such heresy. But why the men who believe in electrons should regard themselves as less credulous than the men who believed in angels is not apparent to me. If they refuse to believe, with the Rouen assessors of 1431, that Joan was a witch, it is not because that explanation is too marvellous, but because it is not marvellous enough.

THE STAGE LIMITS OF HISTORICAL REPRESENTATION

For the story of Joan I refer the reader to the play which follows. It contains all that need be known about her; but as it is for stage use I have had to condense into three and a half hours a series of events which in their historical happening were spread over four times as many months; for the theatre imposes unities of time and place from which Nature in her boundless wastefulness is free. Therefore the reader must not suppose that Joan really put Robert de Baudricourt in her pocket in fifteen minutes, nor that her excommunication, recantation, relapse, and death at the stake were a matter of half an hour or so. Neither do I claim more for my dramatizations of Joan's contemporaries than that some of them are probably slightly more like the originals than those imaginary portraits of all the Popes from Saint Peter onward through the Dark Ages which are still gravely exhibited in the Uffizi in Florence (or were when I

was there last). My Dunois would do equally well for the Duc
d'Alençon. Both left descriptions of Joan so similar that, as a
man always describes himself unconsciously whenever he describes anyone else, I have inferred that these good-natured
young men were very like one another in mind; so I have
lumped the twain into a single figure, thereby saving the theatre
manager a salary and a suit of armor. Dunois' face, still on record
at Châteaudun, is a suggestive help. But I really know no more
about these men and their circle than Shakespear knew about
Falconbridge and the Duke of Austria, or about Macbeth and
Macduff. In view of the things they did in history, and have
to do again in the play, I can only invent appropriate characters for them in Shakespear's manner.

A VOID IN THE ELIZABETHAN DRAMA

I have, however, one advantage over the Elizabethans. I write
in full view of the Middle Ages, which may be said to have
been rediscovered in the middle of the nineteenth century after
an eclipse of about four hundred and fifty years. The Renascence of antique literature and art in the sixteenth century, and
the lusty growth of Capitalism, between them buried the Middle Ages; and their resurrection is a second Renascence. Now
there is not a breath of medieval atmosphere in Shakespear's
histories. His John of Gaunt is like a study of the old age of
Drake. Although he was a Catholic by family tradition, his
figures are all intensely Protestant, individualist, sceptical, self-
centered in everything but their love affairs, and completely
personal and selfish even in them. His kings are not statesmen:
his cardinals have no religion: a novice can read his plays from
one end to the other without learning that the world is finally
governed by forces expressing themselves in religions and laws
which make epochs rather than by vulgarly ambitious individuals who make rows. The divinity which shapes our ends, rough
hew them how we will, is mentioned fatalistically only to be
forgotten immediately like a passing vague apprehension. To

Shakespear as to Mark Twain, Cauchon would have been a ty-
rant and a bully instead of a Catholic, and the inquisitor Lemaître would have been a Sadist instead of a lawyer. Warwick
would have had no more feudal quality than his successor the
King Maker has in the play of Henry VI. We should have seen
them all completely satisfied that if they would only to their
own selves be true they could not then be false to any man (a
precept which represents the reaction against medievalism at its
intensest) as if they were beings in the air, without public responsibilities of any kind. All Shakespear's characters are so:
that is why they seem natural to our middle classes, who are
comfortable and irresponsible at other people's expense, and are
neither ashamed of that condition nor even conscious of it. Nature abhors this vacuum in Shakespear; and I have taken care to
let the medieval atmosphere blow through my play freely.
Those who see it performed will not mistake the startling event
it records for a mere personal accident. They will have before
them not only the visible and human puppets, but the Church,
the Inquisition, the Feudal System, with divine inspiration always beating against their too inelastic limits: all more terrible
in their dramatic force than any of the little mortal figures
clanking about in plate armor or moving silently in the frocks
and hoods of the order of St Dominic.

TRAGEDY, NOT MELODRAMA

There are no villains in the piece. Crime, like disease, is not
interesting: it is something to be done away with by general
consent, and that is all about it. It is what men do at their best,
with good intentions, and what normal men and women find
that they must and will do in spite of their intentions, that really
concern us. The rascally bishop and the cruel inquisitor of
Mark Twain and Andrew Lang are as dull as pickpockets; and
they reduce Joan to the level of the even less interesting person
whose pocket is picked. I have represented both of them as capable and eloquent exponents of The Church Militant and The

Church Litigant, because only by doing so can I maintain my
drama on the level of high tragedy and save it from becoming
a mere police court sensation. A villain in a play can never be
anything more than a *diabolus ex machina,* possibly a more exciting expedient than a *deus ex machina,* but both equally
mechanical, and therefore interesting only as mechanism. It is, I
repeat, what normally innocent people do that concerns us; and
if Joan had not been burnt by normally innocent people in the
energy of their righteousness her death at their hands would
have no more significance than the Tokyo earthquake, which
burnt a great many maidens. The tragedy of such murders is
that they are not committed by murderers. They are judicial
murders, pious murders; and this contradiction at once brings an
element of comedy into the tragedy: the angels may weep at the
murder, but the gods laugh at the murderers.

THE INEVITABLE FLATTERIES OF TRAGEDY

Here then we have a reason why my drama of Saint Joan's
career, though it may give the essential truth of it, gives an in-
exact picture of some accidental facts. It goes almost without
saying that the old Jeanne d'Arc melodramas, reducing everything to a conflict of villain and hero, or in Joan's case villain
and heroine, not only miss the point entirely, but falsify the
characters, making Cauchon a scoundrel, Joan a prima donna,
and Dunois a lover. But the writer of high tragedy and comedy,
aiming at the innermost attainable truth, must needs flatter
Cauchon nearly as much as the melodramatist vilifies him. Although there is, as far as I have been able to discover, nothing
against Cauchon that convicts him of bad faith or exceptional
severity in his judicial relations with Joan, or of as much anti-
prisoner, pro-police, class and sectarian bias as we now take for
granted in our own courts, yet there is hardly more warrant for
classing him as a great Catholic churchman, completely proof
against the passions roused by the temporal situation. Neither
does the inquisitor Lemaître, in such scanty accounts of him as

are now recoverable, appear quite so able a master of his duties
and of the case before him as I have given him credit for being.
But it is the business of the stage to make its figures more intelligible to themselves than they would be in real life; for by no
other means can they be made intelligible to the audience. And
in this case Cauchon and Lemaître have to make intelligible not
only themselves but the Church and the Inquisition, just as
Warwick has to make the feudal system intelligible, the three
between them having thus to make a twentieth-century audience conscious of an epoch fundamentally different from its own.
Obviously the real Cauchon, Lemaître, and Warwick could
not have done this: they were part of the Middle Ages themselves, and therefore as unconscious of its peculiarities as of the
atomic formula of the air they breathed. But the play would be
unintelligible if I had not endowed them with enough of this
consciousness to enable them to explain their attitude to the
twentieth century. All I claim is that by this inevitable sacrifice of verisimilitude I have secured in the only possible way
sufficient veracity to justify me in claiming that as far as I can
gather from the available documentation, and from such powers of divination as I possess, the things I represent these three
exponents of the drama as saying are the things they actually
would have said if they had known what they were really doing. And beyond this neither drama nor history can go in my
hands.

SOME WELL-MEANT PROPOSALS FOR THE
IMPROVEMENT OF THE PLAY

I have to thank several critics on both sides of the Atlantic,
including some whose admiration for my play is most generously
enthusiastic, for their heartfelt instructions as to how it can be
improved. They point out that by the excision of the epilogue
and all the references to such undramatic and tedious matters
as the Church, the feudal system, the Inquisition, the theory of
heresy and so forth, all of which, they point out, would be

ruthlessly blue pencilled by any experienced manager, the play could be considerably shortened. I think they are mistaken. The experienced knights of the blue pencil, having saved an hour and a half by disembowelling the play, would at once proceed to waste two hours in building elaborate scenery, having real water in the river Loire and a real bridge across it, and staging an obviously sham fight for possession of it, with the victorious French led by Joan on a real horse. The coronation would eclipse all previous theatrical displays, shewing, first, the procession through the streets of Rheims, and then the service in the cathedral, with special music written for both. Joan would be burnt on the stage, as Mr Matheson Lang always is in The Wandering Jew, on the principle that it does not matter in the least why a woman is burnt provided she is burnt, and people can pay to see it done. The intervals between the acts whilst these splendors were being built up and then demolished by the stage carpenters would seem eternal, to the great profit of the refreshment bars. And the weary and demoralized audience would lose their last trains and curse me for writing such inordinately long and intolerably dreary and meaningless plays. But the applause of the press would be unanimous. Nobody who knows the stage history of Shakespear will doubt that this is what would happen if I knew my business so little as to listen to these well intentioned but disastrous counsellors: indeed it probably will happen when I am no longer in control of the performing rights. So perhaps it will be as well for the public to see the play while I am still alive.

THE EPILOGUE

As to the epilogue, I could hardly be expected to stultify myself by implying that Joan's history in the world ended unhappily with her execution, instead of beginning there. It was necessary by hook or crook to shew the canonized Joan as well as the incinerated one; for many a woman has got herself burnt by carelessly whisking a muslin skirt into the drawing room fireplace, but getting canonized is a different matter, and a more important one. So I am afraid the epilogue must stand.

TO THE CRITICS, LEST THEY SHOULD FEEL IGNORED

To a professional critic (I have been one myself) theatre-going is the curse of Adam. The play is the evil he is paid to endure in the sweat of his brow; and the sooner it is over, the better. This would seem to place him in irreconcilable opposition to the paying playgoer, from whose point of view the longer the play, the more entertainment he gets for his money. It does in fact so place him, especially in the provinces, where the playgoer goes to the theatre for the sake of the play solely, and insists so effectively on a certain number of hours' entertainment that touring managers are sometimes seriously embarrassed by the brevity of the London plays they have to deal in.

For in London the critics are reinforced by a considerable body of persons who go to the theatre as many others go to church, to display their best clothes and compare them with other people's; to be in the fashion, and have something to talk about at dinner parties; to adore a pet performer; to pass the evening anywhere rather than at home: in short, for any or every reason except interest in dramatic art as such. In fashionable centres the number of irreligious people who go to church, or unmusical people who go to concerts and operas, and of undramatic people who go to the theatre, is so prodigious that sermons have been cut down to ten minutes and plays to two hours; and, even at that, congregations sit longing for the benediction and audiences for the final curtain, so that they may get away to the lunch or supper they really crave for, after arriving as late as (or later than) the hour of beginning can possibly be made for them.

Thus from the stalls and in the Press an atmosphere of hypocrisy spreads. Nobody says straight out that genuine drama is a tedious nuisance, and that to ask people to endure more than two hours of it (with two long intervals of relief) is an intolerable imposition. Nobody says "I hate classical tragedy and comedy as I hate sermons and symphonies; but I like police news and divorce news and any kind of dancing or decoration that has an aphrodisiac effect on me or on my wife or husband. And whatever superior people may pretend, I cannot associate pleasure with any sort of intellectual activity; and I dont believe anyone else can either." Such things are not said; yet nine-tenths of what is offered as criticism of the drama in the metropolitan Press of Europe and America is nothing but a muddled paraphrase of it. If it does not mean that, it means nothing.

I do not complain of this, though it complains very unreasonably of me. But I can take no more notice of it than Einstein of the people who are incapable of mathematics. I write in the classical manner for those who pay for admission to a theatre because they like classical comedy or tragedy for its own sake, and like it so much when it is good of its kind and well done that they tear themselves away from it with reluctance to catch the very latest train or omnibus that will take them home. Far from arriving late from an eight or half-past eight o'clock dinner so as to escape at least the first half-hour of the performance, they stand in queues outside the theatre doors for hours beforehand in bitingly cold weather to secure a seat. In countries where a play lasts a week, they bring baskets of provisions and sit it out. These are the patrons on whom I depend for my bread. I do not give them performances twelve hours long, because circumstances do not at present make such entertainments feasible; though a performance beginning after breakfast and ending at sunset is as possible physically and artistically in Surrey or Middlesex as in Ober-Ammergau; and an all-night sitting in a theatre would be at least as enjoyable as an all-night sitting in the House of Commons, and much more useful. But in St Joan I have done my best by going to the well-established classical limit of three and a half hours practically continuous playing, barring the one interval imposed by considerations which have nothing

to do with art. I know that this is hard on the pseudo-critics and
on the fashionable people whose playgoing is a hypocrisy. I
cannot help feeling some compassion for them when they assure
me that my play, though a great play, must fail hopelessly, because it does not begin at a quarter to nine and end at eleven.
The facts are overwhelmingly against them. They forget that all
men are not as they are. Still, I am sorry for them; and though
I cannot for their sakes undo my work and help the people who
hate the theatre to drive out the people who love it, yet I may
point out to them that they have several remedies in their own
hands. They can escape the first part of the play by their usual
practice of arriving late. They can escape the epilogue by not
waiting for it. And if the irreducible minimum thus attained
is still too painful, they can stay away altogether. But I depre-
cate this extreme course, because it is good neither for my pocket
nor for their own souls. Already a few of them, noticing that
what matters is not the absolute length of time occupied by a
play, but the speed with which that time passes, are discovering
that the theatre, though purgatorial in its Aristotelian moments,
is not necessarily always the dull place they have so often found
it. What do its discomforts matter when the play makes us
forget them?

AYOT ST LAWRENCE,
   May 1924.

SCENE I

A FINE spring morning on the river Meuse, between Lorraine and Champagne, in the year 1429 A.D., in the castle of Vaucouleurs.

Captain Robert de Baudricourt, a military squire, handsome and physically energetic, but with no will of his own, is disguising that defect in his usual fashion by storming terribly at his steward, a trodden worm, scanty of flesh, scanty of hair, who might be any age from 18 to 55, being the sort of man whom age cannot wither because he has never bloomed.

The two are in a sunny stone chamber on the first floor of the castle. At a plain strong oak table, seated in chair to match, the captain presents his left profile. The steward stands facing him at the other side of the table, if so deprecatory a stance as his can be called standing. The mullioned thirteenth-century window is open behind him. Near it in the corner is a turret with a narrow arched doorway leading to a winding stair which descends to the courtyard. There is a stout fourlegged stool under the table, and a wooden chest under the window.

ROBERT. No eggs! No eggs!! Thousand thunders, man, what do you mean by no eggs?

STEWARD. Sir: it is not my fault. It is the act of God.

ROBERT. Blasphemy. You tell me there are no eggs; and you blame your Maker for it.

STEWARD. Sir: what can I do? I cannot lay eggs.

ROBERT (*sarcastic*) Ha! You jest about it.

STEWARD. No, sir, God knows. We all have to go without eggs just as you have, sir. The hens will not lay.

ROBERT. Indeed! (*Rising*) Now listen to me, you.

STEWARD (*humbly*) Yes, sir.

ROBERT. What am I?

STEWARD. What are you, sir?

ROBERT (*coming at him*) Yes: what am I? Am I Robert, squire of Baudricourt and captain of this castle of Vaucouleurs; or am I a cowboy?

STEWARD. Oh, sir, you know you are a greater man here than the king himself.

ROBERT. Precisely. And now, do you know what you are?

STEWARD. I am nobody, sir, except that I have the honor to be your steward.

ROBERT (*driving him to the wall, adjective by adjective*) You have not only the honor of being my steward, but the privilege of being the worst, most incompetent, drivelling snivelling jibbering jabbering idiot of a steward in France. (*He strides back to the table*).

STEWARD (*cowering on the chest*) Yes, sir: to a great man like you I must seem like that.

ROBERT (*turning*) My fault, I suppose. Eh?

STEWARD (*coming to him deprecatingly*) Oh, sir: you always give my most innocent words such a turn!

ROBERT. I will give your neck a turn if you dare tell me, when I ask you how many eggs there are, that you cannot lay any.

STEWARD (*protesting*) Oh sir, oh sir—

ROBERT. No: not oh sir, oh sir, but no sir, no sir. My three Barbary hens and the black are the best layers in Champagne. And you come and tell me that there are no eggs! Who stole them? Tell me that, before I kick you out through the castle gate for a liar and a seller of my goods to thieves. The milk was short yesterday, too: do not forget that.

STEWARD (*desperate*) I know, sir. I know only too well. There is no milk: there are no eggs: tomorrow there will be nothing.

ROBERT. Nothing! You will steal the lot: eh?

STEWARD. No, sir: nobody will steal anything. But there is a spell on us: we are bewitched.

ROBERT. That story is not good enough for me. Robert de Baudricourt burns witches and hangs thieves. Go. Bring me four dozen eggs and two gallons of milk here in this room before noon, or Heaven have mercy on your bones! I will teach you to make a fool of me. (*He resumes his seat with an air of finality*).

STEWARD. Sir: I tell you there are no eggs. There will be none—not if you were to kill me for it—as long as The Maid is at the door.

ROBERT. The Maid! What maid? What are you talking about?

STEWARD. The girl from Lorraine, sir. From Domrémy.

ROBERT (*rising in fearful wrath*) Thirty thousand thunders! Fifty thousand devils! Do you mean to say that that girl, who had the impudence to ask to see me two days ago, and whom I told you to send back to her father with my orders that he was to give her a good hiding, is here still?

STEWARD. I have told her to go, sir. She wont.

ROBERT. I did not tell you to tell her to go: I told you to throw her out. You have fifty men-at-arms and a dozen lumps of ablebodied servants to carry out my orders. Are they afraid of her?

STEWARD. She is so positive, sir.

ROBERT (*seizing him by the scruff of the neck*) Positive! Now see here. I am going to throw you downstairs.

STEWARD. No, sir. Please.

ROBERT. Well, stop me by being positive. It's quite easy: any slut of a girl can do it.

STEWARD (*hanging limp in his hands*) Sir, sir: you cannot get rid of her by throwing me out. (*Robert has to let him drop. He squats on his knees on the floor, contemplating his master resignedly*). You see, sir, you are much more positive than I am. But so is she.

ROBERT. I am stronger than you are, you fool.

STEWARD. No, sir: it isnt that: it's your strong character, sir. She is weaker than we are: she is only a slip of a girl; but we cannot make her go.

ROBERT. You parcel of curs: you are afraid of her.

STEWARD (*rising cautiously*) No, sir: we are afraid of you; but she puts courage into us. She really doesnt seem to be afraid of anything. Perhaps you could frighten her, sir.

ROBERT (*grimly*) Perhaps. Where is she now?

STEWARD. Down in the courtyard, sir, talking to the soldiers as usual. She is always talking to the soldiers except when she is praying.

ROBERT. Praying! Ha! You believe she prays, you idiot. I know the sort of girl that is always talking to soldiers. She shall talk to me a bit. (*He goes to the window and shouts fiercely through it*) Hallo, you there!

A GIRL'S VOICE (*bright, strong and rough*) Is it me, sir?

ROBERT. Yes, you.

THE VOICE. Be you captain?

ROBERT. Yes, damn your impudence, I be captain. Come up here. (*To the soldiers in the yard*) Shew her the way, you. And shove her along quick. (*He leaves the window, and returns to his place at the table, where he sits magisterially*).

STEWARD (*whispering*) She wants to go and be a soldier herself. She wants you to give her soldier's clothes. Armor, sir! And a sword! Actually! (*He steals behind Robert*).

Joan appears in the turret doorway. She is an ablebodied country girl of 17 or 18, respectably dressed in red, with an uncommon face: eyes very wide apart and bulging as they often do in very imaginative people, a long well-shaped nose with wide nostrils, a short upper lip, resolute but full-lipped mouth, and handsome fighting chin. She comes eagerly to the table, delighted at having penetrated to Baudricourt's presence at last, and full of hope as to the result. His scowl does not check or frighten her in the least. Her voice is normally a hearty coaxing voice, very confident, very appealing, very hard to resist.

JOAN (*bobbing a curtsey*) Good morning, captain squire. Captain: you are to give me a horse and armor and some soldiers, and send me to the Dauphin. Those are your orders from my Lord.

ROBERT (*outraged*) Orders from your lord! And who the devil may your lord be? Go back to him, and tell him that I am neither duke nor peer at his orders: I am squire of Baudricourt; and I take no orders except from the king.

JOAN (*reassuringly*) Yes, squire: that is all right. My Lord is the King of Heaven.

ROBERT. Why, the girl's mad. (*To the steward*) Why didnt you tell me so, you blockhead?

STEWARD. Sir: do not anger her: give her what she wants.

JOAN (*impatient, but friendly*) They all say I am mad until I talk to them, squire. But you see that it is the will of God that you are to do what He has put into my mind.

ROBERT. It is the will of God that I shall send you back to your father with orders to put you under lock and key and thrash the madness out of you. What have you to say to that?

JOAN. You think you will, squire; but you will find it all coming quite different. You said you would not see me; but here I am.

STEWARD (*appealing*) Yes, sir. You see, sir.

ROBERT. Hold your tongue, you.

STEWARD (*abjectly*) Yes, sir.

ROBERT (*to Joan, with a sour loss of confidence*) So you are presuming on my seeing you, are you?

JOAN (*sweetly*) Yes, squire.

ROBERT (*feeling that he has lost ground, brings down his two fists squarely on the table, and inflates his chest imposingly to cure the unwelcome and only too familiar sensation*) Now listen to me. I am going to assert myself.

JOAN (*busily*) Please do, squire. The horse will cost sixteen francs. It is a good deal of money; but I can save it on the armor. I can find a soldier's armor that will fit me well enough: I am very hardy; and I do not need beautiful armor made to my measure like you wear. I shall not want many soldiers: the Dauphin will give me all I need to raise the siege of Orleans.

ROBERT (*flabbergasted*) To raise the siege of Orleans!

JOAN (*simply*) Yes, squire: that is what God is sending me to do. Three men will be enough for you to send with me if they are good men and gentle to me. They have promised to come with me. Polly and Jack and—

ROBERT. Polly!! You impudent baggage, do you dare call squire Bertrand de Poulengey Polly to my face?

JOAN. His friends call him so, squire: I did not know he had any other name. Jack—

ROBERT. That is Monsieur John of Metz, I suppose?

JOAN. Yes, squire. Jack will come willingly: he is a very kind gentleman, and gives me money to give to the poor. I think John Godsave will come, and Dick the Archer, and their servants John of Honecourt and Julian. There will be no trouble for you, squire: I have arranged it all: you have only to give the order.

ROBERT (*contemplating her in a stupor of amazement*) Well, I am damned!

JOAN (*with unruffled sweetness*) No, squire: God is very merciful; and the blessed saints Catherine and Margaret, who speak to me every day (*he gapes*), will intercede for you. You will go to paradise; and your name will be remembered for ever as my first helper.

ROBERT (*to the steward, still much bothered, but changing his tone as he pursues a new clue*) Is this true about Monsieur de Poulengey?

STEWARD (*eagerly*) Yes, sir, and about Monsieur de Metz too. They both want to go with her.

ROBERT (*thoughtful*) Mf! (*He goes to the window, and*

shouts into the courtyard) Hallo! You there: send Monsieur de Poulengey to me, will you? (*He turns to Joan*). Get out; and wait in the yard.

JOAN (*smiling brightly at him*) Right, squire. (*She goes out*).

ROBERT (*to the steward*) Go with her, you, you dithering imbecile. Stay within call; and keep your eye on her. I shall have her up here again.

STEWARD. Do so in God's name, sir. Think of those hens, the best layers in Champagne; and—

ROBERT. Think of my boot; and take your backside out of reach of it.

The steward retreats hastily and finds himself confronted in the doorway by Bertrand de Poulengey, a lymphatic French gentleman-at-arms, aged 36 or thereabout, employed in the department of the provost-marshal, dreamily absent-minded, seldom speaking unless spoken to, and then slow and obstinate in reply: altogether in contrast to the self-assertive, loud-mouthed, superficially energetic, fundamentally will-less Robert. The steward makes way for him, and vanishes.

Poulengey salutes, and stands awaiting orders.

ROBERT (*genially*) It isnt service, Polly. A friendly talk. Sit down. (*He hooks the stool from under the table with his instep*).

Poulengey relaxing, comes into the room; places the stool between the table and the window; and sits down ruminatively. Robert, half sitting on the end of the table, begins the friendly talk.

ROBERT. Now listen to me, Polly. I must talk to you like a father.

Poulengey looks up at him gravely for a moment, but says nothing.

ROBERT. It's about this girl you are interested in. Now, I have seen her. I have talked to her. First, she's mad. That doesnt matter. Second, she's not a farm wench. She's a bourgeoise. That matters a great deal. I know her class exactly. Her father came here last year to represent his village in a lawsuit: he is one of their notables. A farmer. Not a gentleman farmer: he makes money by it, and lives by it. Still, not a laborer. Not a mechanic. He might have a cousin a lawyer, or in the Church. People of this sort may be of no account socially; but they can give a lot of bother to the authorities. That is to say, to me. Now no doubt it seems to you a very simple thing to take this girl away, humbugging her into the belief that you are taking her to the Dauphin. But if you get her into trouble, you may get me into no end of a mess, as I am her father's lord, and responsible for her protection. So friends or no friends, Polly, hands off her.

POULENGEY (*with deliberate impressiveness*) I should as soon think of the Blessed Virgin herself in that way, as of this girl.

ROBERT (*coming off the table*) But she says you and Jack and Dick have offered to go with her. What for? You are not going to tell me that you take her crazy notion of going to the Dauphin seriously, are you?

POULENGEY (*slowly*) There is something about her. They are pretty foulmouthed and foulminded down there in the guardroom, some of them. But there hasnt been a word that has anything to do with her being a woman. They have stopped swearing before her. There is something. Something. It may be worth trying.

ROBERT. Oh, come, Polly! pull yourself together. Commonsense was never your strong point; but this is a little too much. (*He retreats disgustedly*).

POULENGEY (*unmoved*) What is the good of commonsense? If we had any commonsense we should join the Duke of Burgundy and the English king. They hold half the country, right down to the Loire. They have Paris. They have this castle: you know very well that we had to surrender it to the Duke of Bedford, and that you are only holding it on parole. The Dauphin is in Chinon, like a rat in a corner, except that he wont fight.

We dont even know that he is the Dauphin: his mother says he isnt; and she ought to know. Think of that! the queen denying the legitimacy of her own son!

ROBERT. Well, she married her daughter to the English king. Can you blame the woman?

POULENGEY. I blame nobody. But thanks to her, the Dauphin is down and out; and we may as well face it. The English will take Orleans: the Bastard will not be able to stop them.

ROBERT. He beat the English the year before last at Montargis. I was with him.

POULENGEY. No matter: his men are cowed now; and he cant work miracles. And I tell you that nothing can save our side now but a miracle.

ROBERT. Miracles are all right, Polly. The only difficulty about them is that they dont happen nowadays.

POULENGEY. I used to think so. I am not so sure now. (*Rising, and moving ruminatively towards the window*) At all events this is not a time to leave any stone unturned. There is something about the girl.

ROBERT. Oh! You think the girl can work miracles, do you?

POULENGEY. I think the girl herself is a bit of a miracle. Anyhow, she is the last card left in our hand. Better play her than throw up the game. (*He wanders to the turret*).

ROBERT (*wavering*) You really think that?

POULENGEY (*turning*) Is there anything else left for us to think?

ROBERT (*going to him*) Look here, Polly. If you were in my place would you let a girl like that do you out of sixteen francs for a horse?

POULENGEY. I will pay for the horse.

ROBERT. You will!

POULENGEY. Yes: I will back my opinion.

ROBERT. You will really gamble on a forlorn hope to the tune of sixteen francs?

POULENGEY. It is not a gamble.

ROBERT. What else is it?

POULENGEY. It is a certainty. Her words and her ardent faith in God have put fire into me.

ROBERT (*giving him up*) Whew! You are as mad as she is.

POULENGEY (*obstinately*) We want a few mad people now. See where the sane ones have landed us!

ROBERT (*his irresoluteness now openly swamping his affected decisiveness*) I shall feel like a precious fool. Still, if you feel sure—?

POULENGEY. I feel sure enough to take her to Chinon—unless you stop me.

ROBERT. This is not fair. You are putting the responsibility on me.

POULENGEY. It is on you whichever way you decide.

ROBERT. Yes: thats just it. Which way am I to decide? You dont see how awkward this is for me. (*Snatching at a dilatory step with an unconscious hope that Joan will make up his mind for him*) Do you think I ought to have another talk to her?

POULENGEY (*rising*) Yes. (*He goes to the window and calls*) Joan!

JOAN'S VOICE. Will he let us go, Polly?

POULENGEY. Come up. Come in. (*Turning to Robert*) Shall I leave you with her?

ROBERT. No: stay here; and back me up.

Poulengey sits down on the chest. Robert goes back to his magisterial chair, but remains standing to inflate himself more imposingly. Joan comes in, full of good news.

JOAN. Jack will go halves for the horse.

ROBERT. Well!! (*He sits, deflated*)

POULENGEY (*Gravely*) Sit down, Joan.

JOAN (*checked a little, and looking to Robert*) May I?

ROBERT. Do what you are told.

Joan curtsies and sits down on the stool between them. Robert outfaces his perplexity with his most peremptory air.

ROBERT. What is your name?

JOAN (*chattily*) They always call me Jenny in Lorraine. Here in France I am Joan. The soldiers call me The Maid.

ROBERT. What is your surname?

JOAN. Surname? What is that? My father sometimes calls himself d'Arc; but I know nothing about it. You met my father. He—

ROBERT. Yes, yes: I remember. You come from Domrémy in Lorraine, I think.

JOAN. Yes; but what does it matter? we all speak French.

ROBERT. Dont ask questions: answer them. How old are you?

JOAN. Seventeen: so they tell me. It might be nineteen. I dont remember.

ROBERT. What did you mean when you said that St Catherine and St Margaret talked to you every day?

JOAN. They do.

ROBERT. What are they like?

JOAN (*suddenly obstinate*) I will tell you nothing about that: they have not given me leave.

ROBERT. But you actually see them; and they talk to you just as I am talking to you?

JOAN. No: it is quite different. I cannot tell you: you must not talk to me about my voices.

ROBERT. How do you mean? voices?

JOAN. I hear voices telling me what to do. They come from God.

ROBERT. They come from your imagination.

JOAN. Of course. That is how the messages of God come to us.

POULENGEY. Checkmate.

ROBERT. No fear! (*To Joan*) So God says you are to raise the siege of Orleans?

JOAN. And to crown the Dauphin in Rheims Cathedral.

ROBERT (*gasping*) Crown the D——! Gosh!

JOAN. And to make the English leave France.

ROBERT (*sarcastic*) Anything else?

JOAN (*charming*) Not just at present, thank you, squire.

ROBERT. I suppose you think raising a siege is as easy as chasing a cow out of a meadow. You think soldiering is anybody's job?

JOAN. I do not think it can be very difficult if God is on your side, and you are willing to put your life in His hand. But many soldiers are very simple.

ROBERT (*grimly*) Simple! Did you ever see English soldiers fighting?

JOAN. They are only men. God made them just like us; but He gave them their own country and their own language; and it is not His will that they should come into our country and try to speak our language.

ROBERT. Who has been putting such nonsense into your head? Dont you know that soldiers are subject to their feudal lord, and that it is nothing to them or to you whether he is the duke of Burgundy or the king of England or the king of France? What has their language to do with it?

JOAN. I do not understand that a bit. We are all subject to the King of Heaven; and He gave us our countries and our languages, and meant us to keep to them. If it were not so it would be murder to kill an Englishman in battle; and you, squire, would be in great danger of hell fire. You must not think about your duty to your feudal lord, but about your duty to God.

POULENGEY. It's no use, Robert: she can choke you like that every time.

ROBERT. Can she, by Saint Dennis! We shall see. (*To Joan*) We are not talking about God: we are talking about practical affairs. I ask you again, girl, have you ever seen English soldiers fighting? Have you ever seen them plundering, burning, turning the countryside into a desert? Have you heard no tales of their Black Prince who was blacker than the devil himself, or of the English king's father?

JOAN. You must not be afraid, Robert—

ROBERT. Damn you, I am not afraid. And who gave you leave to call me Robert?

JOAN. You were called so in church in the name of our Lord. All the other names are your father's or your brother's or anybody's.

ROBERT. Tcha.

JOAN. Listen to me, squire. At Domrémy we had to fly to the next village to escape from the English soldiers. Three of them were left behind, wounded. I came to know these three poor goddams quite well. They had not half my strength.

ROBERT. Do you know why they are called goddams?

JOAN. No. Everyone calls them goddams.

ROBERT. It is because they are always calling on their God to condemn their souls to perdition. That is what goddam means in their language. How do you like it?

JOAN. God will be merciful to them; and they will act like His good children when they go back to the country He made for them, and made them for. I have heard the tales of the Black Prince. The moment he touched the soil of our country the devil entered into him and made him a black fiend. But at home, in the place made for him by God, he was good. It is always so. If I went into England against the will of God to conquer England, and tried to live there and speak its language, the devil would enter into me; and when I was old I should shudder to remember the wickednesses I did.

ROBERT. Perhaps. But the more devil you were the better you might fight. That is why the goddams will take Orleans. And you cannot stop them, nor ten thousand like you.

JOAN. One thousand like me can stop them. Ten like me can stop them with God on our side. (*She rises impetuously, and goes at him, unable to sit quiet any longer*). You do not understand, squire. Our soldiers are always beaten because they are fighting only to save their skins; and the shortest way to save your skin is to run away. Our knights are thinking only of the money they will make in ransoms: it is not kill or be

killed with them, but pay or be paid. But I will teach them all
to fight that the will of God may be done in France; and then
they will drive the poor goddams before them like sheep. You
and Polly will live to see the day when there will not be an
English soldier on the soil of France; and there will be but one
king there: not the feudal English king, but God's French one.

ROBERT (*to Poulengey*) This may be all rot, Polly; but the
troops might swallow it, though nothing that we can say seems
able to put any fight into them. Even the Dauphin might swallow it. And if she can put fight into him, she can put it into
anybody.

POULENGEY. I can see no harm in trying. Can you? And
there is something about the girl—

ROBERT (*turning to Joan*) Now listen you to me; and (*desperately*) dont cut in before I have time to think.

JOAN (*plumping down on the stool again, like an obedient
schoolgirl*) Yes, squire.

ROBERT. Your orders are, that you are to go to Chinon under
the escort of this gentleman and three of his friends.

JOAN (*radiant, clasping her hands*) Oh, squire! Your head is
all circled with light, like a saint's.

POULENGEY. How is she to get into the royal presence?

ROBERT (*who has looked up for his halo rather apprehensively*) I dont know: how did she get into my presence? If the
Dauphin can keep her out he is a better man than I take him
for. (*Rising*) I will send her to Chinon; and she can say I sent
her. Then let come what may: I can do no more.

JOAN. And the dress? I may have a soldier's dress, maynt I,
squire?

ROBERT. Have what you please. I wash my hands of it.

JOAN (*wildly excited by her success*) Come, Polly. (*She
dashes out*).

ROBERT (*shaking Poulengey's hand*) Goodbye, old man, I
am taking a big chance. Few other men would have done it.
But as you say, there is something about her.

POULENGEY. Yes: there is something about her. Goodbye. (*He goes out*).

Robert, still very doubtful whether he has not been made a fool of by a crazy female, and a social inferior to boot, scratches his head and slowly comes back from the door.

The steward runs in with a basket.

STEWARD. Sir, sir—

ROBERT. What now?

STEWARD. The hens are laying like mad, sir. Five dozen eggs!

ROBERT (*stiffens convulsively; crosses himself; and forms with his pale lips the words*) Christ in heaven! (*Aloud but breathless*) She did come from God.

SCENE II

CHINON, *in Touraine. An end of the throne-room in the castle, curtained off to make an antechamber. The Archbishop of Rheims, close on 50, a full-fed political prelate with nothing of the ecclesiastic about him except his imposing bearing, and the Lord Chamberlain, Monseigneur de la Trémouille, a monstrous arrogant wineskin of a man, are waiting for the Dauphin. There is a door in the wall to the right of the two men. It is late in the afternoon on the 8th of March, 1429. The Archbishop stands with dignity whilst the Chamberlain, on his left, fumes about in the worst of tempers.*

LA TRÉMOUILLE. What the devil does the Dauphin mean by keeping us waiting like this? I dont know how you have the patience to stand there like a stone idol.

THE ARCHBISHOP. You see, I am an archbishop; and an archbishop is a sort of idol. At any rate he has to learn to keep still and suffer fools patiently. Besides, my dear Lord Chamberlain, it is the Dauphin's royal privilege to keep you waiting, is it not?

LA TRÉMOUILLE. Dauphin be damned! saving your reverence. Do you know how much money he owes me?

THE ARCHBISHOP. Much more than he owes me, I have no doubt, because you are a much richer man. But I take it he owes you all you could afford to lend him. That is what he owes me.

LA TRÉMOUILLE. Twentyseven thousand: that was his last haul. A cool twentyseven thousand!

THE ARCHBISHOP. What becomes of it all? He never has a suit of clothes that I would throw to a curate.

LA TRÉMOUILLE. He dines on a chicken or a scrap of mutton.

74

He borrows my last penny; and there is nothing to shew for it (*A page appears in the doorway*). At last!

THE PAGE. No, my lord: it is not His Majesty. Monsieur de Rais is approaching.

LA TRÉMOUILLE. Young Bluebeard! Why announce him?

THE PAGE. Captain La Hire is with him. Something has happened, I think.

Gilles de Rais, a young man of 25, very smart and self-possessed, and sporting the extravagance of a little curled beard dyed blue at a clean-shaven court, comes in. He is determined to make himself agreeable, but lacks natural joyousness, and is not really pleasant. In fact when he defies the Church some eleven years later he is accused of trying to extract pleasure from horrible cruelties, and hanged. So far, however, there is no shadow of the gallows on him. He advances gaily to the Archbishop. The page withdraws.

BLUEBEARD. Your faithful lamb, Archbishop. Good day, my lord. Do you know what has happened to La Hire?

LA TRÉMOUILLE. He has sworn himself into a fit, perhaps.

BLUEBEARD. No: just the opposite. Foul Mouthed Frank, the only man in Touraine who could beat him at swearing, was told by a soldier that he shouldnt use such language when he was at the point of death.

THE ARCHBISHOP. Nor at any other point. But *was* Foul Mouthed Frank on the point of death?

BLUEBEARD. Yes: he has just fallen into a well and been drowned. La Hire is frightened out of his wits.

Captain La Hire comes in: a war dog with no court manners and pronounced camp ones.

BLUEBEARD. I have just been telling the Chamberlain and the Archbishop. The Archbishop says you are a lost man.

LA HIRE (*striding past Bluebeard, and planting himself between the Archbishop and La Trémouille*) This is nothing to joke about. It is worse than we thought. It was not a soldier, but an angel dressed as a soldier.

THE ARCHBISHOP
THE CHAMBERLAIN } (*exclaiming all together*) An angel!
BLUEBEARD

LA HIRE. Yes, an angel. She has made her way from Champagne with half a dozen men through the thick of everything: Burgundians, Goddams, deserters, robbers, and Lord knows who; and they never met a soul except the country folk. I know one of them: de Poulengey. He says she's an angel. If ever I utter an oath again may my soul be blasted to eternal damnation!

THE ARCHBISHOP. A very pious beginning, Captain.

Bluebeard and La Trémouille laugh at him. The page returns.

THE PAGE. His Majesty.

They stand perfunctorily at court attention. The Dauphin, aged 26, really King Charles the Seventh since the death of his father, but as yet uncrowned, comes in through the curtains with a paper in his hands. He is a poor creature physically; and the current fashion of shaving closely, and hiding every scrap of hair under the head-covering or headdress, both by women and men, makes the worst of his appearance. He has little narrow eyes, near together, a long pendulous nose that droops over his thick short upper lip, and the expression of a young dog accustomed to be kicked, yet incorrigible and irrepressible. But he is neither vulgar nor stupid; and he has a cheeky humor which enables him to hold his own in conversation. Just at present he is excited, like a child with a new toy. He comes to the Archbishop's left hand. Bluebeard and La Hire retire towards the curtains.

CHARLES. Oh, Archbishop, do you know what Robert de Baudricourt is sending me from Vaucouleurs?

THE ARCHBISHOP (*contemptuously*) I am not interested in the newest toys.

CHARLES (*indignantly*) It isnt a toy. (*Sulkily*) However, I can get on very well without your interest.

THE ARCHBISHOP. Your Highness is taking offence very unnecessarily.

CHARLES. Thank you. You are always ready with a lecture, arnt you?

LA TRÉMOUILLE (*roughly*) Enough grumbling. What have you got there?

CHARLES. What is that to you?

LA TRÉMOUILLE. It is my business to know what is passing between you and the garrison at Vaucouleurs. (*He snatches the paper from the Dauphin's hand, and begins reading it with some difficulty, following the words with his finger and spelling them out syllable by syllable.*)

CHARLES (*mortified*) You all think you can treat me as you please because I owe you money, and because I am no good at fighting. But I have the blood royal in my veins.

THE ARCHBISHOP. Even that has been questioned, your Highness. One hardly recognizes in you the grandson of Charles the Wise.

CHARLES. I want to hear no more of my grandfather. He was so wise that he used up the whole family stock of wisdom for five generations, and left me the poor fool I am, bullied and insulted by all of you.

THE ARCHBISHOP. Control yourself, sir. These outbursts of petulance are not seemly.

CHARLES. Another lecture! Thank you. What a pity it is that though you are an archbishop saints and angels dont come to see you!

THE ARCHBISHOP. What do you mean?

CHARLES. Aha! Ask that bully there (*pointing to La Trémouille*).

LA TRÉMOUILLE (*furious*) Hold your tongue. Do you hear?

CHARLES. Oh, I hear. You neednt shout. The whole castle

can hear. Why dont you go and shout at the English, and beat them for me?

LA TRÉMOUILLE (*raising his fist*) You young—

CHARLES (*running behind the Archbishop*) Dont you raise your hand to me. It's high treason.

LA HIRE. Steady, Duke! Steady!

THE ARCHBISHOP (*resolutely*) Come, come! this will not do. My lord Chamberlain: please! please! we must keep some sort of order. (*To the Dauphin*) And you, sir: if you cannot rule your kingdom, at least try to rule yourself.

CHARLES. Another lecture! Thank you.

LA TRÉMOUILLE (*handing the paper to the Archbishop*) Here: read the accursed thing for me. He has sent the blood boiling into my head: I cant distinguish the letters.

CHARLES (*coming back and peering round La Trémouille's left shoulder*) I will read it for you if you like. I can read, you know.

LA TRÉMOUILLE (*with intense contempt, not at all stung by the taunt*) Yes: reading is about all you are fit for. Can you make it out, Archbishop?

THE ARCHBISHOP. I should have expected more commonsense from De Baudricourt. He is sending some cracked country lass here—

CHARLES (*interrupting*) No: he is sending a saint: an angel. And she is coming to me: to me, the king, and not to you, Archbishop, holy as you are. She knows the blood royal if you dont. (*He struts up to the curtains between Bluebeard and La Hire*).

THE ARCHBISHOP. You cannot be allowed to see this crazy wench.

CHARLES (*turning*) But I am the king; and I will.

LA TRÉMOUILLE (*brutally*) Then she cannot be allowed to see you. Now!

CHARLES. I tell you I will. I am going to put my foot down—

BLUEBEARD (*laughing at him*) Naughty! What would your wise grandfather say?

CHARLES. That just shews your ignorance, Bluebeard. My grandfather had a saint who used to float in the air when she was praying, and told him everything he wanted to know. My poor father had two saints, Marie de Maillé and the Gasque of Avignon. It is in our family; and I dont care what you say: I will have my saint too.

THE ARCHBISHOP. This creature is not a saint. She is not even a respectable woman. She does not wear women's clothes. She is dressed like a soldier, and rides round the country with soldiers. Do you suppose such a person can be admitted to your Highness's court?

LA HIRE. Stop. (*Going to the Archbishop*) Did you say a girl in armor, like a soldier?

THE ARCHBISHOP. So De Baudricourt describes her.

LA HIRE. But by all the devils in hell—Oh, God forgive me, what am I saying?—by Our Lady and all the saints, this must be the angel that struck Foul Mouthed Frank dead for swearing.

CHARLES (*triumphantly*) You see! A miracle!

LA HIRE. She may strike the lot of us dead if we cross her. For Heaven's sake, Archbishop, be careful what you are doing.

THE ARCHBISHOP (*severely*) Rubbish! Nobody has been struck dead. A drunken blackguard who has been rebuked a hundred times for swearing has fallen into a well, and been drowned. A mere coincidence.

LA HIRE. I do not know what a coincidence is. I do know that the man is dead, and that she told him he was going to die.

THE ARCHBISHOP. We are all going to die, Captain.

LA HIRE (*crossing himself*) I hope not. (*He backs out of the conversation*).

BLUEBEARD. We can easily find out whether she is an angel

or not. Let us arrange when she comes that I shall be the Dauphin, and see whether she will find me out.

CHARLES. Yes: I agree to that. If she cannot find the blood royal I will have nothing to do with her.

THE ARCHBISHOP. It is for the Church to make saints: let De Baudricourt mind his own business, and not dare unsurp the function of his priest. I say the girl shall not be admitted.

BLUEBEARD. But, Archbishop—

THE ARCHBISHOP (*sternly*) I speak in the Church's name. (*To the Dauphin*) Do you dare say she shall?

CHARLES (*intimidated but sulky*) Oh, if you make it an excommunication matter, I have nothing more to say, of course. But you havnt read the end of the letter. De Baudricourt says she will raise the siege of Orleans, and beat the English for us.

LA TRÉMOUILLE. Rot!

CHARLES. Well, will you save Orleans for us, with all your bullying?

LA TRÉMOUILLE (*savagely*) Do not throw that in my face again: do you hear? I have done more fighting than you ever did or ever will. But I cannot be everywhere.

THE DAUPHIN. Well, thats something.

BLUEBEARD (*coming between the Archbishop and Charles*) You have Jack Dunois at the head of your troops in Orleans: the brave Dunois, the handsome Dunois, the wonderful invincible Dunois, the darling of all the ladies, the beautiful bastard. Is it likely that the country lass can do what he cannot do?

CHARLES. Why doesnt he raise the siege, then?

LA HIRE. The wind is against him.

BLUEBEARD. How can the wind hurt him at Orleans? It is not on the Channel.

LA HIRE. It is on the river Loire; and the English hold the bridgehead. He must ship his men across the river and upstream, if he is to take them in the rear. Well, he cannot, because there is a devil of a wind blowing the other way. He is tired of paying the priests to pray for a west wind. What he needs is a miracle. You tell me that what the girl did to Foul Mouthed Frank was no miracle. No matter: it finished Frank. If she changes the wind for Dunois, that may not be a miracle either; but it may finish the English. What harm is there in trying?

THE ARCHBISHOP (*who has read the end of the letter and become more thoughtful*) It is true that De Baudricourt seems extraordinarily impressed.

LA HIRE. De Baudricourt is a blazing ass; but he is a soldier; and if he thinks she can beat the English, all the rest of the army will think so too.

LA TRÉMOUILLE (*to the Archbishop, who is hesitating*) Oh, let them have their way. Dunois' men will give up the town in spite of him if somebody does not put some fresh spunk into them.

THE ARCHBISHOP. The Church must examine the girl before anything decisive is done about her. However, since his Highness desires it, let her attend the Court.

LA HIRE. I will find her and tell her. (*He goes out*).

CHARLES. Come with me, Bluebeard; and let us arrange so that she will not know who I am. You will pretend to be me. (*He goes out through the curtains*).

BLUEBEARD. Pretend to be that thing! Holy Michael! (*He follows the Dauphin*).

LA TRÉMOUILLE. I wonder will she pick him out!

THE ARCHBISHOP. Of course she will.

LA TRÉMOUILLE. Why? How is she to know?

THE ARCHBISHOP. She will know what everybody in Chinon knows: that the Dauphin is the meanest-looking and worst-dressed figure in the Court, and that the man with the blue beard is Gilles de Rais.

LA TRÉMOUILLE. I never thought of that.

THE ARCHBISHOP. You are not so accustomed to miracles as I am. It is part of my profession.

LA TRÉMOUILLE (*puzzled and a little scandalized*) But that would not be a miracle at all.

THE ARCHBISHOP (*calmly*) Why not?

LA TRÉMOUILLE. Well, come! what is a miracle?

THE ARCHBISHOP. A miracle, my friend, is an event which creates faith. That is the purpose and nature of miracles. They may seem very wonderful to the people who witness them, and very simple to those who perform them. That does not matter: if they confirm or create faith they are true miracles.

LA TRÉMOUILLE. Even when they are frauds, do you mean?

THE ARCHBISHOP. Frauds deceive. An event which creates faith does not deceive: therefore it is not a fraud, but a miracle.

LA TRÉMOUILLE (*scratching his neck in his perplexity*) Well, I suppose as you are an archbishop you must be right. It seems a bit fishy to me. But I am no churchman, and dont understand these matters.

THE ARCHBISHOP. You are not a churchman; but you are a diplomatist and a soldier. Could you make our citizens pay war taxes, or our soldiers sacrifice their lives, if they knew what is really happening instead of what seems to them to be happening?

LA TRÉMOUILLE. No, by Saint Dennis: the fat would be in the fire before sundown.

THE ARCHBISHOP. Would it not be quite easy to tell them the truth?

LA TRÉMOUILLE. Man alive, they wouldn't believe it.

THE ARCHBISHOP. Just so. Well, the Church has to rule men for the good of their souls as you have to rule them for the good of their bodies. To do that, the Church must do as you do: nourish their faith by poetry.

LA TRÉMOUILLE. Poetry! I should call it humbug.

THE ARCHBISHOP. You would be wrong, my friend. Parables are not lies because they describe events that have never happened. Miracles are not frauds because they are often—I do not say always—very simple and innocent contrivances by which the priest fortifies the faith of his flock. When this girl picks out the Dauphin among his courtiers, it will not be a miracle for me, because I shall know how it has been done, and my faith will not be increased. But as for the others, if they feel the thrill of the supernatural, and forget their sinful clay in a sudden sense of the glory of God, it will be a miracle and a blessed one. And you will find that the girl herself will be more affected than anyone else. She will forget how she really picked him out. So, perhaps, will you.

LA TRÉMOUILLE. Well, I wish I were clever enough to know how much of you is God's archbishop and how much the most artful fox in Touraine. Come on, or we shall be late for the fun; and I want to see it, miracle or no miracle.

THE ARCHBISHOP (*detaining him a moment*) Do not think that I am a lover of crooked ways. There is a new spirit rising in men: we are at the dawning of a wider epoch. If I were a simple monk, and had not to rule men, I should seek peace for my spirit with Aristotle and Pythagoras rather than with the saints and their miracles.

LA TRÉMOUILLE. And who the deuce was Pythagoras?

THE ARCHBISHOP. A sage who held that the earth is round, and that it moves round the sun.

LA TRÉMOUILLE. What an utter fool! Couldnt he use his eyes?

They go out together through the curtains, which are presently withdrawn, revealing the full depth of the throne-room with the Court assembled. On the right are two Chairs of State on a dais. Bluebeard is standing theatrically on the dais, playing the king, and, like the courtiers, enjoying the joke rather obviously. There is a curtained arch in the wall behind the dais; but the main door, guarded by men-at-arms, is at the other side of the room; and a clear path across is kept and lined by the courtiers. Charles is in this path in the middle of the room. La Hire is on his right. The Archbishop, on his left, has taken his place by the dais: La Trémouille at the other side of it. The Duchess de la Trémouille, pretending to be the Queen, sits in the Consort's chair, with a group of ladies in waiting close by, behind the Archbishop.

The chatter of the courtiers makes such a noise that nobody notices the appearance of the page at the door.

THE PAGE. The Duke of—(*Nobody listens*). The Duke of— (*The chatter continues. Indignant at his failure to command a hearing, he snatches the halberd of the nearest man-at-arms, and thumps the floor with it. The chatter ceases; and everybody looks at him in silence*). Attention (*He restores the halberd to the man-at-arms*). The Duke of Vendôme presents Joan the Maid to his Majesty.

CHARLES (*putting his finger on his lip*) Ssh! (*He hides behind the nearest courtier, peering out to see what happens*).

BLUEBEARD (*majestically*) Let her approach the throne.

Joan, dressed as a soldier, with her hair bobbed and hanging thickly round her face, is led in by a bashful and speechless nobleman, from whom she detaches herself to stop and look round eagerly for the Dauphin.

THE DUCHESS (*To the nearest lady in waiting*) My dear! Her hair!

All the ladies explode in uncontrollable laughter.

BLUEBEARD (*trying not to laugh, and waving his hand in deprecation of their merriment*) Ssh—ssh! Ladies! Ladies!!

JOAN (*not at all embarrassed*) I wear it like this because I am a soldier. Where be Dauphin?

A titter runs through the Court as she walks to the dais.

BLUEBEARD (*condescendingly*) You are in the presence of the Dauphin.

Joan looks at him sceptically for a moment, scanning him hard up and down to make sure. Dead silence, all watching her. Fun dawns in her face.

JOAN. Coom, Bluebeard! Thou canst not fool me. Where be Dauphin?

A roar of laughter breaks out as Gilles, with a gesture of sur-

render, joins in the laugh, and jumps down from the dais be-
side La Trémouille. Joan, also on the broad grin, turns back,
searching along the row of courtiers, and presently makes a
dive, and drags out Charles by the arm.

JOAN (*releasing him and bobbing him a little curtsey*) Gentle
little Dauphin, I am sent to you to drive the English away
from Orleans and from France, and to crown you king in the
cathedral at Rheims, where all true kings of France are
crowned.

CHARLES (*triumphant, to the Court*) You see, all of you: she
knew the blood royal. Who dare say now that I am not my
father's son? (*To Joan*) But if you want me to be crowned at
Rheims you must talk to the Archbishop, not to me. There he
is (*he is standing behind her*)!

JOAN (*turning quickly, overwhelmed with emotion*) Oh, my
lord! (*She falls on both knees before him, with bowed head,
not daring to look up*) My lord: I am only a poor country girl;
and you are filled with the blessedness and glory of God Himself; but you will touch me with your hands, and give me your
blessings, wont you?

BLUEBEARD (*whispering to La Trémouille*) The old fox
blushes.

LA TRÉMOUILLE. Another miracle!

THE ARCHBISHOP (*touched, putting his hand on her head*)
Child: you are in love with religion.

JOAN (*startled: looking up at him*) Am I? I never thought of
that. Is there any harm in it?

THE ARCHBISHOP. There is no harm in it, my child. But there
is danger.

JOAN (*rising, with a sunflush of reckless happiness irradiat-
ing her face*) There is always danger, except in heaven. Oh, my
lord, you have given me such strength, such courage. It must
be a most wonderful thing to be Archbishop.

The Court smiles broadly: even titters a little.

THE ARCHBISHOP (*drawing himself up sensitively*) Gentle-

men: your levity is rebuked by this maid's faith. I am, God
help me, all unworthy; but your mirth is a deadly sin.

Their faces fall. Dead silence.

BLUEBEARD. My lord: we were laughing at her, not at you.

THE ARCHBISHOP. What? Not at my unworthiness but at her
faith! Gilles de Rais: this maid prophesied that the blasphemer
should be drowned in his sin—

JOAN (*distressed*) No!

THE ARCHBISHOP (*silencing her by a gesture*) I prophesy now
that you will be hanged in yours if you do not learn when to
laugh and when to pray.

BLUEBEARD. My lord: I stand rebuked. I am sorry: I can say
no more. But if you prophesy that I shall be hanged, I shall
never be able to resist temptation, because I shall always be telling myself that I may as well be hanged for a sheep as a lamb.

The courtiers take heart at this. There is more tittering.

JOAN (*scandalized*) You are an idle fellow, Bluebeard; and
you have great impudence to answer the Archbishop.

LA HIRE (*with a huge chuckle*) Well said, lass! Well said!

JOAN (*impatiently to the Archbishop*) Oh, my lord, will you
send all these silly folks away so that I may speak to the Dauphin alone?

LA HIRE (*goodhumoredly*) I can take a hint. (*He salutes;
turns on his heel; and goes out*).

THE ARCHBISHOP. Come, gentlemen. The Maid comes with
God's blessing, and must be obeyed.

*The courtiers withdraw, some through the arch, others at the
opposite side. The Archbishop marches across to the door, followed by the Duchess and La Trémouille. As the Archbishop
passes Joan, she falls on her knees, and kisses the hem of his
robe fervently. He shakes his head in instinctive remonstrance;
gathers the robe from her; and goes out. She is left kneeling
directly in the Duchess's way.*

THE DUCHESS (*coldly*) Will you allow me to pass, please?

JOAN (*hastily rising, and standing back*) Beg pardon, maam. I am sure.

The Duchess passes on. Joan stares after her; then whispers to the Dauphin.

JOAN. Be that Queen?

CHARLES. No. She thinks she is.

JOAN (*again staring after the Duchess*) Oo-oo-ooh! (*Her awestruck amazement at the figure cut by the magnificently dressed lady is not wholly complimentary*).

LA TRÉMOUILLE (*very surely*) I'll trouble your Highness not to gibe at my wife. (*He goes out. The others have already gone*).

JOAN (*to the Dauphin*) Who be old Gruff-and-Grum?

CHARLES. He is the Duke de la Trémouille.

JOAN. What be his job?

CHARLES. He pretends to command the army. And whenever I find a friend I can care for, he kills him.

JOAN. Why dost let him?

CHARLES (*petulantly moving to the throne side of the room to escape from her magnetic field*) How can I prevent him? He bullies me. They all bully me.

JOAN. Art afraid?

CHARLES. Yes: I am afraid. It's no use preaching to me about it. It's all very well for these big men with their armor that is too heavy for me, and their swords that I can hardly lift, and their muscle and their shouting and their bad tempers. They like fighting: most of them are making fools of themselves all the time they are not fighting; but I am quiet and sensible; and I dont want to kill people: I only want to be left alone to enjoy myself in my own way. I never asked to be a king: it was pushed on me. So if you are going to say "Son of St Louis: gird on the sword of your ancestors, and lead us to victory" you may spare your breath to cool your porridge; for I cannot do it I am not built that way; and there is an end of it.

JOAN (*trenchant and masterful*) Blethers! We are all like that to begin with. I shall put courage into thee.

CHARLES. But I dont want to have courage put into me. I want to sleep in a comfortable bed, and not live in continual terror of being killed or wounded. Put courage into the others, and let them have their bellyful of fighting; but let me alone.

JOAN. It's no use, Charlie: thou must face what God puts on thee. If thou fail to make thyself king, thoult be a beggar: what else art fit for? Come! Let me see thee sitting on the throne. I have looked forward to that.

CHARLES. What is the good of sitting on the throne when the other fellows give all the orders? However! (*he sits enthroned, a piteous figure*) here is the king for you! Look your fill at the poor devil.

JOAN. Thourt not king yet, lad: thourt but Dauphin. Be not led away by them around thee. Dressing up dont fill empty noddle. I know the people: the real people that make thy bread for thee; and I tell thee they count no man king of France until the holy oil has been poured on his hair, and himself consecrated and crowned in Rheims Cathedral. And thou needs new clothes, Charlie. Why does not Queen look after thee properly?

CHARLES. We're too poor. She wants all the money we can spare to put on her own back. Besides, I like to see her beautifully dressed; and I dont care what I wear myself: I should look ugly anyhow.

JOAN. There is some good in thee, Charlie; but it is not yet a king's good.

CHARLES. We shall see. I am not such a fool as I look. I have my eyes open; and I can tell you that one good treaty is worth ten good fights. These fighting fellows lose all on the treaties that they gain on the fights. If we can only have a treaty, the English are sure to have the worst of it, because they are better at fighting than at thinking.

JOAN. If the English win, it is they that will make the treaty; and then God help poor France! Thou must fight, Charlie, whether thou will or no. I will go first to hearten thee. We must take our courage in both hands: aye, and pray for it with both hands too.

CHARLES (*descending from his throne and again crossing the room to escape from her dominating urgency*) Oh do stop talking about God and praying. I cant bear people who are always praying. Isnt it bad enough to have to do it at the proper times?

JOAN (*pitying him*) Thou poor child, thou hast never prayed in thy life. I must teach thee from the beginning.

CHARLES. I am not a child: I am a grown man and a father; and I will not be taught any more.

JOAN. Aye, you have a little son. He that will be Louis the Eleventh when you die. Would you not fight for him?

CHARLES. No: a horrid boy. He hates me. He hates everybody, selfish little beast! I dont want to be bothered with children. I dont want to be a father; and I dont want to be a son: especially a son of St Louis. I dont want to be any of these fine things you all have your heads full of: I want to be just what I am. Why cant you mind your own business, and let me mind mine?

JOAN (*again contemptuous*) Minding your own business is like minding your own body: it's the shortest way to make yourself sick. What is my business? Helping mother at home. What is thine? Petting lapdogs and sucking sugarsticks. I call that muck. I tell thee it is God's business we are here to do: not our own. I have a message to thee from God; and thou must listen to it, though thy heart break with the terror of it.

CHARLES. I dont want a message; but can you tell me any secrets? Can you do any cures? Can you turn lead into gold, or anything of that sort?

JOAN. I can turn thee into a king, in Rheims Cathedral; and that is a miracle that will take some doing, it seems.

CHARLES. If we go to Rheims, and have a coronation, Anne will want new dresses. We cant afford them. I am all right as I am.

JOAN. As you are! And what is that? Less than my father's poorest shepherd. Thourt not lawful owner of thy own land of France till thou be consecrated.

CHARLES. But I shall not be lawful owner of my own land anyhow. Will the consecration pay off my mortgages? I have pledged my last acre to the Archbishop and that fat bully. I owe money even to Bluebeard.

JOAN (*earnestly*) Charlie: I come from the land, and have gotten my strength working on the land; and I tell thee that the land is thine to rule righteously and keep God's peace in, and not to pledge at the pawnshop as a drunken woman pledges her children's clothes. And I come from God to tell thee to kneel in the cathedral and solemnly give thy kingdom to Him for ever and ever, and become the greatest king in the world as His steward and His bailiff, His soldier and His servant. The very clay of France will become holy: her soldiers will be the soldiers of God: the rebel dukes will be rebels against God: the English will fall on their knees and beg thee let them return to their lawful homes in peace. Wilt be a poor little Judas, and betray me and Him that sent me?

CHARLES (*tempted at last*) Oh, if I only dare!

JOAN. I shall dare, dare, and dare again, in God's name! Art for or against me?

CHARLES (*excited*) I'll risk it. I warn you I shant be able to keep it up; but I'll risk it. You shall see. (*Running to the main door and shouting*) Hallo! Come back, everybody. (*To Joan, as he runs back to the arch opposite*) Mind you stand by and dont let me be bullied. (*Through the arch*) Come along, will you: the whole Court. (*He sits down in the royal chair as they all hurry in to their former places, chattering and wondering*). Now I'm in for it; but no matter: here goes! (*To the page*) Call for silence, you little beast, will you?

THE PAGE (*snatching a halberd as before and thumping with it repeatedly*) Silence for His Majesty the King. The King speaks. (*Peremptorily*) Will you be silent there? (*Silence*).

CHARLES (*rising*) I have given the command of the army to The Maid. The Maid is to do as she likes with it. (*He descends from the dais*).

General amazement. La Hire, delighted, slaps his steel thigh-piece with his gauntlet.

LA TRÉMOUILLE (*turning threateningly towards Charles*) What is this? I command the army.

Joan quickly puts her hand on Charles's shoulder as he instinctively recoils. Charles, with a grotesque effort culminating in an extravagant gesture, snaps his fingers in the Chamberlain's face.

JOAN. Thourt answered, old Gruff-and-Grum. (*Suddenly flashing out her sword as she divines that her moment has come*) Who is for God and His Maid? Who is for Orleans with me?

LA HIRE (*carried away, drawing also*) For God and His Maid! To Orleans!

ALL THE KNIGHTS (*following his lead with enthusiasm*) To Orleans!

Joan, radiant, falls on her knees in thanksgiving to God. They all kneel, except the Archbishop, who gives his benediction with a sign, and La Trémouille, who collapses, cursing.

SCENE III

ORLEANS, May 29th, 1429. Dunois, aged 26, is pacing up and down a patch of ground on the south bank of the silver Loire, commanding a long view of the river in both directions. He has had his lance stuck up with a pennon, which streams in a strong east wind. His shield with its bend sinister lies beside it. He has his commander's baton in his hand. He is well built, carrying his armor easily. His broad brow and pointed chin give him an equilaterally triangular face, already marked by active service and responsibility, with the expression of a good-natured and capable man who has no affectations and no foolish illusions. His page is sitting on the ground, elbows on knees, cheeks on fists, idly watching the water. It is evening; and both man and boy are affected by the loveliness of the Loire.

DUNOIS (*halting for a moment to glance up at the streaming pennon and shake his head wearily before he resumes his pacing*) West wind, west wind, west wind. Strumpet: steadfast when you should be wanton, wanton when you should be steadfast. West wind on the silver Loire: what rhymes to Loire? (*He looks again at the pennon, and shakes his fist at it*) Change, curse you, change, English harlot of a wind, change. West, west, I tell you. (*With a growl he resumes his march in silence, but soon begins again*) West wind, wanton wind, wilful wind, womanish wind, false wind from over the water, will you never blow again?

THE PAGE (*bounding to his feet*) See! There! There she goes!

DUNOIS (*startled from his reverie: eagerly*) Where? Who? The Maid?

THE PAGE. No: the kingfisher. Like blue lightning. She went into the bush.

DUNOIS (*furiously disappointed*) Is that all? You infernal young idiot: I have a mind to pitch you into the river.

THE PAGE (*not afraid, knowing his man*) It looked frightfully jolly, that flash of blue. Look! There goes the other!

DUNOIS (*running eagerly to the river brim*) Where? Where?

THE PAGE (*pointing*) Passing the reeds.

DUNOIS (*delighted*) I see.

They follow the flight till the bird takes cover.

THE PAGE. You blew me up because you were not in time to see them yesterday.

DUNOIS. You knew I was expecting The Maid when you set up your yelping. I will give you something to yelp for next time.

THE PAGE. Arnt they lovely? I wish I could catch them.

DUNOIS. Let me catch you trying to trap them, and I will put you in the iron cage for a month to teach you what a cage feels like. You are an abominable boy.

THE PAGE (*laughs, and squats down as before*)!

DUNOIS (*pacing*) Blue bird, blue bird, since I am friend to thee, change thou the wind for me. No: it does not rhyme. He who has sinned for thee: thats better. No sense in it, though. (*He finds himself close to the page*) You abominable boy! (*He turns away from him*) Mary in the blue snood, kingfisher color: will you grudge me a west wind?

A SENTRY'S VOICE WESTWARD. Halt! Who goes there?

JOAN'S VOICE. The Maid.

DUNOIS. Let her pass. Hither, Maid! To me!

Joan, in splendid armor, rushes in in a blazing rage. The wind drops; and the pennon flaps idly down the lance; but Dunois is too much occupied with Joan to notice it.

JOAN (*bluntly*) Be you Bastard of Orleans?

DUNOIS (*cool and stern, pointing to his shield*) You see the bend sinister. Are you Joan the Maid?

JOAN. Sure.

DUNOIS. Where are your troops?

JOAN. Miles behind. They have cheated me. They have brought me to the wrong side of the river.

DUNOIS. I told them to.

JOAN. Why did you? The English are on the other side!

DUNOIS. The English are on both sides.

JOAN. But Orleans is on the other side. We must fight the English there. How can we cross the river?

DUNOIS (*grimly*) There is a bridge.

JOAN. In God's name, then, let us cross the bridge, and fall on them.

DUNOIS. It seems simple; but it cannot be done.

JOAN. Who says so?

DUNOIS. I say so; and older and wiser heads than mine are of the same opinion.

JOAN (*roundly*) Then your older and wiser heads are fatheads: they have made a fool of you; and now they want to make a fool of me too, bringing me to the wrong side of the river. Do you not know that I bring you better help than ever came to any general or any town?

DUNOIS (*smiling patiently*) Your own?

JOAN. No: the help and counsel of the King of Heaven. Which is the way to the bridge?

DUNOIS. You are impatient, Maid.

JOAN. Is this a time for patience? Our enemy is at our gates; and here we stand doing nothing. Oh, why are you not fighting? Listen to me: I will deliver you from fear. I—

DUNOIS (*laughing heartily, and waving her off*) No, no, my girl: if you delivered me from fear I should be a good knight for a story book, but a very bad commander of the army. Come! let me begin to make a soldier of you. (*He takes her to the water's edge*). Do you see those two forts at this end of the bridge? the big ones?

JOAN. Yes. Are they ours or the goddams'?

DUNOIS. Be quiet, and listen to me. If I were in either of those forts with only ten men I could hold it against an army.

The English have more than ten times ten goddams in those forts to hold them against us.

JOAN. They cannot hold them against God. God did not give them the land under those forts: they stole it from Him. He gave it to us. I will take those forts.

DUNOIS. Single-handed?

JOAN. Our men will take them. I will lead them.

DUNOIS. Not a man will follow you.

JOAN. I will not look back to see whether anyone is following me.

DUNOIS (*recognizing her mettle, and clapping her heartily on the shoulder*) Good. You have the makings of a soldier in you. You are in love with war.

JOAN (*startled*) Oh! And the Archbishop said I was in love with religion.

DUNOIS. I, God forgive me, am a little in love with war myself, the ugly devil! I am like a man with two wives. Do you want to be like a woman with two husbands?

JOAN (*matter-of-fact*) I will never take a husband. A man in Toul took an action against me for breach of promise; but I never promised him. I am a soldier: I do not want to be thought of as a woman. I will not dress as a woman. I do not care for the things women care for. They dream of lovers, and of money. I dream of leading a charge, and of placing the big guns. You soldiers do not know how to use the big guns: you think you can win battles with a great noise and smoke.

DUNOIS (*with a shrug*) True. Half the time the artillery is more trouble than it is worth.

JOAN. Aye, lad; but you cannot fight stone walls with horses: you must have guns, and much bigger guns too.

DUNOIS (*grinning at her familiarity, and echoing it*) Aye, lass; but a good heart and a stout ladder will get over the stoniest wall.

JOAN. I will be first up the ladder when we reach the fort, Bastard. I dare you to follow me.

DUNOIS. You must not dare a staff officer, Joan: only company officers are allowed to indulge in displays of personal courage. Besides, you must know that I welcome you as a saint, not as a soldier. I have daredevils enough at my call, if they could help me.

JOAN. I am not a daredevil: I am a servant of God. My sword is sacred: I found it behind the altar in the church of St Catherine, where God hid it for me; and I may not strike a blow with it. My heart is full of courage, not of anger. I will lead; and your men will follow: that is all I can do. But I must do it: you shall not stop me.

DUNOIS. All in good time. Our men cannot take those forts by a sally across the bridge. They must come by water, and take the English in the rear on this side.

JOAN (*her military sense asserting itself*) Then make rafts and put big guns on them; and let your men cross to us.

DUNOIS. The rafts are ready; and the men are embarked. But they must wait for God.

JOAN. What do you mean? God is waiting for them.

DUNOIS. Let Him send us a wind then. My boats are downstream: they cannot come up against both wind and current. We must wait until God changes the wind. Come: let me take you to the church.

JOAN. No. I love church; but the English will not yield to prayers: they understand nothing but hard knocks and slashes. I will not go to church until we have beaten them.

DUNOIS. You must: I have business for you there.

JOAN. What business?

DUNOIS. To pray for a west wind. I have prayed; and I have given two silver candlesticks; but my prayers are not answered. Yours may be: you are young and innocent.

JOAN. Oh yes: you are right. I will pray: I will tell St Catherine: she will make God give me a west wind. Quick: shew me the way to the church.

THE PAGE (*sneezes violently*) At-cha!!!

JOAN. God bless you, child! Coom, Bastard.

They go out. The page rises to follow. He picks up the shield, and is taking the spear as well when he notices the pennon, which is now streaming eastward.

THE PAGE (*dropping the shield and calling excitedly after them*) Seigneur! Seigneur! Mademoiselle!

DUNOIS (*running back*) What is it? The kingfisher? (*He looks eagerly for it up the river*).

JOAN. (*joining them*) Oh, a kingfisher! Where?

THE PAGE. No: the wind, the wind, the wind (*pointing to the pennon*): That is what made me sneeze.

DUNOIS (*looking at the pennon*) The wind has changed. (*He crosses himself*) God has spoken. (*Kneeling and handing his baton to Joan*) You command the king's army. I am your soldier.

THE PAGE (*looking down the river*) The boats have put off. They are ripping upstream like anything.

DUNOIS (*rising*) Now for the forts. You dared me to follow. Dare you lead?

JOAN (*bursting into tears and flinging her arms round Dunois, kissing him on both cheeks*) Dunois, dear comrade in arms, help me. My eyes are blinded with tears. Set my foot on the ladder, and say "Up, Joan."

DUNOIS (*dragging her out*) Never mind the tears: make for the flash of the guns.

JOAN (*in a blaze of courage*) Ah!

DUNOIS (*dragging her along with him*) For God and Saint Dennis!

THE PAGE (*shrilly*) The Maid! The Maid! God and The Maid! Hurray-ay-ay! (*He snatches up the shield and lance, and capers out after them, mad with excitement*).

SCENE IV

A TENT in the English camp. A bullnecked English chaplain of 50 is sitting on a stool at a table, hard at work writing. At the other side of the table an imposing nobleman, aged 46, is seated in a handsome chair turning over the leaves of an illuminated Book of Hours. The nobleman is enjoying himself: the chaplain is struggling with suppressed wrath. There is an unoccupied leather stool on the nobleman's left. The table is on his right.

THE NOBLEMAN. Now this is what I call workmanship. There is nothing on earth more exquisite than a bonny book, with well-placed columns of rich black writing in beautiful borders, and illuminated pictures cunningly inset. But nowadays, instead of looking at books, people read them. A book might as well be one of those orders for bacon and bran that you are scribbling.

THE CHAPLAIN. I must say, my lord, you take our situation very coolly. Very coolly indeed.

THE NOBLEMAN (*supercilious*) What is the matter?

THE CHAPLAIN. The matter, my lord, is that we English have been defeated.

THE NOBLEMAN. That happens, you know. It is only in history books and ballads that the enemy is always defeated.

THE CHAPLAIN. But we are being defeated over and over again. First, Orleans—

THE NOBLEMAN (*poohpoohing*) Oh, Orleans!

THE CHAPLAIN. I know what you are going to say, my lord: that was a clear case of witchcraft and sorcery. But we are still being defeated. Jargeau, Meung, Beaugency, just like Orleans. And now we have been butchered at Patay, and Sir John Talbot taken prisoner. (*He throws down his pen, almost in tears*) I feel it, my lord: I feel it very deeply. I cannot bear to see my countrymen defeated by a parcel of foreigners.

THE NOBLEMAN. Oh! you are an Englishman, are you?

THE CHAPLAIN. Certainly not, my lord: I am a gentleman. Still, like your lordship, I was born in England; and it makes a difference.

THE NOBLEMAN. You are attached to the soil, eh?

THE CHAPLAIN. It pleases your lordship to be satirical at my expense: your greatness privileges you to be so with impunity. But your lordship knows very well that I am not attached to the soil in a vulgar manner, like a serf. Still, I have a feeling about it; (*with growing agitation*) and I am not ashamed of it; and (*rising wildly*) By God, if this goes on any longer I will fling my cassock to the devil, and take arms myself, and strangle the accursed witch with my own hands.

THE NOBLEMAN (*laughing at him goodnaturedly*) So you shall, chaplain: so you shall, if we can do nothing better. But not yet, not quite yet.

The Chaplain resumes his seat very sulkily.

THE NOBLEMAN (*airily*) I should not care very much about the witch—you see, I have made my pilgrimage to the Holy Land; and the Heavenly Powers, for their own credit, can hardly allow me to be worsted by a village sorceress—but the Bastard of Orleans is a harder nut to crack; and as he has been to the Holy Land too, honors are easy between us as far as that goes.

THE CHAPLAIN. He is only a Frenchman, my lord.

THE NOBLEMAN. A Frenchman! Where did you pick up that expression? Are these Burgundians and Bretons and Picards and Gascons beginning to call themselves Frenchmen, just as our fellows are beginning to call themselves Englishmen? They actually talk of France and England as their countries. Theirs, if you please! What is to become of me and you if that way of thinking comes into fashion?

THE CHAPLAIN. Why, my lord? Can it hurt us?

THE NOBLEMAN. Men cannot serve two masters. If this cant of serving their country once takes hold of them, goodbye to the authority of their feudal lords, and goodbye to the authority of the Church. That is, goodbye to you and me.

THE CHAPLAIN. I hope I am a faithful servant of the Church; and there are only six cousins between me and the barony of Stogumber, which was created by the Conqueror. But is that any reason why I should stand by and see Englishmen beaten by a French bastard and a witch from Lousy Champagne?

THE NOBLEMAN. Easy, man, easy: we shall burn the witch and beat the bastard all in good time. Indeed I am waiting at present for the Bishop of Beauvais, to arrange the burning with him. He has been turned out of his diocese by her faction.

THE CHAPLAIN. You have first to catch her, my lord.

THE NOBLEMAN. Or buy her. I will offer a king's ransom.

THE CHAPLAIN. A king's ransom! For that slut!

THE NOBLEMAN. One has to leave a margin. Some of Charles's people will sell her to the Burgundians; the Burgundians will sell her to us; and there will probably be three or four middlemen who will expect their little commissions.

THE CHAPLAIN. Monstrous. It is all those scoundrels of Jews: they get in every time money changes hands. I would not leave a Jew alive in Christendom if I had my way.

THE NOBLEMAN. Why not? The Jews generally give value. They make you pay; but they deliver the goods. In my experience the men who want something for nothing are invariably Christians.

A page appears.

THE PAGE. The Right Reverend the Bishop of Beauvais: Monseigneur Cauchon.

Cauchon, aged about 60, comes in. The page withdraws. The two Englishmen rise.

THE NOBLEMAN (*with effusive courtesy*) My dear Bishop, how good of you to come! Allow me to introduce myself:

Richard de Beauchamp, Earl of Warwick, at your service.

CAUCHON. Your lordship's fame is well known to me.

WARWICK. This reverend cleric is Master John de Stogumber.

THE CHAPLAIN (*glibly*) John Bowyer Spenser Neville de Stogumber, at your service, my lord: Bachelor of Theology, and Keeper of the Private Seal to His Eminence the Cardinal of Winchester.

WARWICK (*to Cauchon*) You call him the Cardinal of England, I believe. Our king's uncle.

CAUCHON. Messire John de Stogumber: I am always the very good friend of His Eminence. (*He extends his hand to the chaplain, who kisses his ring*).

WARWICK. Do me the honor to be seated. (*He gives Cauchon his chair, placing it at the head of the table*).

Cauchon accepts the place of honor with a grave inclination. Warwick fetches the leather stool carelessly, and sits in his former place. The chaplain goes back to his chair.

Though Warwick has taken second place in calculated deference to the Bishop, he assumes the lead in opening the proceedings as a matter of course. He is still cordial and expansive; but there is a new note in his voice which means that he is coming to business.

WARWICK. Well, my Lord Bishop, you find us in one of our unlucky moments. Charles is to be crowned at Rheims, practically by the young woman from Lorraine; and—I must not deceive you, nor flatter your hopes—we cannot prevent it. I suppose it will make a great difference to Charles's position.

CAUCHON. Undoubtedly. It is a masterstroke of The Maid's.

THE CHAPLAIN (*again agitated*) We were not fairly beaten, my lord. No Englishman is ever fairly beaten.

Cauchon raises his eyebrow slightly, then quickly composes his face.

WARWICK. Our friend here takes the view that the young woman is a sorceress. It would, I presume, be the duty of your reverend lordship to denounce her to the Inquisition, and have her burnt for that offence.

CAUCHON. If she were captured in my diocese: yes.

WARWICK (*feeling that they are getting on capitally*) Just so. Now I suppose there can be no reasonable doubt that she is a sorceress.

THE CHAPLAIN. Not the least. An arrant witch.

WARWICK (*gently reproving the interruption*) We are asking for the Bishop's opinion, Messire John.

CAUCHON. We shall have to consider not merely our own opinions here, but the opinions—the prejudices, if you like—of a French court.

WARWICK (*correcting*) A Catholic court, my lord.

CAUCHON. Catholic courts are composed of mortal men, like other courts, however sacred their function and inspiration may be. And if the men are Frenchmen, as the modern fashion calls them, I am afraid the bare fact that an English army has been defeated by a French one will not convince them that there is any sorcery in the matter.

THE CHAPLAIN. What! Not when the famous Sir John Talbot himself has been defeated and actually taken prisoner by a drab from the ditches of Lorraine!

CAUCHON. Sir John Talbot, we all know, is a fierce and formidable soldier, Messire; but I have yet to learn that he is an able general. And though it pleases you to say that he has been defeated by this girl, some of us may be disposed to give a little of the credit to Dunois.

THE CHAPLAIN (*contemptuously*) The Bastard of Orleans!

CAUCHON. Let me remind—

WARWICK (*interposing*) I know what you are going to say, my lord. Dunois defeated me at Montargis.

CAUCHON (*bowing*) I take that as evidence that the Seigneur Dunois is a very able commander indeed.

WARWICK. Your lordship is the flower of courtesy. I admit, on

our side, that Talbot is a mere fighting animal, and that it probably served him right to be taken at Patay.

THE CHAPLAIN (*chafing*) My lord: at Orleans this woman
had her throat pierced by an English arrow, and was seen to
cry like a child from the pain of it. It was a death wound; yet
she fought all day; and when our men had repulsed all her
attacks like true Englishmen, she walked alone to the wall of
our fort with a white banner in her hand; and our men were
paralyzed, and could neither shoot nor strike whilst the French
fell on them and drove them on to the bridge, which immediately burst into flames and crumbled under them, letting them
down into the river, where they were drowned in heaps. Was
this your bastard's generalship? or were those flames of hell,
conjured up by witchcraft?

WARWICK. You will forgive Messire John's vehemence, my
lord; but he has put our case. Dunois is a great captain, we
admit; but why could he do nothing until the witch came?

CAUCHON. I do not say that there were no supernatural powers on her side. But the names on that white banner were not
the names of Satan and Beelzebub, but the blessed names of
our Lord and His holy mother. And your commander who was
drowned—Clahz-da I think you call him—

WARWICK. Glasdale. Sir William Glasdale.

CAUCHON. Glass-dell, thank you. He was no saint; and many
of our people think that he was drowned for his blasphemies
against The Maid.

WARWICK (*beginning to look very dubious*) Well, what are
we to infer from all this, my lord? Has The Maid converted
you?

CAUCHON. If she had, my lord, I should have known better
than to have trusted myself here within your grasp.

WARWICK (*blandly deprecating*) Oh! oh! My Lord!

CAUCHON. If the devil is making use of this girl—and I believe he is—

WARWICK (*reassured*) Ah! You hear, Messire John? I knew your lordship would not fail us. Pardon my interruption. Proceed.

CAUCHON. If it be so, the devil has longer views than you give him credit for.

WARWICK. Indeed? In what way? Listen to this, Messire John.

CAUCHON. If the devil wanted to damn a country girl, do you think so easy a task would cost him the winning of half a dozen battles? No, my lord: any trumpery imp could do that much if the girl could be damned at all. The Prince of Darkness does not condescend to such cheap drudgery. When he strikes, he strikes at the Catholic Church, whose realm is the whole spiritual world. When he damns, he damns the souls of the entire human race. Against that dreadful design The Church stands ever on guard. And it is as one of the instruments of that design that I see this girl. She is inspired, but diabolically inspired.

THE CHAPLAIN. I told you she was a witch.

CAUCHON (*fiercely*) She is not a witch. She is a heretic.

THE CHAPLAIN. What difference does that make?

CAUCHON. You, a priest, ask me that! You English are strangely blunt in the mind. All these things that you call witchcraft are capable of a natural explanation. The woman's miracles would not impose on a rabbit: she does not claim them as miracles herself. What do her victories prove but that she has a better head on her shoulders than your swearing Glassdells and mad bull Talbots, and that the courage of faith, even though it be a false faith, will always outstay the courage of wrath?

THE CHAPLAIN (*hardly able to believe his ears*) Does your lordship compare Sir John Talbot, three times Governor of Ireland, to a mad bull?!!!

WARWICK. It would not be seemly for you to do so, Messire John, as you are still six removes from a barony. But as I am an earl, and Talbot is only a knight, I may make bold to accept the comparison. (*To the Bishop*) My lord: I wipe the slate as far as witchcraft goes. None the less, we must burn the woman.

CAUCHON. I cannot burn her. The Church cannot take life. And my first duty is to seek this girl's salvation.

WARWICK. No doubt. But you do burn people occasionally.

CAUCHON. No. When The Church cuts off an obstinate heretic as a dead branch from the tree of life, the heretic is handed over to the secular arm. The Church has no part in what the secular arm may see fit to do.

WARWICK. Precisely. And I shall be the secular arm in this case. Well, my lord, hand over your dead branch; and I will see that the fire is ready for it. If you will answer for The Church's part, I will answer for the secular part.

CAUCHON (*with smouldering anger*) I can answer for nothing. You great lords are too prone to treat The Church as a mere political convenience.

WARWICK (*smiling and propitiatory*) Not in England, I assure you.

CAUCHON. In England more than anywhere else. No, my lord: the soul of this village girl is of equal value with yours or your king's before the throne of God; and my first duty is to save it. I will not suffer your lordship to smile at me as if I were repeating a meaningless form of words, and it were well understood between us that I should betray the girl to you. I am no mere political bishop: my faith is to me what your honor is to you; and if there be a loophole through which this baptized child of God can creep to her salvation, I shall guide her to it.

THE CHAPLAIN (*rising in a fury*) You are a traitor.

CAUCHON (*springing up*) You lie, priest. (*Trembling with rage*) If you dare do what this woman has done—set your country above the holy Catholic Church—you shall go to the fire with her.

THE CHAPLAIN. My lord: I—I went too far. I— (*He sits down with a submissive gesture*).

WARWICK (*who has risen apprehensively*) My lord: I apologize to you for the word used by Messire John de Stogumber.

It does not mean in England what it does in France. In your language traitor means betrayer: one who is perfidious, treacherous, unfaithful, disloyal. In our country it means simply one who is not wholly devoted to our English interests.

CAUCHON. I am sorry: I did not understand. (*He subsides into his chair with dignity*).

WARWICK (*resuming his seat, much relieved*) I must apologize on my own account if I have seemed to take the burning of this poor girl too lightly. When one has seen whole countrysides burnt over and over again as mere items in military routine, one has to grow a very thick skin. Otherwise one might go mad: at all events, I should. May I venture to assume that your lordship also, having to see so many heretics burned from time to time, is compelled to take—shall I say a professional view of what would otherwise be a very horrible incident?

CAUCHON. Yes: it is a painful duty: even, as you say, a horrible one. But in comparison with the horror of heresy it is less than nothing. I am not thinking of this girl's body, which will suffer for a few moments only, and which must in any event die in some more or less painful manner, but of her soul, which may suffer to all eternity.

WARWICK. Just so; and God grant that her soul may be saved! But the practical problem would seem to be how to save her soul without saving her body. For we must face it, my lord: if this cult of The Maid goes on, our cause is lost.

THE CHAPLAIN (*his voice broken like that of a man who has been crying*) May I speak, my lord?

WARWICK. Really, Messire John, I had rather you did not, unless you can keep your temper.

THE CHAPLAIN. It is only this. I speak under correction; but The Maid is full of deceit: she pretends to be devout. Her prayers and confessions are endless. How can she be accused of heresy when she neglects no observance of a faithful daughter of The Church?

CAUCHON (*flaming up*) A faithful daughter of The Church! The Pope himself at his proudest dare not presume as this woman presumes. She acts as if she herself were The Church. She brings the message of God to Charles; and The Church must stand aside. She will crown him in the cathedral of Rheims: she, not The Church! She sends letters to the king of England giving him God's command through her to return to his island on pain of God's vengeance, which she will execute. Let me tell you that the writing of such letters was the practice of the accursed Mahomet, the anti-Christ. Has she ever in all her utterances said one word of The Church? Never. It is always God and herself.

WARWICK. What can you expect? A beggar on horseback! Her head is turned.

CAUCHON. Who has turned it? The devil. And for a mighty purpose. He is spreading this heresy everywhere. The man Hus, burnt only thirteen years ago at Constance, infected all Bohemia with it. A man named WcLeef, himself an anointed priest, spread the pestilence in England; and to your shame you let him die in his bed. We have such people here in France too: I know the breed. It is cancerous: if it be not cut out, stamped out, burnt out, it will not stop until it has brought the whole body of human society into sin and corruption, into waste and ruin. By it an Arab camel driver drove Christ and His Church out of Jerusalem, and ravaged his way west like a wild beast until at last there stood only the Pyrenees and God's mercy between France and damnation. Yet what did the camel driver do at the beginning more than this shepherd girl is doing? He had his voices from the angel Gabriel: she has her voices from St Catherine and St Margaret and the Blessed Michael. He declared himself the messenger of God, and wrote in God's name to the kings of the earth. Her letters to them are going forth daily. It is not the Mother of God now to whom we must look for intercession, but to Joan the Maid. What will the world be like when The Church's accumulated wisdom and knowledge and experience, its councils of learned, venerable pious men, are thrust into the kennel by every ignorant laborer or dairymaid whom the devil can puff up with the monstrous self-conceit of being directly inspired from heaven? It will be a world of blood, of fury, of devastation, of each man striving for his own hand: in the end a world wrecked back into barbarism. For now you have only Mahomet and his dupes, and The Maid and her dupes; but what will it be when every girl thinks herself a Joan and every man a Mahomet? I shudder to the very marrow of my bones when I think of it. I have fought it all my life; and I will fight it to the end. Let all this woman's sins be forgiven her except only this sin; for it is the sin against the Holy Ghost; and if she does not recant in the dust before the world, and submit herself to the last inch of her soul to her Church, to the fire she shall go if she once falls into my hand.

WARWICK (*unimpressed*) You feel strongly about it, naturally.

CAUCHON. Do not you?

WARWICK. I am a soldier, not a churchman. As a pilgrim I saw something of the Mahometans. They were not so illbred as I had been led to believe. In some respects their conduct compared favorably with ours.

CAUCHON (*displeased*) I have noticed this before. Men go to the East to convert the infidels. And the infidels pervert them. The Crusader comes back more than half a Saracen. Not to mention that all Englishmen are born heretics.

THE CHAPLAIN. Englishmen heretics!!! (*Appealing to Warwick*) My lord: must we endure this? His lordship is beside himself. How can what an Englishman believes be heresy? It is a contradiction in terms.

CAUCHON. I absolve you, Messire de Stogumber, on the ground of invincible ignorance. The thick air of your country does not breed theologians.

WARWICK. You would not say so if you heard us quarrelling about religion, my lord! I am sorry you think I must be either a heretic or a blockhead because, as a travelled man, I know that the followers of Mahomet profess great respect for our Lord, and are more ready to forgive St Peter for being a fisherman than your lordship is to forgive Mahomet for being a camel driver. But at least we can proceed in this matter without bigotry.

CAUCHON. When men call the zeal of the Christian Church bigotry I know what to think.

WARWICK. They are only east and west views of the same thing.

CAUCHON (*bitterly ironical*) Only east and west! Only!!

WARWICK. Oh, my Lord Bishop, I am not gainsaying you. You will carry The Church with you; but you have to carry the nobles also. To my mind there is a stronger case against The Maid than the one you have so forcibly put. Frankly, I am not afraid of this girl becoming another Mahomet, and superseding The Church by a great heresy. I think you exaggerate that risk. But have you noticed that in these letters of hers, she proposes to all the kings of Europe, as she has already pressed on Charles, a transaction which would wreck the whole social structure of Christendom?

CAUCHON. Wreck The Church. I tell you so.

WARWICK (*whose patience is wearing out*) My lord: pray get The Church out of your head for a moment; and remember that there are temporal institutions in the world as well as spiritual ones. I and my peers represent the feudal aristocracy as you represent The Church. We are the temporal power. Well, do you not see how this girl's idea strikes at us?

CAUCHON. How does her idea strike at you, except as it strikes at all of us, through The Church?

WARWICK. Her idea is that the kings should give their realms to God, and then reign as God's bailiffs.

CAUCHON (*not interested*) Quite sound theologically, my lord. But the king will hardly care, provided he reign. It is an abstract idea: a mere form of words.

WARWICK. By no means. It is a cunning device to supersede the aristocracy, and make the king sole and absolute autocrat. Instead of the king being merely the first among his peers, he becomes their master. That we cannot suffer: we call no man master. Nominally we hold our lands and dignities from the king, because there must be a keystone to the arch of human society; but we hold our lands in our own hands, and defend them with our own swords and those of our own tenants. Now by The Maid's doctrine the king will take our lands—our lands! —and make them a present to God; and God will then vest them wholly in the king.

CAUCHON. Need you fear that? You are the makers of kings after all. York or Lancaster in England, Lancaster or Valois in France: they reign according to your pleasure.

WARWICK. Yes; but only as long as the people follow their feudal lords, and know the king only as a travelling show, owning nothing but the highway that belongs to everybody. If the people's thoughts and hearts were turned to the king, and their lords became only the king's servants in their eyes, the king could break us across his knee one by one; and then what should we be but liveried courtiers in his halls?

CAUCHON. Still you need not fear, my lord. Some men are born kings; and some are born statesmen. The two are seldom the same. Where would the king find counsellors to plan and carry out such a policy for him?

WARWICK (*with a not too friendly smile*) Perhaps in the Church, my lord.

Cauchon, with an equally sour smile, shrugs his shoulders, and does not contradict him.

WARWICK. Strike down the barons; and the cardinals will have it all their own way.

CAUCHON (*conciliatory, dropping his polemical tone*) My lord: we shall not defeat The Maid if we strive against one another. I know well that there is a Will to Power in the world. I know that while it lasts there will be a struggle between the

Emperor and the Pope, between the dukes and the political cardinals, between the barons and the kings. The devil divides us and governs. I see you are no friend to The Church: you are an earl first and last, as I am a churchman first and last. But can we not sink our differences in the face of a common enemy? I see now that what is in your mind is not that this girl has never once mentioned The Church, and thinks only of God and herself, but that she has never once mentioned the peerage, and thinks only of the king and herself.

WARWICK. Quite so. These two ideas of hers are the same idea at bottom. It goes deep, my lord. It is the protest of the individual soul against the interference of priest or peer between the private man and his God. I should call it Protestantism if I had to find a name for it.

CAUCHON (*looking hard at him*) You understand it wonderfully well, my lord. Scratch an Englishman, and find a Protestant.

WARWICK (*playing the pink of courtesy*) I think you are not entirely void of sympathy with The Maid's secular heresy, my lord. I leave you to find a name for it.

CAUCHON. You mistake me, my lord. I have no sympathy with her political presumptions. But as a priest I have gained a knowledge of the minds of the common people; and there you will find yet another most dangerous idea. I can express it only by such phrases as France for the French, England for the English, Italy for the Italians, Spain for the Spanish, and so forth. It is sometimes so narrow and bitter in country folk that it surprises me that this country girl can rise above the idea of her village for its villagers. But she can. She does. When she threatens to drive the English from the soil of France she is undoubtedly thinking of the whole extent of country in which French is spoken. To her the French-speaking people are what Holy Scriptures describe as a nation. Call this side of her heresy Nationalism if you will: I can find you no better name for it. I can only tell you that it is essentially anti-Catholic and anti-

Christian; for the Catholic Church knows only one realm, and that is the realm of Christ's kingdom. Divide that kingdom into nations, and you dethrone Christ. Dethrone Christ, and who will stand between our throats and the sword? The world will perish in a welter of war.

WARWICK. Well, if you will burn the Protestant, I will burn the Nationalist, though perhaps I shall not carry Messire John with me there. England for the English will appeal to him.

THE CHAPLAIN. Certainly England for the English goes without saying: it is the simple law of nature. But this woman denies to England her legitimate conquests, given her by God because of her peculiar fitness to rule over less civilized races for their own good. I do not understand what your lordships mean by Protestant and Nationalist: you are too learned and subtle for a poor clerk like myself. But I know as a matter of plain commonsense that the woman is a rebel; and that is enough for me. She rebels against Nature by wearing man's clothes, and fighting. She rebels against The Church by usurping the divine authority of the Pope. She rebels against God by her damnable league with Satan and his evil spirits against our army. And all these rebellions are only excuses for her great rebellion against England. That is not to be endured. Let her perish. Let her burn. Let her not infect the whole flock. It is expedient that one woman die for the people.

WARWICK (*rising*) My lord: we seem to be agreed.

CAUCHON (*rising also, but in protest*) I will not imperil my soul. I will uphold the justice of The Church. I will strive to the utmost for this woman's salvation.

WARWICK. I am sorry for the poor girl. I hate these severities. I will spare her if I can.

THE CHAPLAIN (*implacably*) I would burn her with my own hands.

CAUCHON (*blessing him*) Sancta simplicitas!

SCENE V

THE AMBULATORY in the cathedral of Rheims, near the door of the vestry. A pillar bears one of the stations of the cross. The organ is playing the people out of the nave after the coronation. Joan is kneeling in prayer before the station. She is beautifully dressed, but still in male attire. The organ ceases as Dunois, also splendidly arrayed, comes into the ambulatory from the vestry.

DUNOIS. Come, Joan! you have had enough praying. After that fit of crying you will catch a chill if you stay here any longer. It is all over: the cathedral is empty; and the streets are full. They are calling for The Maid. We have told them you are staying here alone to pray; but they want to see you again.

JOAN. No: let the king have all the glory.

DUNOIS. He only spoils the show, poor devil. No, Joan: you have crowned him; and you must go through with it.

JOAN (*shakes her head reluctantly*).

DUNOIS (*raising her*) Come come! it will be over in a couple of hours. It's better than the bridge at Orleans: eh?

JOAN. Oh, dear Dunois, how I wish it were the bridge at Orleans again! We lived at that bridge.

DUNOIS. Yes, faith, and died too: some of us.

JOAN. Isnt it strange, Jack? I am such a coward: I am frightened beyond words before a battle; but it is so dull afterwards when there is no danger: oh, so dull! dull! dull!

DUNOIS. You must learn to be abstemious in war, just as you are in your food and drink, my little saint.

JOAN. Dear Jack: I think you like me as a soldier likes his comrade.

DUNOIS. You need it, poor innocent child of God. You have not many friends at court.

JOAN. Why do all these courtiers and knights and churchmen hate me? What have I done to them? I have asked nothing for myself except that my village shall not be taxed; for we cannot afford war taxes. I have brought them luck and victory: I have set them right when they were doing all sorts of stupid things: I have crowned Charles and made him a real king; and all the honors he is handing out have gone to them. Then why do they not love me?

DUNOIS (*rallying her*) Sim-ple-ton! Do you expect stupid people to love you for shewing them up? Do blundering old military dug-outs love the successful young captains who supersede them? Do ambitious politicians love the climbers who take the front seats from them? Do archbishops enjoy being played off their own altars, even by saints? Why, I should be jealous of you myself if I were ambitious enough.

JOAN. You are the pick of the basket here, Jack: the only friend I have among all these nobles. I'll wager your mother was from the country. I will go back to the farm when I have taken Paris.

DUNOIS. I am not so sure that they will let you take Paris.

JOAN (*startled*) What!

DUNOIS. I should have taken it myself before this if they had all been sound about it. Some of them would rather Paris took you, I think. So take care.

JOAN. Jack: the world is too wicked for me. If the goddams and the Burgundians do not make an end of me, the French will. Only for my voices I should lose all heart. That is why I had to steal away to pray here alone after the coronation. I'll tell you something, Jack. It is in the bells I hear my voices. Not to-day, when they all rang: that was nothing but jangling. But here in this corner, where the bells come down from heaven, and the echoes linger, or in the fields, where they come from a distance through the quiet of the countryside, my voices are in them. (*The cathedral clock chimes the quarter*) Hark! (*She becomes rapt*) Do you hear? "Dear-child-of-God": just what you said. At the half-hour they will say "Be-brave-go-on." At the three-quarters they will say "I-am-thy-Help." But it is at the hour, when the great bell goes after "God-will-save-France": it is then that St Margaret and St Catherine and sometimes even the blessed Michael will say things that I cannot tell beforehand. Then, oh then—

DUNOIS (*interrupting her kindly but not sympathetically*) Then, Joan, we shall hear whatever we fancy in the booming of the bell. You make me uneasy when you talk about your voices: I should think you were a bit cracked if I hadnt noticed that you give me very sensible reasons for what you do, though I hear you telling others you are only obeying Madame Saint Catherine.

JOAN (*crossly*) Well, I have to find reasons for you, because you do not believe in my voices. But the voices come first; and I find the reasons after: whatever you may choose to believe.

DUNOIS. Are you angry, Joan?

JOAN. Yes. (*Smiling*) No: not with you. I wish you were one of the village babies.

DUNOIS. Why?

JOAN. I could nurse you for awhile.

DUNOIS. You are a bit of a woman after all.

JOAN. No: not a bit: I am a soldier and nothing else. Soldiers always nurse children when they get a chance.

DUNOIS. That is true. (*He laughs*).

King Charles, with Bluebeard on his left and La Hire on his right, comes from the vestry, where he has been disrobing. Joan shrinks away behind the pillar. Dunois is left between Charles and La Hire.

DUNOIS. Well, your Majesty is an anointed king at last. How do you like it?

CHARLES. I would not go through it again to be emperor of the sun and moon. The weight of those robes! I thought I should have dropped when they loaded that crown on to me. And the famous holy oil they talked so much about was rancid: phew! The Archbishop must be nearly dead: his robes must have weighed a ton: they are stripping him still in the vestry.

DUNOIS (*drily*) Your majesty should wear armor oftener. That would accustom you to heavy dressing.

CHARLES. Yes: the old jibe! Well, I am not going to wear armor: fighting is not my job. Where is The Maid?

JOAN (*coming forward between Charles and Bluebeard, and falling on her knee*) Sire: I have made you king: my work is done. I am going back to my father's farm.

CHARLES (*surprised, but relieved*) Oh, are you? Well, that will be very nice.

Joan rises, deeply discouraged.

CHARLES (*continuing heedlessly*) A healthy life, you know DUNOIS. But a dull one.

BLUEBEARD. You will find the petticoats tripping you up after leaving them off for so long.

LA HIRE. You will miss the fighting. It's a bad habit, but a grand one, and the hardest of all to break yourself of.

CHARLES (*anxiously*) Still, we dont want you to stay if you would really rather go home.

JOAN (*bitterly*) I know well that none of you will be sorry to see me go. (*She turns her shoulder to Charles and walks past him to the more congenial neighborhood of Dunois and La Hire*).

LA HIRE. Well, I shall be able to swear when I want to. But I shall miss you at times.

JOAN. La Hire: in spite of all your sins and swears we shall meet in heaven; for I love you as I love Pitou, my old sheep dog. Pitou could kill a wolf. You will kill the English wolves until they go back to their country and become good dogs of God, will you not?

LA HIRE. You and I together: yes.

JOAN. No: I shall last only a year from the beginning.

ALL THE OTHERS. What!

JOAN. I know it somehow.

DUNOIS. Nonsense!

JOAN. Jack: do you think you will be able to drive them out?

DUNOIS (*with quiet conviction*) Yes: I shall drive them out. They beat us because we thought battles were tournaments and ransom markets. We played the fool while the goddams took war seriously. But I have learnt my lesson, and taken their measure. They have no roots here. I have beaten them before; and I shall beat them again.

JOAN. You will not be cruel to them, Jack?

DUNOIS. The goddams will not yield to tender handling. We did not begin it.

JOAN (*suddenly*) Jack: before I go home, let us take Paris.

CHARLES (*terrified*) Oh no no. We shall lose everything we have gained. Oh dont let us have any more fighting. We can make a very good treaty with the Duke of Burgundy.

JOAN. Treaty! (*She stamps with impatience*).

CHARLES. Well, why not, now that I am crowned and anointed? Oh, that oil!

The Archbishop comes from the vestry, and joins the group between Charles and Bluebeard.

CHARLES. Archbishop: The Maid wants to start fighting again.

THE ARCHBISHOP. Have we ceased fighting, then? Are we at peace?

CHARLES. No: I suppose not; but let us be content with what we have done. Let us make a treaty. Our luck is too good to last; and now is our chance to stop before it turns.

JOAN. Luck! God has fought for us; and you call it luck! And you would stop while there are still Englishmen on this holy earth of dear France!

THE ARCHBISHOP (*sternly*) Maid: the king addressed himself to me, not to you. You forget yourself. You very often forget yourself.

JOAN (*unabashed, and rather roughly*) Then speak, you; and tell him that it is not God's will that he should take his hand from the plough.

THE ARCHBISHOP, If I am not so glib with the name of God as you are, it is because I interpret His will with the authority of The Church and of my sacred office. When you first came you respected it, and would not have dared to speak as you are now speaking. You came clothed with the virtue of humility; and because God blessed your enterprises accordingly, you have stained yourself with the sin of pride. The old Greek tragedy is rising among us. It is the chastisement of hubris.

CHARLES. Yes: she thinks she knows better than everyone else.

JOAN (*distressed, but naïvely incapable of seeing the effect she is producing*) But I do know better than any of you seem to. And I am not proud: I never speak unless I know I am right.

BLUEBEARD ⎱ (*exclaiming   Ha ha!
CHARLES   ⎰   together*)   Just so.

THE ARCHBISHOP. How do you know you are right?

JOAN. I always know. My voices—

CHARLES. Oh, your voices, your voices. Why dont the voices come to me? I am king, not you.

JOAN. They do come to you; but you do not hear them. You have not sat in the field in the evening listening for them. When the angelus rings you cross yourself and have done with it; but if you prayed from your heart, and listened to the thrilling of the bells in the air after they stop ringing, you would hear the voices as well as I do. (*Turning brusquely from him*) But what voices do you need to tell you what the blacksmith can tell you: that you must strike while the iron is hot? I tell you we must make a dash at Compiégne and relieve it as we relieved Orleans. Then Paris will open its gates; or if not, we will break through them. What is your crown worth without your capital?

LA HIRE. That is what I say too. We shall go through them like a red hot shot through a pound of butter. What do you say, Bastard?

DUNOIS. If our cannon balls were all as hot as your head, and we had enough of them, we should conquer the earth, no doubt. Pluck and impetuosity are good servants in war, but bad masters: they have delivered us into the hands of the English every time we have trusted to them. We never know when we are beaten: that is our great fault.

JOAN. You never know when you are victorious: that is a worse fault. I shall have to make you carry looking-glasses in battle to convince you that the English have not cut off all your noses. You would have been besieged in Orleans still, you and your councils of war, if I had not made you attack. You should always attack; and if you only hold on long enough the enemy will stop first. You dont know how to begin a battle; and you dont know how to use your cannons. And I do.

She squats down on the flags with crossed ankles, pouting.

DUNOIS. I know what you think of us, General Joan.

JOAN. Never mind that, Jack. Tell them what you think of me.

DUNOIS. I think that God was on your side; for I have not forgotten how the wind changed, and how our hearts changed when you came; and by my faith I shall never deny that it was in your sign that we conquered. But I tell you as a soldier that God is no man's daily drudge, and no maid's either. If you are worthy of it he will sometimes snatch you out of the jaws of death and set you on your feet again; but that is all: once on your feet you must fight with all your might and all your craft. For he has to be fair to your enemy too: dont forget that. Well, he set us on our feet through you at Orleans; and the glory of it has carried us through a few good battles here to the coronation. But if we presume on it further, and trust to God to do the work we should do ourselves. we shall be defeated; and serve us right!

JOAN. But—

DUNOIS. Sh! I have not finished. Do not think, any of you, that these victories of ours were won without generalship. King Charles: you have said no word in your proclamations of my part in this campaign; and I make no complaint of that; for the people will run after The Maid and her miracles and not after the Bastard's hard work finding troops for her and feeding them. But I know exactly how much God did for us through The Maid, and how much He left me to do by my own wits; and I tell you that your little hour of miracles is over, and that from this time on he who plays the war game best will win— if the luck is on his side.

JOAN. Ah! if, if, if, if! If ifs and ans were pots and pans there'd be no need of tinkers. (*Rising impetuously*) I tell you, Bastard, your art of war is no use, because your knights are no good for real fighting. War is only a game to them, like tennis and all their other games: they make rules as to what is fair and what is not fair, and heap armor on themselves and on the poor horses to keep out the arrows; and when they fall they cant get up, and have to wait for their squires to come and lift them to arrange about the ransom with the man that has poked them off their horse. Cant you see that all the like of that is gone by and done with? What use is armor against gunpowder? And if if was, do you think men that are fighting for France and for God will stop to bargain about ransoms, as half your knights live by doing? No: they will fight to win; and they will give up their lives out of their own hand into the hand of God when they go into battle, as I do. Common folks understand this. They cannot afford armor and cannot pay ransoms; but they follow me half naked into the moat and up the ladder and over the wall. With them it is my life or thine, and God defend the right! You may shake your head, Jack; and Bluebeard may twirl his billygoat's beard and cock his nose at me; but remember the day your knights and captains refused to follow me to attack the English at Orleans! You locked the gates to keep me in; and it was the townsfolk and the common people that followed me, and forced the gate, and shewed you the way to fight in earnest.

BLUEBEARD (*offended*) Not content with being Pope Joan, you must be Caesar and Alexander as well.

THE ARCHBISHOP. Pride will have a fall, Joan.

JOAN. Oh, never mind whether it is pride or not: is it true? is it commonsense?

LA HIRE. It is true. Half of us are afraid of having our handsome noses broken; and the other half are out for paying off their mortgages Let her have her way, Dunois: she does not know everything; but she has got hold of the right end of the stick. Fighting is not what it was; and those who know least about it often make the best job of it.

DUNOIS. I know all that. I do not fight in the old way: I have learnt the lesson of Agincourt, of Poitiers and Crecy. I know how many lives any move of mine will cost; and if the move is worth the cost I make it and pay the cost. But Joan never counts the cost at all: she goes ahead and trusts to God: she thinks she has God in her pocket. Up to now she has had the numbers on her side; and she has won. But I know Joan; and I see that some day she will go ahead when she has only ten men to do the work of a hundred. And then she will find that God is on the side of the big battalions. She will be taken by the enemy. And the lucky man that makes the capture will receive sixteen thousand pounds from the Earl of Ouareek.

JOAN (*flattered*) Sixteen thousand pounds! Eh, laddie, have they offered that for me? There cannot be so much money in the world.

DUNOIS. There is, in England. And now tell me, all of you, which of you will lift a finger to save Joan once the English have got her? I speak first, for the army. The day after she has been dragged from her horse by a goddam or a Burgundian, and he is not struck dead: the day after she is locked in a dungeon, and the bars and bolts do not fly open at the touch of St

Peter's angel: the day when the enemy finds out that she is as vulnerable as I am and not a bit more invincible, she will not be worth the life of a single soldier to us; and I will not risk that life, much as I cherish her as a companion-in-arms.

JOAN. I dont blame you, Jack: you are right. I am not worth one soldier's life if God lets me be beaten; but France may think me worth my ransom after what God has done for her through me.

CHARLES. I tell you I have no money; and this coronation, which is all your fault, has cost me the last farthing I can borrow.

JOAN. The Church is richer than you. I put my trust in The Church.

THE ARCHBISHOP. Woman: they will drag you through the streets, and burn you as a witch.

JOAN (running to him) Oh, my lord, do not say that. It is impossible. I a witch!

THE ARCHBISHOP. Peter Cauchon knows his business. The University of Paris has burnt a woman for saying that what you have done was well done, and according to God.

JOAN (bewildered) But why? What sense is there in it? What I have done is according to God. They could not burn a woman for speaking the truth.

THE ARCHBISHOP. They did.

JOAN. But you know that she was speaking the truth. You would not let them burn me.

THE ARCHBISHOP. How could I prevent them?

JOAN. You would speak in the name of The Church. You are a great prince of The Church. I would go anywhere with your blessing to protect me.

THE ARCHBISHOP. I have no blessing for you while you are proud and disobedient.

JOAN. Oh, why will you go on saying things like that? I am not proud and disobedient. I am a poor girl, and so ignorant that I do not know A from B. How could I be proud? And how can you say that I am disobedient when I always obey my voices, because they come from God.

THE ARCHBISHOP. The voice of God on earth is the voice of the Church Militant; and all the voices that come to you are the echoes of your own wilfulness.

JOAN. It is not true.

THE ARCHBISHOP (*flushing angrily*) You tell the Archbishop in his cathedral that he lies; and yet you say you are not proud and disobedient.

JOAN. I never said you lied. It was you that as good as said my voices lied. When have they ever lied? If you will not believe in them: even if they are only the echoes of my own commonsense, are they not always right? and are not your earthly counsels always wrong?

THE ARCHBISHOP (*indignantly*) It is a waste of time admonishing you.

CHARLES. It always comes back to the same thing. She is right; and everyone else is wrong.

THE ARCHBISHOP. Take this as your last warning. If you perish through setting your private judgment above the instructions of your spiritual directors, The Church disowns you, and leaves you to whatever fate your presumption may bring upon you. The Bastard has told you that if you persist in setting up your military conceit above the counsels of your commanders—

DUNOIS (*interposing*) To put it quite exactly, if you attempt to relieve the garrison in Compiègne without the same superiority in numbers you had at Orleans—

THE ARCHBISHOP. The army will disown you, and will not rescue you. And His Majesty the King has told you that the throne has not a means of ransoming you.

CHARLES. Not a penny.

THE ARCHBISHOP. You stand alone: absolutely alone, trusting to your own conceit, your own ignorance, your own headstrong presumption, your own impiety in hiding all these sins under the cloak of a trust in God. When you pass through these doors into the sunlight, the crowd will cheer you. They will bring you their little children and their invalids to heal: they will kiss your hands and feet, and do what they can, poor simple souls, to turn your head, and madden you with the self-confidence that is leading you to your destruction. But you will be none the less alone: they cannot save you. We and we only can stand between you and the stake at which our enemies have burnt that wretched woman in Paris.

JOAN (*her eyes skyward*) I have better friends and better counsel than yours.

THE ARCHBISHOP. I see that I am speaking in vain to a hardened heart. You reject our protection, and are determined to turn us all against you. In future, then, fend for yourself; and if you fail, God have mercy on your soul.

DUNOIS. That is the truth, Joan. Heed it.

JOAN. Where would you all have been now if I had heeded that sort of truth? There is no help, no counsel, in any of you. Yes: I am alone on earth: I have always been alone. My father told my brothers to drown me if I would not stay to mind his sheep while France was bleeding to death: France might perish if only our lambs were safe. I thought France would have friends at the court of the king of France; and I find only wolves fighting for pieces of her poor torn body. I thought God would have friends everywhere, because He is the friend of everyone; and in my innocence I believed that you who now cast me out would be like strong towers to keep harm from me. But I am wiser now; and nobody is any the worse for being wiser. Do not think you can frighten me by telling me that I am alone. France is alone; and God is alone; and what is my loneliness before the loneliness of my country and my God? I see now that the loneliness of God is His strength: what would He be if He listened to your jealous little counsels? Well, my loneliness shall be my strength too: it is better to be alone with God: His friendship will not fail me, nor His counsel, nor His love. In His strength I will dare, and dare, and dare, until I die. I will go out now to the common people, and let the love in their eyes comfort me for the hate in yours. You will all be glad to see me burnt; but if I go through the fire I shall go through it to their hearts for ever and ever. And so, God be with me!

She goes from them. They stare after her in glum silence for a moment. Then Gilles de Rais twirls his beard.

BLUEBEARD. You know, the woman is quite impossible. I dont dislike her, really; but what are you to do with such a character?

DUNOIS. As God is my judge, if she fell into the Loire I would jump in in full armor to fish her out. But if she plays the fool at Compiègne, and gets caught, I must leave her to her doom.

LA HIRE. Then you had better chain me up; for I could follow her to hell when the spirit rises in her like that.

THE ARCHBISHOP. She disturbs my judgment too: there is a dangerous power in her outbursts. But the pit is open at her feet; and for good or evil we cannot turn her from it.

CHARLES. If only she would keep quiet, or go home!

They follow her dispiritedly.

SCENE VI

ROUEN, 30th May 1431. A great stone hall in the castle, ar-
ranged for a trial-at-law, but not a trial-by-jury, the court being
the Bishop's court with the Inquisition participating: hence
there are two raised chairs side by side for the Bishop and the
Inquisitor as judges. Rows of chairs radiating from them at an
obtuse angle are for the canons, the doctors of law and theology,
and the Dominican monks, who act as assessors. In the angle is
a table for the scribes, with stools. There is also a heavy rough
wooden stool for the prisoner. All these are at the inner end of
the hall. The further end is open to the courtyard through a
row of arches. The court is shielded from the weather by
screens and curtains.

Looking down the great hall from the middle of the inner
end, the judicial chairs and scribes' table are to the right. The
prisoner's stool is to the left. There are arched doors right and
left. It is a fine sunshiny May morning.

Warwick comes in through the arched doorway on the
judges' side, followed by his page.

THE PAGE (*pertly*) I suppose your lordship is aware that we
have no business here. This is an ecclesiastical court; and we
are only the secular arm.

WARWICK. I am aware of that fact. Will it please your impudence to find the Bishop of Beauvais for me, and give him a
hint that he can have a word with me here before the trial, if
he wishes?

THE PAGE (*going*) Yes, my lord.

WARWICK. And mind you behave yourself. Do not address
him as Pious Peter.

THE PAGE. No, my lord. I shall be kind to him, because, when The Maid is brought in, Pious Peter will have to pick a peck of pickled pepper.

Cauchon enters through the same door with a Dominican monk and a canon, the latter carrying a brief.

THE PAGE. The Right Reverend his lordship the Bishop of Beauvais. And two other reverend gentlemen.

WARWICK. Get out; and see that we are not interrupted.

THE PAGE. Right, my lord. (*He vanishes airily*).

CAUCHON. I wish your lordship good-morrow.

WARWICK. Good-morrow to your lordship. Have I had the pleasure of meeting your friends before? I think not.

CAUCHON (*introducing the monk, who is on his right*) This, my lord, is Brother John Lemaître, of the order of St Dominic. He is acting as deputy for the Chief Inquisitor into the evil of heresy in France. Brother John: the earl of Warwick.

WARWICK. Your Reverence is most welcome. We have no Inquisitor in England, unfortunately; though we miss him greatly, especially on occasions like the present.

The Inquisitor smiles patiently, and bows. He is a mild elderly gentleman, but has evident reserves of authority and firmness.

CAUCHON (*introducing the Canon, who is on his left*) This gentleman is Canon John D'Estivet, of the Chapter of Bayeux He is acting as Promoter.

WARWICK. Promoter?

CAUCHON. Prosecutor, you would call him in civil law.

WARWICK. Ah! prosecutor. Quite, quite. I am very glad to make your acquaintance, Canon D'Estivet.

D'Estivet bows. (He is on the young side of middle age, well mannered, but vulpine beneath his veneer).

WARWICK. May I ask what stage the proceedings have reached? It is now more than nine months since The Maid was captured at Compiègne by the Burgundians. It is fully four months since I bought her from the Burgundians for a very handsome sum solely that she might be brought to justice. It is very nearly three months since I delivered her up to you, my Lord Bishop, as a person suspected of heresy. May I suggest that you are taking a rather unconscionable time to make up your minds about a very plain case? Is this trial never going to end?

THE INQUISITOR (*smiling*) It has not yet begun, my lord.

WARWICK. Not yet begun! Why, you have been at it eleven weeks!

CAUCHON. We have not been idle, my lord. We have held fifteen examinations of The Maid: six public and nine private.

THE INQUISITOR (*always patiently smiling*) You see, my lord, I have been present at only two of these examinations. They were proceedings of the Bishop's court solely, and not of the Holy Office. I have only just decided to associate myself—that is, to associate the Holy Inquisition—with the Bishop's court. I did not at first think that this was a case of heresy at all. I regarded it as a political case, and The Maid as a prisoner of war. But having now been present at two of the examinations, I must admit that this seems to be one of the gravest cases of heresy within my experience. Therefore everything is now in order; and we proceed to trial this morning. (*He moves towards the judicial chairs*).

CAUCHON. This moment, if your lordship's convenience allows.

WARWICK (*graciously*) Well, that is good news, gentlemen. I will not attempt to conceal from you that our patience was becoming strained.

CAUCHON. So I gathered from the threats of your soldiers to drown those of our people who favor The Maid.

WARWICK. Dear me! At all events their intentions were friendly to you, my lord.

CAUCHON (*sternly*) I hope not. I am determined that the woman shall have a fair hearing. The justice of The Church is not a mockery, my lord.

THE INQUISITOR (*returning*) Never has there been a fairer examination within my experience, my lord. The Maid needs no lawyers to take her part: she will be tried by her most faithful friends, all ardently desirous to save her soul from perdition.

D'ESTIVET. Sir: I am the Promoter; and it has been my painful duty to present the case against the girl; but believe me, I would throw up my case today and hasten to her defence if I did not know that men far my superiors in learning and piety, in eloquence and persuasiveness, have been sent to reason with her, to explain to her the danger she is running, and the ease with which she may avoid it. (*Suddenly bursting into forensic eloquence, to the disgust of Cauchon and the Inquisitor, who have listened to him so far with patronizing approval*) Men have dared to say that we are acting from hate; but God is our witness that they lie. Have we tortured her? No. Have we ceased to exhort her; to implore her to have pity on herself; to come to the bosom of her Church as an erring but beloved child? Have we—

CAUCHON (*interrupting drily*) Take care, Canon. All that you say is true; but if you make his lordship believe it I will not answer for your life, and hardly for my own.

WARWICK (*deprecating, but by no means denying*) Oh, my lord, you are very hard on us poor English. But we certainly do not share your pious desire to save The Maid: in fact I tell you now plainly that her death is a political necessity which I regret but cannot help. If The Church lets her go—

CAUCHON (*with fierce and menacing pride*) If The Church lets her go, woe to the man, were he the Emperor himself, who dares lay a finger on her! The Church is not subject to political necessity, my lord.

THE INQUISITOR (*interposing smoothly*) You need have no anxiety about the result, my lord. You have an invincible ally in the matter: one who is far more determined than you that she shall burn.

WARWICK. And who is this very convenient partisan, may I ask?

THE INQUISITOR. The Maid herself. Unless you put a gag in her mouth you cannot prevent her from convicting herself ten times over every time she opens it.

D'ESTIVET. That is perfectly true, my lord. My hair bristles on my head when I hear so young a creature utter such blasphemies.

WARWICK. Well, by all means do your best for her if you are quite sure it will be of no avail. (*Looking hard at Cauchon*) I should be sorry to have to act without the blessing of The Church.

CAUCHON (*with a mixture of cynical admiration and contempt*) And yet they say Englishmen are hypocrites! You play for your side, my lord, even at the peril of your soul. I cannot but admire such devotion; but I dare not go so far myself. I fear damnation.

WARWICK. If we feared anything we could never govern England, my lord. Shall I send your people in to you?

CAUCHON. Yes: it will be very good of your lordship to withdraw and allow the court to assemble.

Warwick turns on his heel, and goes out through the courtyard. Cauchon takes one of the judicial seats; and D'Estivet sits at the scribes' table, studying his brief.

CAUCHON (*casually, as he makes himself comfortable*) What scoundrels these English nobles are!

THE INQUISITOR (*taking the other judicial chair on Cauchon's left*) All secular power makes men scoundrels. They are not trained for the work; and they have not the Apostolic Succession. Our own nobles are just as bad.

The Bishop's assessors hurry into the hall, headed by Chaplain de Stogumber and Canon de Courcelles, a young priest of 30. The scribes sit at the table, leaving a chair vacant opposite D'Estivet. Some of the assessors take their seats: others stand chatting, waiting for the proceedings to begin formally. De

Stogumber, aggrieved and obstinate, will not take his seat: neither will the Canon, who stands on his right.

CAUCHON. Good morning, Master de Stogumber. (*To the Inquisitor*) Chaplain to the Cardinal of England.

THE CHAPLAIN (*correcting him*) Of Winchester, my lord. I have to make a protest, my lord.

CAUCHON. You make a great many.

THE CHAPLAIN. I am not without support, my lord. Here is Master de Courcelles, Canon of Paris, who associates himself with me in my protest.

CAUCHON. Well, what is the matter?

THE CHAPLAIN (*sulkily*) Speak you, Master de Courcelles, since I do not seem to enjoy his lordship's confidence. (*He sits down in dudgeon next to Cauchon, on his right*).

COURCELLES. My lord: we have been at great pains to draw up an indictment of The Maid on sixtyfour counts. We are now told that they have been reduced, without consulting us.

THE INQUISITOR. Master de Courcelles: I am the culprit. I am overwhelmed with admiration for the zeal displayed in your sixtyfour counts; but in accusing a heretic, as in other things, enough is enough. Also you must remember that all the members of the court are not so subtle and profound as you, and that some of your very great learning might appear to them to be very great nonsense. Therefore I have thought it well to have your sixtyfour articles cut down to twelve—

COURCELLES (*thunderstruck*) Twelve!!!

THE INQUISITOR. Twelve will, believe me, be quite enough for your purpose.

THE CHAPLAIN. But some of the most important points have been reduced almost to nothing. For instance, The Maid has actually declared that the blessed saints Margaret and Catherine, and the holy Archangel Michael, spoke to her in French. That is a vital point.

THE INQUISITOR. You think, doubtless, that they should have spoken in Latin?

CAUCHON. No: he thinks they should have spoken in English.

THE CHAPLAIN. Naturally, my lord.

THE INQUISITOR. Well, as we are all here agreed, I think, that these voices of The Maid are the voices of evil spirits tempting her to her damnation, it would not be very courteous to you, Master de Stogumber, or to the King of England, to assume that English is the devil's native language. So let it pass. The matter is not wholly omitted from the twelve articles. Pray take your places, gentlemen; and let us proceed to business.

All who have not taken their seats, do so.

THE CHAPLAIN. Well, I protest. That is all.

COURCELLES. I think it hard that all our work should go for nothing. It is only another example of the diabolical influence which this woman exercises over the court. (*He takes his chair, which is on the Chaplain's right*).

CAUCHON. Do you suggest that I am under diabolical influence?

COURCELLES. I suggest nothing, my lord. But it seems to me that there is a conspiracy here to hush up the fact that The Maid stole the Bishop of Senlis's horse.

CAUCHON (*keeping his temper with difficulty*) This is not a police court. Are we to waste our time on such rubbish?

COURCELLES (*rising, shocked*) My lord: do you call the Bishop's horse rubbish?

THE INQUISITOR (blandly) Master de Courcelles: The Maid alleges that she paid handsomely for the Bishop's horse, and that if he did not get the money the fault was not hers. As that may be true, the point is one on which The Maid may well be acquitted.

COURCELLES. Yes, if it were an ordinary horse. But the Bishop's horse! how can she be acquitted for that? (*He sits down again, bewildered and discouraged*).

THE INQUISITOR. I submit to you, with great respect, that if we persist in trying The Maid on trumpery issues on which we may have to declare her innocent, she may escape us on the great main issue of heresy, on which she seems so far to insist on her own guilt. I will ask you, therefore, to say nothing, when The Maid is brought before us, of these stealings of horses, and dancings round fairy trees with the village children, and prayings at haunted wells, and a dozen other things which you were diligently inquiring into until my arrival. There is not a village girl in France against whom you could not prove such things: they all dance round haunted trees, and pray at magic wells. Some of them would steal the Pope's horse if they got the chance. Heresy, gentlemen, heresy is the charge we have to try. The detection and suppression of heresy is my peculiar business: I am here as an inquisitor, not as an ordinary magistrate. Stick to the heresy, gentlemen; and leave the other matters alone.

CAUCHON. I may say that we have sent to the girl's village to make inquiries about her; and there is practically nothing serious against her.

THE CHAPLAIN ⎱ (rising and   Nothing serious, my lord—
COURCELLES   ⎰ clamoring   What! The fairy tree not—
                together)

CAUCHON (out of patience) Be silent, gentlemen; or speak one at a time.

Courcelles collapses into his chair, intimidated.

THE CHAPLAIN (sulkily resuming his seat) That is what The Maid said to us last Friday.

CAUCHON. I wish you had followed her counsel, sir. When I say nothing serious, I mean nothing that men of sufficiently large mind to conduct an inquiry like this would consider serious. I agree with my colleague the Inquisitor that it is on the count of heresy that we must proceed.

LADVENU (a young but ascetically fine-drawn Dominican who is sitting next Courcelles, on his right) But is there any great harm in the girl's heresy? Is it not merely her simplicity? Many saints have said as much as Joan.

THE INQUISITOR (*dropping his blandness and speaking very gravely*) Brother Martin: if you had seen what I have seen of heresy, you would not think it a light thing even in its most apparently harmless and even lovable and pious origins. Heresy begins with people who are to all appearance better than their neighbours. A gentle and pious girl, or a young man who has obeyed the command of our Lord by giving all his riches to the poor, and putting on the garb of poverty, the life of austerity, and the rule of humility and charity, may be the founder of a heresy that will wreck both Church and Empire if not ruthlessly stamped out in time. The records of the holy Inquisition are full of histories we dare not give to the world, because they are beyond the belief of honest men and innocent women; yet they all began with saintly simpletons. I have seen this again and again. Mark what I say: the woman who quarrels with her clothes, and puts on the dress of a man, is like the man who throws off his fur gown and dresses like John the Baptist: they are followed, as surely as the night follows the day, by bands of wild women and men who refuse to wear any clothes at all. When maids will neither marry nor take regular vows, and men reject marriage and exalt their lusts into divine inspirations, then, as surely as the summer follows the spring, they begin with polygamy, and end by incest. Heresy at first seems innocent and even laudable; but it ends in such a monstrous horror of unnatural wickedness that the most tender-hearted among you, if you saw it at work as I have seen it, would clamor against the mercy of The Church in dealing with it. For two hundred years the Holy Office has striven with these diabolical madnesses; and it knows that they begin always by vain and ignorant persons setting up their own judgment against The Church, and taking it upon themselves to be the interpreters of God's will. You must not fall into the common error of mistaking these simpletons for liars and hypocrites. They believe honestly and sincerely that their diabolical inspiration is divine. Therefore you must be on your guard against your natural compassion. You are all, I hope, merciful men: how else could you have devoted your lives to the service of our gentle Savior? You are going to see before you a young girl, pious and chaste; for I must tell you, gentlemen, that the things said of her by our English friends are supported by no evidence, whilst there is abundant testimony that her excesses have been excesses of religion and charity and not of worldliness and wantonness. This girl is not one of those whose hard features are the sign of hard hearts, and whose brazen looks and lewd demeanor condemn them before they are accused. The devilish pride that has led her into her present peril has left no mark on her countenance. Strange as it may seem to you, it has even left no mark on her character outside those special matters in which she is proud; so that you will see a diabolical pride and a natural humility seated side by side in the selfsame soul. Therefore be on your guard. God forbid that I should tell you to harden your hearts; for her punishment if we condemn her will be so cruel that we should forfeit our own hope of divine mercy were there one grain of malice against her in our hearts. But if you hate cruelty—and if any man here does not hate it I command him on his soul's salvation to quit this holy court —I say, if you hate cruelty, remember that nothing is so cruel in its consequences as the toleration of heresy. Remember also that no court of law can be so cruel as the common people are to those whom they suspect of heresy. The heretic in the hands of the Holy Office is safe from violence, is assured of a fair trial, and cannot suffer death, even when guilty, if repentance follows sin. Innumerable lives of heretics have been saved because the Holy Office has taken them out of the hands of the people, and because the people have yielded them up, knowing that the Holy Office would deal with them. Before the Holy Inquisition existed, and even now when its officers are not within reach, the unfortunate wretch suspected of heresy, perhaps quite ignorantly and unjustly, is stoned, torn in pieces, drowned, burned in his house with all his innocent children. without a trial, unshriven, unburied save as a dog is buried: all of them deeds hateful to God and most cruel to man. Gentlemen: I am compassionate by nature as well as by my profession; and though the work I have to do may seem cruel to those who do not know how much more cruel it would be to leave it undone, I would go to the stake myself sooner than do it if I did not know its righteousness, its necessity, its essential mercy. I ask you to address yourself to this trial in that conviction. Anger is a bad counsellor: cast out anger. Pity is sometimes worse: cast out pity. But do not cast out mercy. Remember only that justice comes first. Have you anything to say, my lord, before we proceed to trial?

CAUCHON. You have spoken for me, and spoken better than I could. I do not see how any sane man could disagree with a word that has fallen from you. But this I will add. The crude heresies of which you have told us are horrible; but their horror is like that of the black death: they rage for a while and then die out, because sound and sensible men will not under any incitement be reconciled to nakedness and incest and polygamy and the like. But we are confronted today throughout Europe with a heresy that is spreading among men not weak in mind nor diseased in brain: nay, the stronger the mind, the more obstinate the heretic. It is neither discredited by fantastic extremes nor corrupted by the common lusts of the flesh; but it, too, sets up the private judgment of the single erring mortal against the considered wisdom and experience of The Church. The mighty structure of Catholic Christendom will never be shaken by naked madmen or by the sins of Moab and Ammon. But it may be betrayed from within, and brought to barbarous ruin and desolation, by this arch heresy which the English Commander calls Protestantism.

THE ASSESSORS (*whispering*) Protestantism! What was that? What does the Bishop mean? Is it a new heresy? The English Commander, he said. Did you ever hear of Protestantism? etc., etc.

CAUCHON (*continuing*) And that reminds me. What provision has the Earl of Warwick made for the defence of the secular arm should The Maid prove obdurate, and the people be moved to pity her?

THE CHAPLAIN. Have no fear on that score, my lord. The noble earl has eight hundred men-at-arms at the gates. She will not slip through our English fingers even if the whole city be on her side.

CAUCHON (*revolted*) Will you not add, God grant that she repent and purge her sin?

THE CHAPLAIN. That does not seem to me to be consistent; but of course I agree with your lordship.

CAUCHON (*giving him up with a shrug of contempt*) The court sits.

THE INQUISITOR. Let the accused be brought in.

LADVENU (*calling*) The accused. Let her be brought in.

Joan, chained by the ankles, is brought in through the arched door behind the prisoner's stool by a guard of English soldiers. With them is the Executioner and his assistants. They lead her to the prisoner's stool, and place themselves behind it after taking off her chain. She wears a page's black suit. Her long imprisonment and the strain of examinations which have preceded the trial have left their mark on her; but her vitality still holds: she confronts the court unabashed, without a trace of the awe which their formal solemnity seems to require for the complete success of its impressiveness.

THE INQUISITOR (*kindly*) Sit down, Joan. (*She sits on the prisoner's stool*). You look very pale today. Are you not well?

JOAN. Thank you kindly: I am well enough. But the Bishop sent me some carp; and it made me ill.

CAUCHON. I am sorry. I told them to see that it was fresh.

JOAN. You meant to be good to me, I know; but it is a fish that does not agree with me. The English thought you were trying to poison me—

CAUCHON   } (*together*)   What!
THE CHAPLAIN }   No, my lord.

JOAN (*continuing*) They are determined that I shall be burnt as a witch; and they sent their doctor to cure me; but he was forbidden to bleed me because the silly people believe that a witch's witchery leaves her if she is bled; so he only called me filthy names. Why do you leave me in the hands of the English? I should be in the hands of The Church. And why must I be chained by the feet to a log of wood? Are you afraid I will fly away?

D'ESTIVET (*harshly*) Woman: it is not for you to question the court: it is for us to question you.

COURCELLES. When you were left unchained, did you not try to escape by jumping from a tower sixty feet high? If you cannot fly like a witch, how is it that you are still alive?

JOAN. I suppose because the tower was not so high then. It has grown higher every day since you began asking me questions about it.

D'ESTIVET. Why did you jump from the tower?

JOAN. How do you know that I jumped?

D'ESTIVET. You were found lying in the moat. Why did you leave the tower?

JOAN. Why would anybody leave a prison if they could get out?

D'ESTIVET. You tried to escape?

JOAN. Of course I did; and not for the first time either. If you leave the door of the cage open the bird will fly out.

D'ESTIVET (*rising*) That is a confession of heresy. I call the attention of the court to it.

JOAN. Heresy, he calls it! Am I a heretic because I try to escape from prison?

D'ESTIVET. Assuredly, if you are in the hands of The Church, and you wilfully take yourself out of its hands, you are deserting The Church; and that is heresy.

JOAN. It is great nonsense. Nobody could be such a fool as to think that.

D'ESTIVET. You hear, my lord, how I am reviled in the execution of my duty by this woman. (*He sits down indignantly*).

CAUCHON. I have warned you before, Joan, that you are doing yourself no good by these pert answers.

JOAN. But you will not talk sense to me. I am reasonable if you will be reasonable.

THE INQUISITOR (*interposing*) This is not yet in order. You forget, Master Promoter, that the proceedings have not been formally opened. The time for questions is after she has sworn on the Gospels to tell us the whole truth.

JOAN. You say this to me every time. I have said again and again that I will tell you all that concerns this trial. But I cannot tell you the whole truth: God does not allow the whole truth to be told. You do not understand it when I tell it. It is an old saying that he who tells too much truth is sure to be hanged. I am weary of this argument: we have been over it nine times already. I have sworn as much as I will swear; and I will swear no more.

COURCELLES. My lord: she should be put to torture.

THE INQUISITOR. You hear, Joan? That is what happens to the obdurate. Think before you answer. Has she been shewn the instruments?

THE EXECUTIONER. They are ready, my lord. She has seen them.

JOAN. If you tear me limb from limb until you separate my soul from my body you will get nothing out of me beyond what I have told you. What more is there to tell that you could understand? Besides, I cannot bear to be hurt; and if you hurt me I will say anything you like to stop the pain. But I will take it all back afterwards; so what is the use of it?

LADVENU. There is much in that. We should proceed mercifully.

COURCELLES. But the torture is customary.

THE INQUISITOR. It must not be applied wantonly. If the accused will confess voluntarily, then its use cannot be justified.

COURCELLES. But this is unusual and irregular. She refuses to take the oath.

LADVENU (*disgusted*) Do you want to torture the girl for the mere pleasure of it?

COURCELLES (*bewildered*) But it is not a pleasure. It is the law. It is customary. It is always done.

THE INQUISITOR. That is not so, Master, except when the inquiries are carried on by people who do not know their legal business.

COURCELLES. But the woman is a heretic. I assure you it is always done.

CAUCHON (*decisively*) It will not be done today if it is not necessary. Let there be an end of this. I will not have it said that we proceeded on forced confessions. We have sent our best preachers and doctors to this woman to exhort and implore her to save her soul and body from the fire: we shall not now send the executioner to thrust her into it.

COURCELLES. Your lordship is merciful, of course. But it is a great responsibility to depart from the usual practice.

JOAN. Thou art a rare noodle, Master. Do what was done last time is thy rule, eh?

COURCELLES (*rising*) Thou wanton: dost thou dare call me noodle?

THE INQUISITOR. Patience, Master, patience: I fear you will soon be only too terribly avenged.

COURCELLES (*mutters*) Noodle indeed! (*He sits down, much discontented*).

THE INQUISITOR. Meanwhile, let us not be moved by the rough side of a shepherd lass's tongue.

JOAN. Nay: I am no shepherd lass, though I have helped with the sheep like anyone else. I will do a lady's work in the house —spin or weave—against any woman in Rouen.

THE INQUISITOR. This is not a time for vanity, Joan. You stand in great peril.

JOAN. I know it: have I not been punished for my vanity? If I had not worn my cloth of gold surcoat in battle like a fool, that Burgundian soldier would never have pulled me backwards off my horse; and I should not have been here.

THE CHAPLAIN. If you are so clever at woman's work why do you not stay at home and do it?

JOAN. There are plenty of other women to do it; but there is nobody to do my work.

CAUCHON. Come! We are wasting time on trifles. Joan: I am going to put a most solemn question to you. Take care how you answer; for your life and salvation are at stake on it. Will you for all you have said and done, be it good or bad, accept the judgment of God's Church on earth? More especially as to the acts and words that are imputed to you in this trial by the Promoter here, will you submit your case to the inspired interpretation of the Church Militant?

JOAN. I am a faithful child of The Church. I will obey The Church—

CAUCHON (*hopefully leaning forward*) You will?

JOAN. —provided it does not command anything impossible. *Cauchon sinks back in his chair with a heavy sigh. The Inquisitor purses his lips and frowns. Ladvenu shakes his head pitifully.*

D'ESTIVET. She imputes to The Church the error and folly of commanding the impossible.

JOAN. If you command me to declare that all that I have done and said, and all the visions and revelations I have had, were not from God, then that is impossible: I will not declare it for anything in the world. What God made me do I will never go back on; and what He has commanded or shall command I will not fail to do in spite of any man alive. That is what I mean by impossible. And in case The Church should bid me do anything contrary to the command I have from God, I will not consent to it, no matter what it may be.

THE ASSESSORS (*shocked and indignant*) Oh! The Church contrary to God! What do you say now? Flat heresy. This is beyond everything, etc., etc.

D'ESTIVET (*throwing down his brief*) My lord: do you need anything more than this?

CAUCHON. Woman: you have said enough to burn ten heretics. Will you not be warned? Will you not understand?

THE INQUISITOR. If the Church Militant tells you that your revelations and visions are sent by the devil to tempt you to your damnation, will you not believe that The Church is wiser than you?

JOAN. I believe that God is wiser than I; and it is His commands that I will do. All the things that you call my crimes have come to me by the command of God. I say that I have done them by the order of God: it is impossible for me to say anything else. If any Churchman says the contrary I shall not mind him: I shall mind God alone, whose command I always follow.

LADVENU (*pleading with her urgently*) You do not know what you are saying, child. Do you want to kill yourself? Listen. Do you not believe that you are subject to the Church of God on earth?

JOAN. Yes. When have I ever denied it?

LADVENU. Good. That means, does it not, that you are subject to our Lord the Pope, to the cardinals, the archbishops, and the bishops for whom his lordship stands here today?

JOAN. God must be served first.

D'ESTIVET. Then your voices command you not to submit yourself to the Church Militant?

JOAN. My voices do not tell me to disobey The Church; but God must be served first.

CAUCHON. And you, and not The Church, are to be the judge?

JOAN. What other judgment can I judge by but my own?

THE ASSESSORS (*scandalized*) Oh! (*They cannot find words*).

CAUCHON. Out of your own mouth you have condemned yourself. We have striven for your salvation to the verge of sinning ourselves: we have opened the door to you again and again; and you have shut it in our faces and in the face of God. Dare you pretend, after what you have said, that you are in a state of grace?

JOAN. If I am not, may God bring me to it: if I am, may God keep me in it!

LADVENU. That is a very good reply, my lord.

COURCELLES. Were you in a state of grace when you stole the Bishop's horse?

CAUCHON (*rising in a fury*) Oh, devil take the Bishop's horse and you too! We are here to try a case of heresy; and no sooner do we come to the root of the matter than we are thrown back by idiots who understand nothing but horses. (*Trembling with rage, he forces himself to sit down*).

THE INQUISITOR. Gentlemen, gentlemen: in clinging to these small issues you are The Maid's best advocates. I am not surprised that his lordship has lost patience with you. What does the Promoter say? Does he press these trumpery matters?

D'ESTIVET. I am bound by my office to press everything; but when the woman confesses a heresy that must bring upon her the doom of excommunication, of what consequence is it that she has been guilty also of offences which expose her to minor penances? I share the impatience of his lordship as to these minor charges. Only, with great respect, I must emphasize the gravity of two very horrible and blasphemous crimes which she does not deny. First, she has intercourse with evil spirits, and is therefore a sorceress. Second, she wears men's clothes, which is indecent, unnatural, and abominable; and in spite of our most earnest remonstrances and entreaties, she will not change them even to receive the sacrament.

JOAN. Is blessed St Catherine an evil spirit? Is St Margaret? Is Michael the Archangel?

COURCELLES. How do you know that the spirit which appears to you is an archangel? Does he not appear to you as a naked man?

JOAN. Do you think God cannot afford clothes for him?

The assessors cannot help smiling, especially as the joke is against Courcelles.

LADVENU. Well answered, Joan.

THE INQUISITOR. It is, in effect, well answered. But no evil spirit would be so simple as to appear to a young girl in a guise that would scandalize her when he meant her to take him for a messenger from the Most High. Joan: The Church instructs you that these apparitions are demons seeking your soul's perdition. Do you accept the instruction of The Church?

JOAN. I accept the messenger of God. How could any faithful believer in The Church refuse him?

CAUCHON. Wretched woman: again I ask you, do you know what you are saying?

THE INQUISITOR. You wrestle in vain with the devil for her soul, my lord: she will not be saved. Now as to this matter of the man's dress. For the last time, will you put off that impudent attire, and dress as becomes your sex?

JOAN. I will not.

D'ESTIVET (*pouncing*) The sin of disobedience, my lord.

JOAN (*distressed*) But my voices tell me I must dress as a soldier.

LADVENU. Joan, Joan: does not that prove to you that the voices are the voices of evil spirits? Can you suggest to us one good reason why an angel of God should give you such shameless advice?

JOAN. Why, yes: what can be plainer commonsense? I was a soldier living among soldiers. I am a prisoner guarded by soldiers. If I were to dress as a woman they would think of me as a woman; and then what would become of me? If I dress as a soldier they think of me as a soldier, and I can live with them as I do at home with my brothers. That is why St Catherine tells me I must not dress as a woman until she gives me leave.

COURCELLES. When will she give you leave?

JOAN. When you take me out of the hands of the English soldiers. I have told you that I should be in the hands of The Church, and not left night and day with four soldiers of the Earl of Warwick. Do you want me to live with them in petticoats?

LADVENU. My lord: what she says is, God knows, very wrong and shocking; but there is a grain of worldly sense in it such as might impose on a simple village maiden.

JOAN. If we were as simple in the village as you are in your courts and palaces, there would soon be no wheat to make bread for you.

CAUCHON. That is the thanks you get for trying to save her, Brother Martin.

LADVENU. Joan: we are all trying to save you. His lordship is trying to save you. The Inquisitor could not be more just to you if you were his own daughter. But you are blinded by a terrible pride and self-sufficiency.

JOAN. Why do you say that? I have said nothing wrong. I cannot understand.

THE INQUISITOR. The blessed St Athanasius has laid it down in his creed that those who cannot understand are damned. It is not enough to be simple. It is not enough even to be what simple people call good. The simplicity of a darkened mind is no better than the simplicity of a beast.

JOAN. There is great wisdom in the simplicity of a beast, let me tell you; and sometimes great foolishness in the wisdom of scholars.

LADVENU. We know that, Joan: we are not so foolish as you think us. Try to resist the temptation to make pert replies to us. Do you see that man who stands behind you (*he indicates the Executioner*)?

JOAN (*turning and looking at the man*) Your torturer? But the Bishop said I was not to be tortured.

LADVENU. You are not to be tortured because you have confessed everything that is necessary to your condemnation. That man is not only the torturer: he is also the Executioner. Executioner: let The Maid hear your answers to my questions. Are you prepared for the burning of a heretic this day?

THE EXECUTIONER. Yes, Master.

LADVENU. Is the stake ready?

THE EXECUTIONER. It is. In the market-place. The English have built it too high for me to get near her and make the death easier. It will be a cruel death.

JOAN (*horrified*) But you are not going to burn me now?

THE INQUISITOR. You realize it at last.

LADVENU. There are eight hundred English soldiers waiting to take you to the market-place the moment the sentence of excommunication has passed from the lips of your judges. You are within a few short moments of that doom.

JOAN (*looking round desperately for rescue*) Oh God!

LADVENU. Do not despair, Joan. The Church is merciful. You can save yourself.

JOAN (*hopefully*) Yes: my voices promised me I should not be burnt. St Catherine bade me be bold.

CAUCHON. Woman: are you quite mad? Do you not yet see that your voices have deceived you?

JOAN. Oh no: that is impossible.

CAUCHON. Impossible! They have led you straight to your excommunication, and to the stake which is there waiting for you.

LADVENU (*pressing the point hard*) Have they kept a single promise to you since you were taken at Compiègne? The devil has betrayed you. The Church holds out its arms to you.

JOAN (*despairing*) Oh, it is true: it is true: my voices have deceived me. I have been mocked by devils: my faith is broken. I have dared and dared; but only a fool will walk into a fire:

God, who gave me my commonsense, cannot will me to do that.

LADVENU. Now God be praised that He has saved you at the eleventh hour! (*He hurries to the vacant seat at the scribes' table, and snatches a sheet of paper, on which he sets to work writing eagerly*).

CAUCHON. Amen!

JOAN. What must I do?

CAUCHON. You must sign a solemn recantation of your heresy.

JOAN. Sign? That means to write my name. I cannot write.

CAUCHON. You have signed many letters before.

JOAN. Yes; but someone held my hand and guided the pen. I can make my mark.

THE CHAPLAIN (*who has been listening with growing alarm and indignation*) My lord: do you mean that you are going to allow this woman to escape us?

THE INQUISITOR. The law must take its course, Master de Stogumber. And you know the law.

THE CHAPLAIN (*rising, purple with fury*) I know that there is no faith in a Frenchman. (*Tumult, which he shouts down*). I know what my lord the Cardinal of Winchester will say when he hears of this. I know what the Earl of Warwick will do when he learns that you intend to betray him. There are eight hundred men at the gate who will see that this abominable witch is burnt in spite of your teeth.

THE ASSESSORS (*meanwhile*) What is this? What did he say? He accuses us of treachery! This is past bearing. No faith in a Frenchman! Did you hear that? This is an intolerable fellow. Who is he? Is this what English Churchmen are like? he must be mad or drunk, etc., etc.

THE INQUISITOR (*rising*) Silence, pray! Gentlemen: pray silence! Master Chaplain: bethink you a moment of your holy office: of what you are, and where you are. I direct you to sit down.

THE CHAPLAIN (*folding his arms doggedly, his face working convulsively*) I will NOT sit down.

CAUCHON. Master Inquisitor: this man has called me a traitor to my face before now.

THE CHAPLAIN. So you are a traitor. You are all traitors. You have been doing nothing but begging this damnable witch on your knees to recant all through this trial.

THE INQUISITOR (*placidly resuming his seat*) If you will not sit, you must stand: that is all.

THE CHAPLAIN. I will NOT stand. (*He flings himself back into his chair*).

LADVENU (*rising with the paper in his hand*) My lord: here is the form of recantation for The Maid to sign.

CAUCHON. Read it to her.

JOAN. Do not trouble. I will sign it.

THE INQUISITOR. Woman: you must know what you are putting your hand to. Read it to her, Brother Martin. And let all be silent.

LADVENU (*reading quietly*) "I, Joan, commonly called The Maid, a miserable sinner, do confess that I have most grievously sinned in the following articles. I have pretended to have revelations from God and the angels and the blessed saints, and perversely rejected The Church's warnings that these were temptations by demons. I have blasphemed abominably by wearing an immodest dress, contrary to the Holy Scripture and the canons of The Church. Also I have clipped my hair in the style of a man, and, against all the duties which have made my sex specially acceptable in heaven, taken up the sword, even to the shedding of human blood, inciting men to slay each other, invoking evil spirits to delude them, and stubbornly and most blasphemously imputing these sins to Almighty God. I confess to the sin of sedition, to the sin of idolatry, to the sin of disobedience, to the sin of pride, and to the sin of heresy. All of which sins I now renounce and abjure and depart from, humbly thanking you Doctors and Masters who have brought me back to the truth and into the grace of our Lord. And I will never return to my errors, but will remain in communion with our Holy Church and in obedience to our Holy Father the Pope of Rome. All this I swear by God Almighty and the Holy Gospels, in witness whereto I sign my name to this recantation."

THE INQUISITOR. You understand this, Joan?

JOAN (*listless*) It is plain enough, sir.

THE INQUISITOR. And it is true?

JOAN. It may be true. If it were not true, the fire would not be ready for me in the market-place.

LADVENU (*taking up his pen and a book, and going to her quickly lest she should compromise herself again*) Come, child: let me guide your hand. Take the pen. (*She does so; and they begin to write, using the book as a desk*) J.E.H.A.N.E. So. Now make your mark by yourself.

JOAN (*makes her mark, and gives him back the pen, tormented by the rebellion of her soul against her mind and body*) There!

LADVENU (*replacing the pen on the table, and handing the recantation to Cauchon with a reverence*) Praise be to God, my brothers, the lamb has returned to the flock; and the shepherd rejoices in her more than in ninety and nine just persons. (*He returns to his seat*).

THE INQUISITOR (*taking the paper from Cauchon*) We declare thee by this act set free from the danger of excommunication in which thou stoodest. (*He throws the paper down to the table*).

JOAN. I thank you.

THE INQUISITOR. But because thou hast sinned most presumptuously against God and the Holy Church, and that thou mayst repent thy errors in solitary contemplation, and be shielded from all temptation to return to them, we, for the good of thy soul, and for a penance that may wipe out thy sins and bring thee finally unspotted to the throne of grace, do condemn thee to eat the bread of sorrow and drink the water of affliction to the end of thy earthly days in perpetual imprisonment.

JOAN (*rising in consternation and terrible anger*) Perpetual imprisonment! Am I not then to be set free?

LADVENU (*mildly shocked*) Set free, child, after such wickedness as yours! What are you dreaming of?

JOAN. Give me that writing. (*She rushes to the table; snatches up the paper; and tears it into fragments*) Light your fire: do you think I dread it as much as the life of a rat in a hole? My voices were right.

LADVENU. Joan! Joan!

JOAN. Yes: they told me you were fools (*the word gives great offence*), and that I was not to listen to your fine words nor trust to your charity. You promised me my life; but you lied (*indignant exclamations*). You think that life is nothing but not being stone dead. It is not the bread and water I fear: I can live on bread: when have I asked for more? It is no hardship to drink water if the water be clean. Bread has no sorrow for me, and water no affliction. But to shut me from the light of the sky and the sight of the fields and flowers; to chain my feet so that I can never again ride with the soldiers nor climb the hills; to make me breathe foul damp darkness, and keep from me everything that brings me back to the love of God when your wickedness and foolishness tempt me to hate Him: all this is worse than the furnace in the Bible that was heated seven times. I could do without my warhorse; I could drag about in a skirt; I could let the banners and the trumpets and the knights and soldiers pass me and leave me behind as they leave the other women, if only I could still hear the wind in the trees, the larks in the sunshine, the young lambs crying through the healthy frost, and the blessed blessed church bells that send my angel voices floating to me on the wind. But without these things I cannot live; and by your wanting to take them away from me, or from any human creature, I know that your counsel is of the devil, and that mine is of God.

THE ASSESSORS (*in great commotion*) Blasphemy! blasphemy!

She is possessed. She said our counsel was of the devil. And hers of God. Monstrous! The devil is in our midst, etc., etc.

D'ESTIVET (*shouting above the din*) She is a relapsed heretic, obstinate, incorrigible, and altogether unworthy of the mercy we have shewn her. I call for her excommunication.

THE CHAPLAIN (*to the Executioner*) Light your fire, man. To the stake with her.

The Executioner and his assistants hurry out through the courtyard.

LADVENU. You wicked girl: if your counsel were of God would He not deliver you?

JOAN. His ways are not your ways. He wills that I go through the fire to His bosom; for I am His child, and you are not fit that I should live among you. That is my last word to you.

The soldiers seize her.

CAUCHON (*rising*) Not yet.

They wait. There is a dead silence. Cauchon turns to the Inquisitor with an inquiring look. The Inquisitor nods affirmatively. They rise solemnly, and intone the sentence antiphonally.

CAUCHON. We decree that thou art a relapsed heretic.

THE INQUISITOR. Cast out from the unity of the Church.

CAUCHON. Sundered from her body.

THE INQUISITOR. Infected with the leprosy of heresy.

CAUCHON. A member of Satan.

THE INQUISITOR. We declare that thou must be excommunicate.

CAUCHON. And now we do cast thee out, segregate thee, and abandon thee to the secular power.

THE INQUISITOR. Admonishing the same secular power that it moderate its judgment of thee in respect of death and division of the limbs. (*He resumes his seat*).

CAUCHON. And if any true sign of penitence appear in thee, to permit our Brother Martin to administer to thee the sacrament of penance.

THE CHAPLAIN. Into the fire with the witch. (*He rushes at her, and helps the soldiers to push her out*).

Joan is taken away through the courtyard. The assessors rise in disorder, and follow the soldiers, except Ladvenu, who has hidden his face in his hands.

CAUCHON (*rising again in the act of sitting down*) No, no: this is irregular. The representative of the secular arm should be here to receive her from us.

THE INQUISITOR (*also on his feet again*) That man is an incorrigible fool.

CAUCHON. Brother Martin: see that everything is done in order.

LADVENU. My place is at her side, my lord. You must exercise your own authority. (*He hurries out*).

CAUCHON. These English are impossible: they will thrust her straight into the fire. Look!

He points to the courtyard, in which the glow and flicker of fire can now be seen reddening the May daylight. Only the Bishop and the Inquisitor are left in the court.

CAUCHON (*turning to go*) We must stop that.

THE INQUISITOR (*calmly*) Yes; but not too fast, my lord.

CAUCHON (*halting*) But there is not a moment to lose.

THE INQUISITOR. We have proceeded in perfect order. If the English choose to put themselves in the wrong, it is not our business to put them in the right. A flaw in the procedure may be useful later on: one never knows. And the sooner it is over, the better for that poor girl.

CAUCHON (*relaxing*) That is true. But I suppose we must see this dreadful thing through.

THE INQUISITOR. One gets used to it. Habit is everything. I am accustomed to the fire: it is soon over. But it is a terrible thing to see a young and innocent creature crushed between these mighty forces, The Church and the Law.

CAUCHON. You call her innocent!

THE INQUISITOR. Oh, quite innocent. What does she know

of The Church and the Law? She did not understand a word we were saying. It is the ignorant who suffer. Come, or we shall be late for the end.

CAUCHON (*going with him*) I shall not be sorry if we are: I am not so accustomed as you.

They are going out when Warwick comes in, meeting them.

WARWICK. Oh, I am intruding. I thought it was all over. (*He makes a feint of retiring*).

CAUCHON. Do not go, my lord. It is all over.

THE INQUISITOR. The execution is not in our hands, my lord, but it is desirable that we should witness the end. So by your leave—(*He bows, and goes out through the courtyard*).

CAUCHON. There is some doubt whether your people have observed the forms of law, my lord.

WARWICK. I am told that there is some doubt whether your authority runs in this city, my lord. It is not in your diocese. However, if you will answer for that I will answer for the rest.

CAUCHON. It is to God that we both must answer. Good morning, my lord.

WARWICK. My lord: good morning.

They look at one another for a moment with unconcealed hostility. Then Cauchon follows the Inquisitor out. Warwick looks round. Finding himself alone, he calls for attendance.

WARWICK. Hallo: some attendance here! (*Silence*). Hallo, there! (*Silence*). Hallo! Brian, you young blackguard, where are you? (*Silence*). Guard! (*Silence*). They have all gone to see the burning: even that child.

The silence is broken by someone frantically howling and sobbing.

WARWICK. What in the devil's name—?

The Chaplain staggers in from the courtyard like a demented creature, his face streaming with tears, making the piteous sounds that Warwick has heard. He stumbles to the prisoner's stool, and throws himself upon it with heartrending sobs.

WARWICK (*going to him and patting him on the shoulder*)
What is it, Master John? What is the matter?

THE CHAPLAIN (*clutching at his hands*) My lord, my lord:
for Christ's sake pray for my wretched guilty soul.

WARWICK (*soothing him*) Yes, yes: of course I will. Calmly,
gently—

THE CHAPLAIN (*blubbering miserably*) I am not a bad man,
my lord.

WARWICK. No, no: not at all.

THE CHAPLAIN. I meant no harm. I did not know what it
would be like.

WARWICK (*hardening*) Oh! You saw it, then?

THE CHAPLAIN. I did not know what I was doing. I am a
hotheaded fool; and I shall be damned to all eternity for it.

WARWICK. Nonsense! Very distressing, no doubt; but it was
not your doing.

THE CHAPLAIN (*lamentably*) I let them do it. If I had known,
I would have torn her from their hands. You dont know: you
havent seen: it is so easy to talk when you dont know. You
madden yourself with words: you damn yourself because it
feels grand to throw oil on the flaming hell of your own temper.
But when it is brought home to you; when you see the thing
you have done; when it is blinding your eyes, stifling your
nostrils, tearing your heart, then—then—(*Falling on his knees*)
O God, take away this sight from me! O Christ, deliver me
from this fire that is consuming me! She cried to Thee in the
midst of it: Jesus! Jesus! Jesus! She is in Thy bosom; and I am
in hell for evermore.

WARWICK (*summarily hauling him to his feet*) Come come,
man! you must pull yourself together. We shall have the whole
town talking of this. (*He throws him not too gently into a chair
at the table*) If you have not the nerve to see these things, why
do you not do as I do, and stay away?

THE CHAPLAIN (*bewildered and submissive*) She asked for a

cross. A soldier gave her two sticks tied together. Thank God he was an Englishman! I might have done it; but I did not: I am a coward, a mad dog, a fool. But he was an Englishman too.

WARWICK. The fool! they will burn him too if the priests get hold of him.

THE CHAPLAIN (*shaken with a convulsion*) Some of the people laughed at her. They would have laughed at Christ. They were French people, my lord: I know they were French.

WARWICK. Hush? someone is coming. Control yourself.

Ladvenu comes back through the courtyard to Warwick's right hand, carrying a bishop's cross which he has taken from a church. He is very grave and composed.

WARWICK. I am informed that it is all over, Brother Martin.

LADVENU (*enigmatically*) We do not know, my lord. It may have only just begun.

WARWICK. What does that mean, exactly?

LADVENU. I took this cross from the church for her that she might see it to the last: she had only two sticks that she put into her bosom. When the fire crept round us, and she saw that if I held the cross before her I should be burnt myself, she warned me to get down and save myself. My lord: a girl who could think of another's danger in such a moment was not inspired by the devil. When I had to snatch the cross from her sight, she looked up to heaven. And I do not believe that the heavens were empty. I firmly believe that her Savior appeared to her then in His tenderest glory. She called to Him and died. This is not the end for her, but the beginning.

WARWICK. I am afraid it will have a bad effect on the people.

LADVENU. It had, my lord, on some of them. I heard laughter. Forgive me for saying that I hope and believe it was English laughter.

THE CHAPLAIN (*rising frantically*) No: it was not. There was only one Englishman there that disgraced his country; and that was the mad dog, de Stogumber. (*He rushes wildly out, shrieking*) Let them torture him. Let them burn him. I will go pray among her ashes. I am no better than Judas: I will hang myself.

WARWICK. Quick, Brother Martin: follow him: he will do himself some mischief. After him, quick.

Ladvenu hurries out, Warwick urging him. The Executioner comes in by the door behind the judges' chairs; and Warwick, returning, finds himself face to face with him.

WARWICK. Well, fellow: who are you?

THE EXECUTIONER (*with dignity*) I am not addressed as fellow, my lord. I am the Master Executioner of Rouen: it is a highly skilled mystery. I am come to tell your lordship that your orders have been obeyed.

WARWICK. I crave your pardon, Master Executioner; and I will see that you lose nothing by having no relics to sell. I have your word, have I, that nothing remains, not a bone, not a nail, not a hair?

THE EXECUTIONER. Her heart would not burn, my lord; but everything that was left is at the bottom of the river. You have heard the last of her.

WARWICK (*with a wry smile, thinking of what Ladvenu said*) The last of her? Hm! I wonder!

EPILOGUE

A RESTLESS *fitfully windy night in June* 1456, *full of sum-mer lightning after many days of heat. King Charles the Sev-enth of France, formerly Joan's Dauphin, now Charles the Victorious, aged* 51, *is in bed in one of his royal chateaux. The bed, raised on a dais of two steps, is towards the side of the room so as to avoid blocking a tall lancet window in the middle. Its canopy bears the royal arms in embroidery. Except for the canopy and the huge down pillows there is nothing to distin-guish it from a broad settee with bed-clothes and a valance. Thus its occupant is in full view from the foot.*

Charles is not asleep: he is reading in bed, or rather looking at the pictures in Fouquet's Boccaccio with his knees doubled up to make a reading desk. Beside the bed on his left is a little table with a picture of the Virgin, lighted by candles of painted wax. The walls are hung from ceiling to floor with painted cur-tains which stir at times in the draughts. At first glance the pre-vailing yellow and red in these hanging pictures is somewhat flamelike when the folds breathe in the wind.

The door is on Charles's left, but in front of him close to the corner farthest from him. A large watchman's rattle, hand-somely designed and gaily painted, is in the bed under his hand.

Charles turns a leaf. A distant clock strikes the half-hour softly. Charles shuts the book with a clap; throws it aside; snatches up the rattle; and whirls it energetically, making a deafening clatter. Ladvenu enters, 25 *years older, strange and stark in bearing, and still carrying the cross from Rouen. Charles evidently does not expect him; for he springs out of bed on the farther side from the door.*

CHARLES. Who are you? Where is my gentleman of the bed-chamber? What do you want?

LADVENU (*solemnly*) I bring you glad tidings of great joy. Rejoice, O king; for the taint is removed from your blood, and the stain from your crown. Justice, long delayed, is at last triumphant.

CHARLES. What are you talking about? Who are you?

LADVENU. I am Brother Martin.

CHARLES. And who, saving your reverence, may Brother Martin be?

LADVENU. I held this cross when The Maid perished in the fire. Twentyfive years have passed since then: nearly ten thousand days. And on every one of those days I have prayed God to justify His daughter on earth as she is justified in heaven.

· CHARLES (*reassured, sitting down on the foot of the bed*) Oh, I remember now. I have heard of you. You have a bee in your bonnet about The Maid. Have you been at the inquiry?

LADVENU. I have given my testimony.

CHARLES. Is it over?

LADVENU. It is over.

CHARLES. Satisfactorily?

LADVENU. The ways of God are very strange.

CHARLES. How so?

LADVENU. At the trial which sent a saint to the stake as a heretic and a sorceress, the truth was told; the law was upheld; mercy was shewn beyond all custom; no wrong was done but the final and dreadful wrong of the lying sentence and the pitiless fire. At this inquiry from which I have just come, there was shameless perjury, courtly corruption, calumny of the dead who did their duty according to their lights, cowardly evasion of the issue, testimony made of idle tales that could not impose on a ploughboy. Yet out of this insult to justice, this defamation of The Church, this orgy of lying and foolishness, the truth is set in the noonday sun on the hilltop; the white robe of innocence is cleansed from the smirch of the burning faggots; the holy life is sanctified; the true heart that lived through the flame is consecrated; a great lie is silenced for ever; and a great wrong is set right before all men.

CHARLES. My friend: provided they can no longer say that I was crowned by a witch and a heretic, I shall not fuss about how the trick has been done. Joan would not have fussed about it if it came all right in the end: she was not that sort: I knew her. Is her rehabilitation complete? I made it pretty clear that there was to be no nonsense about it.

LADVENU. It is solemnly declared that her judges were full of corruption, cozenage, fraud, and malice. Four falsehoods.

CHARLES. Never mind the falsehoods: her judges are dead.

LADVENU. The sentence on her is broken, annulled, annihilated, set aside as non-existent, without value or effect.

CHARLES. Good. Nobody can challenge my consecration now, can they?

LADVENU. Not Charlemagne nor King David himself was more sacredly crowned.

CHARLES (rising) Excellent. Think of what that means to me!

LADVENU. I think of what it means to her!

CHARLES. You cannot. None of us ever knew what anything meant to her. She was like nobody else; and she must take care of herself wherever she is; for I cannot take care of her; and neither can you, whatever you may think: you are not big enough. But I will tell you this about her. If you could bring her back to life, they would burn her again within six months, for all their present adoration of her. And you would hold up the cross, too, just the same. So (crossing himself) let her rest; and let you and I mind our own business, and not meddle with hers.

LADVENU. God forbid that I should have no share in her, nor she in me! (He turns and strides out as he came, saying) Henceforth my path will not lie through palaces, nor my conversation be with kings.

CHARLES (following him towards the door, and shouting after

him) Much good may it do you, holy man! (*He returns to the middle of the chamber, where he halts, and says quizzically to himself*) That was a funny chap. How did he get in? Where are my people? (*He goes impatiently to the bed, and swings the rattle. A rush of wind through the open door sets the walls swaying agitatedly. The candles go out. He calls in the darkness*) Hallo! Someone come and shut the windows: everything is being blown all over the place. (*A flash of summer lightning shews up the lancet window. A figure is seen in silhouette against it*) Who is there? Who is that? Help! Murder! (*Thunder. He jumps into bed, and hides under the clothes*).

JOAN'S VOICE. Easy, Charlie, easy. What art making all that noise for? No one can hear thee. Thourt asleep. (*She is dimly seen in a pallid greenish light by the bedside*).

CHARLES (*peeping out*) Joan! Are you a ghost, Joan?

JOAN. Hardly even that, lad. Can a poor burnt-up lass have a ghost? I am but a dream that thourt dreaming. (*The light increases: they become plainly visible as he sits up*) Thou looks older, lad.

CHARLES. I am older. Am I really asleep?

JOAN. Fallen asleep over thy silly book.

CHARLES. That's funny.

JOAN. Not so funny as that I am dead, is it?

CHARLES. Are you really dead?

JOAN. As dead as anybody ever is, laddie. I am out of the body.

CHARLES. Just fancy! Did it hurt much?

JOAN. Did what hurt much?

CHARLES. Being burnt.

JOAN. Oh, that! I cannot remember very well. I think it did at first; but then it all got mixed up; and I was not in my right mind until I was free of the body. But do not thou go handling fire and thinking it will not hurt thee. How hast been ever since?

CHARLES. Oh, not so bad. Do you know, I actually lead my

army out and win battles? Down into the moat up to my waist in mud and blood. Up the ladders with the stones and hot pitch raining down. Like you.

JOAN. No! Did I make a man of thee after all, Charlie?

CHARLES. I am Charles the Victorious now. I had to be brave because you were. Agnes put a little pluck into me too.

JOAN. Agnes! Who was Agnes?

CHARLES. Agnes Sorel. A woman I fell in love with. I dream of her often. I never dreamed of you before.

JOAN. Is she dead, like me?

CHARLES. Yes. But she was not like you. She was very beautiful.

JOAN (laughing heartily) Ha ha! I was no beauty: I was always a rough one: a regular soldier. I might almost as well have been a man. Pity I wasnt: I should not have bothered you all so much then. But my head was in the skies; and the glory of God was upon me; and, man or woman, I should have bothered you as long as your noses were in the mud. Now tell me what has happened since you wise men knew no better than to make a heap of cinders of me?

CHARLES. Your mother and brothers have sued the courts to have your case tried over again. And the courts have declared that your judges were full of corruption and cozenage, fraud and malice.

JOAN. Not they. They were as honest a lot of poor fools as ever burned their betters.

CHARLES. The sentence on you is broken, annihilated, annulled: null, non-existent, without value or effect.

JOAN. I was burned, all the same. Can they unburn me?

CHARLES. If they could, they would think twice before they did it. But they have decreed that a beautiful cross be placed where the stake stood, for your perpetual memory and for your salvation.

JOAN. It is the memory and the salvation that sanctify the cross, not the cross that sanctifies the memory and the salvation.

(*She turns away, forgetting him*) I shall outlast that cross. I shall be remembered when men will have forgotten where Rouen stood.

CHARLES. There you go with your self-conceit, the same as ever! I think you might say a word of thanks to me for having had justice done at last.

CAUCHON (*appearing at the window between them*) Liar!

CHARLES. Thank you.

JOAN. Why, if it isnt Peter Cauchon! How are you, Peter? What luck have you had since you burned me?

CAUCHON. None. I arraign the justice of Man. It is not the justice of God.

JOAN. Still dreaming of justice, Peter? See what justice came to with me! But what has happened to thee? Art dead or alive?

CAUCHON. Dead. Dishonored. They pursued me beyond the grave. They excommunicated my dead body: they dug it up and flung it into the common sewer.

JOAN. Your dead body did not feel the spade and the sewer as my live body felt the fire.

CAUCHON. But this thing that they have done against me hurts justice; destroys faith; saps the foundation of the Church. The solid earth sways like the treacherous sea beneath the feet of men and spirits alike when the innocent are slain in the name of law, and their wrongs are undone by slandering the pure of heart.

JOAN. Well, well, Peter, I hope men will be the better for remembering me; and they would not remember me so well if you had not burned me.

CAUCHON. They will be the worse for remembering me: they will see in me evil triumphing over good, falsehood over truth, cruelty over mercy, hell over heaven. Their courage will rise as they think of you, only to faint as they think of me. Yet God is my witness I was just: I was merciful: I was faithful to my light: I could do no other than I did.

CHARLES (*scrambling out of the sheets and enthroning him-*

self on the side of the bed) Yes: it is always you good men that do the big mischiefs. Look at me! I am not Charles the Good, nor Charles the Wise, nor Charles the Bold. Joan's worshippers may even call me Charles the Coward because I did not pull her out of the fire. But I have done less harm than any of you. You people with your heads in the sky spend all your time trying to turn the world upside down; but I take the world as it is, and say that top-side-up is right-side-up; and I keep my nose pretty close to the ground. And I ask you, what king of France has done better, or been a better fellow in his little way?

JOAN. Art really king of France, Charlie? Be the English gone?

DUNOIS (*coming through the tapestry on Joan's left, the candles relighting themselves at the same moment, and illuminating his armor and surcoat cheerfully*) I have kept my word: the English are gone.

JOAN. Praised be God! now is fair France a province in heaven. Tell me all about the fighting, Jack. Was it thou that led them? Wert thou God's captain to thy death?

DUNOIS. I am not dead. My body is very comfortably asleep in my bed at Chateaudun; but my spirit is called here by yours.

JOAN. And you fought them my way, Jack: eh? Not the old way, chaffering for ransoms; but The Maid's way: staking life against death, with the heart high and humble and void of malice, and nothing counting under God but France free and French. Was it my way, Jack?

DUNOIS. Faith, it was any way that would win. But the way that won was always your way. I give you best, lassie. I wrote a fine letter to set you right at the new trial. Perhaps I should never have let the priests burn you; but I was busy fighting; and it was The Church's business, not mine. There was no use in both of us being burned, was there?

CAUCHON. Ay! put the blame on the priests. But I, who am beyond praise and blame, tell you that the world is saved neither by its priests nor its soldiers, but by God and His Saints.

The Church Militant sent this woman to the fire; but even as she burned, the flames whitened into the radiance of the Church Triumphant.

The clock strikes the third quarter. A rough male voice is heard trolling an improvised tune.

> Rum tum trumpledum,
> Bacon fat and rumpledum,
> Old Saint mumpledum,
> Pull his tail and stumpledum
>   O my Ma—ry Ann!

A ruffianly English soldier comes through the curtains and marches between Dunois and Joan.

DUNOIS. What villainous troubadour taught you that doggrel?

THE SOLDIER. No troubadour. We made it up ourselves as we marched. We were not gentlefolks and troubadours. Music straight out of the heart of the people, as you might say. Rum tum trumpledum, Bacon fat and rumpledum, Old Saint mumpledum, Pull his tail and stumpledum: that dont mean anything, you know; but it keeps you marching. Your servant, ladies and gentlemen. Who asked for a saint?

JOAN. Be you a saint?

THE SOLDIER. Yes, lady, straight from hell.

DUNOIS. A saint, and from hell!

THE SOLDIER. Yes, noble captain: I have a day off. Every year, you know. Thats my allowance for my one good action.

CAUCHON. Wretch! In all the years of your life did you do only one good action?

THE SOLDIER. I never thought about it: it came natural like. But they scored it up for me.

CHARLES. What was it?

THE SOLDIER. Why, the silliest thing you ever heard of. I—

JOAN (*interrupting him by strolling across to the bed, where she sits beside Charles*) He tied two sticks together, and gave them to a poor lass that was going to be burned.

THE SOLDIER. Right. Who told you that?

JOAN. Never mind. Would you know her if you saw her again?

THE SOLDIER. Not I. There are so many girls! and they all expect you to remember them as if there was only one in the world. This one must have been a prime sort; for I have a day off every year for her; and so, until twelve o'clock punctually, I am a saint, at your service, noble lords and lovely ladies.

CHARLES. And after twelve?

THE SOLDIER. After twelve, back to the only place fit for the likes of me.

JOAN (*rising*) Back there! You! that gave the lass the cross!

THE SOLDIER (*excusing his unsoldierly conduct*) Well, she asked for it; and they were going to burn her. She had as good a right to a cross as they had; and they had dozens of them. It was her funeral, not theirs. Where was the harm in it?

JOAN. Man: I am not reproaching you. But I cannot bear to think of you in torment.

THE SOLDIER (*cheerfully*) No great torment, lady. You see I was used to worse.

CHARLES. What! worse than hell?

THE SOLDIER. Fifteen years' service in the French wars. Hell was a treat after that.

Joan throws up her arms, and takes refuge from despair of humanity before the picture of the Virgin.

THE SOLDIER (*continuing*)—Suits me somehow. The day off was dull at first, like a wet Sunday. I dont mind it so much now. They tell me I can have as many as I like as soon as I want them.

CHARLES. What is hell like?

THE SOLDIER. You wont find it so bad, sir. Jolly. Like as if you were always drunk without the trouble and expense of drinking. Tip top company too: emperors and popes and kings and all sorts. They chip me about giving that young judy the cross; but I dont care: I stand up to them proper, and tell them that if she hadnt a better right to it than they, she'd be where they are. That dumbfounds them, that does. All they can do is gnash their teeth, hell fashion; and I just laugh, and go off singing the old chanty: Rum tum trumple—Hullo! Who's that knocking at the door?

They listen. A long gentle knocking is heard.

CHARLES. Come in.

The door opens; and an old priest, white-haired, bent, with a silly but benevolent smile, comes in and trots over to Joan.

THE NEWCOMER. Excuse me, gentle lords and ladies. Do not let me disturb you. Only a poor old harmless English rector. Formerly chaplain to the cardinal: to my lord of Winchester. John de Stogumber, at your service. (*He looks at them inquiringly*) Did you say anything? I am a little deaf, unfortunately. Also a little—well, not always in my right mind, perhaps; but still, it is a small village with a few simple people. I suffice: I suffice: they love me there; and I am able to do a little good. I am well connected, you see; and they indulge me.

JOAN. Poor old John! What brought thee to this state?

DE STOGUMBER. I tell my folks they must be very careful. I say to them, "If you only saw what you think about you would think quite differently about it. It would give you a great shock. Oh, a great shock." And they all say "Yes, parson: we all know you are a kind man, and would not harm a fly." That is a great comfort to me. For I am not cruel by nature, you know.

THE SOLDIER. Who said you were?

DE STOGUMBER. Well, you see, I did a very cruel thing once because I did not know what cruelty was like. I had not seen it, you know. That is the great thing: you must see it. And then you are redeemed and saved.

CAUCHON. Were not the sufferings of our Lord Christ enough for you?

DE STOGUMBER. No. Oh no: not at all. I had seen them in pictures, and read of them in books, and been greatly moved by them, as I thought. But it was no use: it was not our Lord that redeemed me, but a young woman whom I saw actually burned to death. It was dreadful: oh, most dreadful. But it saved me. I have been a different man ever since, though a little astray in my wits sometimes.

CAUCHON. Must then a Christ perish in torment in every age to save those that have no imagination?

JOAN. Well, if I saved all those he would have been cruel to if he had not been cruel to me, I was not burnt for nothing, was I?

DE STOGUMBER. Oh no; it was not you. My sight is bad: I cannot distinguish your features: but you are not she: oh no: she was burned to a cinder: dead and gone, dead and gone.

THE EXECUTIONER (*stepping from behind the bed curtains on Charles's right, the bed being between them*) She is more alive than you, old man. Her heart would not burn; and it would not drown. I was a master at my craft: better than the master of Paris, better than the master of Toulouse; but I could not kill The Maid. She is up and alive everywhere.

THE EARL OF WARWICK (*sallying from the bed curtains on the other side, and coming to Joan's left hand*) Madam: my congratulations on your rehabilitation. I feel that I owe you an apology.

JOAN. Oh, please dont mention it.

WARWICK (*pleasantly*) The burning was purely political. There was no personal feeling against you, I assure you.

JOAN. I bear no malice, my lord.

WARWICK. Just so. Very kind of you to meet me in that way: a touch of true breeding. But I must insist on apologizing very amply. The truth is, these political necessities sometimes turn out to be political mistakes; and this one was a veritable howler;

for your spirit conquered us, madam, in spite of our faggots. History will remember me for your sake, though the incidents of the connection were perhaps a little unfortunate.

JOAN. Ay, perhaps just a little, you funny man.

WARWICK. Still, when they make you a saint, you will owe your halo to me, just as this lucky monarch owes his crown to you.

JOAN (*turning from him*) I shall owe nothing to any man: I owe everything to the spirit of God that was within me. But fancy me a saint! What would St Catherine and St Margaret say if the farm girl was cocked up beside them!

A clerical-looking gentleman in black frockcoat and trousers, and tall hat, in the fashion of the year 1920, suddenly appears before them in the corner on their right. They all stare at him. Then they burst into uncontrollable laughter.

THE GENTLEMAN. Why this mirth, gentlemen?

WARWICK. I congratulate you on having invented a most extraordinarily comic dress.

THE GENTLEMAN. I do not understand. You are all in fancy dress: I am properly dressed.

DUNOIS. All dress is fancy dress, is it not, except our natural skins?

THE GENTLEMAN. Pardon me: I am here on serious business, and cannot engage in frivolous discussions. (*He takes out a paper, and assumes a dry official manner*). I am sent to announce to you that Joan of Arc, formerly known as The Maid, having been the subject of an inquiry instituted by the Bishop of Orleans—

JOAN (*interrupting*) Ah! They remember me still in Orleans.

THE GENTLEMAN (*emphatically, to mark his indignation at the interruption*)—by the Bishop of Orleans into the claim of the said Joan of Arc to be canonized as a saint—

JOAN (*again interrupting*) But I never made any such claim.

THE GENTLEMAN (*as before*)—The Church has examined the claim exhaustively in the usual course, and, having admitted the said Joan successively to the ranks of Venerable and Blessed—

JOAN (*chuckling*) Me venerable!

THE GENTLEMAN. —has finally declared her to have been endowed with heroic virtues and favored with private revelations, and calls the said Venerable and Blessed Joan to the communion of the Church Triumphant as Saint Joan.

JOAN (*rapt*) Saint Joan!

THE GENTLEMAN. On every thirtieth day of May, being the anniversary of the death of the said most blessed daughter of God, there shall in every Catholic church to the end of time be celebrated a special office in commemoration of her; and it shall be lawful to dedicate a special chapel to her, and to place her image on its altar in every such church. And it shall be lawful and laudable for the faithful to kneel and address their prayers through her to the Mercy Seat.

JOAN. Oh no. It is for the saint to kneel. (*She falls on her knees, still rapt*).

THE GENTLEMAN (*putting up his paper, and retiring beside the Executioner*) In Basilica Vaticana, the sixteenth day of May, nineteen hundred and twenty.

DUNOIS (*raising Joan*) Half an hour to burn you, dear Saint; and four centuries to find out the truth about you!

DE STOGUMBER. Sir: I was chaplain to the Cardinal of Winchester once. They always would call him the Cardinal of England. It would be a great comfort to me and to my master to see a fair statue to The Maid in Winchester Cathedral. Will they put one there, do you think?

THE GENTLEMAN. As the building is temporarily in the hands of the Anglican heresy, I cannot answer for that.

A vision of the statue in Winchester Cathedral is seen through the window.

DE STOGUMBER. Oh look! look! that is Winchester.

JOAN. Is that meant to be me? I was stiffer on my feet.

The vision fades.

THE GENTLEMAN. I have been requested by the temporal authorities of France to mention that the multiplication of public statues to The Maid threatens to become an obstruction to traffic. I do so as a matter of courtesy to the said authorities, but must point out on behalf of The Church that The Maid's horse is no greater obstruction to traffic than any other horse.

JOAN. Eh! I am glad they have not forgotten my horse.

A vision of the statue before Rheims Cathedral appears.

JOAN. Is that funny little thing me too?

CHARLES. That is Rheims Cathedral where you had me crowned. It must be you.

JOAN. Who has broken my sword? My sword was never broken. It is the sword of France.

DUNOIS. Never mind. Swords can be mended. Your soul is unbroken; and you are the soul of France.

The vision fades. The Archbishop and the Inquisitor are now seen on the right and left of Cauchon.

JOAN. My sword shall conquer yet: the sword that never struck a blow. Though men destroyed my body, yet in my soul I have seen God.

CAUCHON (*kneeling to her*) The girls in the field praise thee; for thou hast raised their eyes; and they see that there is nothing between them and heaven.

DUNOIS (*kneeling to her*) The dying soldiers praise thee, because thou art a shield of glory between them and the judgment.

THE ARCHBISHOP (*kneeling to her*) The princes of The Church praise thee, because thou hast redeemed the faith their worldinesses have dragged through the mire.

WARWICK (*kneeling to her*) The cunning counsellors praise thee, because thou hast cut the knots in which they have tied their own souls.

DE STOGUMBER (*kneeling to her*) The foolish old men on their deathbeds praise thee, because their sins against thee are turned into blessings.

THE INQUISITOR (*kneeling to her*) The judges in the blindness and bondage of the law praise thee, because thou hast vindicated the vision and the freedom of the living soul.

THE SOLDIER (*kneeling to her*) The wicked out of hell praise thee, because thou hast shewn them that the fire that is not quenched is a holy fire.

THE EXECUTIONER (*kneeling to her*) The tormentors and executioners praise thee, because thou hast shewn that their hands are guiltless of the death of the soul.

CHARLES (*kneeling to her*) The unpretending praise thee, because thou hast taken upon thyself the heroic burdens that are too heavy for them.

JOAN. Woe unto me when all men praise me! I bid you remember that I am a saint, and that saints can work miracles. And now tell me: shall I rise from the dead, and come back to you a living woman?

A sudden darkness blots out the walls of the room as they all spring to their feet in consternation. Only the figures and the bed remain visible.

JOAN. What! Must I burn again? Are none of you ready to receive me?

CAUCHON. The heretic is always better dead. And mortal eyes cannot distinguish the saint from the heretic. Spare them. (*He goes out as he came*).

DUNOIS. Forgive us, Joan: we are not yet good enough for you. I shall go back to my bed. (*He also goes*).

WARWICK. We sincerely regret our little mistake; but political necessities, though occasionally erroneous, are still imperative; so if you will be good enough to excuse me—(*He steals discreetly away*).

THE ARCHBISHOP. Your return would not make me the man you once thought me. The utmost I can say is that though I dare not bless you, I hope I may one day enter into your blessedness. Meanwhile, however—(*He goes*).

THE INQUISITOR. I who am of the dead, testified that day that you were innocent. But I do not see how The Inquisition could possibly be dispensed with under existing circumstances. Therefore—(*He goes*).

DE STOGUMBER. Oh, do not come back: you must not come back. I must die in peace. Give us peace in our time, O Lord! (*He goes*).

THE GENTLEMAN. The possibility of your resurrection was not contemplated in the recent proceedings for your canonization. I must return to Rome for fresh instructions. (*He bows formally, and withdraws*).

THE EXECUTIONER. As a master in my profession I have to consider its interests. And, after all, my first duty is to my wife and children. I must have time to think over this. (*He goes*).

CHARLES. Poor old Joan! They have all run away from you except this blackguard who has to go back to hell at twelve o'clock. And what can I do but follow Jack Dunois' example, and go back to bed too? (*He does so*).

JOAN (*sadly*) Goodnight, Charlie.

CHARLES (*mumbling in his pillow*) Goo ni. (*He sleeps. The darkness envelops the bed*).

JOAN (*to the soldier*) And you, my one faithful? What comfort have you for Saint Joan?

THE SOLDIER. Well, what do they all amount to, these kings and captains and bishops and lawyers and such like? They just leave you in the ditch to bleed to death; and the next thing is, you meet them down there, for all the airs they give themselves. What I say is, you have as good a right to your notions as they have to theirs, and perhaps better. (*Settling himself for a lecture on the subject*) You see, it's like this. If— (*the first stroke of midnight is heard softly from a distant bell*). Excuse me: a pressing appointment— (*He goes on tiptoe*).

The last remaining rays of light gather into a white radiance descending on Joan. The hour continues to strike.

JOAN. O God that madest this beautiful earth, when will it be ready to receive Thy saints? How long, O Lord, how long?

Major Barbara

PREFACE TO MAJOR BARBARA

FIRST AID TO CRITICS

BEFORE dealing with the deeper aspects of Major Barbara, let me, for the credit of English literature, make a protest against an unpatriotic habit into which many of my critics have fallen. Whenever my view strikes them as being at all outside the range of, say, an ordinary suburban churchwarden, they conclude that I am echoing Schopenhauer, Nietzsche, Ibsen, Strindberg, Tolstoy, or some other heresiarch in northern or eastern Europe.

I confess there is something flattering in this simple faith in my accomplishment as a linguist and my erudition as a philosopher. But I cannot countenance the assumption that life and literature are so poor in these islands that we must go abroad for all dramatic material that is not common and all ideas that are not superficial. I therefore venture to put my critics in possession of certain facts concerning my contact with modern ideas.

About half a century ago, an Irish novelist, Charles Lever, wrote a story entitled A Day's Ride: A Life's Romance. It was published by Charles Dickens in Household Words, and proved so strange to the public taste that Dickens pressed Lever to make short work of it. I read scraps of this novel when I was a child; and it made an enduring impression on me. The hero was a very romantic hero, trying to live bravely, chivalrously, and powerfully by dint of mere romance-fed imagination, without courage, without means, without knowledge, without skill, without anything real except his bodily appetites. Even in my childhood I found in this poor devil's unsuccessful encounters with the facts of life, a poignant quality that romantic fiction lacked. The book, in spite of its first failure, is not dead: I saw its title the other day in the catalogue of Tauchnitz.

Now why is it that when I also deal in the tragi-comic irony of the conflict between real life and the romantic imagination, critics never affiliate me to my countryman and immediate forerunner, Charles Lever, whilst they confidently derive me from a Norwegian author of whose language I do not know three words, and of whom I knew nothing until years after the Shavian *Anschauung* was already unequivocally declared in books full of what came, ten years later, to be perfunctorily labelled Ibsenism? I was not Ibsenist even at second hand; for Lever, though he may have read Henri Beyle, *alias* Stendhal, certainly never read Ibsen. Of the books that made Lever popular, such as Charles O'Malley and Harry Lorrequer, I know nothing but the names and some of the illustrations. But the story of the day's ride and life's romance of Potts (claiming alliance with Pozzo di Borgo) caught me and fascinated me as something strange and significant, though I already knew all about Alnaschar and Don Quixote and Simon Tappertit and many another romantic hero mocked by reality. From the plays of Aristophanes to the tales of Stevenson that mockery has been made familiar to all who are properly saturated with letters.

Where, then, was the novelty in Lever's tale? Partly, I think, in a new seriousness in dealing with Potts's disease. Formerly, the contrast between madness and sanity was deemed comic: Hogarth shews us how fashionable people went in parties to Bedlam to laugh at the lunatics. I myself have had a village idiot exhibited to me as something irresistibly funny. On the stage the madman was once a regular comic figure: that was how Hamlet got his opportunity before Shakespear touched him. The originality of Shakespear's version lay in his taking the lunatic sympathetically and seriously, and thereby making an advance towards the eastern consciousness of the fact that lunacy may be inspiration in disguise, since a man who has more brains than his fellows necessarily appears as mad to them as one who has less. But Shakespear did not do for Pistol and

Parolles what he did for Hamlet. The particular sort of madman they represented, the romantic make-believer, lay outside
the pale of sympathy in literature: he was pitilessly despised
and ridiculed here as he was in the east under the name of
Alnaschar, and was doomed to be, centuries later, under the
name of Simon Tappertit. When Cervantes relented over Don
Quixote, and Dickens relented over Pickwick, they did not
become impartial: they simply changed sides, and became
friends and apologists where they had formerly been mockers.

In Lever's story there is a real change of attitude. There is no
relenting towards Potts: he never gains our affections like Don
Quixote and Pickwick: he has not even the infatuate courage
of Tappertit. But we dare not laugh at him, because, somehow,
we recognize ourselves in Potts. We may, some of us, have
enough nerve, enough muscle, enough luck, enough tact or
skill or address or knowledge to carry things off better than he
did; to impose on the people who saw through him; to fascinate
Katinka (who cut Potts so ruthlessly at the end of the story);
but for all that, we know that Potts plays an enormous part in
ourselves and in the world, and that the social problem is not a
problem of story-book heroes of the older pattern, but a problem of Pottses, and of how to make men of them. To fall back
on my old phrase, we have the feeling—one that Alnaschar,
Pistol, Parolles, and Tappertit never gave us—that Potts is a
piece of really scientific natural history as distinguished from
funny story telling. His author is not throwing a stone at a
creature of another and inferior order, but making a confession,
with the effect that the stone hits each of us full in the conscience and causes our self-esteem to smart very sorely. Hence
the failure of Lever's book to please the readers of Household
Words. That pain in the self-esteem nowadays causes critics to
raise a cry of Ibsenism. I therefore assure them that the sensation first came to me from Lever and may have come to him
from Beyle, or at least out of the Stendhalian atmosphere. I
exclude the hypothesis of complete originality on Lever's part,

because a man can no more be completely original in that sense than a tree can grow out of air.

Another mistake as to my literary ancestry is made whenever I violate the romantic convention that all women are angels when they are not devils; that they are better looking than men; that their part in courtship is entirely passive; and that the human female form is the most beautiful object in nature. Schopenhauer wrote a splenetic essay which, as it is neither polite nor profound, was probably intended to knock this nonsense violently on the head. A sentence denouncing the idolized form as ugly has been largely quoted. The English critics have read that sentence; and I must here affirm, with as much gentleness as the implication will bear, that it has yet to be proved that they have dipped any deeper. At all events, whenever an English playwright represents a young and marriageable woman as being anything but a romantic heroine, he is disposed of without further thought as an echo of Schopenhauer. My own case is a specially hard one, because, when I implore the critics who are obsessed with the Schopenhauerian formula to remember that playwrights, like sculptors, study their figures from life, and not from philosophic essays, they reply passionately that I am not a playwright and that my stage figures do not live. But even so, I may and do ask them why, if they must give the credit of my plays to a philosopher, they do not give it to an English philosopher? Long before I ever read a word by Schopenhauer, or even knew whether he was a philosopher or a chemist, the Socialist revival of the eighteen-eighties brought me into contact, both literary and personal, with Ernest Belfort Bax, an English Socialist and philosophic essayist, whose handling of modern feminism would provoke romantic protests from Schopenhauer himself, or even Strindberg. As a matter of fact I hardly noticed Schopenhauer's disparagements of women when they came under my notice later on, so thoroughly had Bax familiarized me with the homoist attitude, and forced me to recognize the extent to which public opinion, and consequently legislation and jurisprudence, is corrupted by feminist sentiment.

Belfort Bax's essays were not confined to the Feminist question. He was a ruthless critic of current morality. Other writers have gained sympathy for dramatic criminals by eliciting the alleged "soul of goodness in things evil"; but Bax would propound some quite undramatic and apparently shabby violation of our commercial law and morality, and not merely defend it with the most disconcerting ingenuity, but actually prove it to be a positive duty that nothing but the certainty of police persecution should prevent every right-minded man from at once doing on principle. The Socialists were naturally shocked, being for the most part morbidly moral people; but at all events they were saved later on from the delusion that nobody but Nietzsche had ever challenged our mercanto-Christian morality. I first heard the name of Nietzsche from a German mathematician, Miss Borchardt, who had read my Quintessence of Ibsenism, and told me that she saw what I had been reading: namely, Nietzsche's Jenseits von Gut und Böse. Which I protest I had never seen, and could not have read with any comfort, for want of the necessary German, if I had seen it.

Nietzsche, like Schopenhauer, is the victim in England of a single much quoted sentence containing the phrase "big blonde beast." On the strength of this alliteration it is assumed that Nietzsche gained his European reputation by a senseless glorification of selfish bullying as the rule of life, just as it is assumed, on the strength of the single word Superman (Übermensch) borrowed by me from Nietzsche, that I look for the salvation of society to the despotism of a single Napoleonic Superman, in spite of my careful demonstration of the folly of that outworn infatuation. But even the less recklessly superficial critics seem to believe that the modern objection to Christianity as a pernicious slave-morality was first put forward by Nietzsche. It was familiar to me before I ever heard of Nietzsche. The late Captain Wilson, author of several queer pamphlets, propagandist of ᵃ metaphysical system called Comprehensionism, and inventor of the term "Crosstianity" to distinguish the retrograde element in Christendom, was wont thirty years ago, in the discussions of the Dialectical Society, to protest earnestly against the beatitudes of the Sermon on the Mount as excuses for cowardice and servility, as destructive of our will, and consequently of our honor and manhood. Now it is true that Captain Wilson's moral criticism of Christianity was not a historical theory of it, like Nietzsche's; but this objection cannot be made to Stuart-Glennie, the successor of Buckle as a philosophic historian, who devoted his life to the elaboration and propagation of his theory that Christianity is part of an epoch (or rather an aberration, since it began as recently as 6000 B.C. and is already collapsing) produced by the necessity in which the numerically inferior white races found themselves to impose their domination on the colored races by priestcraft, making a virtue and a popular religion of drudgery and submissiveness in this world not only as a means of achieving saintliness of character but of securing a reward in heaven. Here was the slave-morality view formulated by a Scotch philosopher of my acquaintance long before we all began chattering about Nietzsche.

As Stuart-Glennie traced the evolution of society to the conflict of races, his theory made some sensation among Socialists—that is, among the only people who were seriously thinking about historical evolution at all—by its collision with the class-conflict theory of Karl Marx. Nietzsche, as I gather, regarded the slave-morality as having been invented and imposed on the world by slaves making a virtue of necessity and a religion of their servitude. Stuart-Glennie regarded the slave-morality as an invention of the superior white race to subjugate the minds of the inferior races whom they wished to exploit, and who would have destroyed them by force of numbers if their minds had not been subjugated. As this process is in operation still, and can be studied at first hand not only in our Church schools and in the struggle between our modern proprietary classes and the proletariat, but in the part played by Christian missionaries in reconciling the black races of Africa to their subjugation by European Capitalism, we can judge for ourselves whether the initiative came from above or below. My object here is not to argue the historical point, but simply to make our theatre critics ashamed of their habit of treating Britain as an intellectual void, and assuming that every philosophical idea, every historic theory, every criticism of our moral, religious and juridical institutions, must necessarily be either a foreign import, or else a fantastic sally (in rather questionable taste) totally unrelated to the existing body of thought. I urge them to remember that this body of thought is the slowest of growths and the rarest of blossomings, and that if there is such a thing on the philosophic plane as a matter of course, it is that no individual can make more than a minute contribution to it. In fact, their conception of clever persons parthenogenetically bringing forth complete original cosmogonies by dint of sheer "brilliancy" is part of that ignorant credulity which is the despair of the honest philosopher, and the opportunity of the religious impostor.

THE GOSPEL OF ST ANDREW UNDERSHAFT

It is this credulity that drives me to help my critics out with Major Barbara by telling them what to say about it. In the millionaire Undershaft I have represented a man who has become intellectually and spiritually as well as practically conscious of the irresistible natural truth which we all abhor and repudiate: to wit, that the greatest of our evils, and the worst of our crimes is poverty, and that our first duty, to which every other consideration should be sacrificed, is not to be poor. "Poor but honest," "the respectable poor," and such phrases are as intolerable and as immoral as "drunken but amiable," "fraudulent but a good afterdinner speaker," "splendidly criminal," or the like. Security, the chief pretence of civilization, cannot exist where the worst of dangers, the danger of poverty, hangs over everyone's head, and where the alleged protection of our persons from violence is only an accidental result of the existence of a police force whose real business is to force the poor man to see his children starve whilst idle people overfeed pet dogs with the money that might feed and clothe them.

It is exceedingly difficult to make people realize that an evil is an evil. For instance, we seize a man and deliberately do him a malicious injury: say, imprison him for years. One would not suppose that it needed any exceptional clearness of wit to recognize in this an act of diabolical cruelty. But in England such a recognition provokes a stare of surprise, followed by an explanation that the outrage is punishment or justice or something else that is all right, or perhaps by a heated attempt to argue that we should all be robbed and murdered in our beds if such stupid villainies as sentences of imprisonment were not committed daily. It is useless to argue that even if this were true, which it is not, the alternative to adding crimes of our own to the crimes from which we suffer is not helpless submission. Chickenpox is an evil; but if I were to declare that we must either submit to it or else repress it sternly by seizing everyone who suffers from it and punishing them by inoculation with smallpox, I should be laughed at; for though nobody could deny that the result would be to prevent chickenpox to some extent by making people avoid it much more carefully, and to effect a further apparent prevention by making them conceal it very anxiously, yet people would have sense enough to see that the deliberate propagation of smallpox was a creation of evil, and must therefore be ruled out in favor of purely humane and hygienic measures. Yet in the precisely parallel case of a man breaking into my house and stealing my wife's diamonds I am expected as a matter of course to steal ten years of his life, torturing him all the time. If he tries to defeat that monstrous retaliation by shooting me, my survivors hang him. The net result suggested by the police statistics is that we inflict atrocious injuries on the burglars we catch in order to make the rest take effectual precautions against detection; so that instead of saving our wives' diamonds from burglary we only greatly decrease our chances of ever getting them back, and increase our chances of being shot by the robber if we are unlucky enough to disturb him at his work.

But the thoughtless wickedness with which we scatter sentences of imprisonment, torture in the solitary cell and on the plank bed, and flogging, on moral invalids and energetic rebels, is as nothing compared to the silly levity with which we tolerate poverty as if it were either a wholesome tonic for lazy people or else a virtue to be embraced as St Francis embraced it. If a man is indolent, let him be poor. If he is drunken, let him be poor. If he is not a gentleman, let him be poor. If he is addicted to the fine arts or to pure science instead of to trade and finance, let him be poor. If he chooses to spend his urban eighteen shillings a week or his agricultural thirteen shillings a week on his beer and his family instead of saving it up for his old age, let him be poor. Let nothing be done for "the undeserving": let him be poor. Serve him right! Also—somewhat inconsistently—blessed are the poor!

Now what does this Let Him Be Poor mean? It means let him be weak. Let him be ignorant. Let him become a nucleus of disease. Let him be a standing exhibition and example of ugliness and dirt. Let him have rickety children. Let him be cheap and let him drag his fellows down to his own price by selling himself to do their work. Let his habitations turn our cities into poisonous congeries of slums. Let his daughters infect our young men with the diseases of the streets, and his sons revenge him by turning the nation's manhood into scrofula, cowardice, cruelty, hypocrisy, political imbecility, and all the other fruits of oppression and malnutrition. Let the undeserving become still less deserving; and let the deserving lay up for himself, not treasures in heaven, but horrors in hell upon earth. This being so, is it really wise to let him be poor? Would he not do ten times less harm as a prosperous burglar, incendiary, ravisher or murderer, to the utmost limits of humanity's comparatively negligible impulses in these directions? Suppose we were to abolish all penalties for such activities, and decide that poverty is the one thing we will not tolerate—that every adult with less than, say, £365 a year, shall be painlessly but inexorably killed, and every hungry half naked child forcibly fattened and clothed, would not that be an enormous improvement on our existing system, which has already destroyed so many civilizations, and is visibly destroying ours in the same way?

Is there any radicle of such legislation in our parliamentary system? Well, there are two measures just sprouting in the political soil, which may conceivably grow to something valuable. One is the institution of a Legal Minimum Wage. The other, Old Age Pensions. But there is a better plan than either of these. Some time ago I mentioned the subject of Universal Old Age Pensions to my fellow Socialist Cobden-Sanderson, famous as an artist-craftsman in bookbinding and printing. "Why not Universal Pensions for Life?" said Cobden-Sanderson. In saying this, he solved the industrial problem at a stroke. At present we say callously to each citizen "If you want money, earn it" as if his having or not having it were a matter that concerned himself alone. We do not even secure for him the opportunity of earning it: on the contrary, we allow our industry to be organized in open dependence on the maintenance of "a reserve army of unemployed" for the sake of "elasticity." The sensible course would be Cobden-Sanderson's: that is, to give every man enough to live well on, so as to guarantee the community against the possibility of a case of the malignant disease of poverty, and then (necessarily) to see that he earned it.

Undershaft, the hero of Major Barbara, is simply a man who, having grasped the fact that poverty is a crime, knows that when society offered him the alternative of poverty or a lucrative trade in death and destruction, it offered him, not a choice between opulent villainy and humble virtue, but between energetic enterprise and cowardly infamy. His conduct stands the Kantian test, which Peter Shirley's does not. Peter Shirley is

what we call the honest poor man. Undershaft is what we call
the wicked rich one: Shirley is Lazarus, Undershaft Dives.
Well, the misery of the world is due to the fact that the great
mass of men act and believe as Peter Shirley acts and believes.
If they acted and believed as Undershaft acts and believes,
the immediate result would be a revolution of incalculable
beneficence. To be wealthy, says Undershaft, is with me a
point of honor for which I am prepared to kill at the risk of
my own life. This preparedness is, as he says, the final test
of sincerity. Like Froissart's medieval hero, who saw that "to
rob and pill was a good life" he is not the dupe of that public
sentiment against killing which is propagated and endowed by
people who would otherwise be killed themselves, or of the
mouth-honor paid to poverty and obedience by rich and in-
subordinate do-nothings who want to rob the poor without
courage and command them without superiority. Froissart's
knight, in placing the achievement of a good life before all the
other duties—which indeed are not duties at all when they
conflict with it, but plain wickednesses—behaved bravely,
admirably, and, in the final analysis, public-spiritedly. Medieval
society, on the other hand, behaved very badly indeed in organizing itself so stupidly that a good life could be achieved by
robbing and pilling. If the knight's contemporaries had been
all as resolute as he, robbing and pilling would have been the
shortest way to the gallows, just as, if we were all as resolute
and clearsighted as Undershaft, an attempt to live by means
of what is called "an independent income" would be the shortest way to the lethal chamber. But as, thanks to our political
imbecility and personal cowardice (fruits of poverty, both), the
best imitation of a good life now procurable is life on an
independent income, all sensible people aim at securing
such an income, and are, of course, careful to legalize and moral-
ize both it and all the actions and sentiments which lead to it
and support it as an institution. What else can they do? They
know, of course, that they are rich because others are poor. But

they cannot help that: it is for the poor to repudiate poverty when they have had enough of it. The thing can be done easily enough: the demonstrations to the contrary made by the economists, jurists, moralists and sentimentalists hired by the rich to defend them, or even doing the work gratuitously out of sheer folly and abjectness, impose only on those who want to be imposed on.

The reason why the independent income-tax payers are not solid in defence of their position is that since we are not medieval rovers through a sparsely populated country, the poverty of those we rob prevents our having the good life for which we sacrifice them. Rich men or aristocrats with a developed sense of life—men like Ruskin and William Morris and Kropotkin—have enormous social appetites and very fastidious personal ones. They are not content with handsome houses: they want handsome cities. They are not content with bediamonded wives and blooming daughters: they complain because the charwoman is badly dressed, because the laundress smells of gin, because the sempstress is anemic, because every man they meet is not a friend and every woman not a romance. They turn up their noses at their neighbors' drains, and are made ill by the architecture of their neighbors' houses. Trade patterns made to suit vulgar people do not please them (and they can get nothing else): they cannot sleep nor sit at ease upon "slaughtered" cabinet maker's furniture. The very air is not good enough for them: there is too much factory smoke in it. They even demand abstract conditions: justice, honor, a noble moral atmosphere, a mystic nexus to replace the cash nexus. Finally they declare that though to rob and pill with your own hand on horseback and in steel coat may have been a good life, to rob and pill by the hands of the policeman, the bailiff, and the soldier, and to underpay them meanly for doing it, is not a good life, but rather fatal to all possibility of even a tolerable one. They call on the poor to revolt, and, finding the poor shocked at their ungentlemanliness, desparingly revile the proletariat for its "damned wantlessness" (*verdammte Bedürfnislosigkeit*).

So far, however, their attack on society has lacked simplicity. The poor do not share their tastes nor understand their art-criticisms. They do not want the simple life, nor the esthetic life; on the contrary, they want very much to wallow in all the costly vulgarities from which the elect souls among the rich turn away with loathing. It is by surfeit and not by abstinence that they will be cured of their hankering after unwholesome sweets. What they do dislike and despise and are ashamed of is poverty. To ask them to fight for the difference between the Christmas number of the Illustrated London News and the Kelmscott Chaucer is silly: they prefer the News. The difference between a stockbroker's cheap and dirty starched white shirt and collar and the comparatively costly and carefully dyed blue shirt of William Morris is a difference so disgraceful to Morris in their eyes that if they fought on the subject at all, they would fight in defence of the starch. "Cease to be slaves, in order that you may become cranks" is not a very inspiring call to arms; nor is it really improved by substituting saints for cranks. Both terms denote men of genius; and the common man does not want to live the life of a man of genius: he would much rather live the life of a pet collie if that were the only alternative. But he does want more money. Whatever else he may be vague about, he is clear about that. He may or may not prefer Major Barbara to the Drury Lane pantomime; but he always prefers five hundred pounds to five hundred shillings.

Now to deplore this preference as sordid, and teach children that it is sinful to desire money, is to strain towards the extreme possible limit of impudence in lying and corruption in hypocrisy. The universal regard for money is the one hopeful fact in our civilization, the one sound spot in our social conscience. Money is the most important thing in the world. It represents health, strength, honor, generosity and beauty as conspicuously and undeniably as the want of it represents illness, weakness, disgrace, meanness and ugliness. Not the least of its virtues is that it destroys base people as certainly as it fortifies and dignifies noble people. It is only when it is cheapened to worthlessness for some and made impossibly dear to others, that it becomes a curse. In short, it is a curse only in such foolish social conditions that life itself is a curse. For the two things are inseparable: money is the counter that enables life to be distributed socially: it *is* life as truly as sovereigns and bank notes are money. The first duty of every citizen is to insist on having money on reasonable terms; and this demand is not complied with by giving four men three shillings each for ten or twelve hours' drudgery and one man a thousand pounds for nothing. The crying need of the nation is not for better morals, cheaper bread, temperance, liberty, culture, redemption of fallen sisters and erring brothers, nor the grace, love and fellowship of the Trinity, but simply for enough money. And the evil to be attacked is not sin, suffering, greed, priestcraft, kingcraft, demagogy, monopoly, ignorance, drink, war, pestilence, nor any other of the scapegoats which reformers sacrifice, but simply poverty.

Once take your eyes from the ends of the earth and fix them on this truth just under your nose; and Andrew Undershaft's views will not perplex you in the least. Unless indeed his constant sense that he is only the instrument of a Will or Life Force which uses him for purposes wider than his own, may puzzle you. If so, that is because you are walking either in artificial Darwinian darkness, or in mere stupidity. All genuinely religious people have that consciousness. To them Undershaft the Mystic will be quite intelligible, and his perfect comprehension of his daughter the Salvationist and her lover the Euripidean republican natural and inevitable. That, however, is not new, even on the stage. What is new, as far as I know, is that article in Undershaft's religion which recognizes in

Money the first need and in poverty the vilest sin of man and society.

This dramatic conception has not, of course, been attained *per saltum*. Nor has it been borrowed from Nietzsche or from any man born beyond the Channel. The late Samuel Butler, in his own department the greatest English writer of the latter half of the XIX century, steadily inculcated the necessity and morality of a conscientious Laodiceanism in religion and of an earnest and constant sense of the importance of money. It drives one almost to despair of English literature when one sees so extraordinary a study of English life as Butler's posthumous Way of All Flesh making so little impression that when, some years later, I produce plays in which Butler's extraordinarily fresh, free and future-piercing suggestions have an obvious share, I am me with nothing but vague cacklings about Ibsen and Nietzsche, and am only too thankful that they are not about Alfred de Musset and Georges Sand. Really, the English do not deserve to have great men. They allowed Butler to die practically unknown, whilst I, a comparatively insignificant Irish journalist, was leading them by the nose into an advertisement of me which has made my own life a burden. In Sicily there is a Via Samuele Butler. When an English tourist sees it, he either asks "Who the devil was Samuele Butler?" or wonders why the Sicilians should perpetuate the memory of the author of Hudibras.

Well, it cannot be denied that the English are only too anxious to recognize a man of genius if somebody will kindly point him out to them. Having pointed myself out in this manner with some success, I now point out Samuel Butler, and trust that in consequence I shall hear a little less in future of the novelty and foreign origin of the ideas which are now making their way into the English theatre through plays written by Socialists. There are living men whose originality and power are as obvious as Butler's and when they die that fact will be discovered

Meanwhile I recommend them to insist on their own merits as an important part of their own business.

THE SALVATION ARMY

When Major Barbara was produced in London, the second act was reported in an important northern newspaper as a withering attack on the Salvation Army, and the despairing ejaculation of Barbara deplored by a London daily as a tasteless blasphemy. And they were set right, not by the professed critics of the theatre, but by religious and philosophical publicists like Sir Oliver Lodge and Dr Stanton Coit, and strenuous Nonconformist journalists like William Stead, who not only understood the act as well as the Salvationists themselves, but also saw it in its relation to the religious life of the nation, a life which seems to lie not only outside the sympathy of many of our theatre critics, but actually outside their knowledge of society. Indeed nothing could be more ironically curious than the confrontation Major Barbara effected of the theatre enthusiasts with the religious enthusiasts. On the one hand was the playgoer, always seeking pleasure, paying exorbitantly for it, suffering unbearable discomforts for it, and hardly ever getting it. On the other hand was the Salvationist, repudiating gaiety and courting effort and sacrifice, yet always in the wildest spirits, laughing, joking, singing, rejoicing, drumming, and tambourining: his life flying by in a flash of excitement, and his death arriving as a climax of triumph. And, if you please, the playgoer despising the Salvationists as a joyless person, shut out from the heaven of the theatre, self-condemned to a life of hideous gloom; and the Salvationist mourning over the playgoer as over a prodigal with vine leaves in his hair, careening outrageously to hell amid the popping of champagne corks and the ribald laughter of sirens! Could misunderstanding be more complete, or sympathy worse misplaced?

Fortunately, the Salvationists are more accessible to the religious character of the drama than the playgoers to the gay energy and artistic fertility of religion. They can see, when it is pointed out to them, that a theatre, as a place where two or three are gathered together, takes from that divine presence an inalienable sanctity of which the grossest and profanest farce can no more deprive it than a hypocritical sermon by a snobbish bishop can desecrate Westminster Abbey. But in our professional playgoers this indispensable preliminary conception of sanctity seems wanting. They talk of actors as mimes and mummers, and, I fear, think of dramatic authors as liars and pandars, whose main business is the voluptuous soothing of the tired city speculator when what he calls the serious business of the day is over. Passion, the life of drama, means nothing to them but primitive sexual excitement: such phrases as "impassioned poetry" or "passionate love of truth" have fallen quite out of their vocabulary and been replaced by "passional crime" and the like. They assume, as far as I can gather, that people in whom passion has a larger scope are passionless and therefore uninteresting. Consequently they come to think of religious people as people who are not interesting and not amusing. And so, when Barbara cuts the regular Salvation Army jokes, and snatches a kiss from her lover across his drum, the devotees of the theatre think they ought to appear shocked, and conclude that the whole play is an elaborate mockery of the Army. And then either hypocritically rebuke me for mocking, or foolishly take part in the supposed mockery!

Even the handful of mentally competent critics got into difficulties over my demonstration of the economic deadlock in which the Salvation Army finds itself. Some of them thought that the Army would not have taken money from a distiller and a cannon founder: others thought it should not have taken it: all assumed more or less definitely that it reduced itself to absurdity or hypocrisy by taking it. On the first point the reply of the Army itself was prompt and conclusive. As one of its officers said, they would take money from the devil himself and be only too glad to get it out of his hands and into God's. They gratefully acknowledged that publicans not only give them money but allow them to collect it in the bar—sometimes even when there is a Salvation meeting outside preaching teetotalism. In fact, they questioned the verisimilitude of the play, not because Mrs Baines took the money, but because Barbara refused it.

On the point that the Army ought not to take such money, its justification is obvious. It must take the money because it cannot exist without money, and there is no other money to be had. Practically all the spare money in the country consists of a mass of rent, interest, and profit, every penny of which is bound up with crime, drink, prostitution, disease, and all the evil fruits of poverty, as inextricably as with enterprise, wealth, commercial probity, and national prosperity. The notion that you can earmark certain coins as tainted is an unpractical individualist superstition. None the less the fact that all our money is tainted gives a very severe shock to earnest young souls when some dramatic instance of the taint first makes them conscious of it. When an enthusiastic young clergyman of the Established Church first realizes that the Ecclesiastical Commissioners receive the rents of sporting public houses, brothels, and sweating dens; or that the most generous contributor at his last charity sermon was an employer trading in female labor cheapened by prostitution as unscrupulously as a hotel keeper trades in waiters' labor cheapened by tips, or commissionaires' labor cheapened by pensions; or that the only patron who can afford to rebuild his church or his schools or give his boys' brigade a gymnasium or a library is the son-in-law of a Chicago meat King, that young clergyman has, like Barbara, a very bad quarter hour. But he cannot help himself by refusing to accept money from anybody except sweet old ladies with independent incomes and gentle and lovely ways of life. He has only to follow up the income of the sweet ladies to its industrial source, and there he will find Mrs Warren's profession and the poisonous canned meat and all the rest of it. His own stipend has the same root.

He must either share the world's guilt or go to another planet. He must save the world's honor if he is to save his own. This is what all the Churches find just as the Salvation Army and Barbara find it in the play. Her discovery that she is her father's accomplice; that the Salvation Army is the accomplice of the distiller and the dynamite maker; that they can no more escape one another than they can escape the air they breathe; that there is no salvation for them through personal righteousness, but only through the redemption of the whole nation from its vicious, lazy, competitive anarchy: this discovery has been made by everyone except the Pharisees and (apparently) the professional playgoers, who still wear their Tom Hood shirts and underpay their washerwomen without the slightest misgiving as to the elevation of their private characters, the purity of their private atmospheres, and their right to repudiate as foreign to themselves the coarse depravity of the garret and the slum. Not that they mean any harm: they only desire to be, in their little private way, what they call gentlemen. They do not understand Barbara's lesson because they have not, like her, learnt it by taking their part in the larger life of the nation.

BARBARA'S RETURN TO THE COLORS

Barbara's return to the colors may yet provide a subject for the dramatic historian of the future. To go back to the Salvation Army with the knowledge that even the Salvationists themselves are not saved yet; that poverty is not blessed, but a most damnable sin; and that when General Booth chose Blood and Fire for the emblem of Salvation instead of the Cross, he was perhaps better inspired than he knew: such knowledge, for the daughter of Andrew Undershaft, will clearly lead to something hopefuller than distributing bread and treacle at the expense of Bodger.

It is a very significant thing, this instinctive choice of the military form of organization, this substitution of the drum for the organ, by the Salvation Army. Does it not suggest that the Sal-

vationists divine that they must actually fight the devil instead
of merely praying at him? At present, it is true, they have not
quite ascertained his correct address. When they do, they may
give a very rude shock to that sense of security which he has
gained from his experience of the fact that hard words, even
when uttered by eloquent essayists and lecturers, or carried
unanimously at enthusiastic public meetings on the motion of
eminent reformers, break no bones. It has been said that the
French Revolution was the work of Voltaire, Rousseau and the
Encyclopedists. It seems to me to have been the work of men
who had observed that virtuous indignation, caustic criticism,
conclusive argument and instructive pamphleteering, even when
done by the most earnest and witty literary geniuses, were as
useless as praying, things going steadily from bad to worse whilst
the Social Contract and the pamphlets of Voltaire were at the
height of their vogue. Eventually, as we know, perfectly respectable citizens and earnest philanthropists connived at the
September massacres because hard experience had convinced
them that if they contented themselves with appeals to humanity and patriotism, the aristocracy, though it would read their
appeals with the greatest enjoyment and appreciation, flattering
and admiring the writers, would none the less continue to con-
spire with foreign monarchists to undo the revolution and restore
the old system with every circumstance of savage vengeance and
ruthless repression of popular liberties.

The nineteenth century saw the same lesson repeated in England. It had its Utilitarians, its Christian Socialists, its Fabians
(still extant): it had Bentham, Mill, Dickens, Ruskin, Carlyle,
Butler, Henry George, and Morris. And the end of all their efforts is the Chicago desc. ed by Mr Upton Sinclair, and the
London in which the people who pay to be amused by my dramatic representation of Peter Shirley turned out to starve at
forty because there are younger slaves to be had for his wages,
do not take, and have not the slightest intention of taking, any
effective step to organize society in such a way as to make that

everyday infamy impossible. I, who had preached and pamphleteered like any Encyclopedist, have to confess that my methods are no use, and would be no use if I were Voltaire, Rousseau, Bentham, Marx, Mill, Dickens, Carlyle, Ruskin, Butler and Morris all rolled into one, with Euripides, More, Montaigne, Molière, Beaumarchais, Swift, Goethe, Ibsen, Tolstoy, Jesus and the prophets all thrown in (as indeed in some sort I actually am, standing as I do on all their shoulders). The problem being to make heroes out of cowards, we paper apostles and artist-magicians have succeeded only in giving cowards all the sensations of heroes whilst they tolerate every abomination, accept every plunder, and submit to every oppression. Christianity, in making a merit of such submission, has marked only that depth in the abyss at which the very sense of shame is lost. The Christian has been like Dickens' doctor in the debtor's prison, who tells the newcomer of its ineffable peace and security: no duns; no tyrannical collectors of rates, taxes, and rent; no importunate hopes nor exacting duties; nothing but the rest and safety of having no farther to fall.

Yet in the poorest corner of this soul-destroying Christendom vitality suddenly begins to germinate again. Joyousness, a sacred gift long dethroned by the hellish laughter of derision and obscenity, rises like a flood miraculously out of the fetid dust and mud of the slums; rousing marches and impetuous dithyrambs rise to the heavens from people among whom the depressing noise called "sacred music" is a standing joke; a flag with Blood and Fire on it is unfurled, not in murderous rancor, but because fire is beautiful and blood a vital and splendid red; Fear, which we flatter by calling Self, vanishes; and transfigured men and women carry their gospel through a transfigured world, calling their leader General, themselves captains and brigadiers, and their whole body an Army: praying, but praying only for refreshment, for strength to fight, and for needful MONEY (a notable sign, that); preaching, but not preaching submission; daring ill-usage and abuse, but not putting up with more of it than is inevitable; and practising what the world will let them practise, including soap and water, color and music. There is danger in such activity; and where there is danger there is hope. Our present security is nothing, and can be nothing, but evil made irresistible.

WEAKNESSES OF THE SALVATION ARMY

For the present, however, it is not my business to flatter the Salvation Army. Rather must I point out to it that it has almost as many weaknesses as the Church of England itself. It is building up a business organization which will compel it eventually to see that its present staff of enthusiast-commanders shall be succeeded by a bureaucracy of men of business who will be no better than bishops, and perhaps a good deal more unscrupulous. That has always happened sooner or later to great orders founded by saints; and the order founded by St William Booth is not exempt from the same danger. It is even more dependent than the Church on rich people who would cut off supplies at once if it began to preach that indispensable revolt against poverty which must also be a revolt against riches. It is hampered by a heavy contingent of pious elders who are not really Salvationists at all, but Evangelicals of the old school. It still, as Commissioner Howard affirms, "sticks to Moses," which is flat nonsense at this time of day if the Commissioner means, as I am afraid he does, that the Book of Genesis contains a trustworthy scientific account of the origin of species, and that the god to whom Jephthah sacrificed his daughter is any less obviously a tribal idol than Dagon or Chemosh.

Further, there is still too much other-worldliness about the Army. Like Frederick's grenadier, the Salvationist wants to live for ever (the most monstrous way of crying for the moon); and though it is evident to anyone who has ever heard General Booth and his best officers that they would work as hard for human salvation as they do at present if they believed that death would be the end of them individually, they and their followers have a bad habit of talking as if the Salvationists were heroically enduring a very bad time on earth as an investment which will bring them in dividends later on in the form, not of a better life to come for the whole world, but of an eternity spent by themselves personally in a sort of bliss which would bore any active person to a second death. Surely the truth is that the Salvationists are unusually happy people. And is it not the very diagnostic of true salvation that it shall overcome the fear of death? Now the man who has come to believe that there is no such thing as death, the change so called being merely the transition to an exquisitely happy and utterly careless life, has not overcome the fear of death at all: on the contrary, it has overcome him so completely that he refuses to die on any terms whatever. I do not call a Salvationist really saved until he is ready to lie down cheerfully on the scrap heap, having paid scot and lot and something over, and let his eternal life pass on to renew its youth in the battalions of the future.

Then there is the nasty lying habit called confession, which the Army encourages because it lends itself to dramatic oratory, with plenty of thrilling incident. For my part, when I hear a convert relating the violences and oaths and blasphemies he was guilty of before he was saved, making out that he was a very terrible fellow then and is the most contrite and chastened of Christians now, I believe him no more than I believe the millionaire who says he came up to London or Chicago as a boy with only three halfpence in his pocket. Salvationists have said to me that Barbara in my play would never have been taken in by so transparent a humbug as Snobby Price; and certainly I do not think Snobby could have taken in any experienced Salvationist on a point on which the Salvationist did not wish to be taken in. But on the point of conversion all Salvationists wish to be taken in; for the more obvious the sinner the more obvious the miracle of his conversion. When you advertize a converted burglar or reclaimed drunkard as one of the attractions at an experience meeting, your burglar can hardly have been too burglarious or your drunkard too drunken. As long as such attractions are relied on, you will have your Snobbies claiming to have beaten their mothers when they were as a matter of prosaic fact habitually beaten by them, and your Rummies of the tamest respectability pretending to a past of reckless and dazzling vice. Even when confessions are sincerely autobiographic we should beware of assuming that the impulse to make them is pious or the interest of the hearers is wholesome. As well might we assume that the poor people who insist on shewing disgusting ulcers to district visitors are convinced hygienists, or that the curiosity which sometimes welcomes such exhibitions is a pleasant and creditable one. One is often tempted to suggest that those who pester our police superintendents with confessions of murder might very wisely be taken at their word and executed, except in the few cases in which a real murderer is seeking to be relieved of his guilt by confession and expiation. For though I am not, I hope, an unmerciful person, I do not think that the inexorability of the deed once done should be disguised by any ritual, whether in the confessional or on the scaffold.

And here my disagreement with the Salvation Army, and with all propagandists of the Cross (which I loathe as I loathe all gibbets) becomes deep indeed. Forgiveness, absolution, atonement, are figments: punishment is only a pretence of cancelling one crime by another; and you can no more have forgiveness without vindictiveness than you can have a cure without a disease. You will never get a high morality from people who conceive that their misdeeds are revocable and pardonable, or in a society where absolution and expiation are officially provided for us all. The demand may be very real; but the supply is spurious. Thus Bill Walker, in my play, having assaulted the Salvation Lass, presently finds himself overwhelmed with an intolerable conviction of sin under the skilled treatment of Barbara. Straightway he begins to try to unassault the lass and deruffianize his deed, first by getting punished for it in kind, and, when that relief is denied him, by fining himself a pound to compen-

sate the girl. He is foiled both ways. He finds the Salvation
Army as inexorable as fact itself. It will not punish him: it will
not take his money. It will not tolerate a redeemed ruffian: it
leaves him no means of salvation except ceasing to be a ruffian.
In doing this, the Salvation Army instinctively grasps the central
truth of Christianity and discards its central superstition: that
central truth being the vanity of revenge and punishment, and
that central superstition the salvation of the world by the gibbet.

For, be it noted, Bill has assaulted an old and starving woman
also; and for this worse offence he feels no remorse whatever, because she makes it clear that her malice is as great as his own.
"Let her have the law of me, as she said she would," says Bill:
"what I done to her is no more on what you might call my
conscience than sticking a pig." This shews a perfectly natural
and wholesome state of mind on his part. The old woman, like
the law she threatens him with, is perfectly ready to play
the game of retaliation with him: to rob him if he steals, to flog
him if he strikes, to murder him if he kills. By example and precept the law and public opinion teach him to impose his will on
others by anger, violence, and cruelty, and to wipe off the moral
score by punishment. That is sound Crosstianity. But this Crosstianity has got entangled with something which Barbara calls
Christianity, and which unexpectedly causes her to refuse to
play the hangman's game of Satan casting out Satan. She refuses
to prosecute a drunken ruffian; she converses on equal terms
with a blackguard to whom no lady should be seen speaking in
the public street: in short, she imitates Christ. Bill's conscience
reacts to this just as naturally as it does to the old woman's
threats. He is placed in a position of unbearable moral inferiority, and strives by every means in his power to escape from it,
whilst he is still quite ready to meet the abuse of the old woman
by attempting to smash a mug on her face. And that is the triumphant justification of Barbara's Christianity as against our
system of judicial punishment and the vindictive villain-thrash-
ings and "poetic justice" of the romantic stage.

For the credit of literature it must be pointed out that the situation is only partly novel. Victor Hugo long ago gave us the epic of the convict and the bishop's candlesticks, of the Crosstian policeman annihilated by his encounter with the Christian Valjean. But Bill Walker is not, like Valjean, romantically changed from a demon into an angel. There are millions of Bill Walkers in all classes of society today; and the point which I, as a professor of natural psychology, desire to demonstrate, is that Bill, without any change in his character or circumstances whatsoever, will react one way to one sort of treatment and another way to another.

In proof I might point to the sensational object lesson provided by our commercial millionaires today. They begin as brigands: merciless, unscrupulous, dealing out ruin and death and slavery to their competitors and employees, and facing desperately the worst that their competitors can do to them. The history of the English factories, the American Trusts, the exploitation of African gold, diamonds, ivory and rubber, outdoes in villainy the worst that has ever been imagined of the buccaneers of the Spanish Main. Captain Kidd would have marooned a modern Trust magnate for conduct unworthy of a gentleman of fortune. The law every day seizes on unsuccessful scoundrels of this type and punishes them with a cruelty worse than their own, with the result that they come out of the torture house more dangerous than they went in, and renew their evil doing (nobody will employ them at anything else) until they are again seized, again tormented, and again let loose, with the same result.

But the successful scoundrel is dealt with very differently, and very Christianly. He is not only forgiven: he is idolized, respected, made much of, all but worshipped. Society returns him good for evil in the most extravagant overmeasure. And with what result? He begins to idolize himself, to respect himself, to live up to the treatment he receives. He preaches sermons; he writes books of the most edifying advice to young men, and actually persuades himself that he got on by taking his own advice; he endows educational institutions; he supports charities; he dies finally in the odor of sanctity, leaving a will which is a monument of public spirit and bounty. And all this without any change in his character. The spots of the leopard and the stripes of the tiger are as brilliant as ever; but the conduct of the world towards him has changed; and his conduct has changed accordingly. You have only to reverse your attitude towards him —to lay hands on his property, revile him, assault him, and he will be a brigand again in a moment, as ready to crush you as you are to crush him, and quite as full of pretentious moral reasons for doing it.

In short, when Major Barbara says that there are no scoundrels, she is right: there are no absolute scoundrels, though there are impracticable people of whom I shall treat presently. Every reasonable man (and woman) is a potential scoundrel and a potential good citizen. What a man is depends on his character; but what he does, and what we think of what he does, depends on his circumstances. The characteristics that ruin a man in one class make him eminent in another. The characters that behave differently in different circumstances behave alike in similar circumstances. Take a common English character like that of Bill Walker. We meet Bill everywhere: on the judicial bench, on the episcopal bench, in the Privy Council, at the War Office and Admiralty, as well as in the Old Bailey dock or in the ranks of casual unskilled labor. And the morality of Bill's characteristics varies with these various circumstances. The faults of the burglar are the qualities of the financier: the manners and habits of a duke would cost a city clerk his situation. In short, though character is independent of circumstances, conduct is not; and our moral judgments of character are not: both are circumstantial. Take any condition of life in which the circumstances are for a mass of men practically alike: felony, the House of Lords, the factory, the stables, the gipsy encampment or where you please! In spite of diversity of character and tempera-

ment, the conduct and morals of the individuals in each group
are as predictable and as alike in the main as if they were a flock
of sheep, morals being mostly only social habits and circumstantial necessities. Strong people know this and count upon it.
In nothing have the master-minds of the world been distinguished from the ordinary suburban season-ticket holder more
than in their straightforward perception of the fact that mankind is practically a single species, and not a menagerie of gentlemen and bounders, villains and heroes, cowards and daredevils,
peers and peasants, grocers and aristocrats, artisans and laborers,
washerwomen and duchesses, in which all the grades of income
and caste represent distinct animals who must not be introduced
to one another or intermarry. Napoleon constructing a galaxy of
generals and courtiers, and even of monarchs, out of his collection of social nobodies; Julius Caesar appointing as governor of
Egypt the son of a freedman—one who but a short time before
would have been legally disqualified for the post even of a
private soldier in the Roman army; Louis XI making his barber
his privy councillor: all these had in their different ways a firm
hold of the scientific fact of human equality, expressed by Barbara in the Christian formula that all men are children of one
father. A man who believes that men are naturally divided into
upper and lower and middle classes morally is making exactly
the same mistake as the man who believes that they are naturally
divided in the same way socially. And just as our persistent attempts to found political institutions on a basis of social inequality have always produced long periods of destructive friction
relieved from time to time by violent explosions of revolution;
so the attempt—will Americans please note—to found moral institutions on a basis of moral inequality can lead to nothing but
unnatural Reigns of the Saints relieved by licentious Restora-
tions; to Americans who have made divorce a public institution
turning the face of Europe into one huge sardonic smile by
refusing to stay in the same hotel with a Russian man of genius
who has changed wives without the sanction of South Dakota;

to grotesque hypocrisy, cruel persecution, and final utter confusion of conventions and compliances with benevolence and
respectability. It is quite useless to declare that all men are born
free if you deny that they are born good. Guarantee a man's
goodness and his liberty will take care of itself. To guarantee
his freedom on condition that you approve of his moral character is formally to abolish all freedom whatsoever, as every
man's liberty is at the mercy of a moral indictment which any
fool can trump up against everyone who violates custom,
whether as a prophet or as a rascal. This is the lesson Democracy
has to learn before it can become anything but the most oppres-
sive of all the priesthoods.

Let us now return to Bill Walker and his case of conscience
against the Salvation Army. Major Barbara, not being a modern
Tetzel, or the treasurer of a hospital, refuses to sell absolution to
Bill for a sovereign. Unfortunately, what the Army can afford
to refuse in the case of Bill Walker, it cannot refuse in the case
of Bodger. Bodger is master of the situation because he holds the
purse strings. "Strive as you will," says Bodger, in effect: "me
you cannot do without. You cannot save Bill Walker without my
money." And the Army answers, quite rightly under the circumstances, "We will take money from the devil himself sooner
than abandon the work of Salvation." So Bodger pays his con-
science-money and gets the absolution that is refused to Bill. In
real life Bill would perhaps never know this. But I, the dramatist
whose business it is to shew the connexion between things that
seem apart and unrelated in the haphazard order of events in
real life, have contrived to make it known to Bill, with the result that the Salvation Army loses its hold of him at once.

But Bill may not be lost, for all that. He is still in the grip of
the facts and of his own conscience, and may find his taste for
blackguardism permanently spoiled. Still, I cannot guarantee
that happy ending. Walk through the poorer quarters of our
cities on Sunday when the men are not working, but resting
and chewing the cud of their reflections. You will find one

expression common to every mature face: the expression of cynicism. The discovery made by Bill Walker about the Salvation Army has been made by everyone there. They have found that every man has his price; and they have been foolishly or corruptly taught to mistrust and despise him for that necessary and salutary condition of social existence. When they learn that General Booth, too, has his price, they do not admire him because it is a high one, and admit the need of organizing society so that he shall get it in an honorable way: they conclude that his character is unsound and that all religious men are hypocrites and allies of their sweaters and oppressors. They know that the large subscriptions which help to support the Army are endowments, not of religion, but of the wicked doctrine of docility in poverty and humility under oppression; and they are rent by the most agonizing of all the doubts of the soul, the doubt whether their true salvation must not come from their most abhorrent passions, from murder, envy, greed, stubbornness, rage, and terrorism, rather than from public spirit, reasonableness, humanity, generosity, tenderness, delicacy, pity and kindness. The confirmation of that doubt, at which our newspapers have been working so hard for years past, is the morality of militarism; and the justification of militarism is that circumstances may at any time make it the true morality of the moment. It is by producing such moments that we produce violent and sanguinary revolutions, such as the one now in progress in Russia and the one which Capitalism in England and America is daily and diligently provoking.

At such moments it becomes the duty of the Churches to evoke all the powers of destruction against the existing order. But if they do this, the existing order must forcibly suppress them. Churches are suffered to exist only on condition that they preach submission to the State as at present capitalistically organized. The Church of England itself is compelled to add to the thirtysix articles in which it formulates its religious tenets, three more in which it apologetically protests that the moment any of these articles comes in conflict with the State it is to be entirely renounced, abjured, violated, abrogated and abhorred, the policeman being a much more important person than any of the Persons of the Trinity. And this is why no tolerated Church nor Salvation Army can ever win the entire confidence of the poor. It must be on the side of the police and the military, no matter what it believes or disbelieves; and as the police and the military are the instruments by which the rich rob and oppress the poor (on legal and moral principles made for the purpose), it is not possible to be on the side of the poor and of the police at the same time. Indeed the religious bodies, as the almoners of the rich, become a sort of auxiliary police, taking off the insurrectionary edge of poverty with coals and blankets, bread and treacle, and soothing and cheering the victims with hopes of immense and inexpensive happiness in another world when the process of working them to premature death in the service of the rich is complete in this.

CHRISTIANITY AND ANARCHISM

Such is the false position from which neither the Salvation Army nor the Church of England nor any other religious organization whatever can escape except through a reconstitution of society. Nor can they merely endure the State passively, washing their hands of its sins. The State is constantly forcing the consciences of men by violence and cruelty. Not content with exacting money from us for the maintenance of its soldiers and policemen, its gaolers and executioners, it forces us to take an active personal part in its proceedings on pain of becoming ourselves the victims of its violence. As I write these lines, a sensational example is given to the world. A royal marriage has been celebrated, first by sacrament in a cathedral, and then by a bullfight having for its main amusement the spectacle of horses gored and disembowelled by the bull, after which, when the bull is so exhausted as to be no longer dangerous, he is killed by a cautious matador. But the ironic contrast between the bullfight and the sacrament of marriage does not move anyone. Another contrast—that between the splendor, the happiness, the atmosphere of kindly admiration surrounding the young couple, and the price paid for it under our abominable social arrangements in the misery, squalor and degradation of millions of other young couples—is drawn at the same moment by a novelist, Mr Upton Sinclair, who chips a corner of the veneering from the huge meat packing industries of Chicago, and shews it to us as a sample of what is going on all over the world underneath the top layer of prosperous plutocracy. One man is sufficiently moved by that contrast to pay his own life as the price of one terrible blow at the responsible parties. His poverty has left him ignorant enough to be duped by the pretence that the innocent young bride and bridegroom, put forth and crowned by plutocracy as the heads of a State in which they have less personal power than any policeman, and less influence than any Chairman of a Trust, are responsible. At them accordingly he launches his sixpennorth of fulminate, missing his mark, but scattering the bowels of as many horses as any bull in the arena, and slaying twentythree persons, besides wounding ninetynine. And of all these, the horses alone are innocent of the guilt he is avenging: had he blown all Madrid to atoms with every adult person in it, not one could have escaped the charge of being an accessory, before, at, and after the fact, to poverty and prostitution, to such wholesale massacre of infants as Herod never dreamt of, to plague, pestilence and famine, battle, murder and lingering death—perhaps not one who had not helped, through example, precept, connivance, and even clamor, to teach the dynamiter his well-learnt gospel of hatred and vengeance, by approving every day of sentences of years of imprisonment so infernal in their unnatural stupidity and panic-stricken cruelty, that their advocates can disavow neither the dagger nor the bomb without stripping the mask of justice and humanity from themselves also.

Be it noted that at this very moment there appears the biography of one of our dukes, who, being a Scot, could argue about politics, and therefore stood out as a great brain among our aristocrats. And what, if you please, was his grace's favorite historical episode, which he declared he never read without intense satisfaction? Why, the young General Bonaparte's pounding of the Paris mob to pieces in 1795, called in playful approval by our respectable classes "the whiff of grapeshot," though Napoleon, to do him justice, took a deeper view of it, and would fain have had it forgotten. And since the Duke of Argyll was not a demon, but a man of like passions with ourselves, by no means rancorous or cruel as men go, who can doubt that all over the world proletarians of the ducal kidney are now revelling in "the whiff of dynamite" (the flavor of the joke seems to evaporate a little, does it not?) because it was aimed at the class they hate even as our argute duke hated what he called the mob.

In such an atmosphere there can be only one sequel to the Madrid explosion. All Europe burns to emulate it. Vengeance! More blood! Tear "the Anarchist beast" to shreds. Drag him to the scaffold. Imprison him for life. Let all civilized States band together to drive his like off the face of the earth; and if any State refuses to join, make war on it. This time the leading London newspaper, anti-Liberal and therefore anti-Russian in politics, does not say "Serve you right" to the victims, as it did, in effect, when Bobrikoff, and De Plehve, and Grand Duke Sergius, were in the same manner unofficially fulminated into fragments. No: fulminate our rivals in Asia by all means, ye brave Russian revolutionaries; but to aim at an English princess! monstrous! hideous! hound down the wretch to his doom; and observe, please, that we are a civilized and merciful people, and, however much we may regret it, must not treat him as Ravaillac and Damiens were treated. And meanwhile, since we have not yet caught him, let us soothe our quivering nerves with the bullfight, and comment in a courtly way on the unfailing tact and good taste of the ladies of our royal houses, who, though

presumably of full normal natural tenderness, have been so effectually broken in to fashionable routine that they can be taken
to see the horses slaughtered as helplessly as they could no doubt
be taken to a gladiator show, if that happened to be the mode
just now.

Strangely enough, in the midst of this raging fire of malice,
the one man who still has faith in the kindness and intelligence
of human nature is the fulminator, now a hunted wretch, with
nothing, apparently, to secure his triumph over all the prisons
and scaffolds of infuriated Europe except the revolver in his
pocket and his readiness to discharge it at a moment's notice
into his own or any other head. Think of him setting out to
find a gentleman and a Christian in the multitude of human
wolves howling for his blood. Think also of this: that at the
very first essay he finds what he seeks, a veritable grandee of
Spain, a noble, high-thinking, unterrified, malice-void soul, in
the guise—of all masquerades in the world!—of a modern editor.
The Anarchist wolf, flying from the wolves of plutocracy,
throws himself on the honor of the man. The man, not being
a wolf (nor a London editor), and therefore not having enough
sympathy with his exploit to be made bloodthirsty by it, does not
throw him back to the pursuing wolves—gives him, instead,
what help he can to escape, and sends him off acquainted at
last with a force that goes deeper than dynamite, though you
cannot buy so much of it for sixpence. That righteous and honorable high human deed is not wasted on Europe, let us hope,
though it benefits the fugitive wolf only for a moment. The
plutocratic wolves presently smell him out. The fugitive shoots
the unlucky wolf whose nose is nearest; shoots himself; and then
convinces the world, by his photograph, that he was no monstrous freak of reversion to the tiger, but a good looking young
man with nothing abnormal about him except his appalling
courage and resolution (that is why the terrified shriek Coward
at him): one to whom murdering a happy young couple on
their wedding morning would have been an unthinkably un-

natural abomination under rational and kindly human circumstances.

Then comes the climax of irony and blind stupidity. The wolves, balked of their meal of fellow-wolf, turn on the man, and proceed to torture him, after their manner, by imprisonment, for refusing to fasten his teeth in the throat of the dynamiter and hold him down until they came to finish him.

Thus, you see, a man may not be a gentleman nowadays even if he wishes to. As to being a Christian, he is allowed some latitude in that matter, because, I repeat, Christianity has two faces. Popular Christianity has for its emblem a gibbet, for its chief sensation a sanguinary execution after torture, for its central mystery an insane vengeance bought off by a trumpery expiation. But there is a nobler and profounder Christianity which affirms the sacred mystery of Equality, and forbids the glaring futility and folly of vengeance, often politely called punishment or justice. The gibbet part of Christianity is tolerated. The other is criminal felony. Connoisseurs in irony are well aware of the fact that the only editor in England who denounces punishment as radically wrong, also repudiates Christianity; calls his paper The Freethinker; and has been imprisoned for "bad taste" under the law against blasphemy.

SANE CONCLUSIONS

And now I must ask the excited reader not to lose his head on one side or the other, but to draw a sane moral from these grim absurdities. It is not good sense to propose that laws against crime should apply to principals only and not to accessories whose consent, counsel, or silence may secure impunity to the principal. If you institute punishment as part of the law, you must punish people for refusing to punish. If you have a police, part of its duty must be to compel everybody to assist the police. No doubt if your laws are unjust, and your policemen agents of oppression, the result will be an unbearable violation of the private consciences of citizens. But that cannot be helped: the remedy is, not to license everybody to thwart the law if they please, but to make laws that will command the public assent, and not to deal cruelly and stupidly with law-breakers. Everybody disapproves of burglars; but the modern burglar, when caught and overpowered by a householder, usually appeals, and often, let us hope, with success, to his captor not to deliver him over to the useless horrors of penal servitude. In other cases the lawbreaker escapes because those who could give him up do not consider his breach of the law a guilty action. Sometimes, even, private tribunals are formed in opposition to the official tribunals; these private tribunals employ assassins as executioners, as was done, for example, by Mahomet before he had established his power officially, and by the Ribbon lodges of Ireland in their long struggle with the landlords. Under such circumstances, the assassin goes free although everybody in the district knows who he is and what he has done. They do not betray him, partly because they justify him exactly as the regular Government justifies its official executioner, and partly because they would themselves be assassinated if they betrayed him: another method learnt from the official government. Given a tribunal, employing a slayer who has no personal quarrel with the slain; and there is clearly no moral difference between official and unofficial killing.

In short, all men are anarchists with regard to laws which are against their consciences, either in the preamble or in the penalty. In London our worst anarchists are the magistrates, because many of them are so old and ignorant that when they are called upon to administer any law that is based on ideas or knowledge less than half a century old, they disagree with it, and being mere ordinary homebred private Englishmen without any respect for law in the abstract, naïvely set the example of violating it. In this instance the man lags behind the law; but when the law lags behind the man, he becomes equally an anarchist. When some huge change in social conditions, such as the industrial revolution of the eighteenth and nineteenth centuries, throws our legal and industrial institutions out of date, Anarchism becomes almost a religion. The whole force of the most energetic geniuses of the time in philosophy, economics, and art, concentrates itself on demonstrations and reminders that morality and law are only conventions, fallible and continually obsolescing. Tragedies in which the heroes are bandits, and comedies in which law-abiding and conventionally moral folk are compelled to satirize themselves by outraging the conscience of the spectators every time they do their duty, appear simultaneously with economic treatises entitled "What is Property? Theft!" and with histories of "The Conflict between Religion and Science."

Now this is not a healthy state of things. The advantages of living in society are proportionate, not to the freedom of the individual from a code, but to the complexity and subtlety of the code he is prepared not only to accept but to uphold as a matter of such vital importance that a lawbreaker at large is hardly to be tolerated on any plea. Such an attitude becomes impossible when the only men who can make themselves heard and remembered throughout the world spend all their energy in raising our gorge against current law, current morality, current respectability, and legal property. The ordinary man, uneducated in social theory even when he is schooled in Latin verse, cannot be set against all the laws of his country and yet persuaded to regard law in the abstract as vitally necessary to society. Once he is brought to repudiate the laws and institutions he knows, he will repudiate the very conception of law and the very groundwork of institutions, ridiculing human rights, extolling brainless methods as "historical," and tolerating nothing except pure empiricism in conduct, with dynamite as the basis of politics and vivisection as the basis of science. That is hideous; but what is to be done? Here am I, for instance, by class a respectable man, by common sense a hater of waste and disorder, by intellectual constitution legally minded to the verge of pedantry, and by temperament apprehensive and economically disposed to the limit of old-maidishness; yet I am, and have always been, and shall now always be, a revolutionary writer, because our laws make law impossible; our liberties destroy all freedom; our property is organized robbery; our morality is an impudent hypocrisy; our wisdom is administered by inexperienced or mal-experienced dupes, our power wielded by cowards and weak-lings, and our honor false in all its points. I am an enemy of the existing order for good reasons; but that does not make my at-tacks any less encouraging or helpful to people who are its ene-mies for bad reasons. The existing order may shriek that if I tell the truth about it, some foolish person may drive it to become still worse by trying to assassinate it. I cannot help that, even if I could see what worse it could do than it is already doing. And the disadvantage of that worst even from its own point of view is that society, with all its prisons and bayonets and whips and ostracisms and starvations, is powerless in the face of the Anar-chist who is prepared to sacrifice his own life in the battle with it. Our natural safety from the cheap and devastating explosives which every Russian student can make, and every Russian gren-adier has learnt to handle in Manchuria, lies in the fact that brave and resolute men, when they are rascals, will not risk their skins for the good of humanity, and, when they are not, are sympathetic enough to care for humanity, abhorring murder, and never committing it until their consciences are outraged beyond endurance. The remedy is, then, simply not to outrage their consciences.

Do not be afraid that they will not make allowances. All men make very large allowances indeed before they stake their own lives in a war to the death with society. Nobody demands or expects the millennium. But there are two things that must be set right, or we shall perish, like Rome, of soul atrophy disguised as empire.

The first is, that the daily ceremony of dividing the wealth of the country among its inhabitants shall be so conducted that no crumb shall, save as a criminal's ration, go to any able-bodied adults who are not producing by their personal exertions not only a full equivalent for what they take, but a surplus sufficient to provide for their superannuation and pay back the debt due for their nurture.

The second is that the deliberate infliction of malicious injuries which now goes on under the name of punishment be abandoned; so that the thief, the ruffian, the gambler, and the beggar, may without inhumanity be handed over to the law, and made to understand that a State which is too humane to punish will also be too thrifty to waste the life of honest men in watching or restraining dishonest ones. That is why we do not imprison dogs. We even take our chance of their first bite. But if a dog delights to bark and bite, it goes to the lethal chamber. That seems to me sensible. To allow the dog to expiate his bite by a period of torment, and then let him loose in a much more savage condition (for the chain makes a dog savage) to bite again and expiate again, having meanwhile spent a great deal of human life and happiness in the task of chaining and feeding and tormenting him, seems to me idiotic and superstitious. Yet that is what we do to men who bark and bite and steal. It would be far more sensible to put up with their vices, as we put up with their illnesses, until they give more trouble than they are worth, at which point we should, with many apologies and expressions of sympathy, and some generosity in complying with their last wishes, place them in the lethal chamber and get rid of them. Under no circumstances should they be allowed to expiate their misdeeds by a manufactured penalty, to subscribe to a charity, or to compensate the victims. If there is to be no punishment there can be no forgiveness. We shall never have real moral responsibility until everyone knows that his deeds are irrevocable, and that his life depends on his usefulness. Hitherto, alas! humanity has never dared face these hard facts. We frantically scatter conscience money and invent systems of conscience banking, with expiatory penalties, atonements, redemptions, salvations, hospital subscription lists and what not, to enable us to contract-out of the moral code. Not content with the old scapegoat and sacrificial lamb, we deify human saviors, and pray to miraculous virgin intercessors. We attribute mercy to the inexorable; sooth our consciences after committing murder by throwing ourselves on the bosom of divine love; and shrink even from our own gallows because we are forced to admit that it, at least, is irrevocable—as if one hour of imprisonment were not as irrevocable as any execution!

If a man cannot look evil in the face without illusion, he will never know what it really is, or combat it effectually. The few men who have been able (relatively) to do this have been called cynics, and have sometimes had an abnormal share of evil in themselves, corresponding to the abnormal strength of their minds; but they have never done mischief unless they intended to do it. That is why great scoundrels have been beneficent rulers whilst amiable and privately harmless monarchs have ruined their countries by trusting to the hocus-pocus of innocence and guilt, reward and punishment, virtuous indignation and pardon, instead of standing up to the facts without either malice or mercy. Major Barbara stands up to Bill Walker in that way, with the result that the ruffian who cannot get hated, has to hate himself. To relieve this agony he tries to get punished; but the Salvationist whom he tries to provoke is as merciless as Barbara, and only prays for him. Then he tries to pay, but can get nobody to take his money. His doom is the doom of Cain, who, failing to find either a savior, a policeman, or an almoner to help him to pretend that his brother's blood no longer cried from the ground, had to live and die a murderer. Cain took care not to commit another murder, unlike our railway shareholders (I am one) who kill and maim shunters by hundreds to save the cost of automatic couplings, and make atonement by annual subscriptions to deserving charities. Had Cain been allowed to pay off his score, he might possibly have killed Adam and Eve for the mere sake of a second luxurious reconciliation with God afterwards. Bodger, you may depend on it, will go on to the end of his life poisoning people with bad whisky, because he can always depend on the Salvation Army or the Church of England to negotiate a redemption for him in consideration of a trifling percentage of his profits.

There is a third condition too, which must be fulfilled before the great teachers of the world will cease to scoff at its religions. Creeds must become intellectually honest. At present there is not a single credible established religion in the world. That is perhaps the most stupendous fact in the whole world-situation. This play of mine, Major Barbara, is, I hope, both true and inspired; but whoever says that it all happened, and that faith in it and understanding of it consist in believing that it is a record of an actual occurrence, is, to speak according to Scripture, a fool and a liar, and is hereby solemnly denounced and cursed as such by me, the author, to all posterity.

London, June 1906.

N.B. The Euripidean verses in the second act of Major Barbara are not by me, nor even directly by Euripides. They are by Professor Gilbert Murray, whose English version of The Bacchæ came into our dramatic literature with all the impulsive power of an original work shortly before Major Barbara was begun. The play, indeed, stands indebted to him in more ways than one.

G.B.S.

ACT I

IT IS *after dinner in January 1906, in the library in Lady Britomart Undershaft's house in Wilton Crescent. A large and comfortable settee is in the middle of the room, upholstered in dark leather. A person sitting on it (it is vacant at present) would have, on his right, Lady Britomart's writing-table, with the lady herself busy at it; a smaller writing-table behind him on his left; the door behind him on Lady Britomart's side; and a window with a window-seat directly on his left. Near the window is an armchair.*

Lady Britomart is a woman of fifty or thereabouts, well dressed and yet careless of her dress, well bred and quite reckless of her breeding, well mannered and yet appallingly outspoken and indifferent to the opinion of her interlocutors, amiable and yet peremptory, arbitrary, and hightempered to the last bearable degree, and withal a very typical managing matron of the upper class, treated as a naughty child until she grew into a scolding mother, and finally settling down with plenty of practical ability and worldly experience, limited in the oddest way with domestic and class limitations, conceiving the universe exactly as if it were a large house in Wilton Crescent, though handling her corner of it very effectively on that assumption, and being quite enlightened and liberal as to the books in the library, the pictures on the walls, the music in the portfolios, and the articles in the papers.

Her son, Stephen, comes in. He is a gravely correct young man under 25, taking himself very seriously, but still in some awe of his mother, from childish habit and bachelor shyness rather than from any weakness of character.

STEPHEN. Whats the matter?

LADY BRITOMART. Presently, Stephen.

Stephen submissively walks to the settee and sits down. He takes up a Liberal weekly called The Speaker.

LADY BRITOMART. Dont begin to read, Stephen. I shall require all your attention.

STEPHEN. It was only while I was waiting—

LADY BRITOMART. Dont make excuses, Stephen. (*He puts down The Speaker*). Now! (*She finishes her writing; rises; and comes to the settee*). I have not kept you waiting very long, I think.

STEPHEN. Not at all, mother.

LADY BRITOMART. Bring me my cushion. (*He takes the cushion from the chair at the desk and arranges it for her as she sits down on the settee*). Sit down. (*He sits down and fingers his tie nervously*). Dont fiddle with your tie, Stephen: there is nothing the matter with it.

STEPHEN. I beg your pardon. (*He fiddles with his watch chain instead*).

LADY BRITOMART. Now are you attending to me, Stephen?

STEPHEN. Of course, mother.

LADY BRITOMART. No: it's n o t of course. I want something much more than your everyday matter-of-course attention. I am going to speak to you very seriously, Stephen. I wish you would let that chain alone.

STEPHEN (*hastily relinquishing the chain*) Have I done anything to annoy you, mother? If so, it was quite unintentional.

LADY BRITOMART (*astonished*) Nonsense! (*With some remorse*) My poor boy, did you think I was angry with you?

STEPHEN. What is it, then, mother? You are making me very uneasy.

LADY BRITOMART (*squaring herself at him rather aggressively*) Stephen: may I ask how soon you intend to realize that you are a grown-up man, and that I am only a woman?

STEPHEN (*amazed*) Only a—

LADY BRITOMART. Dont repeat my words, please: it is a most aggravating habit. You must learn to face life seriously, Stephen. I really cannot bear the whole burden of our family affairs any longer. You must advise me: you must assume the responsibility.

STEPHEN. I!

LADY BRITOMART. Yes, you, of course. You were 24 last June. Youve been at Harrow and Cambridge. Youve been to India and Japan. You must know a lot of things, now; unless you have wasted your time most scandalously. Well, a d v i s e me.

STEPHEN (*much perplexed*) You know I have never interfered in the household—

LADY BRITOMART. No: I should think not. I don't want you to order the dinner.

STEPHEN. I mean in our family affairs.

LADY BRITOMART. Well, you must interfere now; for they are getting quite beyond me.

STEPHEN (*troubled*) I have thought sometimes that perhaps I ought; but really, mother, I know so little about them; and what I do know is so painful—it is so impossible to mention some things to you— (*He stops, ashamed*).

LADY BRITOMART. I suppose you mean your father.

STEPHEN (*almost inaudibly*) Yes.

LADY BRITOMART. My dear: we cant go on all our lives not mentioning him. Of course you were quite right not to open the subject until I asked you to; but you are old enough now to be taken into my confidence, and to help me to deal with him about the girls.

STEPHEN. But the girls are all right. They are engaged.

LADY BRITOMART (*complacently*) Yes: I have made a very good match for Sarah. Charles Lomax will be a millionaire at 35. But that is ten years ahead; and in the meantime his trustees cannot under the terms of his father's will allow him more than £800 a year.

STEPHEN. But the will says also that if he increases his income by his own exertions, they may double the increase.

LADY BRITOMART. Charles Lomax's exertions are much more likely to decrease his income than to increase it. Sarah will have to find at least another £800 a year for the next ten years; and even then they will be as poor as church mice. And what about Barbara? I thought Barbara was going to make the most brilliant career of all of you. And what does she do? Joins the Salvation Army; discharges her maid; lives on a pound a week; and walks in one evening with a professor of Greek whom she has picked up in the street, and who pretends to be a Salvationist, and actually plays the big drum for her in public because he has fallen head over ears in love with her.

STEPHEN. I was certainly rather taken aback when I heard they were engaged. Cusins is a very nice fellow, certainly: nobody would ever guess that he was born in Australia; but—

LADY BRITOMART. Oh, Adolphus Cusins will make a very good husband. After all, nobody can say a word against Greek: it stamps a man at once as an educated gentleman. And my family, thank Heaven, is not a pigheaded Tory one. We are Whigs, and believe in liberty. Let snobbish people say what they please: Barbara shall marry, not the man they like, but the man I like.

STEPHEN. Of course I was thinking only of his income. However, he is not likely to be extravagant.

LADY BRITOMART. Dont be too sure of that, Stephen. I know your quiet, simple, refined, poetic people like Adolphus—quite content with the best of everything! They cost more than your extravagant people, who are always as mean as they are second rate. No: Barbara will need at least £2000 a year. You see it means two additional households. Besides, my dear, y o u must marry soon. I dont approve of the present fashion of philandering bachelors and late marriages; and I am trying to arrange something for you.

STEPHEN. It's very good of you, mother; but perhaps I had better arrange that for myself.

LADY BRITOMART. Nonsense! you are much too young to begin matchmaking: you would be taken in by some pretty little nobody. Of course I dont mean that you are not to be consulted: you know that as well as I do. (*Stephen closes his lips and is silent*). Now don't sulk, Stephen.

STEPHEN. I am not sulking, mother. What has all this got to do with—with—with my father?

LADY BRITOMART. My dear Stephen: where is the money to come from? It is easy enough for you and the other children to live on my income as long as we are in the same house; but I cant keep four families in four separate houses. You know how poor my father is: he has barely seven thousand a year now; and really, if he were not the Earl of Stevenage, he would have to give up society. He can do nothing for us. He says, naturally enough, that it is absurd that he should be asked to provide for the children of a man who is rolling in money. You see, Stephen, your father must be fabulously wealthy, because there is always a war going on somewhere.

STEPHEN. You need not remind me of that, mother. I have hardly ever opened a newspaper in my life without seeing our name in it. The Undershaft torpedo! The Undershaft quick firers! The Undershaft ten inch! The Undershaft disappearing rampart gun! The Undershaft submarine! and now the Undershaft aerial battleship! At Harrow they called me the Woolwich Infant. At Cambridge it was the same. A little brute at King's who was always trying to get up revivals, spoilt my Bible—your first birthday present to me—by writing under my name, "Son and heir to Undershaft and Lazarus, Death and Destruction Dealers: address, Christendom and Judea." But that was not so bad as the way I was kowtowed to everywhere because my father was making millions by selling cannons.

LADY BRITOMART. It is not only the cannons, but the war

loans that Lazarus arranges under cover of giving credit for the cannons. You know, Stephen, it's perfectly scandalous. Those two men, Andrew Undershaft and Lazarus, positively have Europe under their thumbs. That is why your father is able to behave as he does. He is above the law. Do you think Bismarck or Gladstone or Disraeli could have openly defied every social and moral obligation all their lives as your father has? They simply wouldnt have dared. I asked Gladstone to take it up. I asked The Times to take it up. I asked the Lord Chamberlain to take it up. But it was just like asking them to declare war on the Sultan. They w o u l d n t. They said they couldnt touch him. I believe they were afraid.

STEPHEN. What could they do? He does not actually break the law.

LADY BRITOMART. Not break the law! He is always breaking the law. He broke the law when he was born: his parents were not married.

STEPHEN. Mother! Is that true?

LADY BRITOMART. Of course it's true: that was why we separated.

STEPHEN. He married without letting you know this!

LADY BRITOMART (*rather taken aback by this inference*) Oh no. To do Andrew justice, that was not the sort of thing he did. Besides, you know the Undershaft motto: Unashamed. Everybody knew.

STEPHEN. But you said that was why you separated.

LADY BRITOMART. Yes, because he was not content with being a foundling himself: he wanted to disinherit you for another foundling. That was what I couldnt stand.

STEPHEN (*ashamed*) Do you mean for—for—for—

LADY BRITOMART. Dont stammer, Stephen. Speak distinctly.

STEPHEN. But this is so frightful to me, mother. To have to speak to you about such things!

LADY BRITOMART. It's not pleasant for me, either, especially if you are still so childish that you must make it worse by a display of embarrassment. It is only in the middle classes, Stephen, that people get into a state of dumb helpless horror when they find that there are wicked people in the world. In our class, we have to decide what is to be done with wicked people; and nothing should disturb our self-possession. Now ask your question properly.

STEPHEN. Mother: you have no consideration for me. For Heaven's sake either treat me as a child, as you always do, and tell me nothing at all; or tell me everything and let me take it as best I can.

LADY BRITOMART. Treat you as a child! What do you mean? It is most unkind and ungrateful of you to say such a thing. You know I have never treated any of you as children. I have always made you my companions and friends, and allowed you perfect freedom to do and say whatever you liked, so long as you liked what I could approve of.

STEPHEN (*desperately*) I daresay we have been the very imperfect children of a very perfect mother; but I do beg of you to let me alone for once, and tell me about this horrible business of my father wanting to set me aside for another son.

LADY BRITOMART (*amazed*) Another son! I never said anything of the kind. I never dreamt of such a thing. This is what comes of interrupting me.

STEPHEN. But you said—

LADY BRITOMART (*cutting him short*) Now be a good boy, Stephen, and listen to me patiently. The Undershafts are descended from a foundling in the parish of St Andrew Undershaft in the city. That was long ago, in the reign of James the First. Well, this foundling was adopted by an armorer and gunmaker. In the course of time the foundling succeeded to the business; and from some notion of gratitude, or some vow or something, he adopted another foundling, and left the business to him. And that foundling did the same. Ever since that, the cannon business has always been left to an adopted foundling named Andrew Undershaft.

STEPHEN. But did they never marry? Were there no legiti-mate sons?

LADY BRITOMART. Oh yes: they married just as your father did; and they were rich enough to buy land for their own children and leave them well provided for. But they always adopted and trained some foundling to succeed them in the business; and of course they always quarrelled with their wives furiously over it. Your father was adopted in that way; and he pretends to consider himself bound to keep up the tradition and adopt somebody to leave the business to. Of course I was not going to stand that. There may have been some reason for it when the Undershafts could only marry women in their own class, whose sons were not fit to govern great estates. But there could be no excuse for passing over m y son.

STEPHEN (*dubiously*) I am afraid I should make a poor hand of managing a cannon foundry.

LADY BRITOMART. Nonsense! you could easily get a manager and pay him a salary.

STEPHEN. My father evidently had no great opinion of my capacity.

LADY BRITOMART. Stuff, child! you were only a baby: it had nothing to do with your capacity. Andrew did it on principle, just as he did every perverse and wicked thing on principle. When my father remonstrated, Andrew actually told him to his face that history tells us of only two successful institutions: one the Undershaft firm, and the other the Roman Empire under the Antonines. That was because the Antonine emperors all adopted their successors. Such rubbish! The Stevenages are as good as the Antonines, I hope; and you are a Stevenage. But that was Andrew all over. There you have the man! Always clever and unanswerable when he was defending nonsense and wickedness: always awkward and sullen when he had to be-have sensibly and decently.

STEPHEN. Then it was on my account that your home life was broken up, mother. I am sorry.

LADY BRITOMART. Well, dear, there were other differences. I really cannot bear an immoral man. I am not a Pharisee, I hope; and I should not have minded his merely d o i n g wrong things: we are none of us perfect. But your father didnt exactly do wrong things: he said them and thought them: that was what was so dreadful. He really had a sort of religion of wrongness. Just as one doesnt mind men practising immorality so long as they own that they are in the wrong by preaching morality; so I couldnt forgive Andrew for preaching immorality while he practised morality. You would all have grown up without principles, without any knowledge of right and wrong, if he had been in the house. You know, my dear, your father was a very attractive man in some ways. Children did not dislike him; and he took advantage of it to put the wickedest ideas into their heads, and make them quite unmanageable. I did not dislike him myself: very far from it; but nothing can bridge over moral disagreement.

STEPHEN. All this simply bewilders me, mother. People may differ about matters of opinion, or even about religion; but how can they differ about right and wrong? Right is right; and wrong is wrong; and if a man cannot distinguish them properly, he is either a fool or a rascal: thats all.

LADY BRITOMART (*touched*) Thats my own boy (*She pats his cheek*)! Your father never could answer that: he used to laugh and get out of it under cover of some affectionate nonsense. And now that you understand the situation, what do you advise me to do?

STEPHEN. Well, what c a n you do?

LADY BRITOMART. I must get the money somehow.

STEPHEN. We cannot take money from him. I had rather go and live in some cheap place like Bedford Square or even Hampstead than take a farthing of his money.

LADY BRITOMART. But after all, Stephen, our present income comes from Andrew.

STEPHEN (*shocked*) I never knew that.

LADY BRITOMART. Well, you surely didnt suppose your grandfather had anything to give me. The Stevenages could not do everything for you. We gave you social position. Andrew had to contribute s o m e t h i n g. He had a very good bargain, I think.

STEPHEN (*bitterly*) We are utterly dependent on him and his cannons, then?

LADY BRITOMART. Certainly not: the money is settled. But he provided it. So you see it is not a question of taking money from him or not: it is simply a question of how much. I dont want any more for myself.

STEPHEN. Nor do I.

LADY BRITOMART. But Sarah does; and Barbara does. That is, Charles Lomax and Adolphus Cusins will cost them more. So I must put my pride in my pocket and ask for it, I suppose. That is your advice, Stephen, is it not?

STEPHEN. No.

LADY BRITOMART (*sharply*) Stephen!

STEPHEN. Of course if you are determined—

LADY BRITOMART. I am not determined: I ask your advice; and I am waiting for it. I will not have all the responsibility thrown on my shoulders.

STEPHEN (*obstinately*) I would die sooner than ask him for another penny.

LADY BRITOMART (*resignedly*) You mean that I must ask him. Very well, Stephen: it shall be as you wish. You will be glad to know that your grandfather concurs. But he thinks I ought to ask Andrew to come here and see the girls. After all he must have some natural affection for them.

STEPHEN. Ask him here! ! !

LADY BRITOMART. Do n o t repeat my words, Stephen. Where else can I ask him?

STEPHEN. I never expected you to ask him at all.

LADY BRITOMART. Now dont tease, Stephen. Come! you see

that it is necessary that he should pay us a visit, dont you?

STEPHEN (*reluctantly*) I suppose so, if the girls cannot do without his money.

LADY BRITOMART. Thank you, Stephen: I knew you would give me the right advice when it was properly explained to you. I have asked your father to come this evening. (*Stephen bounds from his seat*). Dont jump, Stephen: it fidgets me.

STEPHEN (*in utter consternation*) Do you mean to say that my father is coming here to-night—that he may be here at any moment?

LADY BRITOMART (*looking at her watch*) I said nine. (*He gasps. She rises*). Ring the bell, please. (*Stephen goes to the smaller writing table; presses a button on it; and sits at it with his elbows on the table and his head in his hands, outwitted and overwhelmed*). It is ten minutes to nine yet; and I have to prepare the girls. I asked Charles Lomax and Adolphus to dinner on purpose that they might be here. Andrew had better see them in case he should cherish any delusions as to their being capable of supporting their wives. (*The butler enters: Lady Britomart goes behind the settee to speak to him*). Morrison: go up to the drawing-room and tell everybody to come down here at once. (*Morrison withdraws. Lady Britomart turns to Stephen*). Now remember, Stephen: I shall need all your countenance and authority. (*He rises and tries to recover some vestige of these attributes*). Give me a chair, dear. (*He pushes a chair forward from the wall to where she stands, near the smaller writing table. She sits down; and he goes to the armchair, into which he throws himself*). I dont know how Barbara will take it. Ever since they made her a major in the Salvation Army she has developed a propensity to have her own way and order people about which quite cows me sometimes. It's not ladylike: I'm sure I dont know where she picked it up. Anyhow, Barbara shant bully m e; but still it's just as well that your father should be here before she has time to refuse to meet him

or make a fuss. Dont look nervous, Stephen: it will only encourage Barbara to make difficulties. I am nervous enough,
goodness knows; but I dont shew it.

*Sarah and Barbara come in with their respective young men,
Charles Lomax and Adolphus Cusins. Sarah is slender, bored,
and mundane. Barbara is robuster, jollier, much more energetic.
Sarah is fashionably dressed: Barbara is in Salvation Army uniform. Lomax, a young man about town, is like many other
young men about town. He is afflicted with a frivolous sense of
humor which plunges him at the most inopportune moments
into paroxysms of imperfectly suppressed laughter. Cusins is a
spectacled student, slight, thin haired, and sweet voiced, with
a more complex form of Lomax's complaint. His sense of humor
is intellectual and subtle, and is complicated by an appalling
temper. The life-long struggle of a benevolent temperament and
a high conscience against impulses of inhuman ridicule and
fierce impatience has set up a chronic strain which has visibly
wrecked his constitution. He is a most implacable, determined,
tenacious, intolerant person who by mere force of character presents himself as—and indeed actually is—considerate, gentle,
explanatory, even mild and apologetic, capable possibly of murder, but not of cruelty or coarseness. By the operation of some
instinct which is not merciful enough to blind him with the
illusions of love, he is obstinately bent on marrying Barbara.
Lomax likes Sarah and thinks it will be rather a lark to marry
her. Consequently he has not attempted to resist Lady Britomart's arrangements to that end.*

*All four look as if they had been having a good deal of fun
in the drawing room. The girls enter first, leaving the swains
outside. Sarah comes to the settee. Barbara comes in after her
and stops at the door.*

BARBARA. Are Cholly and Dolly to come in?

LADY BRITOMART (*forcibly*) Barbara: I will not have Charles
called Cholly: the vulgarity of it positively makes me ill.

BARBARA. It's all right, mother: Cholly is quite correct nowadays. Are they to come in?

LADY BRITOMART. Yes, if they will behave themselves.

BARBARA (*through the door*) Come in, Dolly; and behave yourself.

Barbara comes to her mother's writing table. Cusins enters smiling, and wanders towards Lady Britomart.

SARAH (*calling*) Come in, Cholly. (*Lomax enters, controlling his features very imperfectly, and places himself vaguely between Sarah and Barbara*).

LADY BRITOMART (*peremptorily*) Sit down, all of you. (*They sit. Cusins crosses to the window and seats himself there. Lomax takes a chair. Barbara sits at the writing table and Sarah on the settee*). I dont in the least know what you are laughing at, Adolphus. I am surprised at you, though I expected nothing better from Charles Lomax.

CUSINS (*in a remarkably gentle voice*) Barbara has been trying to teach me the West Ham Salvation March.

LADY BRITOMART. I see nothing to laugh at in that; nor should you if you are really converted.

CUSINS (*sweetly*) You were not present. It was really funny, I believe.

LOMAX. Ripping.

LADY BRITOMART. Be quiet, Charles. Now listen to me, children. Your father is coming here this evening.

General stupefaction. Lomax, Sarah, and Barbara rise: Sarah scared, and Barbara amused and expectant.

LOMAX (*remonstrating*) Oh I say!

LADY BRITOMART. You are not called on to say anything, Charles.

SARAH. Are you serious, mother?

LADY BRITOMART. Of course I am serious. It is on your account, Sarah, and also on Charles's. (*Silence. Sarah sits, with a shrug. Charles looks painfully unworthy*). I hope you are not going to object, Barbara.

BARBARA. I! why should I? My father has a soul to be saved like anybody else. He's quite welcome as far as I am concerned. (*She sits on the table, and softly whistles 'Onward, Christian Soldiers'*).

LOMAX (*still remonstrant*) But really, dont you know! Oh I say!

LADY BRITOMART (*frigidly*) What do you wish to convey, Charles?

LOMAX. Well, you must admit that this is a bit thick.

LADY BRITOMART (*turning with ominous suavity to Cusins*) Adolphus: you are a professor of Greek. Can you translate Charles Lomax's remarks into reputable English for us?

CUSINS (*cautiously*) If I may say so, Lady Brit, I think Charles has rather happily expressed what we all feel. Homer, speaking of Autolycus, uses the same phrase. πυκινὸν δόμον ἐλθεῖν means a bit thick.

LOMAX (*handsomely*) Not that I mind, you know, if Sarah dont. (*He sits*).

LADY BRITOMART (*crushingly*) Thank you. Have I y o u r permission, Adolphus, to invite my own husband to my own house?

CUSINS (*gallantly*) You have my unhesitating support in everything you do.

LADY BRITOMART. Tush! Sarah: have you nothing to say?

SARAH. Do you mean that he is coming regularly to live here?

LADY BRITOMART. Certainly not. The spare room is ready for him if he likes to stay for a day or two and see a little more of you; but there are limits.

SARAH. Well, he cant eat us, I suppose. *I* dont mind.

LOMAX (*chuckling*) I wonder how the old man will take it.

LADY BRITOMART. Much as the old woman will, no doubt, Charles.

LOMAX (*abashed*) I didnt mean—at least—

LADY BRITOMART. You didnt t h i n k, Charles. You never do; and the result is, you never mean anything. And now please attend to me, children. Your father will be quite a stranger to us.

LOMAX. I suppose he hasnt seen Sarah since she was a little kid.

LADY BRITOMART. Not since she was a little kid, Charles, as you express it with that elegance of diction and refinement of thought that seem never to desert you. Accordingly—er— (*Impatiently*) Now I have forgotten what I was going to say. That comes of your provoking me to be sarcastic, Charles. Adolphus: will you kindly tell me where I was.

CUSINS (*sweetly*) You were saying that as Mr Undershaft has not seen his children since they were babies, he will form his opinion of the way you have brought them up from their behavior to-night, and that therefore you wish us all to be particularly careful to conduct ourselves well, especially Charles.

LADY BRITOMART (*with emphatic approval*) Precisely.

LOMAX. Look here, Dolly: Lady Brit didnt say that.

LADY BRITOMART (*vehemently*) I did, Charles. Adolphus's recollection is perfectly correct. It is most important that you should be good; and I do beg you for once not to pair off into opposite corners and giggle and whisper while I am speaking to your father.

BARBARA. All right, mother. We'll do you credit. (*She comes off the table, and sits in her chair with ladylike elegance*).

LADY BRITOMART. Remember, Charles, that Sarah will want to feel proud of you instead of ashamed of you.

LOMAX. Oh I say! theres nothing to be exactly proud of, dont you know.

LADY BRITOMART. Well, try and look as if there was.

Morrison, pale and dismayed, breaks into the room in uncon-cealed disorder.

MORRISON. Might I speak a word to you, my lady?

LADY BRITOMART. Nonsense! Shew him up.

MORRISON. Yes, my lady. (*He goes*).

LOMAX. Does Morrison know who it is?

LADY BRITOMART. Of course. Morrison has always been with us.

LOMAX. It must be a regular corker for him, dont you know.

LADY BRITOMART. Is this a moment to get on my nerves, Charles, with your outrageous expressions?

LOMAX. But this is something out of the ordinary, really—

MORRISON (*at the door*) The—er—Mr Undershaft. (*He retreats in confusion*).

Andrew Undershaft comes in. All rise. Lady Britomart meets him in the middle of the room behind the settee.

Andrew is, on the surface, a stoutish, easygoing elderly man, with kindly patient manners, and an engaging simplicity of character. But he has a watchful, deliberate, waiting, listening face, and formidable reserves of power, both bodily and mental, in his capacious chest and long head. His gentleness is partly that of a strong man who has learnt by experience that his natural grip hurts ordinary people unless he handles them very carefully, and partly the mellowness of age and success. He is also a little shy in his present very delicate situation.

LADY BRITOMART. Good evening, Andrew.

UNDERSHAFT. How d'ye do, my dear.

LADY BRITOMART. You look a good deal older.

UNDERSHAFT (*apologetically*) I a m somewhat older. (*Taking her hand with a touch of courtship*) Time has stood still with you.

LADY BRITOMART (*throwing away his hand*) Rubbish! This is your family.

UNDERSHAFT (*surprised*) Is it so large? I am sorry to say my memory is failing very badly in some things. (*He offers his hand with paternal kindness to Lomax*).

LOMAX (*jerkily shaking his hand*) Ahdedoo.

UNDERSHAFT. I can see you are my eldest. I am very glad to meet you again, my boy.

LOMAX (*remonstrating*) No, but look here dont you know— (*Overcome*) Oh I say!

LADY BRITOMART (*recovering from momentary speechlessness*) Andrew: do you mean to say that you dont remember how many children you have?

UNDERSHAFT. Well, I am afraid I— They have grown so much—er. Am I making any ridiculous mistake? I may as well confess: I recollect only one son. But so many things have happened since, of course—er—

LADY BRITOMART (*decisively*) Andrew: you are talking nonsense. Of course you have only one son.

UNDERSHAFT. Perhaps you will be good enough to introduce me, my dear.

LADY BRITOMART. That is Charles Lomax, who is engaged to Sarah.

UNDERSHAFT. My dear sir, I beg your pardon.

LOMAX. Notatall. Delighted, I assure you.

LADY BRITOMART. This is Stephen.

UNDERSHAFT (*bowing*) Happy to make your acquaintance, Mr Stephen. Then (*going to Cusins*) y o u must be my son. (*Taking Cusins' hands in his*) How are you, my young friend? (*To Lady Britomart*) He is very like you, my love.

CUSINS. You flatter me, Mr Undershaft. My name is Cusins: engaged to Barbara. (*Very explicitly*) That is Major Barbara Undershaft, of the Salvation Army. That is Sarah, your second daughter. This is Stephen Undershaft, your son.

UNDERSHAFT. My dear Stephen, I b e g your pardon.

STEPHEN. Not at all.

UNDERSHAFT. Mr Cusins: I am indebted to you for explaining so precisely. (*Turning to Sarah*) Barbara, my dear—

SARAH (*prompting him*) Sarah.

UNDERSHAFT. Sarah, of course. (*They shake hands. He goes over to Barbara*). Barbara—I am right this time, I hope.

BARBARA. Quite right. (*They shake hands*).

LADY BRITOMART (*resuming command*) Sit down, all of you. Sit down, Andrew. (*She comes forward and sits on the settee. Cusins also brings his chair forward on her left. Barbara and Stephen resume their seats. Lomax gives his chair to Sarah and goes for another*).

UNDERSHAFT. Thank you, my love.

LOMAX (*conversationally, as he brings a chair forward between the writing table and the settee, and offers it to Undershaft*) Takes you some time to find out exactly where you are, dont it?

UNDERSHAFT (*accepting the chair, but remaining standing*) That is not what embarrasses me, Mr Lomax. My difficulty is that if I play the part of a father, I shall produce the effect of an intrusive stranger; and if I play the part of a discreet stranger, I may appear a callous father.

LADY BRITOMART. There is no need for you to play any part at all, Andrew. You had much better be sincere and natural.

UNDERSHAFT (*submissively*) Yes, my dear: I daresay that will be best. (*He sits down comfortably*). Well, here I am. Now what can I do for you all?

LADY BRITOMART. You need not do anything, Andrew. You are one of the family. You can sit with us and enjoy yourself.

A painfully conscious pause. Barbara makes a face at Lomax, whose too long suppressed mirth immediately explodes in agonized neighings.

LADY BRITOMART (*outraged*) Charles Lomax: if you can behave yourself, behave yourself. If not, leave the room.

LOMAX. I'm awfully sorry, Lady Brit; but really, you know, upon my soul! (*He sits on the settee between Lady Britomart and Undershaft, quite overcome*).

BARBARA. Why dont you laugh if you want to, Cholly? It's good for your inside.

LADY BRITOMART. Barbara: you have had the education of a lady. Please let your father see that; and dont talk like a street girl.

UNDERSHAFT. Never mind me, my dear. As you know, I am not a gentleman; and I was never educated.

LOMAX (*encouragingly*) Nobody'd know it, I assure you. You look all right, you know.

CUSINS. Let me advise you to study Greek, Mr Undershaft. Greek scholars are privileged men. Few of them know Greek; and none of them know anything else; but their position is unchallengeable. Other languages are the qualifications of waiters and commercial travellers: Greek is to a man of position what the hallmark is to silver.

BARBARA. Dolly: dont be insincere. Cholly: fetch your concertina and play something for us.

LOMAX (*jumps up eagerly, but checks himself to remark doubtfully to Undershaft*) Perhaps that sort of thing isnt in your line, eh?

UNDERSHAFT. I am particularly fond of music.

LOMAX (*delighted*) Are you? Then I'll get it. (*He goes upstairs for the instrument*).

UNDERSHAFT. Do you play, Barbara?

BARBARA. Only the tambourine. But Cholly's teaching me the concertina.

UNDERSHAFT. Is Cholly also a member of the Salvation Army?

BARBARA. No: he says it's bad form to be a dissenter. But I dont despair of Cholly. I made him come yesterday to a meeting at the dock gates, and take the collection in his hat.

UNDERSHAFT (*looks whimsically at his wife*)!!

LADY BRITOMART. It is not my doing, Andrew. Barbara is old enough to take her own way. She has no father to advise her.

BARBARA. Oh yes she has. There are no orphans in the Salvation Army.

UNDERSHAFT. Your father there has a great many children and plenty of experience, eh?

BARBARA (*looking at him with quick interest and nodding*)

Just so. How did y o u come to understand that? (*Lomax is heard at the door trying the concertina*).

LADY BRITOMART. Come in, Charles. Play us something at once.

LOMAX. Righto! (*He sits down in his former place, and preludes*).

UNDERSHAFT. One moment, Mr Lomax. I am rather interested in the Salvation Army. Its motto might be my own: Blood and Fire.

LOMAX (*shocked*) But not your sort of blood and fire, you know.

UNDERSHAFT. My sort of blood cleanses: my sort of fire purifies.

BARBARA. So do ours. Come down to-morrow to my shelter—the West Ham shelter—and see what we're doing. We're going to march to a great meeting in the Assembly Hall at Mile End. Come and see the shelter and then march with us: it will do you a lot of good. Can you play anything?

UNDERSHAFT. In my youth I earned pennies, and even shillings occasionally, in the streets and in public house parlors by my natural talent for stepdancing. Later on, I became a member of the Undershaft orchestral society, and performed passably on the tenor trombone.

LOMAX (*scandalized—putting down the concertina*) Oh I say!

BARBARA. Many a sinner has played himself into heaven on the trombone, thanks to the Army.

LOMAX (*to Barbara, still rather shocked*) Yes; but what about the cannon business, dont you know? (*To Undershaft*) Getting into heaven is not exactly in your line, is it?

LADY BRITOMART. Charles!!!

LOMAX. Well; but it stands to reason, dont it? The cannon business may be necessary and all that: we cant get on without cannons; but it isn't right, you know. On the other hand, there may be a certain amount of tosh about the Salvation Army—I belong to the Established Church myself—but still you cant deny that it's religion; and you cant go against religion, can you? At least unless youre downright immoral, dont you know.

UNDERSHAFT. You hardly appreciate my position, Mr Lomax—

LOMAX (*hastily*) I'm not saying anything against you personally—

UNDERSHAFT. Quite so, quite so. But consider for a moment. Here I am, a profiteer in mutilation and murder. I find myself in a specially amiable humor just now because, this morning, down at the foundry, we blew twenty-seven dummy soldiers into fragments with a gun which formerly destroyed only thirteen.

LOMAX (*leniently*) Well, the more destructive war becomes, the sooner it will be abolished, eh?

UNDERSHAFT. Not at all. The more destructive war becomes the more fascinating we find it. No, Mr Lomax: I am obliged to you for making the usual excuse for my trade; but I am not ashamed of it. I am not one of those men who keep their morals and their business in watertight compartments. All the spare money my trade rivals spend on hospitals, cathedrals, and other receptacles for conscience money, I devote to experiments and researches in improved methods of destroying life and property. I have always done so; and I always shall. Therefore your Christmas card moralities of peace on earth and goodwill among men are of no use to me. Your Christianity, which enjoins you to resist not evil, and to turn the other cheek, would make me a bankrupt. My morality—my religion—must have a place for cannons and torpedoes in it.

STEPHEN (*coldly—almost sullenly*) You speak as if there were half a dozen moralities and religions to choose from, instead of one true morality and one true religion.

UNDERSHAFT. For me there is only one true morality; but it

might not fit you, as you do not manufacture aerial battleships. There is only one true morality for every man; but every man has not the same true morality.

LOMAX (*overtaxed*) Would you mind saying that again? I didnt quite follow it.

CUSINS. It's quite simple. As Euripides says, one man's meat is another man's poison morally as well as physically.

UNDERSHAFT. Precisely.

LOMAX. Oh, t h a t. Yes, yes, yes. True. True.

STEPHEN. In other words, some men are honest and some are scoundrels.

BARBARA. Bosh. There are no scoundrels.

UNDERSHAFT. Indeed? Are there any good men?

BARBARA. No. Not one. There are neither good men nor scoundrels: there are just children of one Father; and the sooner they stop calling one another names the better. You neednt talk to me: I know them. Ive had scores of them through my hands: scoundrels, criminals, infidels, philanthropists, missionaries, county councillors, all sorts. Theyre all just the same sort of sinner; and theres the same salvation ready for them all.

UNDERSHAFT. May I ask have you ever saved a maker of cannons?

BARBARA. No. Will you let me try?

UNDERSHAFT. Well, I will make a bargain with you. If I go to see you to-morrow in your Salvation Shelter, will you come the day after to see me in my cannon works?

BARBARA. Take care. It may end in your giving up the cannons for the sake of the Salvation Army.

UNDERSHAFT. Are you sure it will not end in your giving up the Salvation Army for the sake of cannons?

BARBARA. I will take my chance of that.

UNDERSHAFT. And I will take my chance of the other. (*They shake hands on it*). Where is your shelter?

BARBARA. In West Ham. At the sign of the cross. Ask anybody in Canning Town. Where are your works?

UNDERSHAFT. In Perivale St Andrews. At the sign of the sword. Ask anybody in Europe.

LOMAX. Hadnt I better play something?

BARBARA. Yes. Give us Onward, Christian Soldiers.

LOMAX. Well, thats rather a strong order to begin with, dont you know. Suppose I sing Thourt passing hence, my brother. It's much the same tune.

BARBARA. It's too melancholy. You get saved, Cholly; and youll pass hence, my brother, without making such a fuss about it.

LADY BRITOMART. Really, Barbara, you go on as if religion were a pleasant subject. Do have some sense of propriety.

UNDERSHAFT. I do not find it an unpleasant subject, my dear. It is the only one that capable people really care for.

LADY BRITOMART (*looking at her watch*) Well, if you are determined to have it, I insist on having it in a proper and respectable way. Charles: ring for prayers. (*General amazement. Stephen rises in dismay*).

LOMAX (*rising*) Oh I say!

UNDERSHAFT (*rising*) I am afraid I must be going.

LADY BRITOMART. You cannot go now, Andrew: it would be most improper. Sit down. What will the servants think?

UNDERSHAFT. My dear: I have conscientious scruples. May I suggest a compromise? If Barbara will conduct a little service in the drawing room, with Mr Lomax as organist, I will attend it willingly. I will even take part, if a trombone can be procured.

LADY BRITOMART. Dont mock, Andrew.

UNDERSHAFT (*shocked—to Barbara*) You dont think I am mocking, my love, I hope.

BARBARA. No, of course not; and it wouldnt matter if you were: half the Army came to their first meeting for a lark.

(*Rising*) Come along. (*She throws her arm round her father and sweeps him out, calling to the others from the threshold*). Come, Dolly. Come, Cholly.

Cusins rises.

LADY BRITOMART. I will not be disobeyed by everybody. Adolphus: sit down. (*He does not*). Charles: you may go. You are not fit for prayers: you cannot keep your countenance.

LOMAX. Oh I say! (*He goes out*).

LADY BRITOMART (*continuing*) But you, Adolphus, can behave yourself if you choose to. I insist on your staying.

CUSINS. My dear Lady Brit: there are things in the family prayer book that I couldnt bear to hear you say.

LADY BRITOMART. What things, pray?

CUSINS. Well, you would have to say before all the servants that we have done things we ought not to have done, and left undone things we ought to have done, and that there is no health in us. I cannot bear to hear you doing yourself such an injustice, and Barbara such an injustice. As for myself, I flatly deny it: I have done my best. I shouldnt dare to marry Barbara —I couldnt look you in the face—if it were true. So I must go to the drawing room.

LADY BRITOMART (*offended*) Well, go. (*He starts for the door*). And remember this, Adolphus (*he turns to listen*): I have a strong suspicion that you went to the Salvation Army to worship Barbara and nothing else. And I quite appreciate the clever way in which you systematically humbug me. I have found you out. Take care Barbara doesnt. Thats all.

CUSINS (*with unruffled sweetness*) Dont tell on me. (*He steals out*).

LADY BRITOMART. Sarah: if you want to go, go. Anything's better than to sit there as if you wished you were a thousand miles away.

SARAH (*languidly*) Very well, mamma. (*She goes*).

Lady Britomart, with a sudden flounce, gives way to a little gust of tears.

STEPHEN (*going to her*) Mother: whats the matter?

LADY BRITOMART (*swishing away her tears with her handkerchief*) Nothing. Foolishness. You can go with him, too, if you like, and leave me with the servants.

STEPHEN. Oh, you mustnt think that, mother. I—I dont like him.

LADY BRITOMART. The others do. That is the injustice of a woman's lot. A woman has to bring up her children; and that means to restrain them, to deny them things they want, to set them tasks, to punish them when they do wrong, to do all the unpleasant things. And then the father, who has nothing to do but pet them and spoil them, comes in when all her work is done and steals their affection from her.

STEPHEN. He has not stolen our affection from you. It is only curiosity.

LADY BRITOMART (*violently*) I wont be consoled, Stephen. There is nothing the matter with me. (*She rises and goes towards the door*).

STEPHEN. Where are you going, mother?

LADY BRITOMART. To the drawing room, of course. (*She goes out. Onward, Christian Soldiers, on the concertina, with tambourine accompaniment, is heard when the door opens*). Are you coming, Stephen?

STEPHEN. No. Certainly not. (*She goes. He sits down on the settee, with compressed lips and an expression of strong dislike*).

END OF ACT I

ACT II

*THE YARD of the West Ham shelter of the Salvation Army
is a cold place on a January morning. The building itself, an
old warehouse, is newly whitewashed. Its gabled end projects
into the yard in the middle, with a door on the ground floor,
and another in the loft above it without any balcony or ladder,
but with a pulley rigged over it for hoisting sacks. Those who
come from this central gable end into the yard have the gateway leading to the street on their left, with a stone horse-trough
just beyond it, and, on the right, a penthouse shielding a table
from the weather. There are forms at the table; and on them are
seated a man and a woman, both much down on their luck,
finishing a meal of bread (one thick slice each, with margarine
and golden syrup) and diluted milk.*

*The man, a workman out of employment, is young, agile, a
talker, a poser, sharp enough to be capable of anything in reason except honesty or altruistic considerations of any kind. The
woman is a commonplace old bundle of poverty and hard-worn
humanity. She looks sixty and probably is forty-five. If they
were rich people, gloved and muffed and well wrapped up in
furs and overcoats, they would be numbed and miserable; for it
is a grindingly cold, raw, January day; and a glance at the back-
ground of grimy warehouses and leaden sky visible over the
whitewashed walls of the yard would drive any idle rich person
straight to the Mediterranean. But these two, being no more
troubled with visions of the Mediterranean than of the moon,
and being compelled to keep more of their clothes in the pawnshop, and less on their persons, in winter than in summer, are
not depressed by the cold: rather are they stung into vivacity,
to which their meal has just now given an almost jolly turn.*

The man takes a pull at his mug, and then gets up and moves about the yard with his hands deep in his pockets, occasionally breaking into a stepdance.

THE WOMAN. Feel better arter your meal, sir?

THE MAN. No. Call that a meal! Good enough for you, praps; but wot is it to me, an intelligent workin man.

THE WOMAN. Workin man! Wot are you?

THE MAN. Painter.

THE WOMAN (*sceptically*) Yus, I dessay.

THE MAN. Yus, you dessay! I know. Every loafer that cant do nothink calls isself a painter. Well, I'm a real painter: grainer, finisher, thirty-eight bob a week when I can get it.

THE WOMAN. Then why dont you go and get it?

THE MAN. I'll tell you why. Fust: I'm intelligent—fffff! it's rotten cold here (*he dances a step or two*)—yes; intelligent beyond the station o life into which it has pleased the capitalists to call me; and they dont like a man that sees through em. Second, an intelligent bein needs a doo share of appiness; so I drink somethink cruel when I get the chawnce. Third, I stand by my class and do as little as I can so's to leave arf the job for me fellow workers. Fourth, I'm fly enough to know wots inside the law and wots outside it; and inside it I do as the capitalists do: pinch wot I can lay me ands on. In a proper state of society I am sober, industrious and honest: in Rome, so to speak, I do as the Romans do. Wots the consequence? When trade is bad—and it's rotten bad just now—and the employers az to sack arf their men, they generally start on me.

THE WOMAN. Whats your name?

THE MAN. Price. Bronterre O'Brien Price. Usually called Snobby Price, for short.

THE WOMAN. Snobby's a carpenter, aint it? You said you was a painter.

PRICE. Not that kind of snob, but the genteel sort. I'm too uppish, owing to my intelligence, and my father being a Chartist and a reading, thinking man: a stationer, too. I'm none of your common hewers of wood and drawers of water; and dont you forget it. (*He returns to his seat at the table, and takes up his mug*). Wots y o u r name?

THE WOMAN. Rummy Mitchens, sir.

PRICE (*quaffing the remains of his milk to her*) Your elth, Miss Mitchens.

RUMMY (*correcting him*) Missis Mitchens.

PRICE. Wot! Oh Rummy, Rummy! Respectable married woman, Rummy, gittin rescued by the Salvation Army by pretendin to be a bad un. Same old game!

RUMMY. What am I to do? I cant starve. Them Salvation lasses is dear good girls; but the better you are, the worse they likes to think you were before they rescued you. Why shouldnt they av a bit o credit, poor loves? theyre worn to rags by their work. And where would they get the money to rescue us if we was to let on we're no worse than other people? You know what ladies and gentlemen are.

PRICE. Thievin swine! Wish I ad their job, Rummy, all the same. Wot does Rummy stand for? Pet name praps?

RUMMY. Short for Romola.

PRICE. For wot!?

RUMMY. Romola. It was out of a new book. Somebody me mother wanted me to grow up like.

PRICE. We're companions in misfortune, Rummy. Both of us got names that nobody cawnt pronounce. Consequently I'm Snobby and youre Rummy because Bill and Sally wasnt good enough for our parents. Such is life!

RUMMY. Who saved you, Mr Price? Was it Major Barbara?

PRICE. No: I come here on my own. I'm goin to be Bronterre O'Brien Price, the converted painter. I know wot they like. I'll tell em how I blasphemed and gambled and wopped my poor old mother—

RUMMY (*shocked*) Used you to beat your mother?

PRICE. Not likely. She used to beat me. No matter: you come

and listen to the converted painter, and youll hear how she was a pious woman that taught me me prayers at er knee, an how I used to come home drunk and drag her out o bed be er snow white airs, an lam into er with the poker.

RUMMY. Thats whats so unfair to us women. Your confessions is just as big lies as ours: you dont tell what you really done no more than us; but you men can tell your lies right out at the meetins and be made much of for it; while the sort o confessions we az to make az to be whispered to one lady at a time. It aint right, spite of all their piety.

PRICE. Right! Do you spose the Army 'd be allowed if it went and did right? Not much. It combs our air and makes us good little blokes to be robbed and put upon. But I'll play the game as good as any of em. I'll see somebody struck by lightnin, or hear a voice sayin "Snobby Price: where will you spend eternity?" I'll ave a time of it, I tell you.

RUMMY. You wont be let drink, though.

PRICE. I'll take it out in gorspellin, then. I don't want to drink if I can get fun enough any other way.

Jenny Hill, a pale, overwrought, pretty Salvation lass of 18, comes in through the yard gate, leading Peter Shirley, a half hardened, half worn-out elderly man, weak with hunger.

JENNY (*supporting him*) Come! pluck up. I'll get you something to eat. Youll be all right then.

PRICE (*rising and hurrying officiously to take the old man off Jenny's hands*) Poor old man! Cheer up, brother: youll find rest and peace and appiness ere. Hurry up with the food, miss: e's fair done. (*Jenny hurries into the shelter*). Ere, buck up, daddy! shes fetchin y'a thick slice o breadn treacle, an a mug o skyblue. (*He seats him at the corner of the table*).

RUMMY (*gaily*) Keep up your old art! Never say die!

SHIRLEY. I'm not an old man. I'm only 46. I'm as good as ever I was. The grey patch come in my hair before I was thirty. All it wants is three pennorth o hair dye: am I to be turned on the streets to starve for it? Holy God! Ive worked ten to twelve hours a day since I was thirteen, and paid my way all through; and now am I to be thrown into the gutter and my job given to a young man that can do it no better than me because I've black hair that goes white at the first change?

PRICE (*cheerfully*) No good jawrin about it. Youre only a jumped-up, jerked-off, orspittle-turned-out incurable of an ole workin man: who cares about you? Eh? Make the thievin swine give you a meal: theyve stole many a one from you. Get a bit o your own back. (*Jenny returns with the usual meal*). There you are, brother. Awsk a blessin an tuck that into you.

SHIRLEY (*looking at it ravenously but not touching it, and crying like a child*) I never took anything before.

JENNY (*petting him*) Come, come! the Lord sends it to you: he wasnt above taking bread from his friends; and why should you be? Besides, when we find you a job you can pay us for it if you like.

SHIRLEY (*eagerly*) Yes, yes: thats true. I can pay you back: its only a loan. (*Shivering*) Oh Lord! oh Lord! (*He turns to the table and attacks the meal ravenously*).

JENNY. Well, Rummy, are you more comfortable now?

RUMMY. God bless you, lovey! youve fed my body and saved my soul, havent you? (*Jenny, touched, kisses her*). Sit down and rest a bit: you must be ready to drop.

JENNY. Ive been going hard since morning. But theres more work than we can do. I mustnt stop.

RUMMY. Try a prayer for just two minutes. Youll work all the better after.

JENNY (*her eyes lighting up*) Oh isnt it wonderful how a few minutes prayer revives you! I was quite lightheaded at twelve o'clock, I was so tired; but Major Barbara just sent me to pray for five minutes; and I was able to go on as if I had only just begun. (*To Price*) Did you have a piece of bread?

PRICE (*with unction*) Yes, miss; but Ive got the piece that I value more; and thats the peace that passeth hall hanner-stennin.

RUMMY (*fervently*) Glory Hallelujah!

Bill Walker, a rough customer of about 25, appears at the yard gate and looks malevolently at Jenny.

JENNY. That makes me so happy. When you say that, I feel wicked for loitering here. I must get to work again.

She is hurrying to the shelter, when the new-comer moves quickly up to the door and intercepts her. His manner is so threatening that she retreats as he comes at her truculently, driving her down the yard.

BILL. Aw knaow you. Youre the one that took awy maw girl. Youre the one that set er agen me. Well, I'm gowin to ev er aht. Not that Aw care a carse for er or you: see? Bat Aw'll let er knaow; and Aw'll let y o u knaow. Aw'm gowin to give her a doin thatll teach er to cat awy from me. Nah in wiv you and tell er to cam aht afore Aw cam in and kick er aht. Tell er Bill Walker wants er. She'll knaow wot thet means; and if she keeps me witin itll be worse. You stop to jawr beck at me; and Aw'll stawt on you: d'ye eah? Theres your wy. In you gow. (*He takes her by the arm and slings her towards the door of the shelter. She falls on her hand and knee. Rummy helps her up again*).

PRICE (*rising, and venturing irresolutely towards Bill*) Easy there, mate. She aint doin you no arm.

BILL. Oo are you callin mite? (*Standing over him threateningly*) Youre gowin to stend up for er, aw yer? Put ap your ends.

RUMMY (*running indignantly to him to scold him*) Oh, you great brute— (*He instantly swings his left hand back against her face. She screams and reels back to the trough, where she sits down, covering her bruised face with her hands and rocking herself and moaning with pain*).

JENNY (*going to her*) Oh, God forgive you! How could you strike an old woman like that?

BILL (*seizing her by the hair so violently that she also screams, and tearing her away from the old woman*) You Gawd forgimme again and Aw'll Gawd forgive you one on the jawr thetll stop you pryin for a week. (*Holding her and turning fiercely on Price*) Ev you ennything to sy agen it?

PRICE (*intimidated*) No, matey: she aint anything to do with me.

BILL. Good job for you! Aw'd pat two meals into you and fawt you with one finger arter, you stawved cur. (*To Jenny*) Nah are you gowin to fetch aht Mog Ebbijem; or em Aw to knock your fice off you and fetch her meself?

JENNY (*writhing in his grasp*) Oh please someone go in and tell Major Barbara— (*She screams again as he wrenches her head down; and Price and Rummy flee into the shelter*).

BILL. You want to gow in and tell your Mijor of me, do you?

JENNY. Oh please dont drag my hair. Let me go.

BILL. Do you or downt you? (*She stifles a scream*) Yus or nao?

JENNY. God give me strength—

BILL. (*striking her with his fist in the face*) Gow an shaow her thet, and tell her if she wants one lawk it to cam and interfere with me. (*Jenny, crying with pain, goes into the shed. He goes to the form and addresses the old man*). Eah: finish your mess; and git aht o maw wy.

SHIRLEY (*springing up and facing him fiercely, with the mug in his hand*) You take a liberty with me, and I'll smash you over the face with the mug and cut your eye out. Aint you satisfied—young whelps like you—with takin the bread out o the mouths of your elders that have brought you up and slaved for you, but you must come shovin and cheeking and bullyin in here, where the bread o charity is sickenin in our stummicks?

BILL (*contemptuously, but backing a little*) Wot good are you, you aold palsy mag? Wot good are you?

SHIRLEY. As good as you and better. I'll do a day's work agen you or any fat young soaker of your age. Go and take my job at Horrockses, where I worked for ten year. They want young men there: they cant afford to keep men over forty-five. Theyre very sorry—give you a character and happy to help you to get anything suited to your years—sure a steady man wont be long out of a job. Well, let em try y o u. Theyll find the differ. What do y o u know? Not as much as how to beeyave yourself —layin your dirty fist across the mouth of a respectable woman!

BILL. Downt provowk me to ly it acrost yours: d'ye eah?

SHIRLEY (*with blighting contempt*) Yes: you like an old man to hit, dont you, when youve finished with the women. I aint seen you hit a young one yet.

BILL (*stung*) You loy, you aold soupkitchener, you. There was a yang menn eah. Did Aw offer to itt him or did Aw not?

SHIRLEY. Was he starvin or was he not? Was he a man or only a crosseyed thief an a loafer? Would you hit my son-in-law's brother?

BILL. Oo's ee?

SHIRLEY. Todger Fairmile o Balls Pond. Him that won £20 off the Japanese wrastler at the music hall by standin out 17 minutes 4 seconds agen him.

BILL (*sullenly*) Aw'm nao music awl wrastler. Ken he box?

SHIRLEY. Yes: an you cant.

BILL. Wot! Aw cawnt, cawnt Aw? Wots thet you sy (*threatening him*)?

SHIRLEY (*not budging an inch*) Will you box Todger Fairmile if I put him on to you? Say the word.

BILL (*subsiding with a slouch*) Aw'll stend ap to enny menn alawv, if he was ten Todger Fairmawls. But Aw dont set ap to be a perfeshnal.

SHIRLEY (*looking down on him with unfathomable disdain*) Y o u box! Slap an old woman with the back o your hand! You hadnt even the sense to hit her where a magistrate couldnt see the mark of it, you silly young lump of conceit and ignorance. Hit a girl in the jaw and ony make her cry! If Todger Fairmile'd done it, she wouldnt a got up inside o ten minutes, no more than you would if he got on to you. Yah! I'd set about you myself if I had a week's feedin in me instead o two months' starvation. (*He turns his back on him and sits down moodily at the table*).

BILL (*following him and stooping over him to drive the taunt in*) You loy! youve the bread and treacle in you that you cam eah to beg.

SHIRLEY (*bursting into tears*) Oh God! it's true: I'm only an old pauper on the scrap heap. (*Furiously*) But youll come to it yourself; and then youll know. Youll come to it sooner than a teetotaller like me, fillin yourself with gin at this hour o the mornin!

BILL. Aw'm nao gin drinker, you oald lawr; bat wen Aw want to give my girl a bloomin good awdin Aw lawk to ev a bit o devil in me: see? An eah Aw emm, talking to a rotten aold blawter like you sted o given er wot for. (*Working himself into a rage*) Aw'm gowin in there to fetch her aht. (*He makes vengefully for the shelter door*).

SHIRLEY. Youre goin to the station on a stretcher, more likely; and theyll take the gin and the devil out of you there when they get you inside. You mind what youre about: the major here is the Earl o Stevenage's granddaughter.

BILL (*checked*) Garn!

SHIRLEY. Youll see.

BILL (*his resolution oozing*) Well, Aw aint dan nathin to er.

SHIRLEY. Spose she said you did! who'd believe you?

BILL (*very uneasy, skulking back to the corner of the penthouse*) Gawd! theres no jastice in this cantry. To think wot them people can do! Aw'm as good as er.

SHIRLEY. Tell her so. Its just what a fool like you would do.

Barbara, brisk and businesslike, comes from the shelter with a note book, and addresses herself to Shirley. Bill, cowed, sits down in the corner on a form, and turns his back on them.

BARBARA. Good morning.

SHIRLEY (*standing up and taking off his hat*) Good morning, miss.

BARBARA. Sit down: make yourself at home. (*He hesitates;*

but she puts a friendly hand on his shoulder and makes him obey). Now then! since youve made friends with us, we want to know all about you. Names and addresses and trades.

SHIRLEY. Peter Shirley. Fitter. Chucked out two months ago because I was too old.

BARBARA (*not at all surprised*) Youd pass still. Why didnt you dye your hair?

SHIRLEY. I did. Me age come out at a coroner's inquest on me daughter.

BARBARA. Steady?

SHIRLEY. Teetotaller. Never out of a job before. Good worker. And sent to the knackers like an old horse!

BARBARA. No matter: if you did your part God will do his.

SHIRLEY (*suddenly stubborn*) My religion's no concern of anybody but myself.

BARBARA (*guessing*) I know. Secularist?

SHIRLEY (*hotly*) Did I offer to deny it?

BARBARA. Why should you? My own father's a Secularist, I think. Our Father—yours and mine—fulfils himself in many ways; and I daresay he knew what he was about when he made a Secularist of you. So buck up, Peter! we can always find a job for a steady man like you. (*Shirley, disarmed and a little bewildered, touches his hat. She turns from him to Bill*). Whats y o u r name?

BILL (*insolently*) Wots thet to you?

BARBARA (*calmly making a note*) Afraid to give his name. Any trade?

BILL. Oo's afride to give is nime? (*Doggedly, with a sense of heroically defying the House of Lords in the person of Lord Stevenage*) If you want to bring a chawge agen me, bring it. (*She waits, unruffled*). Moy nime's Bill Walker.

BARBARA (*as if the name were familiar: trying to remember how*) Bill Walker? (*Recollecting*) Oh, I know: youre the man that Jenny Hill was praying for inside just now. (*She enters his name in her note book*).

BILL. Oo's Jenny Ill? And wot call as she to pry for me?

BARBARA. I dont know. Perhaps it was you that cut her lip.

BILL (*defiantly*) Yus, it w a s me that cat her lip. Aw aint afride o y o u.

BARBARA. How could you be, since youre not afraid of God? Youre a brave man, Mr Walker. It takes some pluck to do o u r work here; but none of us dare lift our hand against a girl like that, for fear of her father in heaven.

BILL (*sullenly*) I want nan o your kentin jawr. I spowse you think Aw cam eah to beg from you, like this demmiged lot eah. Not me. Aw downt want your bread and scripe and ketlep. Aw dont blieve in your Gawd, no more than you do yourself.

BARBARA (*sunnily apologetic and ladylike, as on a new footing with him*) Oh, I beg your pardon for putting your name down, Mr Walker. I didnt understand. I'll strike it out.

BILL (*taking this as a slight, and deeply wounded by it*) Eah! you let maw nime alown. Aint it good enaff to be in your book?

BARBARA (*considering*) Well, you see, theres no use putting down your name unless I can do something for you, is there? Whats your trade?

BILL (*still smarting*) Thets nao concern o yours.

BARBARA. Just so. (*Very businesslike*) I'll put you down as (*writing*) the man who—struck—poor little Jenny Hill—in the mouth.

BILL (*rising threateningly*) See eah. Awve ed enaff o this.

BARBARA (*quite sunny and fearless*) What did you come to us for?

BILL. Aw cam for maw gel, see? Aw cam to tike her aht o this and to brike er jawr for er.

BARBARA (*complacently*) You see I was right about your trade. (*Bill, on the point of retorting furiously, finds himself, to his great shame and terror, in danger of crying instead. He sits down again suddenly*). Whats her name?

BILL (*dogged*) Er nime's Mog Ebbijem: thets wot her nime is.

BARBARA. Mog Habbijam! Oh, she's gone to Canning Town, to our barracks there.

BILL (*fortified by his resentment of Mog's perfidy*) Is she? (*Vindictively*) Then Aw'm gowin to Kenintahn arter her. (*He crosses to the gate; hesitates; finally comes back at Barbara*). Are you loyin to me to git shat o me?

BARBARA. I dont want to get shut of you. I want to keep you here and save your soul. Youd better stay: youre going to have a bad time today, Bill.

BILL. Oo's gowin to give it to me? Y o u, preps?

BARBARA. Someone you dont believe in. But youll be glad afterwards.

BILL (*slinking off*) Aw'll gow to Kennintahn to be aht o reach o your tangue. (*Suddenly turning on her with intense malice*) And if Aw downt fawnd Mog there, Aw'll cam beck and do two years for you, selp me Gawd if Aw downt!

BARBARA (*a shade kindlier, if possible*) It's no use, Bill. She's got another bloke.

BILL. Wot!

BARBARA. One of her own converts. He fell in love with her when he saw her with her soul saved, and her face clean, and her hair washed.

BILL (*surprised*) Wottud she wash it for, the carroty slat? It's red.

BARBARA. It's quite lovely now, because she wears a new look in her eyes with it. It's a pity youre too late. The new bloke has put your nose out of joint, Bill.

BILL. Aw'll put his nowse aht o joint for him. Not that Aw care a carse for er, mawnd thet. But Aw'll teach her to drop me as if Aw was dirt. And Aw'll teach him to meddle with maw judy. Wots iz bleedin nime?

BARBARA. Sergeant Todger Fairmile.

SHIRLEY (*rising with grim joy*) I'll go with him, miss. I want to see them two meet. I'll take him to the infirmary when it's over.

BILL (*to Shirley, with undissembled misgiving*) Is thet im you was speakin on?

SHIRLEY. Thats him.

BILL. Im that wrastled in the music awl?

SHIRLEY. The competitions at the National Sportin Club was worth nigh a hundred a year to him. He's gev em up now for religion; so he's a bit fresh for want of the exercise he was accustomed to. He'll be glad to see you. Come along.

BILL. Wots is wight?

SHIRLEY. Thirteen four. (*Bill's last hope expires*).

BARBARA. Go and talk to him, Bill. He'll convert you.

SHIRLEY. He'll convert your head into a mashed potato.

BILL (*sullenly*) Aw aint afride of im. Aw aint afride of ennybody. Bat e can lick me. She's dan me. (*He sits down moodily on the edge of the horse trough*).

SHIRLEY. You aint goin. I thought not. (*He resumes his seat*).

BARBARA (*calling*) Jenny!

JENNY (*appearing at the shelter door with a plaster on the corner of her mouth*) Yes, Major.

BARBARA. Send Rummy Mitchens out to clear away here.

JENNY. I think she's afraid.

BARBARA (*her resemblance to her mother flashing out for a moment*) Nonsense! she must do as she's told.

JENNY (*calling into the shelter*) Rummy: the Major says you must come.

Jenny comes to Barbara, purposely keeping on the side next Bill, lest he should suppose that she shrank from him or bore malice.

BARBARA. Poor little Jenny! Are you tired? (*Looking at the wounded cheek*) Does it hurt?

JENNY. No: it's all right now. It was nothing.

BARBARA (*critically*) It was as hard as he could hit, I expect. Poor Bill! You dont feel angry with him, do you?

JENNY. Oh no, no, no: indeed I dont, Major, bless his poor heart! (*Barbara kisses her; and she runs away merrily into the shelter. Bill writhes with an agonizing return of his new and alarming symptoms, but says nothing. Rummy Mitchens comes from the shelter*).

BARBARA (*going to meet Rummy*) Now Rummy, bustle. Take in those mugs and plates to be washed; and throw the crumbs about for the birds.

Rummy takes the three plates and mugs; but Shirley takes back his mug from her, as there is still some milk left in it.

RUMMY. There aint any crumbs. This aint a time to waste good bread on birds.

PRICE (*appearing at the shelter door*) Gentleman come to see the shelter, Major. Says he's your father.

BARBARA. All right. Coming. (*Snobby goes back into the shelter, followed by Barbara*).

RUMMY (*stealing across to Bill and addressing him in a sub-dued voice, but with intense conviction*) I'd av the lor of you, you flat eared pignosed potwalloper, if she'd let me. Youre no gentleman, to hit a lady in the face. (*Bill, with greater things moving in him, takes no notice*).

SHIRLEY (*following her*) Here! in with you and dont get yourself into more trouble by talking.

RUMMY (*with hauteur*) I aint ad the pleasure o being hintro-duced to you, as I can remember. (*She goes into the shelter with the plates*).

SHIRLEY. Thats the—

BILL (*savagely*) Downt you talk to me, d'ye eah? You lea me alown, or Aw'll do you a mischief. Aw'm not dirt under y o u r feet, ennywy.

SHIRLEY (*calmly*) Dont you be afeerd. You aint such prime company that you need expect to be sought after. (*He is about to go into the shelter when Barbara comes out, with Under-shaft on her right*).

BARBARA. Oh, there you are, Mr Shirley! (*Between them*) This is my father: I told you he was a Secularist, didnt I? Perhaps youll be able to comfort one another.

UNDERSHAFT (*startled*) A Secularist! Not the least in the world: on the contrary, a confirmed mystic.

BARBARA. Sorry, I'm sure. By the way, papa, what i s your religion? in case I have to introduce you again.

UNDERSHAFT. My religion? Well, my dear, I am a Millionaire. That is my religion.

BARBARA. Then I'm afraid you and Mr Shirley wont be able to comfort one another after all. Youre not a Millionaire, are you, Peter?

SHIRLEY. No; and proud of it.

UNDERSHAFT (*gravely*) Poverty, my friend, is not a thing to be proud of.

SHIRLEY (*angrily*) Who made your millions for you? Me and my like. Whats kep us poor? Keepin you rich. I wouldnt have your conscience, not for all your income.

UNDERSHAFT. I wouldn't have your income, not for all your conscience, Mr Shirley. (*He goes to the penthouse and sits down on a form*).

BARBARA (*stopping Shirley adroitly as he is about to retort*) You wouldnt think he was my father, would you, Peter? Will you go into the shelter and lend the lasses a hand for a while: we're worked off our feet.

SHIRLEY (*bitterly*) Yes: I'm in their debt for a meal, ain't I?

BARBARA. Oh, not because youre in their debt, but for love of them, Peter, for love of them. (*He cannot understand, and is rather scandalized*). There! dont stare at me. In with you; and give that conscience of yours a holiday. (*Bustling him into the shelter*).

SHIRLEY (*as he goes in*) Ah! it's a pity you never was trained to use your reason, miss. Youd have been a very taking lecturer on Secularism.

Barbara turns to her father.

UNDERSHAFT. Never mind me, my dear. Go about your work; and let me watch it for a while.

BARBARA. All right.

UNDERSHAFT. For instance, whats the matter with that outpatient over there?

BARBARA (*looking at Bill, whose attitude has never changed, and whose expression of brooding wrath has deepened*) Oh, we shall cure him in no time. Just watch. (*She goes over to Bill and waits. He glances up at her and casts his eyes down again, uneasy, but grimmer than ever*). It w o u l d be nice to just stamp on Mog Habbijam's face, wouldn't it, Bill?

BILL (*starting up from the trough in consternation*) It's a loy: Aw never said so. (*She shakes her head*). Oo taold you wot was in moy mawnd?

BARBARA. Only your new friend.

BILL. Wot new friend?

BARBARA. The devil, Bill. When he gets round people they get miserable, just like you.

BILL (*with a heartbreaking attempt at devil-may-care cheerfulness*) Aw aint miserable. (*He sits down again, and stretches his legs in an attempt to seem indifferent*).

BARBARA. Well, if youre happy, why dont you look happy, as we do?

BILL (*his legs curling back in spite of him*) Aw'm eppy enaff, Aw tell you. Woy cawnt you lea me alown? Wot ev I dan to y o u? Aw aint smashed y o u r fice, ev Aw?

BARBARA (*softly: wooing his soul*) It's not me thats getting at you, Bill.

BILL. Oo else is it?

BARBARA. Somebody that doesnt intend you to smash women's faces, I suppose. Somebody or something that wants to make a man of you.

BILL (*blustering*) Mike a menn o m e! Aint Aw a menn? eh? Oo sez Aw'm not a menn?

BARBARA. Theres a man in you somewhere, I suppose. But

why did he let you hit poor little Jenny Hill? That wasnt very manly of him, was it?

BILL (*tormented*) Ev dan wiv it, Aw tell you. Chack it. Aw'm sick o your Jenny Ill and er silly little fice.

BARBARA. Then why do you keep thinking about it? Why does it keep coming up against you in your mind? Youre not getting converted, are you?

BILL (*with conviction*) Not ME. Not lawkly.

BARBARA. Thats right, Bill. Hold out against it. Put out your strength. Dont lets get you cheap. Todger Fairmile said he wrestled for three nights against his salvation harder than he ever wrestled with the Jap at the music hall. He gave in to the Jap when his arm was going to break. But he didnt give in to his salvation until his heart was going to break. Perhaps youll escape that. You havnt any heart, have you?

BILL. Wot d'ye mean? Woy aint Aw got a awt the sime as ennybody else?

BARBARA. A man with a heart wouldnt have bashed poor little Jenny's face, would he?

BILL (*almost crying*) Ow, w i l l you lea me alown? Ev Aw ever offered to meddle with y o u, that you cam neggin and provowkin me lawk this? (*He writhes convulsively from his eyes to his toes*).

BARBARA (*with a steady soothing hand on his arm and a gentle voice that never lets go*) It's your soul thats hurting you, Bill, and not me. Weve been through it all ourselves. Come with us, Bill. (*He looks wildly round*). To brave manhood on earth and eternal glory in heaven. (*He is on the point of breaking down*). Come. (*A drum is heard in the shelter; and Bill, with a gasp, escapes from the spell as Barbara turns quickly. Adolphus enters from the shelter with a big drum*). Oh! there you are, Dolly. Let me introduce a new friend of mine, Mr Bill Walker. This is my bloke, Bill: Mr Cusins. (*Cusins salutes with his drumstick*).

BILL. Gowin to merry im?

BARBARA. Yes.

BILL (*fervently*) Gawd elp im! Gaw-aw-aw-awd elp im!

BARBARA. Why? Do you think he wont be happy with me?

BILL. Awve aony ed to stend it for a mawnin: e'll ev to stend it for a lawftawm.

CUSINS. That is a frightful reflection, Mr Walker. But I cant tear myself away from her.

BILL. Well, Aw ken. (*To Barbara*) Eah! do you knaow where Aw'm gowin to, and wot Aw'm gowin to do?

BARBARA. Yes: youre going to heaven; and youre coming back here before the week's out to tell me so.

BILL. You loy. Aw'm gowin to Kennintahn, to spit in Todger Fairmawl's eye. Aw beshed Jenny Ill's fice; an nar Aw'll git me aown fice beshed and cam beck and shaow it to er. Ee'll itt me ardern Aw itt er. Thatll mike us square. (*To Adolphus*) Is that fair or is it not? Youre a genlmn: you oughter knaow.

BARBARA. Two black eyes wont make one white one, Bill.

BILL. Aw didnt awst y o u. Cawnt you never keep your mahth shat? Oy awst the genlmn.

CUSINS (*reflectively*) Yes: I think youre right, Mr Walker. Yes: I should do it. It's curious: it's exactly what an ancient Greek would have done.

BARBARA. But what good will it do?

CUSINS. Well, it will give Mr Fairmile some exercise; and it will satisfy Mr Walker's soul.

BILL. Rot! there aint nao sach a thing as a saoul. Ah kin you tell wevver Awve a saoul or not? You never seen it.

BARBARA. Ive seen it hurting you when you went against it.

BILL (*with compressed aggravation*) If you was maw gel and took the word aht o me mahth lawk thet, Aw'd give you sathink youd feel urtin, Aw would. (*To Adolphus*) You tike maw tip, mite. Stop er jawr; or youll doy afoah your tawm. (*With intense expression*) Wore aht: thets wot youll be: wore aht. (*He goes away through the gate*).

CUSINS (*looking after him*) I wonder!

BARBARA. Dolly! (*Indignant, in her mother's manner*).

CUSINS. Yes, my dear, it's very wearing to be in love with you. If it lasts, I quite think I shall die young.

BARBARA. Should you mind?

CUSINS. Not at all. (*He is suddenly softened, and kisses her over the drum, evidently not for the first time, as people cannot kiss over a big drum without practice. Undershaft coughs*).

BARBARA. It's all right, papa, weve not forgotten you. Dolly: explain the place to papa: I havnt time. (*She goes busily into the shelter*).

Undershaft and Adolphus now have the yard to themselves. Undershaft, seated on a form, and still keenly attentive, looks hard at Adolphus. Adolphus looks hard at him.

UNDERSHAFT. I fancy you guess something of what is in my mind, Mr Cusins. (*Cusins flourishes his drumsticks as if in the act of beating a lively rataplan, but makes no sound*). Exactly so. But suppose Barbara finds you out!

CUSINS. You know, I do not admit that I am imposing on Barbara. I am quite genuinely interested in the views of the Salvation Army. The fact is, I am a sort of collector of religions; and the curious thing is that I find I can believe them all. By the way, have you any religion?

UNDERSHAFT. Yes.

CUSINS. Anything out of the common?

UNDERSHAFT. Only that there are two things necessary to Salvation.

CUSINS (*disappointed, but polite*) Ah, the Church Catechism. Charles Lomax also belongs to the Established Church.

UNDERSHAFT. The two things are—

CUSINS. Baptism and—

UNDERSHAFT. No. Money and gunpowder.

CUSINS (*surprised, but interested*) That is the general opinion of our governing classes. The novelty is in hearing any man confess it.

UNDERSHAFT. Just so.

CUSINS. Excuse me: is there any place in your religion for honor, justice, truth, love, mercy and so forth?

UNDERSHAFT. Yes: they are the graces and luxuries of a rich, strong, and safe life.

CUSINS. Suppose one is forced to choose between them and money or gunpowder?

UNDERSHAFT. Choose money a n d gunpowder; for without enough of both you cannot afford the others.

CUSINS. That is your religion?

UNDERSHAFT. Yes.

The cadence of this reply makes a full close in the conversation. Cusins twists his face dubiously and contemplates Undershaft. Undershaft contemplates him.

CUSINS. Barbara wont stand that. You will have to choose between your religion and Barbara.

UNDERSHAFT. So will you, my friend. She will find out that that drum of yours is hollow.

CUSINS. Father Undershaft: you are mistaken: I am a sincere Salvationist. You do not understand the Salvation Army. It is the army of joy, of love, of courage: it has banished the fear and remorse and despair of the old hell-ridden evangelical sects: it marches to fight the devil with trumpet and drum, with music and dancing, with banner and palm, as becomes a sally from heaven by its happy garrison. It picks the waster out of the public house and makes a man of him: it finds a worm wriggling in a back kitchen, and lo! a woman! Men and women of rank too, sons and daughters of the Highest. It takes the poor professor of Greek, the most artificial and self-suppressed of human creatures, from his meal of roots, and lets loose the rhapsodist in him; reveals the true worship of Dionysos to him; sends him down the public street drumming dithyrambs. (*He plays a thundering flourish on the drum*).

UNDERSHAFT. You will alarm the shelter.

CUSINS. Oh, they are accustomed to these sudden ecstasies of piety. However, if the drum worries you— (*He pockets the drumsticks; unhooks the drum; and stands it on the ground opposite the gateway).*

UNDERSHAFT. Thank you.

CUSINS. You remember what Euripides says about your money and gunpowder?

UNDERSHAFT. No.

CUSINS (*declaiming*)

> One and another
> In money and guns may outpass his brother;
> And men in their millions float and flow
> And seethe with a million hopes as leaven;
> And they win their will; or they miss their will;
> And their hopes are dead or are pined for still;
> But whoe'er can know
> As the long days go
> That to live is happy, has found h i s heaven.

My translation: what do you think of it?

UNDERSHAFT. I think, my friend, that if you wish to know, as the long days go, that to live is happy, you must first acquire money enough for a decent life, and power enough to be your own master.

CUSINS. You are damnably discouraging. (*He resumes his declamation*).

> Is it so hard a thing to see
> That the spirit of God—whate'er it be—
> The law that abides and changes not, ages long,
> The Eternal and Nature-born: t h e s e things be strong?
> What else is Wisdom? What of Man's endeavor,
> Or God's high grace so lovely and so great?
> To stand from fear set free? to breathe and wait?
> To hold a hand uplifted over Fate?
> And shall not Barbara be loved for ever?

UNDERSHAFT. Euripides mentions Barbara, does he?

CUSINS. It is a fair translation. The word means Loveliness.

UNDERSHAFT. May I ask—as Barbara's father—how much a year she is to be loved for ever on?

CUSINS. As Barbara's father, that is more your affair than mine. I can feed her by teaching Greek: that is about all.

UNDERSHAFT. Do you consider it a good match for her?

CUSINS (*with polite obstinacy*) Mr Undershaft: I am in many ways a weak, timid, ineffectual person; and my health is far from satisfactory. But whenever I feel that I must have anything, I get it, sooner or later. I feel that way about Barbara. I dont like marriage: I feel intensely afraid of it; and I dont know what I shall do with Barbara or what she will do with me. But I feel that I and nobody else must marry her. Please regard that as settled.—Not that I wish to be arbitrary; but why should I waste your time in discussing what is inevitable?

UNDERSHAFT. You mean that you will stick at nothing: not even the conversion of the Salvation Army to the worship of Dionysos.

CUSINS. The business of the Salvation Army is to save, not to wrangle about the name of the pathfinder. Dionysos or another: what does it matter?

UNDERSHAFT (*rising and approaching him*) Professor Cusins: you are a young man after my own heart.

CUSINS. Mr Undershaft: you are, as far as I am able to gather, a most infernal old rascal; but you appeal very strongly to my sense of ironic humor.

Undershaft mutely offers his hand. They shake.

UNDERSHAFT (*suddenly concentrating himself*) And now to business.

CUSINS. Pardon me. We were discussing religion. Why go back to such an uninteresting and unimportant subject as business?

UNDERSHAFT. Religion is our business at present, because it is through religion alone that we can win Barbara.

CUSINS. Have you, too, fallen in love with Barbara?

UNDERSHAFT. Yes, with a father's love.

CUSINS. A father's love for a grown-up daughter is the most dangerous of all infatuations. I apologize for mentioning my own pale, coy, mistrustful fancy in the same breath with it.

UNDERSHAFT. Keep to the point. We have to win her; and we are neither of us Methodists.

CUSINS. That doesnt matter. The power Barbara wields here —the power that wields Barbara herself—is not Calvinism, not Presbyterianism, not Methodism—

UNDERSHAFT. Not Greek Paganism either, eh?

CUSINS. I admit that. Barbara is quite original in her religion.

UNDERSHAFT (*triumphantly*) Aha! Barbara Undershaft would be. Her inspiration comes from within herself.

CUSINS. How do you suppose it got there?

UNDERSHAFT (*in towering excitement*) It is the Undershaft inheritance. I shall hand on my torch to my daughter. She shall make my converts and preach my gospel—

CUSINS. What! Money and gunpowder!

UNDERSHAFT. Yes, money and gunpowder; freedom and power; command of life and command of death.

CUSINS (*urbanely: trying to bring him down to earth*) This is extremely interesting, Mr Undershaft. Of course you know that you are mad.

UNDERSHAFT (*with redoubled force*) And you?

CUSINS. Oh, mad as a hatter. You are welcome to my secret since I have discovered yours. But I am astonished. Can a madman make cannons?

UNDERSHAFT. Would anyone else than a madman make them? And now (*With surging energy*) question for question. Can a sane man translate Euripides?

CUSINS. No.

UNDERSHAFT (*seizing him by the shoulder*) Can a sane woman make a man of a waster or a woman of a worm?

CUSINS (*reeling before the storm*) Father Colossus— Mammoth Millionaire—

UNDERSHAFT (*pressing him*) Are there two mad people or three in this Salvation shelter to-day?

CUSINS. You mean Barbara is as mad as we are?

UNDERSHAFT (*pushing him lightly off and resuming his equanimity suddenly and completely*) Pooh, Professor! let us call things by their proper names. I am a millionaire; you are a poet; Barbara is a savior of souls. What have we three to do with the common mob of slaves and idolaters? (*He sits down again with a shrug of contempt for the mob*).

CUSINS. Take care! Barbara is in love with the common people. So am I. Have you never felt the romance of that love?

UNDERSHAFT (*cold and sardonic*) Have you ever been in love with Poverty, like St Francis? Have you ever been in love with Dirt, like St Simeon? Have you ever been in love with disease and suffering, like our nurses and philanthropists? Such passions are not virtues, but the most unnatural of all the vices. This love of the common people may please an earl's grand-daughter and a university professor; but I have been a common man and a poor man; and it has no romance for me. Leave it to the poor to pretend that poverty is a blessing: leave it to the coward to make a religion of his cowardice by preaching humility: we know better than that. We three must stand together above the common people: how else can we help their children to climb up beside us? Barbara must belong to us, not to the Salvation Army.

CUSINS. Well, I can only say that if you think you will get her away from the Salvation Army by talking to her as you have been talking to me, you dont know Barbara.

UNDERSHAFT. My friend: I never ask for what I can buy.

CUSINS (*in a white fury*) Do I understand you to imply that you can buy Barbara?

UNDERSHAFT. No; but I can buy the Salvation Army.

CUSINS. Quite impossible.

UNDERSHAFT. You shall see. All religious organizations exist by selling themselves to the rich.

CUSINS. Not the Army. That is the Church of the poor.

UNDERSHAFT. All the more reason for buying it.

CUSINS. I dont think you quite know what the Army does for the poor.

UNDERSHAFT. Oh yes I do. It draws their teeth: that is enough for me—as a man of business—

CUSINS. Nonsense! It makes them sober—

UNDERSHAFT. I prefer sober workmen. The profits are larger.

CUSINS. —honest—

UNDERSHAFT. Honest workmen are the most economical.

CUSINS. —attached to their homes—

UNDERSHAFT. So much the better: they will put up with anything sooner than change their shop.

CUSINS. —happy—

UNDERSHAFT. An invaluable safeguard against revolution.

CUSINS. —unselfish—

UNDERSHAFT. Indifferent to their own interests, which suits me exactly.

CUSINS. —with their thoughts on heavenly things—

UNDERSHAFT (*rising*) And not on Trade Unionism nor Socialism. Excellent.

CUSINS (*revolted*) You really are an infernal old rascal.

UNDERSHAFT (*indicating Peter Shirley, who has just come from the shelter and strolled dejectedly down the yard between them*) And this is an honest man!

SHIRLEY. Yes; and what av I got by it? (*He passes on bitterly and sits on the form, in the corner of the penthouse*).

Snobby Price, beaming sanctimoniously, and Jenny Hill, with a tambourine full of coppers, come from the shelter and go to the drum, on which Jenny begins to count the money.

UNDERSHAFT (*replying to Shirley*) Oh, your employers must have got a good deal by it from first to last. (*He sits on the table, with one foot on the side form, Cusins, overwhelmed, sits down on the same form nearer the shelter. Barbara comes from the shelter to the middle of the yard. She is excited and a little overwrought).*

BARBARA. Weve just had a splendid experience meeting at the other gate in Cripp's lane. Ive hardly ever seen them so much moved as they were by your confession, Mr Price.

PRICE. I could almost be glad of my past wickedness if I could believe that it would elp to keep hathers stright.

BARBARA. So it will, Snobby. How much, Jenny?

JENNY. Four and tenpence, Major.

BARBARA. Oh Snobby, if you had given your poor mother just one more kick, we should have got the whole five shillings!

PRICE. If she heard you say that, miss, she'd be sorry I didnt. But I'm glad. Oh what a joy it will be to her when she hears I'm saved!

UNDERSHAFT. Shall I contribute the odd twopence, Barbara? The millionaire's mite, eh? (*He takes a couple of pennies from his pocket*).

BARBARA. How did you make that twopence?

UNDERSHAFT. As usual. By selling cannons, torpedoes, submarines, and my new patent Grand Duke hand grenade.

BARBARA. Put it back in your pocket. You cant buy your Salvation here for twopence: you must work it out.

UNDERSHAFT. Is twopence not enough? I can afford a little more, if you press me.

BARBARA. Two million millions would not be enough. There is bad blood on your hands; and nothing but good blood can cleanse them. Money is no use. Take it away. (*She turns to Cusins*). Dolly: you must write another letter for me to the papers. (*He makes a wry face*). Yes: I know you dont like it; but it must be done. The starvation this winter is beating us: everybody is unemployed. The General says we must close this shelter if we cant get more money. I force the collections at the meetings until I am ashamed: dont I, Snobby?

PRICE. It's a fair treat to see you work it, Miss. The way you got them up from three-and-six to four-and-ten with that hymn, penny by penny and verse by verse, was a caution. Not a Cheap Jack on Mile End Waste could touch you at it.

BARBARA. Yes; but I wish we could do without it. I am getting at last to think more of the collection than of the people's souls. And what are those hatfuls of pence and halfpence? We want thousands! tens of thousands! hundreds of thousands! I want to convert people, not to be always begging for the Army in a way I'd die sooner than beg for myself.

UNDERSHAFT (*in profound irony*) Genuine unselfishness is capable of anything, my dear.

BARBARA (*unsuspectingly, as she turns away to take the money from the drum and put it in a cash bag she carries*) Yes, isnt it? (*Undershaft looks sardonically at Cusins*).

CUSINS (*aside to Undershaft*) Mephistopheles! Machiavelli!

BARBARA (*tears coming into her eyes as she ties the bag and pockets it*) How are we to feed them? I cant talk religion to a man with bodily hunger in his eyes. (*Almost breaking down*) It's frightful.

JENNY (*running to her*) Major, dear—

BARBARA (*rebounding*) No: dont comfort me. It will be all right. We shall get the money.

UNDERSHAFT. How?

JENNY. By praying for it, of course. Mrs Baines says she prayed for it last night; and she has never prayed for it in vain: never once. (*She goes to the gate and looks out into the street*).

BARBARA (*who has dried her eyes and regained her composure*) By the way, dad, Mrs Baines has come to march with us to our big meeting this afternoon; and she is very anxious to meet you, for some reason or other. Perhaps she'll convert you.

UNDERSHAFT. I shall be delighted, my dear.

JENNY (*at the gate: excitedly*) Major! Major! heres that man back again.

BARBARA. What man?

JENNY. The man that hit me. Oh, I hope he's coming back to join us.

Bill Walker, with frost on his jacket, comes through the gate, his hands deep in his pockets and his chin sunk between his shoulders, like a cleaned-out gambler. He halts between Barbara and the drum.

BARBARA. Hullo, Bill! Back already!

BILL (*nagging at her*) Bin talkin ever sence, ev you?

BARBARA. Pretty nearly. Well, has Todger paid you out for poor Jenny's jaw?

BILL. Nao e aint.

BARBARA. I thought your jacket looked a bit snowy.

BILL. Sao it is snaowy. You want to knaow where the snaow cam from, downt you?

BARBARA. Yes.

BILL. Well, it cam from orf the grahnd in Pawkinses Corner in Kennintahn. It got rabbed orf be maw shaoulders: see?

BARBARA. Pity you didnt rub some off with your knees, Bill! That would have done you a lot of good.

BILL (*with sour mirthless humor*) Aw was sivin anather menn's knees at the tawm. E was kneelin on moy ed, e was.

JENNY. Who was kneeling on your head?

BILL. Todger was. E was pryin for me: pryin camfortable wiv me as a cawpet. Sow was Mog. Sao was the aol bloomin meetin. Mog she sez "Ow Lawd brike is stabborn sperrit; bat downt urt is dear art." Thet was wot she said. "Downt urt is dear art"! An er blowk—thirteen stun four!—kneelin wiv all is wight on me. Fanny, aint it?

JENNY. Oh no. We're so sorry, Mr Walker.

BARBARA (*enjoying it frankly*) Nonsense! of course it's funny. Served you right, Bill! You must have done something to him first.

BILL (*doggedly*) Aw did wot Aw said Aw'd do. Aw spit in is eye. E looks ap at the skoy and sez, "Ow that Aw should be fahnd worthy to be spit upon for the gospel's sike!" e sez; an

Mog sez "Glaory Allelloolier!"; an then e called me Braddher, an dahned me as if Aw was a kid and e was me mather worshin me a Setterda nawt. Aw ednt jast nao shaow wiv im at all. Arf the street pryed; an the tather arf larfed fit to split theirselves. (*To Barbara*) There! are you settisfawd nah?

BARBARA (*her eyes dancing*) Wish I'd been there, Bill.

BILL. Yus: youd a got in a hextra bit o talk on me, wouldnt you?

JENNY. I'm so sorry, Mr Walker.

BILL (*fiercely*) Downt you gow bein sorry for me: youve no call. Listen eah. Aw browk your jawr.

JENNY. No, it didn't hurt me: indeed it didn't, except for a moment. It was only that I was frightened.

BILL. Aw downt want to be forgive be you, or be ennybody. Wot Aw did Aw'll py for. Aw trawd togat me aown jawr browk to settisfaw you—

JENNY (*distressed*) Oh no—

BILL (*impatiently*) Tell y' Aw did: cawnt you listen to wots bein taold you? All Aw got be it was being mide a sawt of in the pablic street for me pines. Well, if Aw cawnt settisfaw you one wy, Aw ken anather. Listen eah! Aw ed two quid sived agen the frost; an Awve a pahnd of it left. A mite o mawn last week ed words with the judy e's gowin to merry. E give er wotfor; an e's bin fawnd fifteen bob. E ed a rawt to itt er cause they was gowin to be merrid; bat Aw ednt nao rawt to itt you; sao put anather fawv bob on an cal it a pahnd's worth. (*He produces a sovereign*). Eahs the manney. Tike it; and lets ev no more o your forgivin an pryin and your Mijor jawrin me. Let wot Aw dan be dan an pide for; and let there be a end of it.

JENNY. Oh, I couldnt take it, Mr Walker. But if you would give a shilling or two to poor Rummy Mitchens! you really did hurt her; and she's old.

BILL (*contemptuously*) Not lawkly. Aw'd give her anather as soon as look at er. Let her ev the lawr o me as she threatened! S h e aint forgiven me: not mach. Wot Aw dan to er is not on me mawnd—wot she (*indicating Barbara*) mawt call on me conscience—no more than stickin a pig. It's this Christian gime o yours that Aw wownt ev plyed agen me: this bloomin forgivin an neggin an jawrin that mikes a menn thet sore that iz lawf's a burdn to im. Aw wownt ev it, Aw tell you; sao tike your manney and stop thraowin your silly beshed fice hap agen me.

JENNY. Major: may I take a little of it for the Army?

BARBARA. No: the Army is not to be bought. We want your soul, Bill; and we'll take nothing less.

BILL (*bitterly*) Aw knaow. Me an maw few shillins is not good enaff for you. Youre a earl's grendorter, you are. Nathink less than a anderd pahnd for you.

UNDERSHAFT. Come, Barbara! you could do a great deal of good with a hundred pounds. If you will set this gentleman's mind at ease by taking his pound, I will give the other ninety-nine.

Bill, dazed by such opulence, instinctively touches his cap.

BARBARA. Oh, youre too extravagant, papa. Bill offers twenty pieces of silver. All you need offer is the other ten. That will make the standard price to buy anybody who's for sale. I'm not; and the Army's not. (*To Bill*) Youll never have another quiet moment, Bill, until you come round to us. You cant stand out against your salvation.

BILL (*sullenly*) Aw cawnt stend aht agen music awl wrastlers and awtful tangued women. Awve offered to py. Aw can do no more. Tike it or leave it. There it is. (*He throws the sovereign on the drum, and sits down on the horse-trough. The coin fascinates Snobby Price, who takes an early opportunity of dropping his cap on it*).

Mrs Baines comes from the shelter. She is dressed as a Salvation Army Commissioner. She is an earnest looking woman of about 40, with a caressing, urgent voice, and an appealing manner.

BARBARA. This is my father, Mrs Baines. (*Undershaft comes*

from the table, taking his hat off with marked civility). Try what you can do with him. He wont listen to me, because he remembers what a fool I was when I was a baby. (*She leaves them together and chats with Jenny*).

MRS BAINES. Have you been shewn over the shelter, Mr Undershaft? You know the work we're doing, of course.

UNDERSHAFT (*very civilly*) The whole nation knows it, Mrs Baines.

MRS BAINES. No, sir: the whole nation does not know it, or we should not be crippled as we are for want of money to carry our work through the length and breadth of the land. Let me tell you that there would have been rioting this winter in London but for us.

UNDERSHAFT. You really think so?

MRS BAINES. I know it, I remember 1886, when you rich gentlemen hardened your hearts against the cry of the poor. They broke the windows of your clubs in Pall Mall.

UNDERSHAFT (*gleaming with approval of their method*) And the Mansion House Fund went up next day from thirty thousand pounds to seventy-nine thousand! I remember quite well.

MRS BAINES. Well, wont you help me to get at the people? They wont break windows then. Come here, Price. Let me shew you to this gentleman. (*Price comes to be inspected*). Do you remember the window breaking?

PRICE. My ole father thought it was the revolution, maam.

MRS BAINES. Would you break windows now?

PRICE. Oh no maam. The windows of eaven av bin opened to me. I know now that the rich man is a sinner like myself.

RUMMY (*appearing above at the loft door*) Snobby Price!

SNOBBY. Wot is it?

RUMMY. Your mother's askin for you at the other gate in Crippses Lane. She's heard about your confession. (*Price turns pale*).

MRS BAINES. Go, Mr Price; and pray with her.

JENNY. You can go through the shelter, Snobby.

PRICE (*to Mrs Baines*) I couldn't face her now, maam, with all the weight of my sins fresh on me. Tell her she'll find her son at ome, waitin for her in prayer. (*He skulks off through the gate, incidentally stealing the sovereign on his way out by picking up his cap from the drum*).

MRS BAINES (*with swimming eyes*) You see how we take the anger and the bitterness against you out of their hearts, Mr Undershaft.

UNDERSHAFT. It is certainly most convenient and gratifying to all large employers of labor, Mrs Baines.

MRS BAINES. Barbara: Jenny: I have good news: most wonderful news. (*Jenny runs to her*). My prayers have been answered. I told you they would, Jenny, didnt I?

JENNY. Yes, yes.

BARBARA (*moving nearer to the drum*) Have we got money enough to keep the shelter open?

MRS BAINES. I hope we shall have enough to keep all the shelters open. Lord Saxmundham has promised us five thousand pounds—

BARBARA. Hooray!

JENNY. Glory!

MRS BAINES. —if—

BARBARA. "If!" If what?

MRS BAINES. —if five other gentlemen will give a thousand each to make it up to ten thousand.

BARBARA. Who is Lord Saxmundham? I never heard of him.

UNDERSHAFT (*who has pricked up his ears at the peer's name, and is now watching Barbara curiously*) A new creation, my dear. You have heard of Sir Horace Bodger?

BARBARA. Bodger! Do you mean the distiller? Bodger's whisky!

UNDERSHAFT. That is the man. He is one of the greatest of our public benefactors. He restored the cathedral at Hakington. They made him a baronet for that. He gave half a million to the funds of his party: they made him a baron for that.

SHIRLEY. What will they give him for the five thousand?

UNDERSHAFT. There is nothing left to give him. So the five thousand, I should think, is to save his soul.

MRS BAINES. Heaven grant it may! Oh Mr Undershaft, you have some very rich friends. Cant you help us towards the other five thousand? We are going to hold a great meeting this afternoon at the Assembly Hall in the Mile End Road. If I could only announce that one gentleman had come forward to support Lord Saxmundham, others would follow. Dont you know somebody? couldnt you? wouldnt you? (*her eyes fill with tears*) oh, think of those poor people, Mr Undershaft: think of how much it means to them, and how little to a great man like you.

UNDERSHAFT (*sardonically gallant*) Mrs Baines: you are irresistible. I cant disappoint you; and I cant deny myself the satisfaction of making Bodger pay up. You shall have your five thousand pounds.

MRS BAINES. Thank God!

UNDERSHAFT. You dont thank m e?

MRS BAINES. Oh sir, dont try to be cynical: dont be ashamed of being a good man. The Lord will bless you abundantly; and our prayers will be like a strong fortification round you all the days of your life. (*With a touch of caution*) You will let me have the cheque to shew at the meeting, wont you? Jenny: go in and fetch a pen and ink. (*Jenny runs to the shelter door*).

UNDERSHAFT. Do not disturb Miss Hill: I have a fountain pen. (*Jenny halts. He sits at the table and writes the cheque. Cusins rises to make room for him. They all watch him silently*).

BILL (*cynically, aside to Barbara, his voice and accent horribly debased*) Wot prawce Selvytion nah?

BARBARA. Stop. (*Undershaft stops writing: they all turn to her in surprise*). Mrs Baines: are you really going to take this money?

MRS BAINES (*astonished*) Why not, dear?

BARBARA. Why not! Do you know what my father is? Have you forgotten that Lord Saxmundham is Bodger the whisky man? Do you remember how we implored the County Council to stop him from writing Bodger's Whisky in letters of fire against the sky; so that the poor drink-ruined creatures on the Embankment could not wake up from their snatches of sleep without being reminded of their deadly thirst by that wicked sky sign? Do you know that the worst thing I have had to fight here is not the devil, but Bodger, Bodger, Bodger, with his whisky, his distilleries, and his tied houses? Are you going to make our shelter another tied house for him, and ask me to keep it?

BILL. Rotten dranken whisky it is too.

MRS BAINES. Dear Barbara: Lord Saxmundham has a soul to be saved like any of us. If heaven has found the way to make a good use of his money, are we to set ourselves up against the answer to our prayers?

BARBARA. I know he has a soul to be saved. Let him come down here; and I'll do my best to help him to his salvation. But he wants to send his cheque down to buy us, and go on being as wicked as ever.

UNDERSHAFT (*with a reasonableness which Cusins alone perceives to be ironical*) My dear Barbara: alcohol is a very necessary article. It heals the sick—

BARBARA. It does nothing of the sort.

UNDERSHAFT. Well, it assists the doctor: that is perhaps a less questionable way of putting it. It makes life bearable to millions of people who could not endure their existence if they were quite sober. It enables Parliament to do things at eleven at night that no sane person would do at eleven in the morning. Is it Bodger's fault that this inestimable gift is deplorably abused by less than one per cent of the poor? (*He turns again to the table; signs the cheque; and crosses it*).

MRS BAINES. Barbara: will there be less drinking or more if all those poor souls we are saving come tomorrow and find the doors of our shelters shut in their faces? Lord Saxmundham gives us the money to stop drinking—to take his own business from him.

CUSINS (*impishly*) Pure self-sacrifice on Bodger's part, clearly! Bless dear Bodger! (*Barbara almost breaks down as Adolphus, too, fails her*).

UNDERSHAFT (*tearing out the cheque and pocketing the book as he rises and goes past Cusins to Mrs Baines*) I also, Mrs Baines, may claim a little disinterestedness. Think of my business! think of the widows and orphans! the men and lads torn to pieces with shrapnel and poisoned with lyddite (*Mrs Baines shrinks; but he goes on remorselessly*)! the oceans of blood, not one drop of which is shed in a really just cause! the ravaged crops! the peaceful peasants forced, women and men, to till their fields under the fire of opposing armies on pain of starvation! the bad blood of the fierce little cowards at home who egg on others to fight for the gratification of their national vanity! All this makes money for me: I am never richer, never busier than when the papers are full of it. Well, it is your work to preach peace on earth and goodwill to men. (*Mrs Baines's face lights up again*). Every convert you make is a vote against war. (*Her lips move in prayer*). Yet I give you this money to help you to hasten my own commercial ruin. (*He gives her the cheque*).

CUSINS (*mounting the form in an ecstasy of mischief*) The millennium will be inaugurated by the unselfishness of Undershaft and Bodger. Oh be joyful! (*He takes the drum-sticks from his pocket and flourishes them*).

MRS BAINES (*taking the cheque*) The longer I live the more proof I see that there is an Infinite Goodness that turns everything to the work of salvation sooner or later. Who would have thought that any good could have come out of war and drink? And yet their profits are brought today to the feet of salvation to do its blessed work. (*She is affected to tears*).

JENNY (*running to Mrs Baines and throwing her arms round her*) Oh dear! how blessed, how glorious it all is!

CUSINS (*in a convulsion of irony*) Let us seize this unspeakable moment. Let us march to the great meeting at once. Excuse me just an instant. (*He rushes into the shelter. Jenny takes her tambourine from the drum head*).

MRS BAINES. Mr Undershaft: have you ever seen a thousand people fall on their knees with one impulse and pray? Come with us to the meeting. Barbara shall tell them that the Army is saved, and saved through you.

CUSINS (*returning impetuously from the shelter with a flag and a trombone, and coming between Mrs Baines and Undershaft*) You will carry the flag down the first street, Mrs. Baines. (*He gives her the flag*). Mr. Undershaft is a gifted trombonist: he shall intone an Olympian diapason to the West Ham Salvation March. (*Aside to Undershaft, as he forces the trombone on him*). Blow, Machiavelli, blow.

UNDERSHAFT (*aside to him, as he takes the trombone*) The trumpet in Zion! (*Cusins rushes to the drum, which he takes up and puts on. Undershaft continues, aloud*) I will do my best. I could vamp a bass if I knew the tune.

CUSINS. It is a wedding chorus from one of Donizetti's operas; but we have converted it. We convert everything to good here, including Bodger. You remember the chorus. "For thee immense rejoicing—immenso giubilo—immenso giubilo." (*With drum obbligato*) Rum tum ti tum tum, tum tum ti ta—

BARBARA. Dolly: you are breaking my heart.

CUSINS. What is a broken heart more or less here? Dionysos Undershaft has descended. I am possessed.

MRS BAINES. Come, Barbara: I must have my dear Major to carry the flag with me.

JENNY. Yes, yes, Major darling.

Cusins snatches the tambourine out of Jenny's hand and mutely offers it to Barbara.

BARBARA (*coming forward a little as she puts the offer behind her with a shudder, whilst Cusins recklessly tosses the tambourine back to Jenny and goes to the gate*) I cant come.

JENNY. Not come!

MRS BAINES (*with tears in her eyes*) Barbara: do you think I am wrong to take the money?

BARBARA (*impulsively going to her and kissing her*) No, no: God help you, dear, you must: you are saving the Army. Go; and may you have a great meeting!

JENNY. But arnt you coming?

BARBARA. No. (*She begins taking off the silver S brooch from her collar*).

MRS BAINES. Barbara: what are you doing?

JENNY. Why are you taking your badge off? You cant be going to leave us, Major.

BARBARA (*quietly*) Father: come here.

UNDERSHAFT (*coming to her*) My dear! (*Seeing that she is going to pin the badge on his collar, he retreats to the penthouse in some alarm*).

BARBARA (*following him*) Dont be frightened. (*She pins the badge on and steps back towards the table, shewing him to the others*). There! It's not much for £5000, is it?

MRS BAINES. Barbara: if you wont come and pray w i t h us, promise me you will pray f o r us.

BARBARA. I cant pray now. Perhaps I shall never pray again.

MRS BAINES. Barbara!

JENNY. Major!

BARBARA (*almost delirious*) I cant bear any more. Quick march!

CUSINS (*calling to the procession in the street outside*) Off we go. Play up, there! I m m e n s o g i u b i l o. (*He gives the time with his drum; and the band strikes up the march, which rapidly becomes more distant as the procession moves briskly away*).

MRS BAINES. I must go, dear. Youre overworked: you will be

all right tomorrow. We'll never lose you. Now Jenny: step out with the old flag. Blood and Fire! (*She marches out through the gate with her flag*).

JENNY. Glory Hallelujah! (*Flourishing her tambourine and marching*).

UNDERSHAFT (*to Cusins, as he marches out past him easing the slide of his trombone*) "My ducats and my daughter"!

CUSINS (*following him out*) Money and gunpowder!

BARBARA. Drunkenness and Murder! My God: why hast thou forsaken me?

She sinks on the form with her face buried in her hands. The march passes away into silence. Bill Walker steals across to her.

BILL (*taunting*) Wot prawce selvytion nah?

SHIRLEY. Dont you hit her when she's down.

BILL. She itt me wen aw wiz dahn. Waw shouldnt Aw git a bit o me aown beck?

BARBARA (*raising her head*) I didnt take y o u r money, Bill. (*She crosses the yard to the gate and turns her back on the two men to hide her face from them*).

BILL (*sneering after her*) Naow, it warnt enaff for you. (*Turning to the drum, he misses the money*) Ellow! If you aint took it sammun else ez. Weres it gorn? Bly me if Jenny Ill didnt tike it arter all!

RUMMY (*screaming at him from the loft*) You lie, you dirty blackguard! Snobby Price pinched it off the drum when he took up his cap. I was up here all the time an see im do it.

BILL. Wot! Stowl maw manney! Waw didnt you call thief on him, you silly aold macker you?

RUMMY. To serve you aht for ittin me acrost the fice. It's cost y'pahnd, that az. (*Raising a pæan of squalid triumph*) I done you. I'm even with you. Ive ad it aht o y—(*Bill snatches up Shirley's mug and hurls it at her. She slams the loft door and vanishes. The mug smashes against the door and falls in fragments*).

BILL (*beginning to chuckle*) Tell us, aol menn, wot o'clock this mawnin was it wen im as they call Snobby Prawce was sived?

BARBARA (*turning to him more composedly, and with unspoiled sweetness*) About half past twelve, Bill. And he pinched your pound at a quarter to two. I know. Well, you cant afford to lose it. I'll send it to you.

BILL (*his voice and accent suddenly improving*) Not if Aw wiz to stawve for it. Aw aint to be bought.

SHIRLEY. Aint you? Youd sell yourself to the devil for a pint o beer; ony there aint no devil to make the offer.

BILL (*unshamed*) Sao Aw would, mite, and often ev, cheerful. But she cawnt baw me. (*Approaching Barbara*) You wanted maw saoul, did you? Well, you aint got it.

BARBARA. I nearly got it, Bill. But weve sold it back to you for ten thousand pounds.

SHIRLEY. And dear at the money!

BARBARA. No, Peter: it was worth more than money.

BILL (*salvationproof*) It's nao good: you cawnt get rahnd me nah. Aw downt blieve in it; and Awve seen tody that Aw was rawt. (*Going*) Sao long, aol soupkitchener! Ta, ta, Mijor Earl's Grendorter! (*Turning at the gate*) Wot prawce selvytion nah? Snobby Prawce! Ha! ha!

BARBARA (*offering her hand*) Goodbye, Bill.

BILL (*taken aback, half plucks his cap off; then shoves it on again defiantly*) Git aht. (*Barbara drops her hand, discouraged. He has a twinge of remorse*). But thets aw rawt, you knaow. Nathink pasnl. Naow mellice. Sao long, Judy. (*He goes*).

BARBARA. No malice. So long, Bill.

SHIRLEY (*shaking his head*) You make too much of him, Miss, in your innocence.

BARBARA (*going to him*) Peter: I'm like you now. Cleaned out, and lost my job.

SHIRLEY. Youve youth an hope. Thats two better than me.

BARBARA. I'll get you a job, Peter. Thats hope for you: the youth will have to be enough for me. (*She counts her money*).

I have just enough left for two teas at Lockharts, a Rowton doss for you, and my tram and bus home. (*He frowns and rises with offended pride. She takes his arm*). Dont be proud, Peter: it's sharing between friends. And promise me youll talk to me and not let me cry. (*She draws him towards the gate*).

SHIRLEY. Well, I'm not accustomed to talk to the like of you—

BARBARA (*urgently*) Yes, yes: you must talk to me. Tell me about Tom Paine's books and Bradlaugh's lectures. Come along.

SHIRLEY. Ah, if you would only read Tom Paine in the proper spirit, Miss! (*They go out through the gate together*).

END OF ACT II

ACT III

NEXT DAY *after lunch Lady Britomart is writing in the library in Wilton Crescent. Sarah is reading in the armchair near the window. Barbara, in ordinary fashionable dress, pale and brooding, is on the settee. Charles Lomax enters. He starts on seeing Barbara fashionably attired and in low spirits.*

LOMAX. Youve left off your uniform!

Barbara says nothing; but an expression of pain passes over her face.

LADY BRITOMART (*warning him in low tones to be careful*) Charles!

LOMAX (*much concerned, coming behind the settee and bending sympathetically over Barbara*) I'm awfully sorry, Barbara. You know I helped you all I could with the concertina and so forth. (*Momentously*) Still, I have never shut my eyes to the fact that there is a certain amount of tosh about the Salvation Army. Now the claims of the Church of England—

LADY BRITOMART. Thats enough, Charles. Speak of something suited to your mental capacity.

LOMAX. But surely the Church of England is suited to all our capacities.

BARBARA (*pressing his hand*) Thank you for your sympathy, Cholly. Now go ánd spoon with Sarah.

LOMAX (*dragging a chair from the writing table and seating himself affectionately by Sarah's side*) How is my ownest to-day?

SARAH. I wish you wouldnt tell Cholly to do things, Barbara. He always comes straight and does them. Cholly: we're going to the works this afternoon.

LOMAX. What works?

SARAH. The cannon works.

LOMAX. What? your governor's shop!

SARAH. Yes.

LOMAX. Oh I say!

Cusins enters in poor condition. He also starts visibly when he sees Barbara without her uniform.

BARBARA. I expected you this morning, Dolly. Didnt you guess that?

CUSINS (*sitting down beside her*) I'm sorry. I have only just breakfasted.

SARAH. But weve just finished lunch.

BARBARA. Have you had one of your bad nights?

CUSINS. No: I had rather a good night: in fact, one of the most remarkable nights I have ever passed.

BARBARA. The meeting?

CUSINS. No: after the meeting.

LADY BRITOMART. You should have gone to bed after the meeting. What were you doing?

CUSINS. Drinking.

LADY BRITOMART.	Adolphus!
SARAH.	Dolly!
BARBARA.	Dolly!
LOMAX.	Oh I say!

LADY BRITOMART. What were you drinking, may I ask?

CUSINS. A most devilish kind of Spanish burgundy, warranted free from added alcohol: a Temperance burgundy in fact. Its richness in natural alcohol made any addition superfluous.

BARBARA. Are you joking, Dolly?

CUSINS (*patiently*). No. I have been making a night of it with the nominal head of this household: that is all.

LADY BRITOMART. Andrew made you drunk!

CUSINS. No: he only provided the wine. I think it was Dionysos who made me drunk. (*To Barbara*) I told you I was possessed.

LADY BRITOMART. Youre not sober yet. Go home to bed at once.

CUSINS. I have never before ventured to reproach you, Lady Brit; but how could you marry the Prince of Darkness?

LADY BRITOMART. It was much more excusable to marry him than to get drunk with him. That is a new accomplishment of Andrew's, by the way. He usent to drink.

CUSINS. He doesnt now. He only sat there and completed the wreck of my moral basis, the rout of my convictions, the purchase of my soul. He cares for you, Barbara. That is what makes him so dangerous to me.

BARBARA. That has nothing to do with it, Dolly. There are larger loves and diviner dreams than the fireside ones. You know that, dont you?

CUSINS. Yes: that is our understanding. I know it. I hold to it. Unless he can win me on that holier ground he may amuse me for a while; but he can get no deeper hold, strong as he is.

BARBARA. Keep to that; and the end will be right. Now tell me what happened at the meeting?

CUSINS. It was an amazing meeting. Mrs Baines almost died of emotion. Jenny Hill simply gibbered with hysteria. The Prince of Darkness played his trombone like a madman: its brazen roarings were like the laughter of the damned. 117 conversions took place then and there. They prayed with the most touching sincerity and gratitude for Bodger, and for the anonymous donor of the £5000. Your father would not let his name be given.

LOMAX. That was rather fine of the old man, you know. Most chaps would have wanted the advertisement.

CUSINS. He said all the charitable institutions would be down on him like kites on a battle field if he gave his name.

LADY BRITOMART. Thats Andrew all over. He never does a proper thing without giving an improper reason for it.

CUSINS. He convinced me that I have all my life been doing improper things for proper reasons.

LADY BRITOMART. Adolphus: now that Barbara has left the Salvation Army, you had better leave it too. I will not have you playing that drum in the streets.

CUSINS. Your orders are already obeyed, Lady Brit.

BARBARA. Dolly: were you ever really in earnest about it? Would you have joined if you had never seen me?

CUSINS (*disingenuously*) Well—er—well, possibly, as a collector of religions—

LOMAX (*cunningly*) Not as a drummer, though, you know. You are a very clearheaded brainy chap, Dolly; and it must have been apparent to you that there is a certain amount of tosh about—

LADY BRITOMART. Charles: if you must drivel, drivel like a grown-up man and not like a schoolboy.

LOMAX (*out of countenance*) Well, drivel is drivel, dont you know, whatever a man's age.

LADY BRITOMART. In good society in England, Charles, men drivel at all ages by repeating silly formulas with an air of wisdom. Schoolboys make their own formulas out of slang, like you. When they reach your age, and get political private secretaryships and things of that sort, they drop slang and get their formulas out of The Spectator or The Times. You had better confine yourself to The Times. You will find that there is a certain amount of tosh about The Times; but at least its language is reputable.

LOMAX (*overwhelmed*) You are so awfully strongminded, Lady Brit—

LADY BRITOMART. Rubbish! (*Morrison comes in*). What is it?

MORRISON. If you please, my lady, Mr Undershaft has just drove up to the door.

LADY BRITOMART. Well, let him in. (*Morrison hesitates*). Whats the matter with you?

MORRISON. Shall I announce him, my lady; or is he at home here, so to speak, my lady?

LADY BRITOMART. Announce him.

MORRISON. Thank you, my lady. You wont mind my asking, I hope. The occasion is in a manner of speaking new to me.

LADY BRITOMART. Quite right. Go and let him in.

MORRISON. Thank you, my lady. (*He withdraws*).

LADY BRITOMART. Children: go and get ready. (*Sarah and Barbara go upstairs for their out-of-door wraps*). Charles: go and tell Stephen to come down here in five minutes: you will find him in the drawing room. (*Charles goes*). Adolphus: tell them to send round the carriage in about fifteen minutes. (*Adolphus goes*).

MORRISON (*at the door*) Mr Undershaft.

Undershaft comes in. Morrison goes out.

UNDERSHAFT. Alone! How fortunate!

LADY BRITOMART (*rising*) Dont be sentimental, Andrew. Sit down. (*She sits on the settee: he sits beside her, on her left. She comes to the point before he has time to breathe*). Sarah must have £800 a year until Charles Lomax comes into his property. Barbara will need more, and need it permanently, because Adolphus hasnt any property.

UNDERSHAFT (*resignedly*) Yes, my dear: I will see to it. Anything else? for yourself, for instance?

LADY BRITOMART. I want to talk to you about Stephen.

UNDERSHAFT (*rather wearily*) Dont, my dear. Stephen doesnt interest me.

LADY BRITOMART. He does interest me. He is our son.

UNDERSHAFT. Do you really think so? He has induced us to bring him into the world; but he chose his parents very incongruously, I think. I see nothing of myself in him, and less of you.

LADY BRITOMART. Andrew: Stephen is an excellent son, and a most steady, capable, highminded young man. You are simply trying to find an excuse for disinheriting him.

UNDERSHAFT. My dear Biddy: the Undershaft tradition disinherits him. It would be dishonest of me to leave the cannon foundry to my son.

LADY BRITOMART. It would be most unnatural and improper of you to leave it to anyone else, Andrew. Do you suppose this wicked and immoral tradition can be kept up for ever? Do you pretend that Stephen could not carry on the foundry just as well as all the other sons of the big business houses?

UNDERSHAFT. Yes: he could learn the office routine without understanding the business, like all the other sons; and the firm would go on by its own momentum until the real Undershaft—probably an Italian or a German—would invent a new method and cut him out.

LADY BRITOMART. There is nothing that any Italian or German could do that Stephen could not do. And Stephen at least has breeding.

UNDERSHAFT. The son of a foundling! Nonsense!

LADY BRITOMART. My son, Andrew! And even you may have good blood in your veins for all you know.

UNDERSHAFT. True. Probably I have That is another argument in favor of a foundling.

LADY BRITOMART. Andrew: dont be aggravating. And dont be wicked. At present you are both.

UNDERSHAFT. This conversation is part of the Undershaft tradition, Biddy. Every Undershaft's wife has treated him to it ever since the house was founded. It is mere waste of breath. If the tradition be ever broken it will be for an abler man than Stephen.

LADY BRITOMART (*pouting*) Then go away.

UNDERSHAFT (*deprecatory*) Go away!

LADY BRITOMART. Yes: go away. If you will do nothing for Stephen, you are not wanted here. Go to your foundling, whoever he is; and look after h i m.

UNDERSHAFT. The fact is, Biddy—

LADY BRITOMART. Dont call me Biddy. I dont call you Andy.

UNDERSHAFT. I will not call my wife Britomart: it is not good sense. Seriously, my love, the Undershaft tradition has landed me in a difficulty. I am getting on in years; and my partner

Lazarus has at last made a stand and insisted that the succession must be settled one way or the other; and of course he is quite right. You see, I havnt found a fit successor yet.

LADY BRITOMART (*obstinately*) There is Stephen.

UNDERSHAFT. Thats just it: all the foundlings I can find are exactly like Stephen.

LADY BRITOMART. Andrew!!

UNDERSHAFT. I want a man with no relations and no schooling: that is, a man who would be out of the running altogether if he were not a strong man. And I cant find him. Every blessed foundling nowadays is snapped up in his infancy by Barnardo homes, or School Board officers, or Boards of Guardians; and if he shews the least ability, he is fastened on by schoolmasters; trained to win scholarships like a racehorse; crammed with secondhand ideas; drilled and disciplined in docility and what they call good taste; and lamed for life so that he is fit for nothing but teaching. If you want to keep the foundry in the family, you had better find an eligible foundling and marry him to Barbara.

LADY BRITOMART. Ah! Barbara! Your pet! You would sacrifice Stephen to Barbara.

UNDERSHAFT. Cheerfully. And you, my dear, would boil Barbara to make soup for Stephen.

LADY BRITOMART. Andrew: this is not a question of our likings and dislikings: it is a question of duty. It is your duty to make Stephen your successor.

UNDERSHAFT. Just as much as it is your duty to submit to your husband. Come, Biddy! these tricks of the governing class are of no use with me. I am one of the governing class myself; and it is waste of time giving tracts to a missionary. I have the power in this matter; and I am not to be humbugged into using it for your purposes.

LADY BRITOMART. Andrew: you can talk my head off; but you cant change wrong into right. And your tie is all on one side. Put it straight.

UNDERSHAFT (*disconcerted*) It wont stay unless it's pinned—
(*He fumbles at it with childish grimaces*).

Stephen comes in.

STEPHEN (*at the door*) I beg your pardon. (*About to retire*).

LADY BRITOMART. No: come in, Stephen. (*Stephen comes forward to his mother's writing table*).

UNDERSHAFT (*not very cordially*) Good afternoon.

STEPHEN (*coldly*) Good afternoon.

UNDERSHAFT (*to Lady Britomart*) He knows all about the tradition, I suppose?

LADY BRITOMART. Yes. (*To Stephen*). It is what I told you last night, Stephen.

UNDERSHAFT (*sulkily*) I understand you want to come into the cannon business.

STEPHEN. I go into trade! Certainly not.

UNDERSHAFT (*opening his eyes, greatly eased in mind and manner*) Oh! in that case—

LADY BRITOMART. Cannons are not trade, Stephen. They are enterprise.

STEPHEN. I have no intention of becoming a man of business in any sense. I have no capacity for business and no taste for it. I intend to devote myself to politics.

UNDERSHAFT (*rising*) My dear boy: this is an immense relief to me. And I trust it may prove an equally good thing for the country. I was afraid you would consider yourself disparaged and slighted. (*He moves towards Stephen as if to shake hands with him*).

LADY BRITOMART (*rising and interposing*) Stephen: I cannot allow you to throw away an enormous property like this.

STEPHEN (*stiffly*) Mother: there must be an end of treating me as a child, if you please. (*Lady Britomart recoils, deeply wounded by his tone*). Until last night I did not take your attitude seriously, because I did not think you meant it seriously. But I find now that you left me in the dark as to matters which you should have explained to me years ago. I am extremely hurt and offended. Any further discussion of my intentions had better take place with my father, as between one man and another.

LADY BRITOMART. Stephen! (*She sits down again, her eyes filling with tears*).

UNDERSHAFT (*with grave compassion*) You see, my dear, it is only the big men who can be treated as children.

STEPHEN. I am sorry, mother, that you have forced me—

UNDERSHAFT (*stopping him*) Yes, yes, yes, yes: thats all right, Stephen. She wont interfere with you any more: your independence is achieved: you have won your latchkey. Dont rub it in; and above all, dont apologize. (*He resumes his seat*). Now what about your future, as between one man and another—I beg your pardon, Biddy: as between two men and a woman.

LADY BRITOMART (*who has pulled herself together strongly*) I quite understand, Stephen. By all means go your own way if you feel strong enough. (*Stephen sits down magisterially in the chair at the writing table with an air of affirming his majority*).

UNDERSHAFT. It is settled that you do not ask for the succession to the cannon business.

STEPHEN. I hope it is settled that I repudiate the cannon business.

UNDERSHAFT. Come, come! dont be so devilishly sulky: it's boyish. Freedom should be generous. Besides, I owe you a fair start in life in exchange for disinheriting you. You cant become prime minister all at once. Havent you a turn for something? What about literature, art and so forth?

STEPHEN. I have nothing of the artist about me, either in faculty or character, thank Heaven!

UNDERSHAFT. A philosopher, perhaps? Eh?

STEPHEN. I make no such ridiculous pretension.

UNDERSHAFT. Just so. Well, there is the army, the navy, the

Church, the Bar. The Bar requires some ability. What about the Bar?

STEPHEN. I have not studied law. And I am afraid I have not the necessary push—I believe that is the name barristers give to their vulgarity—for success in pleading.

UNDERSHAFT. Rather a difficult case, Stephen. Hardly any-thing left but the stage, is there? (*Stephen makes an impatient movement*). Well, come! is there a n y t h i n g you know or care for?

STEPHEN (*rising and looking at him steadily*) I know the difference between right and wrong.

UNDERSHAFT (*hugely tickled*) You dont say so! What! no capacity for business, no knowledge of law, no sympathy with art, no pretension to philosophy; only a simple knowledge of the secret that has puzzled all the philosophers, baffled all the lawyers, muddled all the men of business, and ruined most of the artists: the secret of right and wrong. Why, man, youre a genius, a master of masters, a god! At twenty-four, too!

STEPHEN (*keeping his temper with difficulty*) You are pleased to be facetious. I pretend to nothing more than any honorable English gentleman claims as his birthright. (*He sits down angrily*).

UNDERSHAFT. Oh, thats everybody's birthright. Look at poor little Jenny Hill, the Salvation lassie! she would think you were laughing at her if you asked her to stand up in the street and teach grammar or geography or mathematics or even draw-ing room dancing; but it never occurs to her to doubt that she can teach morals and religion. You are all alike, you respectable people. You cant tell me the bursting strain of a ten-inch gun, which is a very simple matter; but you all think you can tell me the bursting strain of a man under temptation. You darent handle high explosives; but youre all ready to handle honesty and truth and justice and the whole duty of man, and kill one another at that game. What a country! What a world!

LADY BRITOMART (*uneasily*) What do you think he had better do, Andrew?

UNDERSHAFT. Oh, just what he wants to do. He knows nothing and he thinks he knows everything. That points clearly to a political career. Get him a private secretaryship to someone who can get him an Under Secretaryship; and then leave him alone. He will find his natural and proper place in the end on the Treasury Bench.

STEPHEN (*springing up again*) I am sorry, sir, that you force me to forget the respect due to you as my father. I am an Englishman and I will not hear the Government of my country insulted. (*He thrusts his hands in his pockets, and walks angrily across to the window*).

UNDERSHAFT (*with a touch of brutality*) The government of your country! I am the government of your country: I, and Lazarus. Do you suppose that you and half a dozen amateurs like you, sitting in a row in that foolish gabble shop, can govern Undershaft and Lazarus? No, my friend: you will do what pays u s. You will make war when it suits us, and keep peace when it doesnt. You will find out that trade requires certain measures when we have decided on those measures. When I want anything to keep my dividends up, you will discover that my want is a national need. When other people want something to keep my dividends down, you will call out the police and military. And in return you shall have the support and applause of my newspapers, and the delight of imagining that you are a great statesman. Government of your country! Be off with you, my boy, and play with your caucuses and leading articles and historic parties and great leaders and burning questions and the rest of your toys. I am going back to my counting house to pay the piper and call the tune.

STEPHEN (*actually smiling, and putting his hand on his father's shoulder with indulgent patronage*) Really, my dear father, it is impossible to be angry with you. You don't know how absurd all this sounds to m e. You are very properly proud of having been industrious enough to make money; and it is greatly to your credit that you have made so much of it. But it has kept you in circles where you are valued for your money and deferred to for it, instead of in the doubtless very old-fashioned and behind-the-times public school and university where I formed my habits of mind. It is natural for you to think that money governs England; but you must allow me to think I know better.

UNDERSHAFT. And what d o e s govern England, pray?

STEPHEN. Character, father, character.

UNDERSHAFT. Whose character? Yours or mine?

STEPHEN. Neither yours nor mine, father, but the best elements in the English national character.

UNDERSHAFT. Stephen: Ive found your profession for you. Youre a born journalist. I'll start you with a hightoned weekly review. There!

Before Stephen can reply Sarah, Barbara, Lomax, and Cusins come in ready for walking. Barbara crosses the room to the window and looks out. Cusins drifts amiably to the armchair. Lomax remains near the door, whilst Sarah comes to her mother.

Stephen goes to the smaller writing table and busies himself with his letters.

SARAH. Go and get ready, mamma: the carriage is waiting. (*Lady Britomart leaves the room*).

UNDERSHAFT (*to Sarah*) Good day, my dear. Good afternoon, Mr Lomax.

LOMAX (*vaguely*) Ahdedoo.

UNDERSHAFT (*to Cusins*) Quite well after last night, Euripides, eh?

CUSINS. As well as can be expected.

UNDERSHAFT. Thats right. (*To Barbara*). So you are coming to see my death and devastation factory, Barbara?

BARBARA (*at the window*) You came yesterday to see my salvation factory. I promised you a return visit.

LOMAX (*coming forward between Sarah and Undershaft*)

Youll find it awfully interesting. Ive been through the Wool-wich Arsenal; and it gives you a ripping feeling of security, you know, to think of the lot of beggars we could kill if it came to fighting. (*To Undershaft, with sudden solemnity*). Still, it must be rather an awful reflection for you, from the religious point of view as it were. Youre getting on, you know, and all that.

SARAH. You dont mind Cholly's imbecility, papa, do you?

LOMAX (*much taken aback*) Oh I say!

UNDERSHAFT. Mr Lomax looks at the matter in a very proper spirit, my dear.

LOMAX. Just so. Thats all I meant, I assure you.

SARAH. Are you coming, Stephen?

STEPHEN. Well, I am rather busy—er—(*Magnanimously*) Oh well, yes: I'll come. That is, if there is room for me.

UNDERSHAFT. I can take two with me in a little motor I am experimenting with for field use. You wont mind its being rather unfashionable. It's not painted yet; but it's bullet proof.

LOMAX (*appalled at the prospect of confronting Wilton Crescent in an unpainted motor*) Oh I s a y!

SARAH. The carriage for me, thank you. Barbara doesnt mind what shes seen in.

LOMAX. I say, Dolly old chap: do you really mind the car being a guy? Because of course if you do I'll go in it. Still—

CUSINS. I prefer it.

LOMAX. Thanks awfully, old man. Come, my ownest. (*He hurries out to secure his seat in the carriage. Sarah follows him*).

CUSINS (*moodily walking across to Lady Britomart's writing table*) Why are we two coming to this Works Department of Hell? that is what I ask myself.

BARBARA. I have always thought of it as a sort of pit where lost creatures with blackened faces stirred up smoky fires and were driven and tormented by my father. Is it like that, dad?

UNDERSHAFT (*scandalized*) My dear! It is a spotlessly clean and beautiful hillside town.

CUSINS. With a Methodist chapel? Oh d o say theres a Methodist chapel.

UNDERSHAFT. There are two: a Primitive one and a sophisticated one. There is even an Ethical Society; but it is not much patronized, as my men are all strongly religious. In the High Explosives Sheds they object to the presence of Agnostics as unsafe.

CUSINS. And yet they dont object to you!

BARBARA. Do they obey all your orders?

UNDERSHAFT. I never give them any orders. When I speak to one of them it is "Well, Jones, is the baby doing well? and has Mrs Jones made a good recovery?" "Nicely, thank you, sir." And thats all.

CUSINS. But Jones has to be kept in order. How do you maintain discipline among your men?

UNDERSHAFT. I dont. They do. You see, the one thing Jones wont stand is any rebellion from the man under him, or any assertion of social equality between the wife of the man with 4 shillings a week less than himself, and Mrs Jones! Of course they all rebel against me, theoretically. Practically, every man of them keeps the man just below him in his place. I never meddle with them. I never bully them. I dont even bully Lazarus. I say that certain things are to be done; but I dont order anybody to do them. I dont say, mind you, that there is no ordering about and snubbing and even bullying. The men snub the boys and order them about; the carmen snub the sweepers; the artisans snub the unskilled laborers; the foremen drive and bully both the laborers and artisans; the assistant engineers find fault with the foremen; the chief engineers drop on the assistants; the departmental managers worry the chiefs; and the clerks have tall hats and hymnbooks and keep up the social tone by refusing to associate on equal terms with anybody. The result is a colossal profit, which comes to me.

CUSINS (*revolted*) You really are a—well, what I was saying yesterday.

BARBARA. What was he saying yesterday?

UNDERSHAFT. Never mind, my dear. He thinks I have made you unhappy. Have I?

BARBARA. Do you think I can be happy in this vulgar silly dress? I! who have worn the uniform. Do you understand what you have done to me? Yesterday I had a man's soul in my hand. I set him in the way of life with his face to salvation. But when we took your money he turned back to drunkenness and derision. (*With intense conviction*) I will never forgive you that. If I had a child, and you destroyed its body with your explosives—if you murdered Dolly with your horrible guns—I could forgive you if my forgiveness would open the gates of heaven to you. But to take a human soul from me, and turn it into the soul of a wolf! that is worse than any murder.

UNDERSHAFT. Does my daughter despair so easily? Can you strike a man to the heart and leave no mark on him?

BARBARA (*her face lighting up*) Oh, you are right: he can never be lost now: where was my faith?

CUSINS. Oh, clever clever devil!

BARBARA. You may be a devil; but God speaks through you sometimes. (*She takes her father's hands and kisses them*). You have given me back my happiness: I feel it deep down now, though my spirit is troubled.

UNDERSHAFT. You have learnt something. That always feels at first as if you had lost something.

BARBARA. Well, take me to the factory of death; and let me learn something more. There must be some truth or other behind all this frightful irony. Come, Dolly. (*She goes out*).

CUSINS. My guardian angel! (*To Undershaft*) Avaunt! (*He follows Barbara*).

STEPHEN (*quietly, at the writing table*) You must not mind

Cusins, father. He is a very amiable good fellow; but he is a Greek scholar and naturally a little eccentric.

UNDERSHAFT. Ah, quite so. Thank you, Stephen. Thank you. (*He goes out*).

Stephen smiles patronizingly; buttons his coat responsibly; and crosses the room to the door. Lady Britomart, dressed for out-of-doors, opens it before he reaches it. She looks round for the others; looks at Stephen; and turns to go without a word.

STEPHEN (*embarrassed*) Mother—

LADY BRITOMART. Dont be apologetic, Stephen. And dont forget that you have outgrown your mother. (*She goes out*).

Perivale St Andrews lies between two Middlesex hills, half climbing the northern one. It is an almost smokeless town of white walls, roofs of narrow green slates or red tiles, tall trees, domes, campaniles, and slender chimney shafts, beautifully situated and beautiful in itself. The best view of it is obtained from the crest of a slope about half a mile to the east, where the high explosives are dealt with. The foundry lies hidden in the depths between, the tops of its chimneys sprouting like huge skittles into the middle distance. Across the crest runs an emplacement of concrete, with a firestep, and a parapet which suggests a fortification, because there is a huge cannon of the obsolete Woolwich Infant pattern peering across it at the town. The cannon is mounted on an experimental gun carriage: possibly the original model of the Undershaft disappearing rampart gun alluded to by Stephen. The firestep, being a convenient place to sit, is furnished here and there with straw disc cushions; and at one place there is the additional luxury of a fur rug.

Barbara is standing on the firestep, looking over the parapet towards the town. On her right is the cannon; on her left the end of a shed raised on piles, with a ladder of three or four steps up to the door, which opens outwards and has a little wooden landing at the threshold, with a fire bucket in the

*corner of the landing. Several dummy soldiers more or less
mutilated, with straw protruding from their gashes, have been
shoved out of the way under the landing. A few others are
nearly upright against the shed; and one has fallen forward
and lies, like a grotesque corpse, on the emplacement. The
parapet stops short of the shed, leaving a gap which is the beginning of the path down the hill through the foundry to the
town. The rug is on the firestep near this gap. Down on the
emplacement behind the cannon is a trolley carrying a huge
conical bombshell with a red band painted on it. Further to
the right is the door of an office, which, like the sheds, is of
the lightest possible construction.*

Cusins arrives by the path from the town.

BARBARA. Well?

CUSINS. Not a ray of hope. Everything perfect! wonderful!
real! It only needs a cathedral to be a heavenly city instead of a
hellish one.

BARBARA. Have you found out whether they have done anything for old Peter Shirley?

CUSINS. They have found him a job as gatekeeper and time-
keeper. He's frightfully miserable. He calls the timekeeping
brainwork, and says he isnt used to it; and his gate lodge is so
splendid that he's ashamed to use the rooms, and skulks in the
scullery.

BARBARA. Poor Peter!

Stephen arrives from the town. He carries a field-glass.

STEPHEN (*enthusiastically*) Have you two seen the place?
Why did you leave us?

CUSINS. I wanted to see everything I was not intended to
see; and Barbara wanted to make the men talk.

STEPHEN. Have you found anything discreditable?

CUSINS. No. They call him Dandy Andy and are proud of
his being a cunning old rascal; but it's all horribly, frightfully,
immorally, unanswerably perfect.

Sarah arrives.

SARAH. Heavens! what a place! (*She crosses to the trolley*). Did you see the nursing home!? (*She sits down on the shell*).

STEPHEN. Did you see the libraries and schools!?

SARAH. Did you see the ball room and the banqueting chamber in the Town Hall!?

STEPHEN. Have you gone into the insurance fund, the pension fund, the building society, the various applications of co-operation!?

Undershaft comes from the office, with a sheaf of telegrams in his hand.

UNDERSHAFT. Well, have you seen everything? I'm sorry I was called away. (*Indicating the telegrams*) Good news from Manchuria.

STEPHEN. Another Japanese victory?

UNDERSHAFT. Oh, I dont know. Which side wins does not concern us here. No: the good news is that the aerial battleship is a tremendous success. At the first trial it has wiped out a fort with three hundred soldiers in it.

CUSINS (*from the platform*) Dummy soldiers?

UNDERSHAFT (*striding across to Stephen and kicking the prostrate dummy brutally out of his way*) No: the real thing.

Cusins and Barbara exchange glances. Then Cusins sits on the step and buries his face in his hands. Barbara gravely lays her hand on his shoulder. He looks up at her in whimsical desperation.

UNDERSHAFT. Well, Stephen, what do you think of the place?

STEPHEN. Oh, magnificent. A perfect triumph of modern industry. Frankly, my dear father, I have been a fool: I had no idea of what it all meant: of the wonderful forethought, the power of organization, the administrative capacity, the financial genius, the colossal capital it represents. I have been repeating to myself as I came through your streets "Peace hath her victories no less renowned than War." I have only one misgiving about it all.

UNDERSHAFT. Out with it.

STEPHEN. Well, I cannot help thinking that all this provision for every want of your workmen may sap their independence and weaken their sense of responsibility. And greatly as we enjoyed our tea at that splendid restaurant—how they gave us all that luxury and cake and jam and cream for threepence I really cannot imagine!—still you must remember that restaurants break up home life. Look at the continent, for instance! Are you sure so much pampering is really good for the men's characters?

UNDERSHAFT. Well you see, my dear boy, when you are organizing civilization you have to make up your mind whether trouble and anxiety are good things or not. If you decide that they are, then, I take it, you simply dont organize civilization; and there you are, with trouble and anxiety enough to make us all angels! But if you decide the other way, you may as well go through with it. However, Stephen, our characters are safe here. A sufficient dose of anxiety is always provided by the fact that we may be blown to smithereens at any moment.

SARAH. By the way, papa, where do you make the explosives?

UNDERSHAFT. In separate little sheds, like that one. When one of them blows up, it costs very little; and only the people quite close to it are killed.

Stephen, who is quite close to it, looks at it rather scaredly, and moves away quickly to the cannon. At the same moment the door of the shed is thrown abruptly open; and a foreman in overalls and list slippers comes out on the little landing and holds the door for Lomax, who appears in the doorway.

LOMAX (*with studied coolness*) My good fellow: you neednt get into a state of nerves. Nothing's going to happen to you; and I suppose it wouldnt be the end of the world if anything did. A little bit of British pluck is what y o u want, old chap. (*He descends and strolls across to Sarah*).

UNDERSHAFT (*to the foreman*) Anything wrong, Bilton?

BILTON (*with ironic calm*) Gentleman walked into the high explosives shed and lit a cigaret, sir: thats all.

UNDERSHAFT. Ah, quite so. (*Going over to Lomax*) Do you happen to remember what you did with the match?

LOMAX. Oh come! I'm not a fool. I took jolly good care to blow it out before I chucked it away.

BILTON. The top of it was red hot inside, sir.

LOMAX. Well, suppose it was! I didn't chuck it into any of y o u r messes.

UNDERSHAFT. Think no more of it, Mr Lomax. By the way, would you mind lending me your matches?

LOMAX (*offering his box*) Certainly.

UNDERSHAFT. Thanks. (*He pockets the matches*).

LOMAX (*lecturing to the company generally*) You know, these high explosives dont go off like gunpowder, except when theyre in a gun. When theyre spread loose, you can put a match to them without the least risk: they just burn quietly like a bit of paper. (*Warming to the scientific interest of the subject*) Did you know that, Undershaft? Have you ever tried?

UNDERSHAFT. Not on a large scale, Mr. Lomax. Bilton will give you a sample of gun cotton when you are leaving if you ask him. You can experiment with it at home. (*Bilton looks puzzled*).

SARAH. Bilton will do nothing of the sort, papa. I suppose it's your business to blow up the Russians and Japs; but you might really stop short of blowing up poor Cholly. (*Bilton gives it up and retires into the shed*).

LOMAX. My ownest, there is no danger. (*He sits beside her on the shell*).

Lady Britomart arrives from the town with a bouquet.

LADY BRITOMART (*impetuously*) Andrew: you shouldnt have let me see this place.

UNDERSHAFT. Why, my dear?

LADY BRITOMART. Never mind why: you shouldnt have:

thats all. To think of all that (*indicating the town*) being yours! and that you have kept it to yourself all these years!

UNDERSHAFT. It does not belong to me. I belong to it. It is the Undershaft inheritance.

LADY BRITOMART. It is not. Your ridiculous cannons and that noisy banging foundry may be the Undershaft inheritance; but all that plate and linen, all that furniture and those houses and orchards and gardens belong to us. They belong to m e: they are not a man's business. I wont give them up. You must be out of your senses to throw them all away; and if you persist in such folly, I will call in a doctor.

UNDERSHAFT (*stooping to smell the bouquet*) Where did you get the flowers, my dear?

LADY BRITOMART. Your men presented them to me in your William Morris Labor Church.

CUSINS. Oh! It needed only that. A Labor Church! (*He mounts the firestep distractedly, and leans with his elbows on the parapet, turning his back to them*).

LADY BRITOMART. Yes, with Morris's words in mosaic letters ten feet high round the dome. NO MAN IS GOOD ENOUGH TO BE ANOTHER MAN'S MASTER. The cynicism of it!

UNDERSHAFT. It shocked the men at first, I am afraid. But now they take no more notice of it than of the ten commandments in church.

LADY BRITOMART. Andrew: you are trying to put me off the subject of the inheritance by profane jokes. Well, you shant. I dont ask it any longer for Stephen: he has inherited far too much of your perversity to be fit for it. But Barbara has rights as well as Stephen. Why should not Adolphus succeed to the inheritance? I could manage the town for him; and he can look after the cannons, if they are really necessary.

UNDERSHAFT. I should ask nothing better if Adolphus were a foundling. He is exactly the sort of new blood that is wanted in English business. But he's not a foundling; and theres an end of it. (*He makes for the office door*).

CUSINS (*turning to them*) Not quite. (*They all turn and stare at him*). I think— Mind! I am not committing myself in any way as to my future course—but I t h i n k the foundling difficulty can be got over. (*He jumps down to the emplacement*).

UNDERSHAFT (*coming back to him*) What do you mean?

CUSINS. Well, I have something to say which is in the nature of a confession.

SARAH.

LADY BRITOMART.   } Confession!

BARBARA.

STEPHEN.

LOMAX. Oh I say!

CUSINS. Yes, a confession. Listen, all. Until I met Barbara I thought myself in the main an honorable, truthful man, because I wanted the approval of my conscience more than I wanted anything else. But the moment I saw Barbara, I wanted her far more than the approval of my conscience.

LADY BRITOMART. Adolphus!

CUSINS. It is true. You accused me yourself, Lady Brit, of joining the Army to worship Barbara; and so I did. She bought my soul like a flower at a street corner; but she bought it for herself.

UNDERSHAFT. What! Not for Dionysos or another?

CUSINS. Dionysos and all the others are in herself. I adored what was divine in her, and was therefore a true worshipper. But I was romantic about her too. I thought she was a woman of the people, and that a marriage with a professor of Greek would be far beyond the wildest social ambitions of her rank.

LADY BRITOMART. Adolphus!!

LOMAX. Oh I s a y!!!

CUSINS. When I learnt the horrible truth—

LADY BRITOMART. What do you mean by the horrible truth, pray?

CUSINS. That she was enormously rich; that her grandfather

was an earl; that her father was the Prince of Darkness—

UNDERSHAFT. Chut!

CUSINS. —and that I was only an adventurer trying to catch a rich wife, then I stooped to deceive her about my birth.

BARBARA (rising) Dolly!

LADY BRITOMART. Your birth! Now Adolphus, dont dare to make up a wicked story for the sake of these wretched cannons. Remember: I have seen photographs of your parents; and the Agent General for South Western Australia knows them personally and has assured me that they are most respectable married people.

CUSINS. So they are in Australia; but here they are outcasts Their marriage is legal in Australia, but not in England. My mother is my father's deceased wife's sister; and in this island I am consequently a foundling. (Sensation).

BARBARA. Silly! (She climbs to the cannon, and leans, listening, in the angle it makes with the parapet).

CUSINS. Is the subterfuge good enough, Machiavelli?

UNDERSHAFT (thoughtfully) Biddy: this may be a way out of the difficulty.

LADY BRITOMART. Stuff! A man cant make cannons any the better for being his own cousin instead of his proper self. (She sits down on the rug with a bounce that expresses her downright contempt for their casuistry).

UNDERSHAFT (to Cusins) You are an educated man. That is against the tradition.

CUSINS. Once in ten thousand times it happens that the schoolboy is a born master of what they try to teach him. Greek has not destroyed my mind: it has nourished it. Besides, I did not learn it at an English public school.

UNDERSHAFT. Hm! Well, I cannot afford to be too particular: you have cornered the foundling market. Let it pass. You are eligible, Euripides: you are eligible.

BARBARA. Dolly: yesterday morning, when Stephen told us all about the tradition, you became very silent; and you have been strange and excited ever since. Were you thinking of your birth then?

CUSINS. When the finger of Destiny suddenly points at a man in the middle of his breakfast, it makes him thoughtful.

UNDERSHAFT. Aha! You have had your eye on the business, my young friend, have you?

CUSINS. Take care! There is an abyss of moral horror between me and your accursed aerial battleships.

UNDERSHAFT. Never mind the abyss for the present. Let us settle the practical details and leave your final decision open. You know that you will have to change your name. Do you object to that?

CUSINS. Would any man named Adolphus—any man called Dolly!—object to be called something else?

UNDERSHAFT. Good. Now, as to money! I propose to treat you handsomely from the beginning. You shall start at a thousand a year.

CUSINS (with sudden heat, his spectacles twinkling with mischief) A thousand! You dare offer a miserable thousand to the son-in-law of a millionaire! No, by Heavens, Machiavelli! you shall not cheat m e. You cannot do without me; and I can do without you. I must have two thousand five hundred a year for two years. At the end of that time, if I am a failure, I go. But if I am a success, and stay on, you must give me the other five thousand.

UNDERSHAFT. What other five thousand?

CUSINS. To make the two years up to five thousand a year. The two thousand five hundred is only half pay in case I should turn out a failure. The third year I must have ten per cent on the profits.

UNDERSHAFT (taken aback) Ten per cent! Why, man, do you know what my profits are?

CUSINS. Enormous, I hope: otherwise I shall require twenty-five per cent.

UNDERSHAFT. But, Mr Cusins, this is a serious matter of

business. You are not bringing any capital into the concern.

CUSINS. What! no capital! Is my mastery of Greek no capital? Is my access to the subtlest thought, the loftiest poetry yet attained by humanity, no capital? My character! my intellect! my life! my career! what Barbara calls my soul! are these no capital? Say another word; and I double my salary.

UNDERSHAFT. Be reasonable—

CUSINS (*peremptorily*) Mr Undershaft: you have my terms. Take them or leave them.

UNDERSHAFT (*recovering himself*) Very well. I note your terms; and I offer you half.

CUSINS (*disgusted*) Half!

UNDERSHAFT (*firmly*) Half.

CUSINS. You call yourself a gentleman; and you offer me half!!

UNDERSHAFT. I do not call myself a gentleman; but I offer you half.

CUSINS. This to your future partner! your successor! your son-in-law!

BARBARA. You are selling your own soul, Dolly, not mine. Leave me out of the bargain, please.

UNDERSHAFT. Come! I will go a step further for Barbara's sake. I will give you three fifths; but that is my last word.

CUSINS. Done!

LOMAX. Done in the eye! Why, I get only eight hundred, you know.

CUSINS. By the way, Mac, I am a classical scholar, not an arithmetical one. Is three fifths more than half or less?

UNDERSHAFT. More, of course.

CUSINS. I would have taken two hundred and fifty. How you can succeed in business when you are willing to pay all that money to a University don who is obviously not worth a junior clerk's wages!—well! What will Lazarus say?

UNDERSHAFT. Lazarus is a gentle romantic Jew who cares for nothing but string quartets and stalls at fashionable theatres.

He will be blamed for your rapacity in money matters, poor fellow! as he has hitherto been blamed for mine. You are a shark of the first order, Euripides. So much the better for the firm!

BARBARA. Is the bargain closed, Dolly? Does your soul belong to him now?

CUSINS. No: the price is settled: that is all. The real tug of war is still to come. What about the moral question?

LADY BRITOMART. There is no moral question in the matter at all, Adolphus. You must simply sell cannons and weapons to people whose cause is right and just, and refuse them to foreigners and criminals.

UNDERSHAFT (*determinedly*) No: none of that. You must keep the true faith of an Armorer, or you dont come in here.

CUSINS. What on earth is the true faith of an Armorer?

UNDERSHAFT. To give arms to all men who offer an honest price for them, without respect of persons or principles: to aristocrat and republican, to Nihilist and Tsar, to Capitalist and Socialist, to Protestant and Catholic, to burglar and policeman, to black man, white man and yellow man, to all sorts and conditions, all nationalities, all faiths, all follies, all causes and all crimes. The first Undershaft wrote up in his shop IF GOD GAVE THE HAND, LET NOT MAN WITHHOLD THE SWORD. The second wrote up ALL HAVE THE RIGHT TO FIGHT: NONE HAVE THE RIGHT TO JUDGE. The third wrote up TO MAN THE WEAPON: TO HEAVEN THE VICTORY. The fourth had no literary turn; so he did not write up anything; but he sold cannons to Napoleon under the nose of George the Third. The fifth wrote up PEACE SHALL NOT PREVAIL SAVE WITH A SWORD IN HER HAND. The sixth, my master, was the best of all. He wrote up NOTHING IS EVER DONE IN THIS WORLD UNTIL MEN ARE PREPARED TO KILL ONE ANOTHER IF IT IS NOT DONE. After that, there was nothing left for the seventh to say. So he wrote up, simply, UNASHAMED.

CUSINS. My good Machiavelli, I shall certainly write something up on the wall; only, as I shall write it in Greek, you wont be able to read it. But as to your Armorer's faith, if I take my neck out of the noose of my own morality I am not going to put it into the noose of yours. I shall sell cannons to whom I please and refuse them to whom I please. So there!

UNDERSHAFT. From the moment when you become Andrew Undershaft, you will never do as you please again. Dont come here lusting for power, young man.

CUSINS. If power were my aim I should not come here for it. Y o u have no power.

UNDERSHAFT. None of my own, certainly.

CUSINS. I have more power than you, more will. You do not drive this place: it drives you. And what drives the place?

UNDERSHAFT (*enigmatically*) A will of which I am a part.

BARBARA (*startled*) Father! Do you know what you are saying; or are you laying a snare for my soul?

CUSINS. Dont listen to his metaphysics, Barbara. The place is driven by the most rascally part of society, the money hunters, the pleasure hunters, the military promotion hunters; and he is their slave.

UNDERSHAFT. Not necessarily. Remember the Armorer's Faith. I will take an order from a good man as cheerfully as from a bad one. If you good people prefer preaching and shirking to buying my weapons and fighting the rascals, dont blame me. I can make cannons: I cannot make courage and conviction. Bah! you tire me, Euripides, with your morality mongering. Ask Barbara: she understands. (*He suddenly reaches up and takes Barbara's hands, looking powerfully into her eyes*). Tell him, my love, what power really means.

BARBARA (*hypnotized*) Before I joined the Salvation Army, I was in my own power; and the consequence was that I never knew what to do with myself. When I joined it, I had not time enough for all the things I had to do.

UNDERSHAFT (*approvingly*) Just so. And why was that, do you suppose?

BARBARA. Yesterday I should have said, because I was in the power of God. (*She resumes her self-possession, withdrawing her hands from his with a power equal to his own*). But you came and shewed me that I was in the power of Bodger and Undershaft. Today I feel—oh! how can I put it into words? Sarah: do you remember the earthquake at Cannes, when we were little children?—how little the surprise of the first shock matters compared to the dread and horror of waiting for the second? That is how I feel in this place today. I stood on the rock I thought eternal; and without a word of warning it reeled and crumbled under me. I was safe with an infinite wisdom watching me, an army marching to Salvation with me; and in a moment, at a stroke of your pen in a cheque book, I stood alone; and the heavens were empty. That was the first shock of the earthquake: I am waiting for the second.

UNDERSHAFT. Come, come, my daughter! dont make too much of your little tinpot tragedy. What do we do here when we spend years of work and thought and thousands of pounds of solid cash on a new gun or an aerial battleship that turns out just a hairsbreadth wrong after all? Scrap it. Scrap it without wasting another hour or another pound on it. Well, you have made for yourself something that you call a morality or a religion or what not. It doesnt fit the facts. Well, scrap it. Scrap it and get one that does fit. That is what is wrong with the world at present. It scraps its obsolete steam engines and dynamos; but it wont scrap its old prejudices and its old moralities and its old religions and its old political constitutions. Whats the result? In machinery it does very well; but in morals and religion and politics it is working at a loss that brings it nearer bankruptcy every year. Dont persist in that folly. If your old religion broke down yesterday, get a newer and a better one for tomorrow.

BARBARA. Oh how gladly I would take a better one to my soul! But you offer me a worse one. (*Turning on him with sudden vehemence*) Justify yourself: shew me some light through the darkness of this dreadful place, with its beautifully clean workshops, and respectable workmen, and model homes.

UNDERSHAFT. Cleanliness and respectability do not need justification, Barbara: they justify themselves. I see no darkness here, no dreadfulness. In your Salvation shelter I saw poverty, misery, cold and hunger. You gave them bread and treacle and dreams of heaven. I give from thirty shillings a week to twelve thousand a year. They find their own dreams; but I look after the drainage.

BARBARA. And their souls?

UNDERSHAFT. I save their souls just as I saved yours.

BARBARA (*revolted*) Y o u saved my soul! What do you mean?

UNDERSHAFT. I fed you and clothed you and housed you. I took care that you should have money enough to live handsomely—more than enough; so that you could be wasteful, careless, generous. That saved your soul from the seven deadly sins.

BARBARA (*bewildered*) The seven deadly sins!

UNDERSHAFT. Yes, the deadly seven. (*Counting on his fingers*) Food, clothing, firing, rent, taxes, respectability and children. Nothing can lift those seven millstones from Man's neck but money; and the spirit cannot soar until the millstones are lifted. I lifted them from your spirit. I enabled Barbara to become Major Barbara; and I saved her from the crime of poverty.

CUSINS. Do you call poverty a crime?

UNDERSHAFT. The worst of crimes. All the other crimes are virtues beside it: all the other dishonors are chivalry itself by comparison. Poverty blights whole cities; spreads horrible pestilences; strikes dead the very souls of all who come within sight, sound or smell of it. What y o u call crime is nothing: a murder here and a theft there, a blow now and a curse then: what do they matter? they are only the accidents and illnesses of life: there are not fifty genuine professional criminals in London. But there are millions of poor people, abject people, dirty people, ill fed, ill clothed people. They poison us morally and physically: they kill the happiness of society: they force us to do away with our own liberties and to organize unnatural cruelties for fear they should rise against us and drag us down into their abyss. Only fools fear crime: we all fear poverty. Pah! (*turning on Barbara*) you talk of your half-saved ruffian in West Ham: you accuse me of dragging his soul back to per- dition. Well, bring him to me here; and I will drag his soul back again to salvation for you. Not by words and dreams; but by thirtyeight shillings a week, a sound house in a handsome street, and a permanent job. In three weeks he will have a fancy waistcoat; in three months a tall hat and a chapel sitting; before the end of the year he will shake hands with a duchess at a Primrose League meeting, and join the Conservative Party.

BARBARA. And will he be the better for that?

UNDERSHAFT. You know he will. Dont be a hypocrite, Bar- bara. He will be better fed, better housed, better clothed, better behaved; and his children will be pounds heavier and bigger. That will be better than an American cloth mattress in a shel- ter, chopping firewood, eating bread and treacle, and being forced to kneel down from time to time to thank heaven for it: knee drill, I think you call it. It is cheap work converting starving men with a Bible in one hand and a slice of bread in the other. I will undertake to convert West Ham to Mahomet- anism on the same terms. Try your hand on m y men: their souls are hungry because their bodies are full.

BARBARA. And leave the east end to starve?

UNDERSHAFT (*his energetic tone dropping into one of bitter and brooding remembrance*) I was an east ender. I moralized and starved until one day I swore that I would be a full-fed free man at all costs—that nothing should stop me except a bul- let, neither reason nor morals nor the lives of other men. I said "Thou shalt starve ere I starve"; and with that word I became free and great. I was a dangerous man until I had my will: now I am a useful, beneficent, kindly person. That is the history of most self-made millionaires, I fancy. When it is the history of every Englishman we shall have an England worth living in.

LADY BRITOMART. Stop making speeches, Andrew. This is not the place for them.

UNDERSHAFT (*punctured*) My dear: I have no other means of conveying my ideas.

LADY BRITOMART. Your ideas are nonsense. You got on because you were selfish and unscrupulous.

UNDERSHAFT. Not at all. I had the strongest scruples about poverty and starvation. Your moralists are quite unscrupulous about both: they make virtues of them. I had rather be a thief than a pauper. I had rather be a murderer than a slave. I dont want to be either; but if you force the alternative on me, then, by Heaven, I'll choose the braver and more moral one. I hate poverty and slavery worse than any other crimes whatsoever. And let me tell you this. Poverty and slavery have stood up for centuries to your sermons and leading articles: they will not stand up to my machine guns. Dont preach at them: dont reason with them. Kill them.

BARBARA. Killing. Is that your remedy for everything?

UNDERSHAFT. It is the final test of conviction, the only lever strong enough to overturn a social system, the only way of saying Must. Let six hundred and seventy fools loose in the street; and three policemen can scatter them. But huddle them together in a certain house in Westminster; and let them go through certain ceremonies and call themselves certain names until at last they get the courage to kill; and your six hundred and seventy fools become a government. Your pious mob fills up ballot papers and imagines it is governing its masters; but the ballot paper that really governs is the paper that has a bullet wrapped up in it.

CUSINS. That is perhaps why, like most intelligent people, I never vote.

UNDERSHAFT. Vote! Bah! When you vote, you only change the names of the cabinet. When you shoot, you pull down governments, inaugurate new epochs, abolish old orders and set up new. Is that historically true, Mr Learned Man, or is it not?

CUSINS. It is historically true. I loathe having to admit it. I repudiate your sentiments. I abhor your nature. I defy you in every possible way. Still, it is true. But it ought not to be true.

UNDERSHAFT. Ought! ought! ought! ought! ought! Are you going to spend your life saying ought, like the rest of our moralists? Turn your oughts into shalls, man. Come and make explosives with me. Whatever can blow men up can blow society up. The history of the world is the history of those who had courage enough to embrace this truth. Have you the courage to embrace it, Barbara?

LADY BRITOMART. Barbara, I positively forbid you to listen to your father's abominable wickedness. And you, Adolphus, ought to know better than to go about saying that wrong things are true. What does it matter whether they are true if they are wrong?

UNDERSHAFT. What does it matter whether they are wrong if they are true?

LADY BRITOMART (*rising*) Children: come home instantly. Andrew: I am exceedingly sorry I allowed you to call on us. You are wickeder than ever. Come at once.

BARBARA (*shaking her head*) It's no use running away from wicked people, mamma.

LADY BRITOMART. It is every use. It shews your disapprobation of them.

BARBARA. It does not save them.

LADY BRITOMART. I can see that you are going to disobey me. Sarah: are you coming home or are you not?

SARAH. I daresay it's very wicked of papa to make cannons; but I dont think I shall cut him on that account.

LOMAX (*pouring oil on the troubled waters*) The fact is, you know, there is a certain amount of tosh about this notion of wickedness. It doesnt work. You must look at facts. Not that

I would say a word in favor of anything wrong; but then, you see, all sorts of chaps are always doing all sorts of things; and we have to fit them in somehow, dont you know. What I mean is that you cant go cutting everybody; and thats about what it comes to. (*Their rapt attention to his eloquence makes him nervous*). Perhaps I dont make myself clear.

LADY BRITOMART. You are lucidity itself, Charles. Because Andrew is successful and has plenty of money to give to Sarah, you will flatter him and encourage him in his wickedness.

LOMAX (*unruffled*) Well, where the carcase is, there will the eagles be gathered, dont you know. (*To Undershaft*) Eh? What?

UNDERSHAFT. Precisely. By the way, m a y I call you Charles?

LOMAX. Delighted. Cholly is the usual ticket.

UNDERSHAFT (*to Lady Britomart*) Biddy—

LADY BRITOMART (*violently*) Dont dare call me Biddy. Charles Lomax: you are a fool. Adolphus Cusins: you are a Jesuit. Stephen: you are a prig. Barbara: you are a lunatic. Andrew: you are a vulgar tradesman. Now you all know my opinion; and my conscience is clear, at all events. (*She sits down with a vehemence that the rug fortunately softens*).

UNDERSHAFT. My dear: you are the incarnation of morality. (*She snorts*). Your conscience is clear and your duty done when you have called everybody names. Come, Euripides! it is getting late; and we all want to go home. Make up your mind.

CUSINS. Understand this, you old demon—

LADY BRITOMART. Adolphus!

UNDERSHAFT. Let him alone, Biddy. Proceed, Euripides.

CUSINS. You have me in a horrible dilemma. I want Barbara.

UNDERSHAFT. Like all young men, you greatly exaggerate the difference between one young woman and another.

BARBARA. Quite true, Dolly.

CUSINS. I also want to avoid being a rascal.

UNDERSHAFT (*with biting contempt*) You lust for personal righteousness, for self-approval, for what you call a good conscience, for what Barbara calls salvation, for what I call patronizing people who are not so lucky as yourself.

CUSINS. I do not: all the poet in me recoils from being a good man. But there are things in me that I must reckon with. Pity—

UNDERSHAFT. Pity! The scavenger of misery.

CUSINS. Well, love.

UNDERSHAFT. I know. You love the needy and the outcast: you love the oppressed races, the negro, the Indian ryot, the underdog everywhere. Do you love the Japanese? Do you love the French? Do you love the English?

CUSINS. No. Every true Englishman detests the English. We are the wickedest nation on earth; and our success is a moral horror.

UNDERSHAFT. That is what comes of your gospel of love, is it?

CUSINS. May I not love even my father-in-law?

UNDERSHAFT. Who wants your love, man? By what right do you take the liberty of offering it to me? I will have your due heed and respect, or I will kill you. But your love! Damn your impertinence!

CUSINS (grinning) I may not be able to control my affections, Mac.

UNDERSHAFT. You are fencing, Euripides. You are weakening: your grip is slipping. Come! try your last weapon. Pity and love have broken in your hand: forgiveness is still left.

CUSINS. No: forgiveness is a beggar's refuge. I am with you there: we must pay our debts.

UNDERSHAFT. Well said. Come! you will suit me. Remember the words of Plato.

CUSINS (starting) Plato! Y o u dare quote Plato to m e!

UNDERSHAFT. Plato says, my friend, that society cannot be saved until either the Professors of Greek take to making gunpowder, or else the makers of gunpowder become Professors of Greek.

CUSINS. Oh, tempter, cunning tempter!

UNDERSHAFT. Come! choose, man, choose.

CUSINS. But perhaps Barbara will not marry me if I make the wrong choice.

BARBARA. Perhaps not.

CUSINS (*desperately perplexed*) You hear!

BARBARA. Father: do you love nobody?

UNDERSHAFT. I love my best friend.

LADY BRITOMART. And who is that, pray?

UNDERSHAFT. My bravest enemy. That is the man who keeps me up to the mark.

CUSINS. You know, the creature is really a sort of poet in his way. Suppose he is a great man, after all!

UNDERSHAFT. Suppose you stop talking and make up your mind, my young friend.

CUSINS. But you are driving me against my nature. I hate war.

UNDERSHAFT. Hatred is the coward's revenge for being intimidated. Dare you make war on war? Here are the means: my friend Mr Lomax is sitting on them.

LOMAX (*springing up*) Oh I say! You dont mean that this thing is loaded, do you? My ownest: come off it.

SARAH (*sitting placidly on the shell*) If I am to be blown up, the more thoroughly it is done the better. Dont fuss, Cholly.

LOMAX (*to Undershaft, strongly remonstrant*) Your own daughter, you know.

UNDERSHAFT. So I see. (*To Cusins*) Well, my friend, may we expect you here at six tomorrow morning?

CUSINS (*firmly*) Not on any account. I will see the whole establishment blown up with its own dynamite before I will get up at five. My hours are healthy, rational hours: eleven to five.

UNDERSHAFT. Come when you please: before a week you will come at six and stay until I turn you out for the sake of your health. (*Calling*) Bilton! (*He turns to Lady Britomart, who rises*). My dear: let us leave these two young people to themselves for a moment. (*Bilton comes from the shed*). I am going to take you through the gun cotton shed.

BILTON (*barring the way*) You cant take anything explosive in here, sir.

LADY BRITOMART. What do you mean? Are you alluding to me?

BILTON (*unmoved*) No, maam. Mr Undershaft has the other gentleman's matches in his pocket.

LADY BRITOMART (*abruptly*) Oh! I beg your pardon. (*She goes into the shed*).

UNDERSHAFT. Quite right, Bilton, quite right: here you are. (*He gives Bilton the box of matches*). Come, Stephen. Come, Charles. Bring Sarah. (*He passes into the shed*).

Bilton opens the box and deliberately drops the matches into the fire-bucket.

LOMAX. Oh I say! (*Bilton stolidly hands him the empty box*). Infernal nonsense! Pure scientific ignorance! (*He goes in*).

SARAH. Am I all right, Bilton?

BILTON. Youll have to put on list slippers, miss: thats all. Weve got em inside. (*She goes in*).

STEPHEN (*very seriously to Cusins*) Dolly, old fellow, think. Think before you decide. Do you feel that you are a sufficiently practical man? It is a huge undertaking, an enormous responsibility. All this mass of business will be Greek to you.

CUSINS. Oh, I think it will be much less difficult than Greek.

STEPHEN. Well, I just want to say this before I leave you to yourselves. Dont let anything I have said about right and wrong prejudice you against this great chance in life. I have satisfied myself that the business is one of the highest character and a credit to our company. (*Emotionally*) I am very proud of my father. I— (*Unable to proceed, he presses Cusins' hand and goes hastily into the shed, followed by Bilton*).

Barbara and Cusins, left alone together, look at one another silently.

CUSINS. Barbara: I am going to accept this offer.

BARBARA. I thought you would.

CUSINS. You understand, dont you, that I had to decide without consulting you. If I had thrown the burden of the choice on you, you would sooner or later have despised me for it.

BARBARA. Yes: I did not want you to sell your soul for me any more than for this inheritance.

CUSINS. It is not the sale of my soul that troubles me: I have sold it too often to care about that. I have sold it for a professorship. I have sold it for an income. I have sold it to escape being imprisoned for refusing to pay taxes for hangmen's ropes and unjust wars and things that I abhor. What is all human conduct but the daily and hourly sale of our souls for trifles? What I am now selling it for is neither money nor position nor comfort, but for reality and for power.

BARBARA. You know that you will have no power, and that he has none.

CUSINS. I know. It is not for myself alone. I want to make power for the world.

BARBARA. I want to make power for the world too; but it must be spiritual power.

CUSINS. I think all power is spiritual: these cannons will not go off by themselves. I have tried to make spiritual power by teaching Greek. But the world can never be really touched by a dead language and a dead civilization. The people must have power; and the people cannot have Greek. Now the power that is made here can be wielded by all men.

BARBARA. Power to burn women's houses down and kill their sons and tear their husbands to pieces.

CUSINS. You cannot have power for good without having power for evil too. Even mother's milk nourishes murderers as well as heroes. This power which only tears men's bodies to pieces has never been so horribly abused as the intellectual power, the imaginative power, the poetic, religious power that enslave men's souls. As a teacher of Greek I gave the intellectual man weapons against the common man. I now want to give the common man weapons against the intellectual man. I love the common people. I want to arm them against the lawyers, the doctors, the priests, the literary men, the professors, the artists, and the politicians, who, once in authority, are more disastrous and tyrannical than all the fools, rascals, and impostors. I want a power simple enough for common men to use, yet strong enough to force the intellectual oligarchy to use its genius for the general good.

BARBARA. Is there no higher power than that (*pointing to the shell*).

CUSINS. Yes; but that power can destroy the higher powers just as a tiger can destroy a man: therefore Man must master that power first. I admitted this when the Turks and Greeks were last at war. My best pupil went out to fight for Hellas. My parting gift to him was not a copy of Plato's Republic, but a revolver and a hundred Undershaft cartridges. The blood of every Turk he shot—if he shot any—is on my head as well as on Undershaft's. That act committed me to this place for ever. Your father's challenge has beaten me. Dare I make war on war? I dare. I must. I will. And now, is it all over between us?

BARBARA (*touched by his evident dread of her answer*) Silly baby Dolly! How could it be!

CUSINS (*overjoyed*) Then you—you—you— Oh for my drum! (*He flourishes imaginary drumsticks*).

BARBARA (*angered by his levity*) Take care, Dolly, take care. Oh, if only I could get away from you and from father and from it all! if I could have the wings of a dove and fly away to heaven!

CUSINS. And leave me!

BARBARA. Yes, you, and all the other naughty mischievous children of men. But I cant. I was happy in the Salvation Army for a moment. I escaped from the world into a paradise of enthusiasm and prayer and soul saving; but the moment our money ran short, it all came back to Bodger: it was he who

saved our people: he, and the Prince of Darkness, my papa.
Undershaft and Bodger: their hands stretch everywhere: when
we feed a starving fellow creature, it is with their bread, because there is no other bread; when we tend the sick, it is in
the hospitals they endow; if we turn from the churches they
build, we must kneel on the stones of the streets they pave. As
long as that lasts, there is no getting away from them. Turning our backs on Bodger and Undershaft is turning our backs
on life.

CUSINS. I thought you were determined to turn your back
on the wicked side of life.

BARBARA. There is no wicked side: life is all one. And I never
wanted to shirk my share in whatever evil must be endured,
whether it be sin or suffering. I wish I could cure you of
middle-class ideas, Dolly.

CUSINS (*gasping*) Middle cl—! A snub! A social snub to m e!
from the daughter of a foundling!

BARBARA. That is why I have no class, Dolly: I come straight
out of the heart of the whole people. If I were middle-class I
should turn my back on my father's business; and we should
both live in an artistic drawing room, with you reading the
reviews in one corner, and I in the other at the piano, playing
Schumann: both very superior persons, and neither of us a bit
of use. Sooner than that, I would sweep out the guncotton
shed, or be one of Bodger's barmaids. Do you know what
would have happened if you had refused papa's offer?

CUSINS. I wonder!

BARBARA. I should have given you up and married the man
who accepted it. After all, my dear old mother has more sense
than any of you. I felt like her when I saw this place—felt that
I must have it—that never, never, never could I let it go; only
she thought it was the houses and the kitchen ranges and the
linen and china, when it was really all the human souls to be
saved: not weak souls in starved bodies, sobbing with gratitude
for a scrap of bread and treacle, but fullfed, quarrelsome, snob-

bish, uppish creatures, all standing on their little rights and dignities, and thinking that my father ought to be greatly obliged to them for making so much money for him—and so he ought. That is where salvation is really wanted. My father shall never throw it in my teeth again that my converts were bribed with bread. (*She is transfigured*). I have got rid of the bribe of bread. I have got rid of the bribe of heaven. Let God's work be done for its own sake: the work he had to create us to do because it cannot be done except by living men and women. When I die, let him be in my debt, not I in his; and let me forgive him as becomes a woman of my rank.

CUSINS. Then the way of life lies through the factory of death?

BARBARA. Yes, through the raising of hell to heaven and of man to God, through the unveiling of an eternal light in the Valley of The Shadow. (*Seizing him with both hands*) Oh, did you think my courage would never come back? did you believe that I was a deserter? that I, who have stood in the streets, and taken my people to my heart, and talked of the holiest and greatest things with them, could ever turn back and chatter foolishly to fashionable people about nothing in a drawing room? Never, never, never, never: Major Barbara will die with the colors. Oh! and I have my dear little Dolly boy still; and he has found me my place and my work. Glory Hallelujah! (*She kisses him*).

CUSINS. My dearest: consider my delicate health. I cannot stand as much happiness as you can.

BARBARA. Yes: it is not easy work being in love with me, is it? But it's good for you. (*She runs to the shed, and calls, childlike*) Mamma! Mamma! (*Bilton comes out of the shed, followed by Undershaft*). I want Mamma.

UNDERSHAFT. She is taking off her list slippers, dear. (*He passes on to Cusins*). Well? What does she say?

CUSINS. She has gone right up into the skies.

LADY BRITOMART (*coming from the shed and stopping on the*

steps, obstructing Sarah, who follows with Lomax. Barbara clutches like a baby at her mother's skirt) Barbara: when will you learn to be independent and to act and think for yourself? I know as well as possible what that cry of "Mamma, Mamma," means. Always running to me!

SARAH (*touching Lady Britomart's ribs with her finger tips and imitating a bicycle horn*) Pip! pip!

LADY BRITOMART (*highly indignant*) How dare you say Pip! pip! to me, Sarah? You are both very naughty children. What do you want, Barbara?

BARBARA. I want a house in the village to live in with Dolly. (*Dragging at the skirt*) Come and tell me which one to take.

UNDERSHAFT (*to Cusins*) Six o'clock tomorrow morning, Euripides.

Androcles and the Lion

A FABLE PLAY

PREFACE ON THE PROSPECTS
OF CHRISTIANITY

WHY NOT GIVE CHRISTIANITY A TRIAL;

THE QUESTION seems a hopeless one after 2000 years of resolute adherence to the old cry of "Not this man, but Barabbas." Yet it is beginning to look as if Barabbas was a failure, in spite of his strong right hand, his victories, his empires, his millions of money, and his moralities and churches and political constitutions. "This man" has not been a failure yet; for nobody has ever been sane enough to try his way. But he has had one quaint triumph. Barabbas has stolen his name and taken his cross as a standard. There is a sort of compliment in that. There is even a sort of loyalty in it, like that of the brigand who breaks every law and yet claims to be a patriotic subject of the king who makes them. We have always had a curious feeling that though we crucified Christ on a stick, he somehow managed to get hold of the right end of it, and that if we were better men we might try his plan. There have been one or two grotesque attempts at it by inadequate people, such as the Kingdom of God in Munster, which was ended by a crucifixion so much more atrocious than the one on Calvary that the bishop who took the part of Annas went home and died of horror. But responsible people have never made such attempts. The moneyed, respectable, capable world has been steadily anti-Christian and Barabbasque since the crucifixion; and the specific doctrine of Jesus has not in all that time been put into political or general social practice. I am no more a Christian than Pilate was, or you, gentle reader; and yet, like Pilate, I greatly prefer Jesus to Annas and Caiaphas; and I am ready to admit that after contemplating the world and human nature for nearly sixty years, I see no way out of the world's misery but the way which would have been found by Christ's will if he had undertaken the work of a modern practical statesman.

Pray do not at this early point lose patience with me and shut the book. I assure you I am as sceptical and scientific and modern a thinker as you will find anywhere. I grant you I know a great deal more about economics and politics than Jesus did, and can do things he could not do. I am by all Barabbasque standards a person of much better character and standing, and greater practical sense. I have no sympathy with vagabonds and talkers who try to reform society by taking men away from their regular productive work and making vagabonds and talkers of them too; and if I had been Pilate I should have recognized as plainly as he the necessity for suppressing attacks on the existing social order, however corrupt that order might be, by people with no knowledge of government and no power to construct political machinery to carry out their views, acting on the very dangerous delusion that the end of the world was at hand. I make no defence of such Christians as Savonarola and John of Leyden: they were scuttling the ship before they had learned how to build a raft; and it became necessary to throw them overboard to save the crew. I say this to set myself right with respectable society; but I must still insist that if Jesus could have worked out the practical problems of a Communist constitution, an admitted obligation to deal with crime without revenge or punishment, and a full assumption by humanity of divine responsibilities, he would have conferred an incalculable benefit on mankind, because these distinctive demands of his are now turning out to be good sense and sound economics.

I say distinctive, because his common humanity and his subjection to time and space (that is, to the Syrian life of his period) involved his belief in many things, true and false, that in no way distinguish him from other Syrians of that time. But such common beliefs do not constitute specific Christianity any more than wearing a beard, working in a carpenter's shop, or believing that the earth is flat and that the stars could drop on it

from heaven like hailstones. Christianity interests practical
statesmen now because of the doctrines that distinguished Christ
from the Jews and the Barabbasques generally, including ourselves.

WHY JESUS MORE THAN ANOTHER?

I do not imply, however, that these doctrines were peculiar to
Christ. A doctrine peculiar to one man would be only a craze,
unless its comprehension depended on a development of human
faculty so rare that only one exceptionally gifted man possessed
it. But even in this case it would be useless, because incapable
of spreading. Christianity is a step in moral evolution which is
independent of any individual preacher. If Jesus had never existed (and that he ever existed in any other sense than that in
which Shakespear's Hamlet existed has been vigorously questioned) Tolstoy would have thought and taught and quarrelled
with the Greek Church all the same. Their creed has been frag-
mentarily practised to a considerable extent in spite of the fact
that the laws of all countries treat it, in effect, as criminal. Many
of its advocates have been militant atheists. But for some reason
the imagination of white mankind has picked out Jesus of Nazareth as *the* Christ, and attributed all the Christian doctrines
to him; and as it is the doctrine and not the man that matters,
and, as, besides, one symbol is as good as another provided everyone attaches the same meaning to it, I raise, for the moment, no
question as to how far the gospels are original, and how far they
consist of Greek and Chinese interpolations. The record that
Jesus said certain things is not invalidated by a demonstration
that Confucius said them before him. Those who claim a literal
divine paternity for him cannot be silenced by the discovery
that the same claim was made for Alexander and Augustus. And
I am not just now concerned with the credibility of the gospels
as records of fact; for I am not acting as a detective, but turning
our modern lights on to certain ideas and doctrines in them
which disentangle themselves from the rest because they are

flatly contrary to common practice, common sense and common
belief, and yet have, in the teeth of dogged incredulity and
recalcitrance, produced an irresistible impression that Christ,
though rejected by his posterity as an unpractical dreamer, and
executed by his contemporaries as a dangerous anarchist and
blasphemous madman, was greater than his judges.

WAS JESUS A COWARD?

I know quite well that this impression of superiority is not
produced on everyone, even of those who profess extreme susceptibility to it. Setting aside the huge mass of inculcated Christ-
worship which has no real significance because it has no intelligence, there is, among people who are really free to think
for themselves on the subject, a great deal of hearty dislike of
Jesus and of contempt for his failure to save himself and overcome his enemies by personal bravery and cunning as Mahomet
did. I have heard this feeling expressed far more impatiently by
persons brought up in England as Christians than by Mahometans, who are, like their prophet, very civil to Jesus, and allow
him a place in their esteem and veneration at least as high as
we accord to John the Baptist. But this British bulldog contempt
is founded on a complete misconception of his reasons for submitting voluntarily to an ordeal of torment and death. The
modern Secularist is often so determined to regard Jesus as a
man like himself and nothing more, that he slips unconsciously
into the error of assuming that Jesus shared that view. But it is
quite clear from the New Testament writers (the chief authorities for believing that Jesus ever existed) that Jesus at the time
of his death believed himself to be the Christ, a divine personage. It is therefore absurd to criticize his conduct before Pilate as
if he were Colonel Roosevelt or Admiral von Tirpitz or even
Mahomet. Whether you accept his belief in his divinity as fully
as Simon Peter did, or reject it as a delusion which led him to
submit to torture and sacrifice his life without resistance in the
conviction that he would presently rise again in glory, you are

equally bound to admit that, far from behaving like a coward or a sheep, he shewed considerable physical fortitude in going through a cruel ordeal against which he could have defended himself as effectually as he cleared the money-changers out of the temple. "Gentle Jesus, meek and mild" is a snivelling modern invention, with no warrant in the gospels. St Matthew would as soon have thought of applying such adjectives to Judas Maccabeus as to Jesus; and even St Luke, who makes Jesus polite and gracious, does not make him meek. The picture of him as an English curate of the farcical comedy type, too meek to fight a policeman, and everybody's butt, may be useful in the nursery to soften children; but that such a figure could ever have become a centre of the world's attention is too absurd for discussion: grown men and women may speak kindly of a harmless creature who utters amiable sentiments and is a helpless nincompoop when he is called on to defend them; but they will not follow him, nor do what he tells them, because they do not wish to share his defeat and disgrace.

WAS JESUS A MARTYR?

It is important therefore that we should clear our minds of the notion that Jesus died, as some of us are in the habit of declaring, for his social and political opinions. There have been many martyrs to those opinions; but he was not one of them, nor, as his words shew, did he see any more sense in martyrdom than Galileo did. He was executed by the Jews for the blasphemy of claiming to be a God; and Pilate, to whom this was a mere piece of superstitious nonsense, let them execute him as the cheapest way of keeping them quiet, on the formal plea that he had committed treason against Rome by saying that he was the King of the Jews. He was not falsely accused, nor denied full opportunities of defending himself. The proceedings were quite straightforward and regular; and Pilate, to whom the appeal lay, favored him and despised his judges, and was evidently willing enough to be conciliated. But instead of denying the charge, Jesus repeated the offence. He knew what he was doing: he had alienated numbers of his own disciples and been stoned in the streets for doing it before. He was not lying: he believed literally what he said. The horror of the High Priest was perfectly natural: he was a Primate confronted with a heterodox street preacher uttering what seemed to him an appalling and impudent blasphemy. The fact that the blasphemy was to Jesus a simple statement of fact, and that it has since been accepted as such by all western nations, does not invalidate the proceedings, nor give us the right to regard Annas and Caiaphas as worse men than the Archbishop of Canterbury and the Head Master of Eton. If Jesus had been indicted in a modern court, he would have been examined by two doctors; found to be obsessed by a delusion; declared incapable of pleading; and sent to an asylum: that is the whole difference. But please note that when a man is charged before a modern tribunal (to take a case that happened the other day) of having asserted and maintained that he was an officer returned from the front to receive the Victoria Cross at the hands of the King, although he was in fact a mechanic, nobody thinks of treating him as afflicted with a delusion. He is punished for false pretences, because his assertion is credible and therefore misleading. Just so, the claim to divinity made by Jesus was to the High Priest, who looked forward to the coming of a Messiah, one that might conceivably have been true, and might therefore have misled the people in a very dangerous way. That was why he treated Jesus as an impostor and a blasphemer where we should have treated him as a madman.

THE GOSPELS WITHOUT PREJUDICE

All this will become clear if we read the gospels without prejudice. When I was young it was impossible to read them without fantastic confusion of thought. The confusion was so utterly confounded that it was called the proper spirit to read the Bible in. Jesus was a baby; and he was older than creation.

He was a man who could be persecuted, stoned, scourged, and killed; and he was a god, immortal and all-powerful, able to raise the dead and call millions of angels to his aid. It was a sin to doubt either view of him: that is, it was a sin to reason about him; and the end was that you did not reason about him, and read about him only when you were compelled. When you heard the gospel stories read in church, or learnt them from painters and poets, you came out with an impression of their contents that would have astonished a Chinaman who had read the story without prepossession. Even sceptics who were specially on their guard, put the Bible in the dock, and read the gospels with the object of detecting discrepancies in the four narratives to shew that the writers were as subject to error as the writers of yesterday's newspaper.

All this has changed greatly within two generations. Today the Bible is so little read that the language of the Authorized Version is rapidly becoming obsolete; so that even in the United States, where the old tradition of the verbal infallibility of "the book of books" lingers more strongly than anywhere else except perhaps in Ulster, retranslations into modern English have been introduced perforce to save its bare intelligibility. It is quite easy today to find cultivated persons who have never read the New Testament, and on whom therefore it is possible to try the experiment of asking them to read the gospels and state what they have gathered as to the history and views and character of Christ.

THE GOSPELS NOW UNINTELLIGIBLE TO NOVICES

But it will not do to read the gospels with a mind furnished only for the reception of, say, a biography of Goethe. You will not make sense of them, nor even be able without impatient weariness to persevere in the task of going steadily through them, unless you know something of the history of the human imagination as applied to religion. Not long ago I asked a writer of distinguished intellectual competence whether he had made a study of the gospels since his childhood. His reply was that he had lately tried, but "found it all such nonsense that I could not stick it." As I do not want to send anyone to the gospels with this result, I had better here give a brief exposition of how much of the history of religion is needed to make the gospels and the conduct and ultimate fate of Jesus intelligible and interesting.

WORLDLINESS OF THE MAJORITY

The first common mistake to get rid of is that mankind consists of a great mass of religious people and a few eccentric atheists. It consists of a huge mass of worldly people, and a small percentage of persons deeply interested in religion and concerned about their own souls and other people's; and this section consists mostly of those who are passionately affirming the established religion and those who are passionately attacking it, the genuine philosophers being very few. Thus you never have a nation of millions of Wesleys and one Tom Paine. You have a million Mr Worldly Wisemans, one Wesley, with his small congregation, and one Tom Paine, with *his* smaller congregation. The passionately religious are a people apart; and if they were not hopelessly outnumbered by the worldly, they would turn the world upside down, as St Paul was reproached, quite justly, for wanting to do. Few people can number among their personal acquaintances a single atheist or a single Plymouth Brother. Unless a religious turn in ourselves has led us to seek the little Societies to which these rare birds belong, we pass our lives among people who, whatever creeds they may repeat, and in whatever temples they may avouch their respectability and wear their Sunday clothes, have robust consciences, and hunger and thirst, not for righteousness, but for rich feeding and comfort and social position and attractive mates and ease and pleasure and respect and consideration: in short, for love and money. To these people one morality is as good as another provided they are used to it and can put up with its restrictions without unhappiness; and in the maintenance of this morality they will fight and punish and coerce without scruple. They may not be the salt of the earth, these Philistines; but they are the substance of civilization; and they save society from ruin by criminals and conquerors as well as by Savonarolas and Knipperdollings. And as they know, very sensibly, that a little religion is good for children and serves morality, keeping the poor in good humor or in awe by promising rewards in heaven or threatening torments in hell, they encourage the religious people up to a certain point: for instance, if Savonarola only tells the ladies of Florence that they ought to tear off their jewels and finery and sacrifice them to God, they offer him a cardinal's hat, and praise him as a saint; but if he induces them to actually do it, they burn him as a public nuisance.

RELIGION OF THE MINORITY. SALVATIONISM

The religion of the tolerated religious minority has always been essentially the same religion: that is why its changes of name and form have made so little difference. That is why, also, a nation so civilized as the English can convert negroes to their faith with great ease, but cannot convert Mahometans or Jews. The negro finds in civilized Salvationism an unspeakably more comforting version of his crude creed; but neither Saracen nor Jew sees any advantage in it over his own version. The Crusader was surprised to find the Saracen quite as religious and moral as himself, and rather more than less civilized. The Latin Christian has nothing to offer the Greek Christian that Greek Christianity has not already provided. They are all, at root, Salvationists.

Let us trace this religion of Salvation from its beginnings. So many things that man does not himself contrive or desire are always happening: death, plagues, tempests, blights, floods, sunrise and sunset, growths and harvests and decay, and Kant's two wonders of the starry heavens above us and the moral law within us, that we conclude that somebody must be doing it all, or that somebody is doing the good and somebody else doing the evil, or that armies of invisible persons, beneficent and malevolent, are doing it; hence you postulate gods and devils, angels and demons. You propitiate these powers with presents, called sacrifices, and flatteries, called praises. Then the Kantian moral law within you makes you conceive your god as a judge; and straightway you try to corrupt him, also with presents and flatteries. This seems shocking to us; but our objection to it is quite a recent development: no longer ago than Shakespear's time it was thought quite natural that litigants should give presents to human judges; and the buying off of divine wrath by actual money payments to priests, or, in the reformed churches which discountenance this, by subscriptions to charities and church building and the like, is still in full swing. Its practical disadvantage is that though it makes matters very easy for the rich, it cuts off the poor from all hope of divine favor. And this quickens the moral criticism of the poor to such an extent, that they soon find the moral law within them revolting against the idea of buying off the deity with gold and gifts, though they are still quite ready to buy him off with the paper money of praise and professions of repentance. Accordingly, you will find that though a religion may last unchanged for many centuries in primitive communities where the conditions of life leave no room for poverty and riches, and the process of propitiating the supernatural powers is as well within the means of the least of the members as within those of the headman, yet when commercial civilization arrives, and capitalism divides the people into a few rich and a great many so poor that they can barely live, a movement for religious reform will arise among the poor, and will be essentially a movement for cheap or entirely gratuitous salvation.

To understand what the poor mean by propitiation, we must examine for a moment what they mean by justice.

THE DIFFERENCE BETWEEN ATONEMENT
AND PUNISHMENT

The primitive idea of justice is partly legalized revenge and partly expiation by sacrifice. It works out from both sides in the notion that two blacks make a white, and that when a wrong has been done, it should be paid for by an equivalent suffering. It seems to the Philistine majority a matter of course that this compensating suffering should be inflicted on the wrongdoer for the sake of its deterrent effect on other would-be wrongdoers; but a moment's reflection will shew that this utilitarian application corrupts the whole transaction. For example, the shedding of innocent blood cannot be balanced by the shedding of guilty blood. Sacrificing a criminal to propitiate God for the murder of one of his righteous servants is like sacrificing a mangy sheep or an ox with the rinderpest: it calls down divine wrath instead of appeasing it. In doing it we offer God as a sacrifice the gratification of our own revenge and the protection of our own lives without cost to ourselves; and cost to ourselves is the essence of sacrifice and expiation. However much the Philistines have succeeded in confusing these things in practice, they are to the Salvationist sense distinct and even contrary. The Baronet's cousin in Dickens's novel, who, perplexed by the failure of the police to discover the murderer of the baronet's solicitor, said "Far better hang wrong fellow than no fellow," was not only expressing a very common sentiment, but trembling on the brink of the rarer Salvationist opinion that it is much better to hang the wrong fellow: that, in fact, the wrong fellow is the right fellow to hang.

The point is a cardinal one, because until we grasp it not only does historical Christianity remain unintelligible to us, but those who do not care a rap about historical Christianity may be led into the mistake of supposing that if we discard revenge, and treat murderers exactly as God treated Cain: that is, exempt them from punishment by putting a brand on them as unworthy

to be sacrificed, and let them face the world as best they can
with that brand on them, we should get rid both of punishment
and sacrifice. It would not at all follow: on the contrary, the
feeling that there must be an expiation of the murder might
quite possibly lead to our putting some innocent person—the
more innocent the better—to a cruel death to balance the account with divine justice.

SALVATION AT FIRST A CLASS PRIVILEGE;
AND THE REMEDY

Thus, even when the poor decide that the method of pur-
chasing salvation by offering rams and goats or bringing gold to
the altar must be wrong because they cannot afford it, we still
do not feel "saved" without a sacrifice and a victim. In vain do
we try to substitute mystical rites that cost nothing, such as
circumcision, or, as a substitute for that, baptism. Our sense of
justice still demands an expiation, a sacrifice, a sufferer for our
sins. And this leaves the poor man still in his old difficulty; for
if it was impossible for him to procure rams and goats and shek-
els, how much more impossible is it for him to find a neighbor
who will voluntarily suffer for his sins: one who will say cheerfully "You have committed a murder. Well, never mind: I am
willing to be hanged for it in your stead"?

Our imagination must come to our rescue. Why not, instead
of driving ourselves to despair by insisting on a separate atonement by a separate redeemer for every sin, have one great atonement and one great redeemer to compound for the sins of the
world once for all? Nothing easier, nothing cheaper. The yoke
is easy, the burden light. All you have to do when the redeemer
is once found (or invented by the imagination) is to believe in
the efficacy of the transaction, and you are saved. The rams and
goats cease to bleed; the altars which ask for expensive gifts
and continually renewed sacrifices are torn down; and the
Church of the single redeemer and the single atonement rises on

the ruins of the old temples, and becomes a single Church of the Christ.

RETROSPECTIVE ATONEMENT; AND THE EXPECTATION OF THE REDEEMER

But this does not happen at once. Between the old costly religion of the rich and the new gratuitous religion of the poor there comes an interregnum in which the redeemer, though conceived by the human imagination, is not yet found. He is awaited and expected under the names of the Christ, the Messiah, Baldur the Beautiful, or what not; but he has not yet come. Yet the sinners are not therefore in despair. It is true that they cannot say, as we say, "The Christ has come, and has redeemed us"; but they can say "The Christ will come, and will redeem us," which, as the atonement is conceived as retrospective, is equally consoling. There are periods when nations are seething with this expectation and crying aloud with prophecy of the Redeemer through their poets. To feel that atmosphere we have only to take up the Bible and read Isaiah at one end of such a period and Luke and John at the other.

COMPLETION OF THE SCHEME BY LUTHER AND CALVIN

We now see our religion as a quaint but quite intelligible evolution from crude attempts to propitiate the destructive forces of Nature among savages to a subtle theology with a costly ritual of sacrifice possible only to the rich as a luxury, and finally to the religion of Luther and Calvin. And it must be said for the earlier forms that they involved very real sacrifices. The sacrifice was not always vicarious, and is not yet universally so. In India men pay with their own skins, torturing themselves hideously to attain holiness. In the west, saints amazed the world with their austerities and self-scourgings and confessions and vigils. But Luther delivered us from all that. His reformation was a

triumph of imagination and a triumph of cheapness. It brought
you complete salvation and asked you for nothing but faith. Luther did not know what he was doing in the scientific sociological way in which we know it; but his instinct served him
better than knowledge could have done; for it was instinct
rather than theological casuistry that made him hold so resolutely to Justification by Faith as the trump card by which he
should beat the Pope, or, as he would have put it, the sign in
which he should conquer. He may be said to have abolished the
charge for admission to heaven. Paul had advocated this; but
Luther and Calvin did it.

JOHN BARLEYCORN

There is yet another page in the history of religion which
must be conned and digested before the career of Jesus can be
fully understood. People who can read long books will find it
in Frazer's Golden Bough. Simpler folk will find it in the peasant's song of John Barleycorn, now made accessible to our drawing room amateurs in the admirable collections of Somersetshire
Folk Songs by Mr Cecil Sharp. From Frazer's *magnum opus*
you will learn how the same primitive logic which makes the
Englishman believe today that by eating a beefsteak he can acquire the strength and courage of the bull, and to hold that
belief in the face of the most ignominious defeats by vegetarian
wrestlers and racers and bicyclists, led the first men who conceived God as capable of incarnation to believe that they could
acquire a spark of his divinity by eating his flesh and drinking
his blood. And from the song of John Barleycorn you may
learn how the miracle of the seed, the growth, and the harvest,
still the most wonderful of all the miracles and as inexplicable
as ever, taught the primitive husbandman, and, as we must now
affirm, taught him quite rightly, that God is in the seed, and
that God is immortal. And thus it became the test of Godhead
that nothing that you could do to it could kill it, and that when
you buried it, it would rise again in renewed life and beauty

and give mankind eternal life on condition that it was eaten and drunk, and again slain and buried, to rise again for ever and ever. You may, and indeed must, use John Barleycorn "right barbarouslee," cutting him "off at knee" with your scythes, scourging him with your flails, burying him in the earth; and he will not resist you nor reproach you, but will rise again in golden beauty amidst a great burst of sunshine and bird music, and save you and renew your life. And from the interweaving of these two traditions with the craving for the Redeemer, you at last get the conviction that when the Redeemer comes he will be immortal; he will give us his body to eat and his blood to drink; and he will prove his divinity by suffering a barbarous death without resistance or reproach, and rise from the dead and return to the earth in glory as the giver of life eternal.

LOOKING FOR THE END OF THE WORLD

Yet another persistent belief has beset the imagination of the religious ever since religion spread among the poor, or, rather, ever since commercial civilization produced a hopelessly poor class cut off from enjoyment in this world. That belief is that the end of this world is at hand, and that it will presently pass away and be replaced by a kingdom of happiness, justice, and bliss in which the rich and the oppressors and the unjust shall have no share. We are all familiar with this expectation: many of us cherish some pious relative who sees in every great calamity a sign of the approaching end. Warning pamphlets are in constant circulation: advertisements are put in the papers and paid for by those who are convinced, and who are horrified at the indifference of the irreligious to the approaching doom. And revivalist preachers, now as in the days of John the Baptist, seldom fail to warn their flocks to watch and pray, as the great day will steal upon them like a thief in the night, and cannot be long deferred in a world so wicked. This belief also associates itself with Barleycorn's second coming; so that the two events become identified at last.

There is the other and more artificial side of this belief, on which it is an inculcated dread. The ruler who appeals to the prospect of heaven to console the poor and keep them from insurrection also curbs the vicious by threatening them with hell. In the Koran we find Mahomet driven more and more to this expedient of government; and experience confirms his evident belief that it is impossible to govern without it in certain phases of civilization. We shall see later on that it gives a powerful attraction to the belief in a Redeemer, since it adds to remorse of conscience, which hardened men bear very lightly, a definite dread of hideous and eternal torture.

THE HONOR OF DIVINE PARENTAGE

One more tradition must be noted. The consummation of praise for a king is to declare that he is the son of no earthly father, but of a god. His mother goes into the temple of Apollo, and Apollo comes to her in the shape of a serpent, or the like. The Roman emperors, following the example of Augustus, claimed the title of God. Illogically, such divine kings insist a good deal on their royal human ancestors. Alexander, claiming to be the son of Apollo, is equally determined to be the son of Philip. As the gospels stand, St Matthew and St Luke give genealogies (the two are different) establishing the descent of Jesus through Joseph from the royal house of David, and yet declare that not Joseph but the Holy Ghost was the father of Jesus. It is therefore now held that the story of the Holy Ghost is a later interpolation borrowed from the Greek and Roman imperial tradition. But experience shews that simultaneous faith in the descent from David and the conception by the Holy Ghost is possible. Such double beliefs are entertained by the human mind without uneasiness or consciousness of the contradiction involved. Many instances might be given: a familiar one to my generation being that of the Tichborne claimant, whose attempt to pass himself off as a baronet was supported by an association of laborers on the ground that the Tichborne family, in resisting it, were trying to do a laborer out of his rights. It is quite possible that Matthew and Luke may have been unconscious of the contradiction: indeed the interpolation theory does not remove the difficulty, as the interpolators themselves must have been unconscious of it. A better ground for suspecting interpolation is that St Paul knew nothing of the divine birth, and taught that Jesus came into the world at his birth as the son of Joseph, but rose from the dead after three days as the son of God. Here again, few notice the discrepancy: the three views are accepted simultaneously without intellectual discomfort. We can provisionally entertain half a dozen contradictory versions of an event if we feel either that it does not greatly matter, or that there is a category attainable in which the contradictions are reconciled.

But that is not the present point. All that need be noted here is that the legend of divine birth was sure to be attached sooner or later to very eminent persons in Roman imperial times, and that modern theologians, far from discrediting it, have very logically affirmed the miraculous conception not only of Jesus but of his mother.

With no more scholarly equipment than a knowledge of these habits of the human imagination, anyone may now read the four gospels without bewilderment, and without the contemptuous incredulity which spoils the temper of many modern atheists, or the senseless credulity which sometimes makes pious people force us to shove them aside in emergencies as impracticable lunatics when they ask us to meet violence and injustice with dumb submission in the belief that the strange demeanor of Jesus before Pilate was meant as an example of normal human conduct. Let us admit that without the proper clues the gospels are, to a modern educated person, nonsensical and incredible, whilst the apostles are unreadable. But with the clues, they are fairly plain sailing. Jesus becomes an intelligible and consistent person. His reasons for going "like a lamb to the slaughter" instead of saving himself as Mahomet did, become quite clear. The narrative becomes as credible as any other historical narrative of its period.

MATTHEW
THE ANNUNCIATION:
THE MASSACRE: THE FLIGHT

Let us begin with the gospel of Matthew, bearing in mind that it does not profess to be the evidence of an eyewitness. It is a chronicle, founded, like other chronicles, on such evidence and records as the chronicler could get hold of. The only one of the evangelists who professes to give first-hand evidence as an eyewitness naturally takes care to say so; and the fact that Matthew makes no such pretension, and writes throughout as a chronicler, makes it clear that he is telling the story of Jesus as Holinshed told the story of Macbeth, except that, for a reason to be given later on, he must have collected his material and completed his book within the lifetime of persons contemporary with Jesus. Allowance must also be made for the fact that the gospel is written in the Greek language, whilst the first-hand traditions and the actual utterances of Jesus must have been in Aramic, the dialect of Palestine. These distinctions are important, as you will find if you read Holinshed or Froissart and then read Benvenuto Cellini. You do not blame Holinshed or Froissart for believing and repeating the things they had read or been told, though you cannot always believe these things yourself. But when Cellini tells you that he saw this or did that, and you find it impossible to believe him, you lose patience with him, and are disposed to doubt everything in his autobiography. Do not forget, then, that Matthew is Holinshed and not Benvenuto. The very first pages of his narrative will put your attitude to the test.

Matthew tells us that the mother of Jesus was betrothed to a man of royal pedigree named Joseph, who was rich enough to live in a house in Bethlehem to which kings could bring gifts of gold without provoking any comment. An angel announces to Joseph that Jesus is the son of the Holy Ghost, and that he must not accuse her of infidelity because of her bearing a son of which he is not the father; but this episode disappears from the subsequent narrative: there is no record of its having been told to Jesus, nor any indication of his having any knowledge of it. The narrative, in fact, proceeds in all respects as if the annunciation formed no part of it.

Herod the Tetrarch, believing that a child has been born who will destroy him, orders all the male children to be slaughtered; and Jesus escapes by the flight of his parents into Egypt, whence they return to Nazareth when the danger is over. Here it is necessary to anticipate a little by saying that none of the other evangelists accepts this story, as none of them except John, who throws over Matthew altogether, shares his craze for treating history and biography as mere records of the fulfilment of ancient Jewish prophecies. This craze no doubt led him to seek for some legend bearing out Hosea's "Out of Egypt have I called my son," and Jeremiah's Rachel weeping for her children: in fact, he says so. Nothing that interests us nowadays turns on the credibility of the massacre of the innocents and the flight into Egypt. We may forget them, and proceed to the important part of the narrative, which skips at once to the manhood of Jesus.

JOHN THE BAPTIST

At this moment, a Salvationist prophet named John is stirring the people very strongly. John has declared that the rite of circumcision is insufficient as a dedication of the individual to God, and has substituted the rite of baptism. To us, who are accustomed to baptism as a matter of course, and to whom circumcision is a rather ridiculous foreign practice of no consequence, the sensational effects of such a heresy as this on the Jews is not apparent: it seems to us as natural that John should have baptized people as that the rector of our village should do so. But, as St Paul found to his cost later on, the discarding of

circumcision for baptism was to the Jews as startling a heresy as
the discarding of transubstantiation in the Mass was to the Catholics of the XVI century.

JESUS JOINS THE BAPTISTS

Jesus entered as a man of thirty (Luke says) into the religious
life of his time by going to John the Baptist and demanding
baptism from him, much as certain well-to-do young gentlemen
forty years ago "joined the Socialists." As far as established Jewry
was concerned, he burnt his boats by this action, and cut himself off from the routine of wealth, respectability, and ortho-
doxy. He then began preaching John's gospel, which, apart
from the heresy of baptism, the value of which lay in its bringing the Gentiles (that is, the uncircumcized) within the pale
of salvation, was a call to the people to repent of their sins, as
the kingdom of heaven was at hand. Luke adds that he also
preached the communism of charity; told the surveyors of taxes
not to over-assess the taxpayers; and advised soldiers to be content with their wages and not to be violent or lay false accusa-
tions. There is no record of John going beyond this.

THE SAVAGE JOHN AND THE
CIVILIZED JESUS

Jesus went beyond it very rapidly, according to Matthew.
Though, like John, he became an itinerant preacher, he de-
parted widely from John's manner of life. John went into the
wilderness, not into the synagogues; and his baptismal font was
the river Jordan. He was an ascetic, clothed in skins and living
on locusts and wild honey, practising a savage austerity. He
courted martyrdom, and met it at the hands of Herod. Jesus saw
no merit either in asceticism or martyrdom. In contrast to John
he was essentially a highly-civilized, cultivated person. According to Luke, he pointed out the contrast himself, chaffing the
Jews for complaining that John must be possessed by the devil
because he was a teetotaller and vegetarian, whilst, because Jesus

was neither one nor the other, they reviled him as a gluttonous man and a winebibber, the friend of the officials and their mistresses. He told straitlaced disciples that they would have trouble enough from other people without making any for themselves, and that they should avoid martyrdom and enjoy themselves whilst they had the chance. "When they persecute you in this city," he says, "flee into the next." He preaches in the synagogues and in the open air indifferently, just as they come. He repeatedly says, "I desire mercy and not sacrifice," meaning evidently to clear himself of the inveterate superstition that suffering is gratifying to God. "Be not, as the Pharisees, of a sad countenance," he says. He is convivial, feasting with Roman officials and sinners. He is careless of his person, and is remonstrated with for not washing his hands before sitting down to table. The followers of John the Baptist, who fast, and who expect to find the Christians greater ascetics than themselves, are disappointed at finding that Jesus and his twelve friends do not fast; and Jesus tells them that they should rejoice in him instead of being melancholy. He is jocular, and tells them they will all have as much fasting as they want soon enough, whether they like it or not. He is not afraid of disease, and dines with a leper. A woman, apparently to protect him against infection, pours a costly unguent on his head, and is rebuked because what it cost might have been given to the poor. He poohpoohs that lowspirited view, and says, as he said when he was reproached for not fasting, that the poor are always there to be helped, but that he is not there to be anointed always, implying that you should never lose a chance of being happy when there is so much misery in the world. He breaks the Sabbath; is impatient of conventionality when it is uncomfortable or obstructive; and outrages the feelings of the Jews by breaches of it. He is apt to accuse people who feel that way of hypocrisy. Like the late Samuel Butler, he regards disease as a department of sin, and on curing a lame man, says "Thy sins are forgiven" instead of "Arise and walk," subsequently maintaining, when the Scribes reproach him for assuming power to forgive sin as well as to cure disease, that the two come to the same thing. He has no modest affectations, and claims to be greater than Solomon or Jonah. When reproached, as Bunyan was, for resorting to the art of fiction when teaching in parables, he justifies himself on the ground that art is the only way in which the people can be taught. He is, in short, what we should call an artist and a Bohemian in his manner of life.

JESUS NOT A PROSELYTIST

A point of considerable practical importance today is that he expressly repudiates the idea that forms of religion, once rooted, can be weeded out and replanted with the flowers of a foreign faith. "If you try to root up the tares you will root up the wheat as well." Our proselytizing missionary enterprises are thus flatly contrary to his advice; and their results appear to bear him out in his view that if you convert a man brought up in another creed, you inevitably demoralize him. He acts on this view himself, and does not convert his disciples from Judaism to Christianity. To this day a Christian would be in religion a Jew initiated by baptism instead of circumcision, and accepting Jesus as the Messiah, and his teachings as of higher authority than those of Moses, but for the action of the Jewish priests, who, to save Jewry from being submerged in the rising flood of Christianity after the capture of Jerusalem and the destruction of the Temple, set up what was practically a new religious order, with new Scriptures and elaborate new observances, and to their list of the accursed added one Jeschu, a bastard magician, whose comic rogueries brought him to a bad end like Punch or Til Eulenspiegel: an invention which cost them dear when the Christians got the upper hand of them politically. The Jew as Jesus, himself a Jew, knew him, never dreamt of such things, and could follow Jesus without ceasing to be a Jew.

THE TEACHINGS OF JESUS

So much for his personal life and temperament. His public career as a popular preacher carries him equally far beyond John the Baptist. He lays no stress on baptism or vows, and preaches conduct incessantly. He advocates communism, the widening of the private family with its cramping ties into the great family of mankind under the fatherhood of God, the abandonment of revenge and punishment, the counteracting of evil by good instead of by a hostile evil, and an organic conception of society in which you are not an independent individual but a member of society, your neighbor being another member, and each of you members one of another, as two fingers on a hand, the obvious conclusion being that unless you love your neighbor as yourself and he reciprocates you will both be the worse for it. He conveys all this with extraordinary charm, and entertains his hearers with fables (parables) to illustrate them. He has no synagogue or regular congregation, but travels from place to place with twelve men whom he has called from their work as he passed, and who have abandoned it to follow him.

THE MIRACLES

He has certain abnormal powers by which he can perform miracles. He is ashamed of these powers, but, being extremely compassionate, cannot refuse to exercise them when afflicted people beg him to cure them, when multitudes of people are hungry, and when his disciples are terrified by storms on the lakes. He asks for no reward, but begs the people not to mention these powers of his. There are two obvious reasons for his dislike of being known as a worker of miracles. One is the natural objection of all men who possess such powers, but have far more important business in the world than to exhibit them, to be regarded primarily as charlatans, besides being pestered to give exhibitions to satisfy curiosity. The other is that his view of the

effect of miracles upon his mission is exactly that taken later on
by Rousseau. He perceives that they will discredit him and di-
vert attention from his doctrine by raising an entirely irrelevant
issue between his disciples and his opponents.

Possibly my readers may not have studied Rousseau's Letters
Written From The Mountain, which may be regarded as the
classic work on miracles as credentials of divine mission. Rousseau shews, as Jesus foresaw, that the miracles are the main ob-
tacle to the acceptance of Christianity, because their incredibil-
ty (if they were not incredible they would not be miracles)
makes people sceptical as to the whole narrative, credible
enough in the main, in which they occur, and suspicious of
the doctrine with which they are thus associated. "Get rid of the
miracles," said Rousseau, "and the whole world will fall at the
feet of Jesus Christ." He points out that miracles offered as evidence of divinity, and failing to convince, make divinity ridiculous. He says, in effect, there is nothing in making a lame man
walk: thousands of lame men have been cured and have walked
without any miracle. Bring me a man with only one leg and
make another grow instantaneously on him before my eyes, and
I will be really impressed; but mere cures of ailments that have
often been cured before are quite useless as evidence of anything else than desire to help and power to cure.

Jesus, according to Matthew, agreed so entirely with Rousseau, and felt the danger so strongly, that when people who
were not ill or in trouble came to him and asked him to exercise
his powers as a sign of his mission, he was irritated beyond measure, and refused with an indignation which they, not seeing
Rousseau's point, must have thought very unreasonable. To be
called "an evil and adulterous generation" merely for asking a
miracle worker to give an exhibition of his powers, is rather a
startling experience. Mahomet, by the way, also lost his temper
when people asked him to perform miracles. But Mahomet expressly disclaimed any unusual powers; whereas it is clear from
Matthew's story that Jesus (unfortunately for himself, as he

thought) had some powers of healing. It is also obvious that the exercise of such powers would give rise to wild tales of magical feats which would expose their hero to condemnation as an impostor among people whose good opinion was of great consequence to the movement started by his mission.

But the deepest annoyance arising from the miracles would be the irrelevance of the issue raised by them. Jesus's teaching has nothing to do with miracles. If his mission had been simply to demonstrate a new method of restoring lost eyesight, the miracle of curing the blind would have been entirely relevant. But to say "You should love your enemies; and to convince you of this I will now proceed to cure this gentleman of cataract" would have been, to a man of Jesus's intelligence, the proposition of an idiot. If it could be proved today that not one of the miracles of Jesus actually occurred, that proof would not invalidate a single one of his didactic utterances; and conversely, if it could be proved that not only did the miracles actually occur, but that he had wrought a thousand other miracles a thousand times more wonderful, not a jot of weight would be added to his doctrine. And yet the intellectual energy of sceptics and divines has been wasted for generations in arguing about the miracles on the assumption that Christianity is at stake in the controversy as to whether the stories of Matthew are false or true. According to Matthew himself, Jesus must have known this only too well; for wherever he went he was assailed with a clamor for miracles, though his doctrine created bewilderment.

So much for the miracles! Matthew tells us further, that Jesus declared that his doctrines would be attacked by Church and State, and that the common multitude were the salt of the earth and the light of the world. His disciples, in their relations with the political and ecclesiastical organizations, would be as sheep among wolves.

MATTHEW IMPUTES BIGOTRY TO JESUS

Matthew, like most biographers, strives to identify the opinions and prejudices of his hero with his own. Although he describes Jesus as tolerant even to carelessness, he draws the line at the Gentile, and represents Jesus as a bigoted Jew who regards his mission as addressed exclusively to "the lost sheep of the house of Israel." When a woman of Canaan begged Jesus to cure her daughter, he first refused to speak to her, and then told her brutally that "It is not meet to take the children's bread and cast it to the dogs." But when the woman said, "Truth, Lord; yet the dogs eat of the crumbs which fall from their master's table," she melted the Jew out of him and made Christ a Christian. To the woman whom he had just called a dog he said, "O woman, great is thy faith: be it unto thee even as thou wilt." This is somehow one of the most touching stories in the gospel; perhaps because the woman rebukes the prophet by a touch of his own finest quality. It is certainly out of character; but as the sins of good men are always out of character, it is not safe to reject the story as invented in the interest of Matthew's determination that Jesus shall have nothing to do with the Gentiles. At all events, there the story is; and it is by no means the only instance in which Matthew reports Jesus, in spite of the charm of his preaching, as extremely uncivil in private intercourse.

THE GREAT CHANGE

So far the history is that of a man sane and interesting apart from his special gifts as orator, healer, and prophet. But a startling change occurs. One day, after the disciples have discouraged him for a long time by their misunderstandings of his mission, and their speculations as to whether he is one of the old prophets come again, and if so, which, his disciple Peter suddenly solves the problem by exclaiming, "Thou art the Christ, the son of the living God." At this Jesus is extraordinarily pleased and excited. He declares that Peter has had a revelation straight from God. He makes a pun on Peter's name, and declares him the founder of his Church. And he accepts his destiny as a god by announcing that he will be killed when he goes to Jerusalem; for if he is really the Christ, it is a necessary part of his legendary destiny that he shall be slain. Peter, not understanding this, rebukes him for what seems mere craven melancholy; and Jesus turns fiercely on him and cries, "Get thee behind me, Satan."

Jesus now becomes obsessed with a conviction of his divinity, and talks about it continually to his disciples, though he forbids them to mention it to others. They begin to dispute among themselves as to the position they shall occupy in heaven when his kingdom is established. He rebukes them strenuously for this, and repeats his teaching that greatness means service and not domination; but he himself, always instinctively somewhat haughty, now becomes arrogant, dictatorial, and even abusive, never replying to his critics without an insulting epithet, and even cursing a fig-tree which disappoints him when he goes to it for fruit. He assumes all the traditions of the folk-lore gods, and announces that, like John Barleycorn, he will be barbarously slain and buried, but will rise from the earth and return to life. He attaches to himself the immemorial tribal ceremony of eating the god, by blessing bread and wine and handing them to his disciples with the words "This is my body: this is my blood." He forgets his own teaching and threatens eternal fire and eternal punishment. He announces, in addition to his Barleycorn resurrection, that he will come to the world a second time in glory and establish his kingdom on earth. He fears that this may lead to the appearance of impostors claiming to be himself, and declares explicitly and repeatedly that no matter what wonders these impostors may perform, his own coming will be unmistakable, as the stars will fall from heaven, and trumpets be blown by angels. Further he declares that this will take place during the lifetime of persons then present.

JERUSALEM AND THE MYSTICAL SACRIFICE

In this new frame of mind he at last enters Jerusalem amid great popular curiosity; drives the moneychangers and sacrifice sellers out of the temple in a riot; refuses to interest himself in the beauties and wonders of the temple building on the ground that presently not a stone of it shall be left on another; reviles the high priests and elders in intolerable terms; and is arrested by night in a garden to avoid a popular disturbance. He makes no resistance, being persuaded that it is part of his destiny as a god to be murdered and to rise again. One of his followers shews fight, and cuts off the ear of one of his captors. Jesus rebukes him, but does not attempt to heal the wound, though he declares that if he wished to resist he could easily summon twelve million angels to his aid. He is taken before the high priest and by him handed over to the Roman governor, who is puzzled by his silent refusal to defend himself in any way, or to contradict his accusers or their witnesses, Pilate having naturally no idea that the prisoner conceives himself as going through an inevitable process of torment, death, and burial as a prelude to resurrection. Before the high priest he has also been silent except that when the priest asks him is he the Christ, the Son of God, he replies that they shall all see the Son of Man sitting at the right hand of power, and coming on the clouds of heaven. He maintains this attitude with frightful fortitude whilst they scourge him, mock him, torment him, and finally crucify him between two thieves. His prolonged agony of thirst and pain on the cross at last breaks his spirit, and he dies with a cry of "My God: why hast Thou forsaken me?"

NOT THIS MAN BUT BARABBAS

Meanwhile he has been definitely rejected by the people as well as by the priests. Pilate, pitying him, and unable to make out exactly what he has done (the blasphemy that has horrified the high priest does not move the Roman), tries to get him off by reminding the people that they have, by custom, the right to have a prisoner released at that time, and suggests that he should release Jesus. But they insist on his releasing a prisoner named Barabbas instead, and on having Jesus crucified. Matthew gives no clue to the popularity of Barabbas, describing him simply as "a notable prisoner." The later gospels make it clear, very significantly, that his offence was sedition and insurrection; that he was an advocate of physical force; and that he had killed his man. The choice of Barabbas thus appears as a popular choice of the militant advocate of physical force as against the unresisting advocate of mercy.

THE RESURRECTION

Matthew then tells how after three days an angel opened the family vault of one Joseph, a rich man of Arimathea, who had buried Jesus in it, whereupon Jesus rose and returned from Jerusalem to Galilee and resumed his preaching with his disciples, assuring them that he would now be with them to the end of the world.

At that point the narrative abruptly stops. The story has no ending.

DATE OF MATTHEW'S NARRATIVE

One effect of the promise of Jesus to come again in glory during the lifetime of some of his hearers is to date the gospel without the aid of any scholarship. It must have been written during the lifetime of Jesus's contemporaries: that is, whilst it was still possible for the promise of his Second Coming to be fulfilled. The death of the last person who had been alive when Jesus said "There be some of them that stand here that shall in no wise taste death til they see the Son of Man coming in his kingdom" destroyed the last possibility of the promised Second Coming, and bore out the incredulity of Pilate and the Jews. And as Matthew writes as one believing in that Second Coming, and in fact left his story unfinished to be ended by it, he must have produced his gospel within a lifetime of the crucifixion. Also, he must have believed that reading books would be one of the pleasures of the kingdom of heaven on earth.

CLASS TYPE OF MATTHEW'S JESUS

One more circumstance must be noted as gathered from Matthew. Though he begins his story in such a way as to suggest that Jesus belonged to the privileged classes, he mentions later on that when Jesus attempted to preach in his own country, and had no success there, the people said, "Is not this the carpenter's son?" But Jesus's manner throughout is that of an aristocrat, or at the very least the son of a rich bourgeois, and by no means a lowly-minded one at that. We must be careful therefore to conceive Joseph, not as a modern proletarian carpenter working for weekly wages, but as a master craftsman of royal descent. John the Baptist may have been a Keir Hardie; but the Jesus of Matthew is of the Ruskin-Morris class.

This haughty characterization is so marked that if we had no other documents concerning Jesus than the gospel of Matthew, we should not feel as we do about him. We should have been much less loth to say, "There is a man here who was sane until Peter hailed him as the Christ, and who then became a monomaniac." We should have pointed out that his delusion is a very common delusion among the insane, and that such insanity is quite consistent with the retention of the argumentative cunning and penetration which Jesus displayed in Jerusalem after his delusion had taken complete hold of him. We should feel horrified at the scourging and mocking and crucifixion just as we should if Ruskin had been treated in that way when he also went mad, instead of being cared for as an invalid. And we should have had no clear perception of any special significance in his way of calling the Son of God the Son of Man. We should have noticed that he was a Communist; that he regarded much of what we call law and order as machinery for robbing the poor under legal forms; that he thought domestic ties a snare for the soul; that he agreed with the proverb "The nearer the Church, the farther from God"; that he saw very plainly that the masters of the community should be its servants and not its oppressors and parasites; and that though he did not tell us not to fight our enemies, he did tell us to love them, and warned us that they who draw the sword shall perish by the sword. All this shews a great power of seeing through vulgar illusions, and a capacity for a higher morality than has yet been established in any civilized community; but it does not place Jesus above Confucius or Plato, not to mention more modern philosophers and moralists.

MARK
THE WOMEN DISCIPLES AND THE
ASCENSION

Let us see whether we can get anything more out of Mark, whose gospel, by the way, is supposed to be older than Matthew's. Mark is brief; and it does not take long to discover that he adds nothing to Matthew except the ending of the story by Christ's ascension into heaven, and the news that many women had come with Jesus to Jerusalem, including Mary Magdalene, out of whom he had cast seven devils. On the other hand Mark says nothing about the birth of Jesus, and does not touch his career until his adult baptism by John. He apparently regards Jesus as a native of Nazareth, as John does, and not of Bethlehem, as Matthew and Luke do, Bethlehem being the city of David, from whom Jesus is said by Matthew and Luke to be descended. He describes John's doctrine as "Baptism of repentance unto remission of sins": that is, a form of Salvationism. He tells us that Jesus went into the synagogues and taught, not as the Scribes but as one having authority: that is, we infer, he preaches his own doctrine as an original moralist instead of repeating what the books say. He describes the miracle of Jesus reaching the boat by walking across the sea, but says nothing about Peter trying to do the same. Mark sees what he relates

more vividly than Matthew, and gives touches of detail that
bring the event more clearly before the reader. He says, for instance, that when Jesus walked on the waves to the boat, he was
passing it by when the disciples called out to him. He seems to
feel that Jesus's treatment of the woman of Canaan requires
some apology, and therefore says that she was a Greek of Syrophenician race, which probably excused any incivility to her in
Mark's eyes. He represents the father of the boy whom Jesus
cured of epilepsy after the transfiguration as a sceptic who says
"Lord, I believe: help thou mine unbelief." He tells the story of
the widow's mite, omitted by Matthew. He explains that Barabbas was "lying bound with them that made insurrection, men
who in the insurrection had committed murder." Joseph of
Arimathea, who buried Jesus in his own tomb, and who is described by Matthew as a disciple, is described by Mark as "one
who also himself was looking for the kingdom of God," which
suggests that he was an independent seeker. Mark earns our
gratitude by making no mention of the old prophecies, and
thereby not only saves time, but avoids the absurd implication
that Christ was merely going through a predetermined ritual,
like the works of a clock, instead of living. Finally Mark reports
Christ as saying, after his resurrection, that those who believe
in him will be saved and those who do not, damned; but it is
impossible to discover whether he means anything by a state of
damnation beyond a state of error. The paleographers regard
this passage as tacked on by a later scribe.

On the whole Mark leaves the modern reader where Matthew
left him.

LUKE

LUKE THE LITERARY ARTIST

When we come to Luke, we come to a later story-teller, and
one with a stronger natural gift for his art. Before you have read
twenty lines of Luke's gospel you are aware that you have passed
from the chronicler writing for the sake of recording im-

portant facts, to the artist, telling the story for the sake of telling it. At the very outset he achieves the most charming idyll in the Bible: the story of Mary crowded out of the inn into the stable and laying her newly-born son in the manger, and of the shepherds abiding in the field keeping watch over their flocks by night, and how the angel of the Lord came upon them, and the glory of the Lord shone around them, and suddenly there was with the angel a multitude of the heavenly host. These shepherds go to the stable and take the place of the kings in Matthew's chronicle. So completely has this story conquered and fascinated our imagination that most of us suppose all the gospels to contain it; but it is Luke's story and his alone: none of the others have the smallest hint of it.

THE CHARM OF LUKE'S NARRATIVE

Luke gives the charm of sentimental romance to every incident. The Annunciation, as described by Matthew, is made to Joseph, and is simply a warning to him not to divorce his wife for misconduct. In Luke's gospel it is made to Mary herself, at much greater length, with a sense of the ecstasy of the bride of the Holy Ghost. Jesus is refined and softened almost out of recognition: the stern peremptory disciple of John the Baptist, who never addresses a Pharisee or a Scribe without an insulting epithet, becomes a considerate, gentle, sociable, almost urbane person; and the Chauvinist Jew becomes a pro-Gentile who is thrown out of the synagogue in his own town for reminding the congregation that the prophets had sometimes preferred Gentiles to Jews. In fact they try to throw him down from a sort of Tarpeian rock which they use for executions; but he makes his way through them and escapes: the only suggestion of a feat of arms on his part in the gospels. There is not a word of the Syrophenician woman. At the end he is calmly superior to his sufferings; delivers an address on his way to execution with unruffled composure; does not despair on the cross; and dies with perfect dignity, commending his spirit to God, after praying for

the forgiveness of his persecutors on the ground that "They
know not what they do." According to Matthew, it is part of the
bitterness of his death that even the thieves who are crucified
with him revile him. According to Luke, only one of them does
this; and he is rebuked by the other, who begs Jesus to remember him when he comes into his kingdom. To which Jesus replies, "This day shalt thou be with me in Paradise," implying
that he will spend the three days of his death there. In short,
every device is used to get rid of the ruthless horror of the Matthew chronicle, and to relieve the strain of the Passion by touching episodes, and by representing Christ as superior to human
suffering. It is Luke's Jesus who has won our hearts.

THE TOUCH OF PARISIAN ROMANCE

Luke's romantic shrinking from unpleasantness, and his sentimentality, are illustrated by his version of the woman with the
ointment. Matthew and Mark describe it as taking place in the
house of Simon the Leper, where it is objected to as a waste
of money. In Luke's version the leper becomes a rich Pharisee; the woman becomes a Dame aux Camellias; and nothing is said about money and the poor. The woman washes the
feet of Jesus with her tears and dries them with her hair; and he
is reproached for suffering a sinful woman to touch him. It is
almost an adaptation of the unromantic Matthew to the Parisian stage. There is a distinct attempt to increase the feminine
interest all through. The slight lead given by Mark is taken up
and developed. More is said about Jesus's mother and her feelings. Christ's following of women, just mentioned by Mark to
account for their presence at his tomb, is introduced earlier; and
some of the women are named; so that we are introduced to
Joanna the wife of Chuza, Herod's steward, and Susanna. There
is the quaint little domestic episode between Mary and Martha.
There is the parable of the Prodigal Son, appealing to the indul-
gence romance has always shewn to Charles Surface and Des
Grieux. Women follow Jesus to the cross; and he makes them

a speech beginning "Daughters of Jerusalem." Slight as these changes may seem, they make a great change in the atmosphere. The Christ of Matthew could never have become what is vulgarly called a woman's hero (though the truth is that the popular demand for sentiment, as far as it is not simply human, is more manly than womanly); but the Christ of Luke has made possible those pictures which now hang in many ladies' chambers, in which Jesus is represented exactly as he is represented in the Lourdes cinematograph, by a handsome actor. The only touch of realism which Luke does not instinctively suppress for the sake of producing this kind of amenity is the reproach addressed to Jesus for sitting down to table without washing his hands; and that is retained because an interesting discourse hangs on it.

WAITING FOR THE MESSIAH

Another new feature in Luke's story is that it begins in a world in which everyone is expecting the advent of the Christ. In Matthew and Mark, Jesus comes into a normal Philistine world like our own of today. Not until the Baptist foretells that one greater than himself shall come after him does the old Jewish hope of a Messiah begin to stir again; and as Jesus begins as a disciple of John, and is baptized by him, nobody connects him with that hope until Peter has the sudden inspiration which produces so startling an effect on Jesus. But in Luke's gospel men's minds, and especially women's minds, are full of eager expectation of a Christ not only before the birth of Jesus, but before the birth of John the Baptist, the event with which Luke begins his story. Whilst Jesus and John are still in their mothers' wombs, John leaps at the approach of Jesus when the two mothers visit one another. At the circumcision of Jesus pious men and women hail the infant as the Christ.

The Baptist himself is not convinced; for at quite a late period in his former disciple's career he sends two young men to ask Jesus is he really the Christ. This is noteworthy because Jesus immediately gives them a deliberate exhibition of miracles, and bids them tell John what they have seen, and ask him what he thinks *now*. This is in complete contradiction to what I have called the Rousseau view of miracles as inferred from Matthew. Luke shews all a romancer's thoughtlessness about miracles: he regards them as "signs": that is, as proofs of the divinity of the person performing them, and not merely of thaumaturgic powers. He revels in miracles just as he revels in parables: they make such capital stories. He cannot allow the calling of Peter, James, and John from their boats to pass without a comic miraculous overdraft of fishes, with the net sinking the boats and provoking Peter to exclaim, "Depart from me; for I am a sinful man, O Lord," which should probably be translated, "I want no more of your miracles: natural fishing is good enough for my boats."

There are some other novelties in Luke's version. Pilate sends Jesus to Herod, who happens to be in Jerusalem just then, because Herod had expressed some curiosity about him; but nothing comes of it: the prisoner will not speak to him. When Jesus is ill received in a Samaritan village James and John propose to call down fire from heaven and destroy it; and Jesus replies that he is come not to destroy lives but to save them. The bias of Jesus against lawyers is emphasized, and also his resolution not to admit that he is more bound to his relatives than to strangers. He snubs a woman who blesses his mother. As this is contrary to the traditions of sentimental romance, Luke would presumably have avoided it had he not become persuaded that the brotherhood of Man and the Fatherhood of God are superior even to sentimental considerations. The story of the lawyer asking what are the two chief commandments is changed by making Jesus put the question to the lawyer instead of answering it.

As to doctrine, Luke is only clear when his feelings are touched. His logic is weak; for some of the sayings of Jesus are pieced together wrongly, as anyone who has read them in the right order and context in Matthew will discover at once. He does not make anything new out of Christ's mission, and, like the other evangelists, thinks that the whole point of it is that Jesus was the long expected Christ, and that he will presently come back to earth and establish his kingdom, having duly died and risen again after three days. Yet Luke not only records the teaching as to communism and the discarding of hate, which have, of course, nothing to do with the Second Coming, but quotes one very remarkable saying which is not compatible with it, which is, that people must not go about asking where the kingdom of heaven is, and saying "Lo, here!" and "Lo, there!" because the kingdom of heaven is within them. But Luke has no sense that this belongs to a quite different order of thought to his Christianity, and retains undisturbed his view of the kingdom as a locality as definite as Jerusalem or Madagascar.

JOHN
A NEW STORY AND A NEW CHARACTER

The gospel of John is a surprise after the others. Matthew, Mark and Luke describe the same events in the same order (the variations in Luke are negligible), and their gospels are therefore called the synoptic gospels. They tell substantially the same story of a wandering preacher who at the end of his life came to Jerusalem. John describes a preacher who spent practically his whole adult life in the capital, with occasional visits to the provinces. His circumstantial account of the calling of Peter and the sons of Zebedee is quite different from the others; and he says nothing about their being fishermen. He says expressly that Jesus, though baptized by John, did not himself practise baptism, and that his disciples did. Christ's agonized appeal against his doom in the garden of Gethsemane becomes a cold-blooded suggestion made in the temple at a much earlier period. Jesus argues much more; complains a good deal of the unreasonableness and dislike with which he is met; is by no means silent before Caiaphas and Pilate; lays much greater stress on his resurrection and on the eating of his body (losing all his disciples except the twelve in consequence); says many apparently contradictory and nonsensical things to which no ordinary reader can now find any clue; and gives the impression of an educated, not to say sophisticated mystic, different both in character and schooling from the simple and downright preacher of Matthew and Mark, and the urbane easyminded charmer of Luke. Indeed, the Jews say of him "How knoweth this man letters, having never learnt?"

JOHN THE IMMORTAL EYE-WITNESS

John, moreover, claims to be not only a chronicler but a witness. He declares that he is "the disciple whom Jesus loved," and that he actually leaned on the bosom of Jesus at the last supper and asked in a whisper which of them it was that should betray him. Jesus whispered that he would give a sop to the traitor, and thereupon handed one to Judas, who ate it and immediately became possessed by the devil. This is more natural than the other accounts, in which Jesus openly indicates Judas without eliciting any protest or exciting any comment. It also implies that Jesus deliberately bewitched Judas in order to bring about his own betrayal. Later on John claims that Jesus said to Peter "If I will that John tarry til I come, what is that to thee?" and John, with a rather obvious mock modesty, adds that he must not claim to be immortal, as the disciples concluded; for Christ did not use that expression, but merely remarked "If I will that he tarry til I come." No other evangelist claims personal intimacy with Christ, or even pretends to be his contemporary (there is no ground for identifying Matthew the publican with Matthew the Evangelist); and John is the only evangelist whose account of Christ's career and character is hopelessly irreconcilable with Matthew's. He is almost as bad as Matthew, by the way, in his repeated explanations of Christ's actions as having no other purpose than to fulfill the old prophecies. The impression is more unpleasant, because, as John, unlike Matthew, is educated, subtle, and obsessed with artificial intellectual mystifications, the discovery that he is stupid or superficial in so simple a matter strikes one with distrust and dislike, in spite of his great literary charm, a good example of which is his transfiguration of the harsh episode of the Syrophenician woman into the pleasant story of the woman of Samaria. This perhaps is why his claim to be John the disciple, or to be a contemporary of Christ or even of any survivor of Christ's generation, has been disputed, and finally, it seems, disallowed. But I repeat, I take no note here of the disputes of experts as to the date of the gospels, not because I am not acquainted with them, but because, as the earliest codices are Greek manuscripts of the fourth century A. D., and the Syrian ones are translations from the Greek, the paleographic expert has no difficulty in arriving at whatever conclusion happens to suit his beliefs or disbeliefs; and he never succeeds in convincing the other experts except when they believe or disbelieve exactly as he does. Hence I conclude that the dates of the original narratives cannot be ascertained, and that we must make the best of the evangelists' own accounts of themselves. There is, as we have seen, a very marked difference between them, leaving no doubt that we are dealing with four authors of well-marked diversity; but they all end in an attitude of expectancy of the Second Coming which they agree in declaring Jesus to have positively and unequivocally promised within the lifetime of his contemporaries. Any believer compiling a gospel after the last of these contemporaries had passed away, would either reject and omit the tradition of that promise on the ground that since it was not fulfilled, and could never now be fulfilled, it could not have been made, or else have had to confess to the Jews, who were the keenest critics of the Christians, that Jesus was either an impostor or the victim of a delusion. Now all the evangelists except Matthew expressly declare themselves to be believers; and Matthew's narrative is obviously not that of a sceptic. I therefore assume as a matter of common sense that, interpolations apart, the gospels are derived from narratives written in the first century A. D. I include John, because though it may be claimed that he hedged his position by claiming that Christ, who specially loved him, endowed him with a miraculous life until the Second Coming, the conclusion being that John is alive at this moment, I cannot believe that a literary forger could hope to save the situation by so outrageous a pretension. Also, John's narrative is in many passages nearer to the realities of public life than the simple chronicle of Matthew or the sentimental romance of Luke. This may be because John was obviously more a man of the world than the others, and knew, as mere chroniclers and romancers never know, what actually happens away from books and desks. But it may also be because he saw and heard what happened instead of collecting traditions about it. The paleographers and daters of first quotations may say what they please: John's claim to give evidence as an eyewitness whilst the others are only compiling history is supported by a certain verisimilitude which appeals to me as one who has preached a new doctrine and argued about it, as well as written stories. This verisimilitude may be dramatic art backed by knowledge of public life; but even at that we must not forget that the best dramatic art is the operation of a divinatory instinct for truth. Be that as it may, John was certainly not the man to believe in the Second Coming and yet give a date for it after that date had passed. There is really no escape from the conclusion that the originals of all the gospels date from the period within which there was still a possibility of the Second Coming occurring at the promised time.

THE PECULIAR THEOLOGY OF JESUS

In spite of the suspicions roused by John's idiosyncrasies, his narrative is of enormous importance to those who go to the gospels for a credible modern religion. For it is John who adds to the other records such sayings as that "I and my father are one"; that "God is a spirit"; that the aim of Jesus is not only that the people should have life, but that they should have it "more abundantly" (a distinction much needed by people who think a man is either alive or dead, and never consider the important question how much alive he is); and that men should bear in mind what they were told in the 82nd Psalm: that they are gods, and are responsible for the doing of the mercy and justice of God. The Jews stoned him for saying these things, and, when he remonstrated with them for stupidly stoning one who had done nothing to them but good works, replied "For a good work we stone thee not; but for blasphemy, because that thou, being a man, makest thyself God." He insists (referring to the 82nd Psalm) that if it is part of their own religion that they are gods on the assurance of God himself, it cannot be blasphemy for him, whom the Father sanctified and sent into the world, to say "I am the son of God." But they will not have this at any price; and he has to escape from their fury. Here the point is obscured by the distinction made by Jesus between himself and other men. He says, in effect, "If you are gods, then, *à fortiori*, I am a god." John makes him say this, just as he makes him say "I am the light of the world." But Matthew makes him say to the people "Ye are the light of the world." John has no grip of the significance of these scraps which he has picked up: he is far more interested in a notion of his own that men can escape death and do even more extraordinary things than Christ himself: in fact, he actually represents Jesus as promising this explicitly, and is finally led into the audacious hint that he, John, is himself immortal in the flesh. Still, he does not miss the significant sayings altogether. However inconsistent they may be with the doctrine he is consciously driving at, they appeal to some sub-intellectual instinct in him that makes him stick them in, like a child sticking tinsel stars on the robe of a toy angel.

John does not mention the ascension; and the end of his narratives leaves Christ restored to life, and appearing from time to time among his disciples. It is on one of these occasions

that John describes the miraculous draught of fishes which
Luke places at the other end of Christ's career, at the call of the
sons of Zebedee.

JOHN AGREED AS TO THE TRIAL AND CRUCIFIXION

Although John, following his practice of shewing Jesus's skill
as a debater, makes him play a less passive part at his trial, he
still gives substantially the same account of it as all the rest. And
the question that would occur to any modern reader never
occurs to him, any more than it occurred to Matthew, Mark,
or Luke. That question is, Why on earth did not Jesus defend
himself, and make the people rescue him from the High Priest?
He was so popular that they were unable to prevent him
driving the moneychangers out of the temple, or to arrest him
for it. When they did arrest him afterwards, they had to do it
at night in a garden. He could have argued with them as he
had often done in the temple, and justified himself both to the
Jewish law and to Caesar. And he had physical force at his
command to back up his arguments: all that was needed was a
speech to rally his followers; and he was not gagged. The reply
of the evangelists would have been that all these inquiries are
idle, because if Jesus had wished to escape, he could have saved
himself all that trouble by doing what John describes him as
doing: that is, casting his captors to the earth by an exertion of
his miraculous power. If you asked John why he let them get
up again and torment and execute him, John would have replied that it was part of the destiny of God to be slain and
buried and to rise again, and that to have avoided this destiny
would have been to repudiate his Godhead. And that is the
only apparent explanation. Whether you believe with the
evangelists that Christ could have rescued himself by a miracle,
or, as a modern Secularist, point out that he could have defended himself effectually, the fact remains that according to
all the narratives he did not do so. He had to die like a god, not

to save himself "like one of the princes." [1] The consensus on this point is important, because it proves the absolute sincerity of Jesus's declaration that he was a god. No impostor would have accepted such dreadful consequences without an effort to save himself. No impostor would have been nerved to endure them by the conviction that he would rise from the grave and live again after three days. If we accept the story at all, we must believe this, and believe also that his promise to return in glory and establish his kingdom on earth within the lifetime of men then living, was one which he believed that he could, and indeed must fulfil. Two evangelists declare that in his last agony he despaired, and reproached God for forsaking him. The other two represent him as dying in unshaken conviction and charity with the simple remark that the ordeal was finished. But all four testify that his faith was not deceived, and that he actually rose again after three days. And I think it unreasonable to doubt that all four wrote their narratives in full faith that the other promise would be fulfilled too, and that they themselves might live to witness the Second Coming.

CREDIBILITY OF THE GOSPELS

It will be noted by the older among my readers, who are sure to be obsessed more or less by elderly wrangles as to whether the gospels are credible as matter-of-fact narratives, that I have hardly raised this question, and have accepted the credible and incredible with equal complacency. I have done this because credibility is a subjective condition, as the evolution of religious belief clearly shews. Belief is not dependent on evidence and reason. There is as much evidence that the

[1] Jesus himself had referred to that psalm (LXXXII) in which men who have judged unjustly and accepted the persons of the wicked (including by anticipation practically all the white inhabitants of the British Isles and the North American continent, to mention no other places) are condemned in the words, "I have said, ye are gods; and all of ye are children of the Most High; but ye shall die like men, and fall like one of the princes."

miracles occurred as that the battle of Waterloo occurred, or that a large body of Russian troops passed through England in 1914 to take part in the war on the western front. The reasons for believing in the murder of Pompey are the same as the reasons for believing in the raising of Lazarus. Both have been believed and doubted by men of equal intelligence. Miracles, in the sense of phenomena we cannot explain, surround us on every hand: life itself is the miracle of miracles. Miracles in the sense of events that violate the normal course of our experience are vouched for every day: the flourishing Church of Christ Scientist is founded on a multitude of such miracles. Nobody believes all the miracles: everybody believes some of them. I cannot tell why men who will not believe that Jesus ever existed yet believe firmly that Shakespear was Bacon. I cannot tell why people who believe that angels appeared and fought on our side at the battle of Mons, and who believe that miracles occur quite frequently at Lourdes, nevertheless boggle at the miracle of the liquefaction of the blood of St Januarius, and reject it as a trick of priestcraft. I cannot tell why people who will not believe Matthew's story of three kings bringing costly gifts to the cradle of Jesus, believe Luke's story of the shepherds and the stable. I cannot tell why people, brought up to believe the Bible in the old literal way as an infallible record and revelation, and rejecting that view later on, begin by rejecting the Old Testament, and give up the belief in a brimstone hell before they give up (if they ever do) the belief in a heaven of harps, crowns, and thrones. I cannot tell why people who will not believe in baptism on any terms believe in vaccination with the cruel fanaticism of inquisitors. I am convinced that if a dozen sceptics were to draw up in parallel columns a list of the events narrated in the gospels which they consider credible and incredible respectively, their lists would be different in several particulars. Belief is literally a matter of taste.

FASHIONS IN BELIEF

Now matters of taste are mostly also matters of fashion. We are conscious of a difference between medieval fashions in belief and modern fashions. For instance, though we are more credulous than men were in the Middle Ages, and entertain such crowds of fortune-tellers, magicians, miracle workers, agents of communication with the dead, discoverers of the elixir of life, transmuters of metals, and healers of all sorts, as the Middle Ages never dreamed of as possible, yet we will not take our miracles in the form that convinced the Middle Ages. Arithmetical numbers appealed to the Middle Ages just as they do to us, because they are difficult to deal with, and because the greatest masters of numbers, the Newtons and Leibnitzes, rank among the greatest men. But there are fashions in numbers too. The Middle Ages took a fancy to some familiar number like seven; and because it was an odd number, and the world was made in seven days, and there are seven stars in Charles's Wain, and for a dozen other reasons, they were ready to believe anything that had a seven or a seven times seven in it. Seven deadly sins, seven swords of sorrow in the heart of the Virgin, seven champions of Christendom, seemed obvious and reasonable things to believe in simply because they were seven. To us, on the contrary, the number seven is the stamp of superstition. We will believe in nothing less than millions. A medieval doctor gained his patient's confidence by telling him that his vitals were being devoured by seven worms. Such a diagnosis would ruin a modern physician. The modern physician tells his patient that he is ill because every drop of his blood is swarming with a million microbes; and the patient believes him abjectly and instantly. Had a bishop told William the Conqueror that the sun was seventy-seven miles distant from the earth, William would have believed him not only out of respect for the Church, but because he would have felt that seventy-seven miles was the proper distance. The Kaiser,

knowing just as little about it as the Conqueror, would send
that bishop to an asylum. Yet he (I presume) unhesitatingly
accepts the estimate of ninety-two and nine-tenths millions of
miles, or whatever the latest big figure may be.

CREDIBILITY AND TRUTH

And here I must remind you that our credulity is not to be
measured by the truth of the things we believe. When men
believed that the earth was flat, they were not credulous: they
were using their common sense, and, if asked to prove that the
earth was flat, would have said simply, "Look at it." Those who
refuse to believe that it is round are exercising a wholesome
scepticism. The modern man who believes that the earth is
round is grossly credulous. Flat Earth men drive him to fury by
confuting him with the greatest ease when he tries to argue
about it. Confront him with a theory that the earth is cylin-
drical, or annular, or hour-glass shaped, and he is lost. The
thing he believes may be true, but that is not why he believes
it: he believes it because in some mysterious way it appeals to
his imagination. If you ask him why he believes that the sun is
ninety-odd million miles off, either he will have to confess that
he doesn't know, or he will say that Newton proved it. But he
has not read the treatise in which Newton proved it, and does
not even know that it was written in Latin. If you press an
Ulster Protestant as to why he regards Newton as an infallible
authority, and St Thomas Aquinas or the Pope as superstitious
liars whom, after his death, he will have the pleasure of watching from his place in heaven whilst they roast in eternal flame,
or if you ask me why I take into serious consideration Colonel
Sir Almroth Wright's estimates of the number of streptococci
contained in a given volume of serum whilst I can only laugh
at the earlier estimates of the number of angels that can be
accommodated on the point of a needle, no reasonable reply is
possible except that somehow sevens and angels are out of fashion, and billions and streptococci are all the rage. I simply can-

not tell you why Bacon, Montaigne, and Cervantes had a quite different fashion of credulity and incredulity from the Venerable Bede and Piers Plowman and the divine doctors of the Aquinas-Aristotle school, who were certainly no stupider, and had the same facts before them. Still less can I explain why, if we assume that these leaders of thought had all reasoned out their beliefs, their authority seemed conclusive to one generation and blasphemous to another, neither generation having followed the reasoning or gone into the facts of the matter for itself at all.

It is therefore idle to begin disputing with the reader as to what he should believe in the gospels and what he should disbelieve. He will believe what he can, and disbelieve what he must. If he draws any lines at all, they will be quite arbitrary ones. St John tells us that when Jesus explicitly claimed divine honors by the sacrament of his body and blood, so many of his disciples left him that their number was reduced to twelve. Many modern readers will not hold out so long: they will give in at the first miracle. Others will discriminate. They will accept the healing miracles, and reject the feeding of the multitude. To some the walking on the water will be a legendary exaggeration of a swim, ending in an ordinary rescue of Peter; and the raising of Lazarus will be only a similar glorification of a commonplace feat of artificial respiration, whilst others will scoff at it as a planned imposture in which Lazarus acted as a confederate. Between the rejection of the stories as wholly fabulous and the acceptance of them as the evangelists themselves mean them to be accepted, there will be many shades of belief and disbelief, of sympathy and derision. It is not a question of being a Christian or not. A Mahometan Arab will accept literally and without question parts of the narrative which an English Archbishop has to reject or explain away; and many Theosophists and lovers of the wisdom of India, who never enter a Christian Church except as sightseers, will revel in parts of John's gospel which mean nothing to a pious matter-of-fact

Bradford manufacturer. Every reader takes from the Bible what he can get. In submitting a précis of the gospel narratives I have not implied any estimate either of their credibility or of their truth. I have simply informed him or reminded him, as the case may be, of what those narratives tell us about their hero.

CHRISTIAN ICONOLATRY AND THE PERIL OF THE ICONOCLAST

I must now abandon this attitude, and make a serious draft on the reader's attention by facing the question whether, if and when the medieval and Methodist will-to-believe the Salvationist and miraculous side of the gospel narratives fails us, as it plainly has failed the leaders of modern thought, there will be anything left of the mission of Jesus: whether, in short, we may not throw the gospels into the waste-paper basket, or put them away on the fiction shelf of our libraries. I venture to reply that we shall be, on the contrary, in the position of the man in Bunyan's riddle who found that "the more he threw away, the more he had." We get rid, to begin with, of the idolatrous or iconographic worship of Christ. By this I mean literally that worship which is given to pictures and statues of him, and to finished and unalterable stories about him. The test of the prevalence of this is that if you speak or write of Jesus as a real live person, or even as a still active God, such worshippers are more horrified than Don Juan was when the statue stepped from its pedestal and came to supper with him. You may deny the divinity of Jesus; you may doubt whether he ever existed; you may reject Christianity for Judaism, Mahometanism, Shintoism, or Fire Worship; and the iconolaters, placidly contemptuous, will only classify you as a freethinker or a heathen. But if you venture to wonder how Christ would have looked if he had shaved and had his hair cut, or what size in shoes he took, or whether he swore when he stood on a nail in the carpenter's shop, or could not button his robe when he was in a hurry, or whether he laughed over the repartees by which he baffled the priests when they tried to trap him into sedition and blasphemy, or even if you tell any part of his story in the vivid terms of modern colloquial slang, you will produce an extraordinary dismay and horror among the iconolaters. You will have made the picture come out of its frame, the statue descend from its pedestal, the story become real, with all the incalculable consequences that may flow from this terrifying miracle. It is at such moments that you realize that the iconolaters have never for a moment conceived Christ as a real person who meant what he said, as a fact, as a force like electricity, only needing the invention of suitable political machinery to be applied to the affairs of mankind with revolutionary effect.

Thus it is not disbelief that is dangerous in our society: it is belief. The moment it strikes you (as it may any day) that Christ is not the lifeless harmless image he has hitherto been to you, but a rallying centre for revolutionary influences which all established States and Churches fight, you must look to yourselves; for you have brought the image to life; and the mob may not be able to bear that horror.

THE ALTERNATIVE TO BARABBAS

But mobs must be faced if civilization is to be saved. It did not need the present war to shew that neither the iconographic Christ nor the Christ of St Paul has succeeded in effecting the salvation of human society. Whilst I write, the Turks are said to be massacring the Armenian Christians on an unprecedented scale; but Europe is not in a position to remonstrate; for her Christians are slaying one another by every device which civilization has put within their reach as busily as they are slaying the Turks. Barabbas is triumphant everywhere; and the final use he makes of his triumph is to lead us all to suicide with heroic gestures and resounding lies. Now those who, like myself, see the Barabbasque social organization as a failure, and are convinced that the Life Force (or whatever you choose to call it) cannot be finally beaten by any failure, and will even supersede humanity by evolving a higher species if we cannot master the problems raised by the multiplication of our own numbers, have always known that Jesus had a real message, and have felt the fascination of his character and doctrine. Not that we should nowadays dream of claiming any supernatural authority for him, much less the technical authority which attaches to an educated modern philosopher and jurist. But when, having entirely got rid of Salvationist Christianity, and even contracted a prejudice against Jesus on the score of his involuntary connection with it, we engage on a purely scientific study of economics, criminology, and biology, and find that our practical conclusions are virtually those of Jesus, we are distinctly pleased and encouraged to find that we were doing him an injustice, and that the nimbus that surrounds his head in the pictures may be interpreted some day as a light of science rather than a declaration of sentiment or a label of idolatry.

The doctrines in which Jesus is thus confirmed are, roughly, the following:

1. The kingdom of heaven is within you. You are the son of God; and God is the son of man. God is a spirit, to be worshipped in spirit and in truth, and not an elderly gentleman to be bribed and begged from. We are members one of another; so that you cannot injure or help your neighbor without injuring or helping yourself. God is your father: you are here to do God's work; and you and your father are one.

2. Get rid of property by throwing it into the common stock. Dissociate your work entirely from money payments. If you let a child starve you are letting God starve. Get rid of all anxiety about tomorrow's dinner and clothes, because you cannot serve two masters: God and Mammon.

3. Get rid of judges and punishment and revenge. Love your neighbor as yourself, he being a part of yourself. And love your enemies: they are your neighbors.

4. Get rid of your family entanglements. Every mother you

meet is as much your mother as the woman who bore you. Every man you meet is as much your brother as the man she bore after you. Dont waste your time at family funerals grieving for your relatives: attend to life, not to death: there are as good fish in the sea as ever came out of it, and better. In the kingdom of heaven, which, as aforesaid, is within you, there is no marriage nor giving in marriage, because you cannot devote your life to two divinities: God and the person you are married to.

Now these are very interesting propositions; and they become more interesting every day, as experience and science drive us more and more to consider them favorably. In considering them, we shall waste our time unless we give them a reasonable construction. We must assume that the man who saw his way through such a mass of popular passion and illusion as stands between us and a sense of the value of such teaching was quite aware of all the objections that occur to an average stockbroker in the first five minutes. It is true that the world is governed to a considerable extent by the considerations that occur to stockbrokers in the first five minutes; but as the result is that the world is so badly governed that those who know the truth can hardly bear to live in it, an objection from an average stockbroker constitutes in itself a *prima facie* case for any social reform.

THE REDUCTION TO MODERN PRACTICE
OF CHRISTIANITY

All the same, we must reduce the ethical counsels and proposals of Jesus to modern practice if they are to be of any use to us. If we ask our stockbroker to act simply as Jesus advised his disciples to act, he will reply, very justly, "You are advising me to become a tramp." If we urge a rich man to sell all that he has and give it to the poor, he will inform us that such an operation is impossible. If he sells his shares and his lands, their purchaser will continue all those activities which oppress

the poor. If all the rich men take the advice simultaneously
the shares will fall to zero and the lands be unsaleable. If one
man sells out and throws the money into the slums, the only
result will be to add himself and his dependents to the list of
the poor, and to do no good to the poor beyond giving a chance
few of them a drunken spree. We must therefore bear in mind
that whereas, in the time of Jesus, and in the ages which grew
darker and darker after his death until the darkness, after a
brief false dawn in the Reformation and the Renascence, cul-
minated in the commercial night of the nineteenth century, it
was believed that you could not make men good by Act of
Parliament, we now know that you cannot make them good in
any other way, and that a man who is better than his fellows
is a nuisance. The rich man must sell up not only himself but
his whole class; and that can be done only through the Chan-
cellor of the Exchequer. The disciple cannot have his bread
without money until there is bread for everybody without
money; and that requires an elaborate municipal organization
of the food supply, rate supported. Being members one of another means One Man One Vote, and One Woman One Vote,
and universal suffrage and equal incomes and all sorts of mod-
dern political measures. Even in Syria in the time of Jesus his
teachings could not possibly have been realized by a series of
independent explosions of personal righteousness on the part of
the separate units of the population. Jerusalem could not have
done what even a village community cannot do, and what
Robinson Crusoe himself could not have done if his conscience,
and the stern compulsion of Nature, had not imposed a common rule on the half dozen Robinson Crusoes who struggled
within him for not wholly compatible satisfactions. And what
cannot be done in Jerusalem or Juan Fernandez cannot be done
in London, New York, Paris, and Berlin.

   In short, Christianity, good or bad, right or wrong, must
perforce be left out of the question in human affairs until it

is made practically applicable to them by complicated political devices; and to pretend that a field preacher under the governorship of Pontius Pilate, or even Pontius Pilate himself in council with all the wisdom of Rome, could have worked out applications of Christianity or any other system of morals for the twentieth century, is to shelve the subject much more effectually than Nero and all its other persecutors ever succeeded in doing. Personal righteousness, and the view that you cannot make people moral by Act of Parliament, is, in fact, the favorite defensive resort of the people who, consciously or subconsciously, are quite determined not to have their property meddled with by Jesus or any other reformer.

MODERN COMMUNISM

Now let us see what modern experience and sociology have to say to the suggestion of Jesus that you should get rid of your property by throwing it into the common stock. One can hear the Pharisees of Jerusalem and Chorazin and Bethsaida saying, "My good fellow, if you were to divide up the wealth of Judea equally today, before the end of the year you would have rich and poor, poverty and affluence, just as you have today; for there will always be the idle and the industrious, the thrifty and the wasteful, the drunken and the sober; and, as you yourself have very justly observed, the poor we shall have always with us." And we can hear the reply, "Woe unto you, liars and hypocrites; for ye have this very day divided up the wealth of the country yourselves, as must be done every day (for man liveth not otherwise than from hand to mouth, nor can fish and eggs endure for ever); and ye have divided it unjustly; also ye have said that my reproach to you for having the poor always with you was a law unto you that this evil should persist and stink in the nostrils of God to all eternity; wherefore I think that Lazarus will yet see you beside Dives in hell." Modern Capitalism has made short work of the primitive pleas for in-

equality. The Pharisees themselves have organized communism
in capital. Joint stock is the order of the day. An attempt to
return to individual properties as the basis of our production
would smash civilization more completely than ten revolutions.
You cannot get the fields tilled today until the farmer becomes
a co-operator. Take the shareholder to his railway, and ask him
to point out to you the particular length of rail, the particular
seat in the railway carriage, the particular lever in the engine
that is his very own and nobody elses; and he will shun you as
a madman, very wisely. And if, like Ananias and Sapphira, you
try to hold back your little shop or what not from the common
stock, represented by the Trust, or Combine, or Kartel, the
Trust will presently freeze you out and rope you in and finally
strike you dead industrially as thoroughly as St Peter himself.
There is no longer any practical question open as to Communism in production: the struggle today is over the distribution of the product: that is, over the daily dividing-up which
is the first necessity of organized society.

REDISTRIBUTION

Now it needs no Christ to convince anybody today that our
system of distribution is wildly and monstrously wrong. We
have million-dollar babies side by side with paupers worn out
by a long life of unremitted drudgery. One person in every five
dies in a workhouse, a public hospital, or a madhouse. In cities
like London the proportion is very nearly one in two. Naturally
so outrageous a distribution has to be effected by violence pure
and simple. If you demur, you are sold up. If you resist the
selling up you are bludgeoned and imprisoned, the process being euphemistically called the maintenance of law and order.
Iniquity can go no further. By this time nobody who knows the
figures of the distribution defends them. The most bigoted British Conservative hesitates to say that his king should be much
poorer than Mr Rockefeller, or to proclaim the moral superiority of prostitution to needlework on the ground that it pays

better. The need for a drastic redistribution of income in all civilized countries is now as obvious and as generally admitted as the need for sanitation.

SHALL HE WHO MAKES, OWN?

It is when we come to the question of the proportions in which we are to redistribute that controversy begins. We are bewildered by an absurdly unpractical notion that in some way a man's income should be given to him, not to enable him to live, but as a sort of Sunday School Prize for good behavior. And this folly is complicated by a less ridiculous but quite as unpractical belief that it is possible to assign to each person the exact portion of the national income that he or she has produced. To a child it seems that the blacksmith has made a horse-shoe, and that therefore the horse-shoe is his. But the blacksmith knows that the horse-shoe does not belong solely to him, but to his landlord, to the rate collector and taxgatherer, to the men from whom he bought the iron and anvil and the coals, leaving only a scrap of its value for himself; and this scrap he has to exchange with the butcher and baker and the clothier for the things that he really appropriates as living tissue or its wrappings, paying for all of them more than their cost; for these fellow traders of his have also their landlords and moneylenders to satisfy. If, then, such simple and direct village examples of apparent individual production turn out on a moment's examination to be the products of an elaborate social organization, what is to be said of such products as dreadnoughts, factory-made pins and needles, and steel pens? If God takes the dreadnought in one hand and a steel pen in the other, and asks Job who made them, and to whom they should belong by maker's right, Job must scratch his puzzled head with a potsherd and be dumb, unless indeed it strikes him that God is the ultimate maker, and that all we have a right to do with the product is to feed his lambs.

LABOR TIME

So maker's right as an alternative to taking the advice of
Jesus would not work. In practice nothing was possible in that
direction but to pay a worker by labor time: so much an hour
or day or week or year. But how much? When that question
came up, the only answer was "as little as he can be starved
into accepting," with the ridiculous results already mentioned,
and the additional anomaly that the largest share went to the
people who did not work at all, and the least to those who
worked hardest. In England nine-tenths of the wealth goes into
the pockets of one-tenth of the population.

THE DREAM OF DISTRIBUTION
ACCORDING TO MERIT

Against this comes the protest of the Sunday School theorists
"Why not distribute according to merit?" Here one imagines
Jesus, whose smile has been broadening down the ages as attempt after attempt to escape from his teaching has led to
deeper and deeper disaster, laughing outright. Was ever so idi
otic a project mooted as the estimation of virtue in money? The
London School of Economics is, we must suppose, to set examination papers with such questions as, "Taking the money
value of the virtues of Jesus as 100, and of Judas Iscariot as zero,
give the correct figures for, respectively, Pontius Pilate, the
proprietor of the Gadarene swine, the widow who put her mite
in the poor-box, Mr Horatio Bottomley, Shakespear, Mr Jack
Johnson, Sir Isaac Newton, Palestrina, Offenbach, Sir Thomas
Lipton, Mr Paul Cinquevalli, your family doctor, Florence
Nightingale, Mrs Siddons, your charwoman, the Archbishop
of Canterbury, and the common hangman." Or "The late Mr
Barney Barnato received as his lawful income three thousand
times as much money as an English agricultural laborer of
good general character. Name the principal virtues in which
Mr Barnato exceeded the laborer three thousandfold; and give

in figures the loss sustained by civilization when Mr Barnato was driven to despair and suicide by the reduction of his multiple to one thousand." The Sunday School idea, with its principle "to each the income he deserves," is really too silly for discussion. Hamlet disposed of it three hundred years ago. "Use every man after his deserts, and who shall scape whipping?" Jesus remains unshaken as the practical man; and we stand exposed as the fools, the blunderers, the unpractical visionaries. The moment you try to reduce the Sunday School idea to figures you find that it brings you back to the hopeless plan of paying for a man's time; and your examination paper will read "The time of Jesus was worth nothing (he complained that the foxes had holes and the birds of the air nests whilst he had not a place to lay his head). Dr Crippen's time was worth, say, three hundred and fifty pounds a year. Criticize this arrangement; and, if you dispute its justice, state in pounds, dollars, francs and marks, what their relative time wages ought to have been." Your answer may be that the question is in extremely bad taste and that you decline to answer it. But you cannot object to being asked how many minutes of a bookmaker's time are worth two hours of an astronomer's?

VITAL DISTRIBUTION

In the end you are forced to ask the question you should have asked at the beginning. What do you give a man an income for? Obviously to keep him alive. Since it is evident that the first condition on which he can be kept alive without enslaving somebody else is that he shall produce an equivalent for what it costs to keep him alive, we may quite rationally compel him to abstain from idling by whatever means we employ to compel him to abstain from murder, arson, forgery, or any other crime. The one supremely foolish thing to do with him is to do nothing: that is, to be as idle, lazy, and heartless in dealing with him as he is in dealing with us. Even if we provided work for him instead of basing, as we do, our whole industrial system on successive competitive waves of overwork with their ensuing troughs of unemployment, we should still sternly deny him the alternative of not doing it; for the result must be that he will become poor and make his children poor if he has any; and poor people are cancers in the common-wealth, costing far more than if they were handsomely pensioned off as incurables. Jesus had more sense than to propose anything of the sort. He said to his disciples, in effect, "Do your work for love; and let the other people lodge and feed and clothe you for love." Or, as we should put it nowadays, "for nothing." All human experience and all natural uncommercial-ized human aspiration point to this as the right path. The Greeks said, "First secure an independent income; and then practise virtue." We all strive towards an independent income. We all know as well as Jesus did that if we have to take thought for the morrow as to whether there shall be anything to eat or drink it will be impossible for us to think of nobler things, or live a higher life than that of a mole, whose life is from begin-ning to end a frenzied pursuit of food. Until the community is organized in such a way that the fear of bodily want is for-gotten as completely as the fear of wolves already is in civ-ilized capitals, we shall never have a decent social life. Indeed the whole attraction of our present arrangement lies in the fact that it does relieve a handful of us from this fear; but as the relief is effected stupidly and wickedly by making the favored handful parasitic on the rest, they are smitten with the de-generacy which seems to be the inevitable biological penalty of complete parasitism. They corrupt culture and statecraft instead of contributing to them, their excessive leisure being as mis-chievous as the excessive toil of the laborers. Anyhow, the moral is clear. The two main problems of organized society: how to produce subsistence enough for all its members, and how to prevent the theft of that subsistence by idlers, should be care-fully dissociated; for the triumphant solution of the first by our inventors and chemists has been offset by the disastrous failure of our rulers to solve the other. Optimism on this point is only wilful blindness: we all have the hard fact of the failure before us. The only people who cling to the lazy delusion that it is possible to find a just distribution that will work automatically are those who postulate some revolutionary change like land nationalization, which by itself would obviously only force into greater urgency the problem of how to distribute the product of the land among all the individuals in the community.

EQUAL DISTRIBUTION

When that problem is at last faced, the question of the proportion in which the national income shall be distributed can have only one answer. All our shares must be equal. It has always been so: it always will be so. It is true that the incomes of robbers vary considerably from individual to individual; and the variation is reflected in the incomes of their parasites. The commercialization of certain exceptional talents has also produced exceptional incomes, direct and derivative. Persons who live on rent of land and capital are economically, though not legally, in the category of robbers, and have grotesquely different incomes. But in the huge mass of mankind variation of income from individual to individual is unknown, because it is ridiculously impracticable. As a device for persuading a carpenter that a judge is a creature of superior nature to himself, to be deferred and submitted to even to the death, we may give a carpenter a hundred pounds a year and a judge five thousand; but the wage for one carpenter is the wage for all the carpenters: the salary for one judge is the salary for all the judges.

THE CAPTAIN AND THE CABIN BOY

Nothing, therefore, is really in question, or ever has been, but the differences between class incomes. Already there is economic equality between captains, and economic equality between cabin boys. What is at issue still is whether there shall be economic equality between captains and cabin boys. What would Jesus have said? Presumably he would have said that if your only object is to produce a captain and a cabin boy for the purpose of transferring you from Liverpool to New York, or to manœuvre a fleet and carry powder from the magazine to the gun, then you need give no more than a shilling to the cabin boy for every pound you give to the more expensively trained captain. But if in addition to this you desire to allow the two human souls which are inseparable from the captain and the cabin boy, and which alone differentiate them from the donkey-engine, to develop all their possibilities, then you may find the cabin boy costing rather more than the captain, because cabin boy's work does not do so much for the soul as captain's work. Consequently you will have to give him at least as much as the captain unless you definitely wish him to be a lower creature, in which case the sooner you are hanged as an abortionist the better. That is the fundamental argument.

THE POLITICAL AND BIOLOGICAL OBJECTIONS TO INEQUALITY

But there are other reasons for objecting to class stratification of income which have heaped themselves up since the time of Jesus. In politics it defeats every form of government except that of a necessarily corrupt oligarchy. Democracy in the most democratic modern republics: France and the United States for example, is an imposture and a delusion. It reduces justice and law to a farce: law becomes merely an instrument for keeping the poor in subjection; and accused workmen are tried, not by a jury of their peers, but by conspiracies of their exploiters. The press is the press of the rich and the curse of the poor: it becomes dangerous to teach men to read. The priest becomes the mere complement of the policeman in the machinery by which the countryhouse oppresses the village. Worst of all, marriage becomes a class affair: the infinite variety of choice which nature offers to the young in search of a mate is narrowed to a handful of persons of similar income; and beauty and health become the dreams of artists and the advertisements of quacks instead of the normal conditions of life. Society is not only divided but actually destroyed in all directions by inequality of income between classes: such stability as it has is due to the huge blocks of people between whom there is equality of income.

JESUS AS ECONOMIST

It seems therefore that we must begin by holding the right to an income as sacred and equal, just as we now begin by holding the right to life as sacred and equal. Indeed the one right is only a restatement of the other. To hang me for cutting a dock laborer's throat after making much of me for leaving him to starve when I do not happen to have a ship for him to unload is idiotic; for as he does far less mischief with his throat cut than when he is starving, a rational society would esteem the cutthroat more highly than the capitalist. The thing has become so obvious, and the evil so unendurable, that if our attempt at civilization is not to perish like all the previous ones, we shall have to organize our society in such a way as to be able to say to every person in the land, "Take no thought, saying What shall we eat? or What shall we drink? or Wherewithal shall we be clothed?" We shall then no longer have a race of men whose hearts are in their pockets and safes and at their bankers. As Jesus said, where your treasure is, there will your heart be also. That was why he recommended that money should cease to be a treasure, and that we should take steps to make ourselves utterly reckless of it, setting our minds free for higher uses. In other words, that we should all be gentlemen and take care of our country because our country takes care of us, instead of the commercialized cads we are, doing everything and anything for money, and selling our souls and bodies by the pound and the inch after wasting half the day haggling over the price. Decidedly, whether you think Jesus was

God or not, you must admit that he was a first-rate political economist.

JESUS AS BIOLOGIST

He was also, as we now see, a first-rate biologist. It took a century and a half of evolutionary preachers, from Buffon and Goethe to Butler and Bergson, to convince us that we and our father are one; that as the kingdom of heaven is within us we need not go about looking for it and crying Lo here! and Lo there!; that God is not a picture of a pompous person in white robes in the family Bible, but a spirit; that it is through this spirit that we evolve towards greater abundance of life; that we are the lamps in which the light of the world burns: that, in short, we are gods though we die like men. All that is today sound biology and psychology; and the efforts of Natural Selectionists like Weismann to reduce evolution to mere automatism have not touched the doctrine of Jesus, though they have made short work of the theologians who conceived God as a magnate keeping men and angels as Lord Rothschild keeps buffaloes and emus at Tring.

MONEY THE MIDWIFE OF SCIENTIFIC COMMUNISM

It may be asked here by some simple-minded reader why we should not resort to crude Communism as the disciples were told to do. This would be quite practicable in a village where production was limited to the supply of the primitive wants which nature imposes on all human beings alike. We know that people need bread and boots without waiting for them to come and ask for these things and offer to pay for them. But when civilization advances to the point at which articles are produced that no man absolutely needs and that only some men fancy or can use, it is necessary that individuals should be able to have things made to their order and at their own cost. It is safe to provide bread for everybody because everybody wants and eats bread; but it would be absurd to provide microscopes and trombones, pet snakes and polo mallets, alembics and test tubes for everybody, as nine-tenths of them would be wasted; and the nine-tenths of the population who do not use such things would object to their being provided at all. We have in the invaluable instrument called money a means of enabling every individual to order and pay for the particular things he desires over and above the things he must consume in order to remain alive, plus the things the State insists on his having and using whether he wants to or not: for example, clothes, sanitary arrangements, armies and navies. In large communities, where even the most eccentric demands for manufactured articles average themselves out until they can be foreseen within a negligible margin of error, direct communism (Take what you want without payment, as the people do in Morris's News From Nowhere) will, after a little experience, be found not only practicable but highly economical to an extent that now seems impossible. The sportsmen, the musicians, the physicists, the biologists will get their apparatus for the asking as easily as their bread, or, as at present, their paving, street lighting, and bridges; and the deaf man will not object to contribute to communal flutes when the musician has to contribute to communal ear trumpets. There are cases (for example, radium) in which the demand may be limited to the merest handful of laboratory workers, and in which nevertheless the whole community must pay because the price is beyond the means of any individual worker. But even when the utmost allowance is made for extensions of communism that now seem fabulous, there will still remain for a long time to come regions of supply and demand in which men will need and use money or individual credit, and for which, therefore, they must have individual incomes. Foreign travel is an obvious instance. We are so far from even national communism still, that we shall probably have considerable developments of local communism before it becomes possible for a Manchester man to go up to London for a day without taking any money with him. The modern practical form of the communism of Jesus is therefore, for the present, equal distribution of the surplus of the national income that is not absorbed by simple communism.

JUDGE NOT

In dealing with crime and the family, modern thought and experience have thrown no fresh light on the views of Jesus. When Swift had occasion to illustrate the corruption of our civilization by making a catalogue of the types of scoundrels it produces, he always gave judges a conspicuous place alongside of them they judged. And he seems to have done this not as a restatement of the doctrine of Jesus, but as the outcome of his own observation and judgment. One of Mr Gilbert Chesterton's stories has for its hero a judge who, whilst trying a criminal case, is so overwhelmed by the absurdity of his position and the wickedness of the things it forces him to do, that he throws off the ermine there and then, and goes out into the world to live the life of an honest man instead of that of a cruel idol. There has also been a propaganda of a soulless stupidity called Determinism, representing man as a dead object driven hither and thither by his environment, antecedents, circumstances, and so forth, which nevertheless does remind us that there are limits to the number of cubits an individual can add to his stature morally or physically, and that it is silly as well as cruel to torment a man five feet high for not being able to pluck fruit that is within the reach of men of average height. I have known a case of an unfortunate child being beaten for not being able to tell the time after receiving an elaborate explanation of the figures on a clock dial, the fact being that she was short-sighted and could not see them. This is a typical illustration of the absurdities and cruelties into which we are led by the counter-stupidity to Determinism: the doctrine of Free Will. The notion that people can be good if they like, and that you should give them a powerful additional motive for

goodness by tormenting them when they do evil, would soon
reduce itself to absurdity if its application were not kept within
the limits which nature sets to the self-control of most of us.
Nobody supposes that a man with no ear for music or no
mathematical faculty could be compelled on pain of death,
however cruelly inflicted, to hum all the themes of Beethoven's
symphonies or to complete Newton's work on fluxions.

LIMITS TO FREE WILL

Consequently such of our laws as are not merely the intim-
idations by which tyrannies are maintained under pretext of
law, can be obeyed through the exercise of a quite common
degree of reasoning power and self-control. Most men and
women can endure the ordinary annoyances and disappoint-
ments of life without committing murderous assaults. They conclude therefore that any person can refrain from such assaults
if he or she chooses to, and proceed to reinforce self-control by
threats of severe punishment. But in this they are mistaken.
There are people, some of them possessing considerable powers
of mind and body, who can no more restrain the fury into
which a trifling mishap throws them than a dog can restrain
himself from snapping if he is suddenly and painfully pinched.
People fling knives and lighted paraffin lamps at one another
in a dispute over a dinner-table. Men who have suffered several long sentences of penal servitude for murderous assaults
will, the very day after they are released, seize their wives and
cast them under drays at an irritating word. We have not only
people who cannot resist an opportunity of stealing for the sake
of satisfying their wants, but even people who have a specific
mania for stealing, and do it when they are in no need of the
things they steal. Burglary fascinates some men as sailoring fascinates some boys. Among respectable people how many are
there who can be restrained by the warnings of their doctors
and the lessons of experience from eating and drinking more
than is good for them? It is true that between self-controlled

people and ungovernable people there is a narrow margin of
moral malingerers who can be made to behave themselves by
the fear of consequences; but it is not worth while maintaining
an abominable system of malicious, deliberate, costly and degrading ill-treatment of criminals for the sake of these marginal
cases. For practical dealing with crime, Determinism or Predes-
tination is quite a good working rule. People without self-control enough for social purposes may be killed, or may be kept
in asylums with a view to studying their condition and ascer-
taining whether it is curable. To torture them and give ourselves virtuous airs at their expense is ridiculous and barbarous;
and the desire to do it is vindictive and cruel. And though
vindictiveness and cruelty are at least human qualities when
they are frankly proclaimed and indulged, they are loathsome
when they assume the robes of Justice. Which, I take it, is why
Shakespear's Isabella gave such a dressing-down to Judge An-
gelo, and why Swift reserved the hottest corner of his hell for
judges. Also, of course, why Jesus said "Judge not that ye be
not judged" and "If any man hear my words and believe not,
I judge him not" because "he hath one that judgeth him":
namely, the Father who is one with him.

When we are robbed we generally appeal to the criminal
law, not considering that if the criminal law were effective
we should not have been robbed. That convicts us of vengeance.

I need not elaborate the argument further. I have dealt with
it sufficiently elsewhere. I have only to point out that we have
been judging and punishing ever since Jesus told us not to; and
I defy anyone to make out a convincing case for believing that
the world has been any better than it would have been if
there had never been a judge, a prison, or a gallows in it all
that time. We have simply added the misery of punishment
to the misery of crime, and the cruelty of the judge to the
cruelty of the criminal. We have taken the bad man, and made
him worse by torture and degradation, incidentally making our-

selves worse in the process. It does not seem very sensible, does it? It would have been far easier to kill him as kindly as possible, or to label him and leave him to his conscience, or to treat him as an invalid or a lunatic is now treated (it is only of late years, by the way, that madmen have been delivered from the whip, the chain, and the cage); and this, I presume, is the form in which the teaching of Jesus could have been put into practice.

JESUS ON MARRIAGE AND THE FAMILY

When we come to marriage and the family, we find Jesus making the same objection to that individual appropriation of human beings which is the essence of matrimony as to the individual appropriation of wealth. A married man, he said, will try to please his wife, and a married woman to please her husband, instead of doing the work of God. This is another version of "Where your treasure is, there will your heart be also." Eighteen hundred years later we find a very different person from Jesus, Talleyrand to wit, saying the same thing. A married man with a family, said Talleyrand, will do anything for money. Now this, though not a scientifically precise statement, is true enough to be a moral objection to marriage. As long as a man has a right to risk his life or his livelihood for his ideas he needs only courage and conviction to make his integrity unassailable. But he forfeits that right when he marries. It took a revolution to rescue Wagner from his Court appointment at Dresden; and his wife never forgave him for being glad and feeling free when he lost it and threw her back into poverty. Millet might have gone on painting potboiling nudes to the end of his life if his wife had not been of a heroic turn herself. Women, for the sake of their children and parents, submit to slaveries and prostitutions that no unattached woman would endure.

This was the beginning and the end of the objection of Jesus to marriage and family ties, and the explanation of his

conception of heaven as a place where there should be neither
marrying nor giving in marriage. Now there is no reason to
suppose that when he said this he did not mean it. He did
not, as St Paul did afterwards in his name, propose celibacy
as a rule of life; for he was not a fool, nor, when he denounced
marriage, had he yet come to believe, as St Paul did, that the
end of the world was at hand and there was therefore no more
need to replenish the earth. He must have meant that the race
should be continued without dividing with women and men
the allegiance the individual owes to God within him. This
raises the practical problem of how we are to secure the spiritual freedom and integrity of the priest and the nun without
their barrenness and uncompleted experience. Luther the priest
did not solve the problem by marrying a nun: he only testified
in the most convincing and practical way to the fact that
celibacy was a worse failure than marriage.

WHY JESUS DID NOT MARRY

To all appearance the problem oppresses only a few excep·
tional people. Thoroughly conventional women married to
thoroughly conventional men should not be conscious of any
restriction: the chain not only leaves them free to do whatever
they want to do, but greatly facilitates their doing it. To them
an attack on marriage is not a blow struck in defence of their
freedom but at their rights and privileges. One would expect
that they would not only demur vehemently to the teachings of
Jesus in this matter, but object strongly to his not having been
a married man himself. Even those who regard him as a god
descended from his throne in heaven to take on humanity
for a time might reasonably declare that the assumption of humanity must have been incomplete at its most vital point if he
were a celibate. But the facts are flatly contrary. The mere
thought of Jesus as a married man is felt to be blasphemous by
the most conventional believers; and even those of us to whom
Jesus is no supernatural personage, but a prophet only as Ma-

homet was a prophet, feel that there was something more dignified in the bachelordom of Jesus than in the spectacle of Mahomet lying distracted on the floor of his harem whilst his wives
stormed and squabbled and hen-pecked round him. We are
not surprised that when Jesus called the sons of Zebedee to follow him, he did not call their father, and that the disciples, like
Jesus himself, were all men without family entanglements. It
is evident from his impatience when people excused themselves from following him because of their family funerals, or
when they assumed that his first duty was to his mother, that he
had found family ties and domestic affections in his way at
every turn, and had become persuaded at last that no man
could follow his inner light until he was free from their compulsion. The absence of any protest against this tempts us to
declare that on this question of marriage there are no conventional people; and that everyone of us is at heart a good Christian sexually.

INCONSISTENCY OF THE SEX INSTINCT

But the question is not so simple as that. Sex is an exceedingly subtle and complicated instinct; and the mass of mankind
neither know nor care much about freedom of conscience, which
is what Jesus was thinking about, and are concerned almost to
obsession with sex, as to which Jesus said nothing. In our
sexual natures we are torn by an irresistible attraction and an
overwhelming repugnance and disgust. We have two tyran-
nous physical passions: concupiscence and chastity. We become
mad in pursuit of sex: we become equally mad in the persecution of that pursuit. Unless we gratify our desire the race is lost:
unless we restrain it we destroy ourselves. We are thus led to
devise marriage institutions which will at the same time secure
opportunities for the gratification of sex and raise up innumerable obstacles to it; which will sanctify it and brand it as
infamous; which will identify it with virtue and with sin simultaneously. Obviously it is useless to look for any consistency

in such institutions; and it is only by continual reform and read-
justment, and by a considerable elasticity in their enforcement,
that a tolerable result can be arrived at. I need not repeat here
the long and elaborate examination of them that I prefixed to
my play entitled Getting Married. Here I am concerned only
with the views of Jesus on the question; and it is necessary, in
order to understand the attitude of the world towards them,
that we should not attribute the general approval of the decision of Jesus to remain unmarried as an endorsement of his
views. We are simply in a state of confusion on the subject; but
it is part of the confusion that we should conclude that Jesus
was a celibate, and shrink even from the idea that his birth was
a natural one, yet cling with ferocity to the sacredness of the institution which provides a refuge from celibacy.

FOR BETTER FOR WORSE

Jesus, however, did not express a complicated view of marriage. His objection to it was quite simple, as we have seen.
He perceived that nobody could live the higher life unless
money and sexual love were obtainable without sacrificing it;
and he saw that the effect of marriage as it existed among the
Jews (and as it still exists among ourselves) was to make the
couples sacrifice every higher consideration until they had fed
and pleased one another. The worst of it is that this dangerous
preposterousness in marriage, instead of improving as the general conduct of married couples improves, becomes much worse.
The selfish man to whom his wife is nothing but a slave, the
selfish woman to whom her husband is nothing but a scapegoat and a breadwinner, are not held back from spiritual or any
other adventures by fear of their effect on the welfare of their
mates. Their wives do not make recreants and cowards of them:
their husbands do not chain them to the cradle and the cooking
range when their feet should be beautiful on the mountains.
It is precisely as people become more kindly, more conscientious,
more ready to shoulder the heavier part of the burden (which

means that the strong shall give way to the weak and the slow hold back the swift), that marriage becomes an intolerable obstacle to individual evolution. And that is why the revolt against marriage of which Jesus was an exponent always recurs when civilization raises the standard of marital duty and affection, and at the same time produces a greater need for individual freedom in pursuit of a higher evolution.

THE REMEDY

This, fortunately, is only one side of marriage; and the question arises, can it not be eliminated? The reply is reassuring: of course it can. There is no mortal reason in the nature of things why a married couple should be economically dependent on one another. The Communism advocated by Jesus, which we have seen to be entirely practicable, and indeed inevitable if our civilization is to be saved from collapse, gets rid of that difficulty completely. And with the economic dependence will go the force of the outrageous claims that derive their real sanction from the economic pressure behind them. When a man allows his wife to turn him from the best work he is capable of doing, and to sell his soul at the highest commercial prices obtainable; when he allows her to entangle him in a social routine that is wearisome and debilitating to him, or tie him to her apron strings when he needs that occasional solitude which is one of the most sacred of human rights, he does so because he has no right to impose eccentric standards of expenditure and unsocial habits on her, and because these conditions have produced by their pressure so general a custom of chaining wedded couples to one another that married people are coarsely derided when their partners break the chain. And when a woman is condemned by her parents to wait in genteel idleness and uselessness for a husband when all her healthy social instincts call her to acquire a profession and work, it is again her economic dependence on them that makes their tyranny effective.

THE CASE FOR MARRIAGE

Thus, though it would be too much to say that everything that is obnoxious in marriage and family life will be cured by Communism, yet it can be said that it will cure what Jesus objected to in these institutions. He made no comprehensive study of them: he only expressed his own grievance with an overwhelming sense that it is a grievance so deep that all the considerations on the other side are as dust in the balance. Obviously there are such considerations, and very weighty ones too. When Talleyrand said that a married man with a family is capable of anything, he meant anything evil; but an optimist may declare, with equal half truth, that a married man is capable of anything good; that marriage turns vagabonds into steady citizens; and that men and women will, for love of their mates and children, practise virtues that unattached individuals are incapable of. It is true that too much of this domestic virtue is self-denial, which is not a virtue at all; but then the following of the inner light at all costs is largely self-indulgence, which is just as suicidal, just as weak, just as cowardly as self-denial. Ibsen, who takes us into the matter far more resolutely than Jesus, is unable to find any golden rule: both Brand and Peer Gynt come to a bad end; and though Brand does not do as much mischief as Peer, the mischief he does do is of extraordinary intensity.

CELIBACY NO REMEDY

We must, I think, regard the protest of Jesus against marriage and family ties as the claim of a particular kind of individual to be free from them because they hamper his own work intolerably. When he said that if we are to follow him in the sense of taking up his work we must give up our family ties, he was simply stating a fact; and to this day the Roman Catholic priest, the Buddhist lama, and the fakirs of all the eastern denominations accept the saying. It is also accepted by the physically enterprising, the explorers, the restlessly energetic of all kinds: in short, by the adventurous. The greatest sacrifice in marriage is the sacrifice of the adventurous attitude towards life: the being settled. Those who are born tired may crave for settlement; but to fresher and stronger spirits it is a form of suicide.

Now to say of any institution that it is incompatible with both the contemplative and adventurous life is to disgrace it so vitally that all the moralizings of all the Deans and Chapters cannot reconcile our souls to its slavery. The unmarried Jesus and the unmarried Beethoven, the unmarried Joan of Arc, Clare, Teresa, Florence Nightingale seem as they should be; and the saying that there is always something ridiculous about a married philosopher becomes inevitable. And yet the celibate is still more ridiculous than the married man: the priest, in accepting the alternative of celibacy, disables himself; and the best priests are those who have been men of this world before they became men of the world to come. But as the taking of vows does not annul an existing marriage, and a married man cannot become a priest, we are again confronted with the absurdity that the best priest is a reformed rake. Thus does marriage, itself intolerable, thrust us upon intolerable alternatives. The practical solution is to make the individual economically independent of marriage and the family, and to make marriage as easily dissoluble as any other partnership: in other words, to accept the conclusions to which experience is slowly driving both our sociologists and our legislators. This will not instantly cure all the evils of marriage, nor root up at one stroke its detestable tradition of property in human bodies. But it will leave Nature free to effect a cure; and in free soil the root may wither and perish.

This disposes of all the opinions and teachings of Jesus which are still matters of controversy. They are all in line with the best modern thought. He told us what we have to do; and we have had to find the way to do it. Most of us are still, as most were in

his own time, extremely recalcitrant, and are being forced
along that way by painful pressure of circumstances, protesting
at every step that nothing will induce us to go; that it is a
ridiculous way, a disgraceful way, a socialistic way, an atheistic
way, an immoral way, and that the vanguard ought to be
ashamed of themselves and must be made to turn back at once.
But they find that they have to follow the vanguard all the
same if their lives are to be worth living.

AFTER THE CRUCIFIXION

Let us now return to the New Testament narrative; for what
happened after the disappearance of Jesus is instructive. Unfortunately, the crucifixion was a complete political success. I
remember that when I described it in these terms once before,
I greatly shocked a most respectable newspaper in my native
town, the Dublin Daily Express, because my journalistic phrase
shewed that I was treating it as an ordinary event like Home
Rule or the Insurance Act: that is (though this did not occur
to the editor), as a real event which had really happened, instead of a portion of the Church service. I can only repeat, assuming as I am that it *was* a real event and did actually happen,
that it was as complete a success as any in history. Christianity
as a specific doctrine was slain with Jesus, suddenly and utterly.
He was hardly cold in his grave, or high in his heaven (as you
please), before the apostles dragged the tradition of him down
to the level of the thing it has remained ever since. And that
thing the intelligent heathen may study, if they would be in-
structed in it by modern books, in Samuel Butler's novel, The
Way of All Flesh.

THE VINDICTIVE MIRACLES AND THE
STONING OF STEPHEN

Take, for example, the miracles. Of Jesus alone of all the
Christian miracle workers there is no record, except in certain gospels that all men reject, of a malicious or destructive

miracle. A barren fig-tree was the only victim of his anger. Every one of his miracles on sentient subjects was an act of kindness. John declares that he healed the wound of the man whose ear was cut off (by Peter, John says) at the arrest in the garden. One of the first things the apostles did with their miraculous power was to strike dead a wretched man and his wife who had defrauded them by holding back some money from the common stock. They struck people blind or dead without remorse, judging because they had been judged. They healed the sick and raised the dead apparently in a spirit of pure display and advertisement. Their doctrine did not contain a ray of that light which reveals Jesus as one of the redeemers of men from folly and error. They cancelled him, and went back straight to John the Baptist and his formula of securing remission of sins by repentance and the rite of baptism (being born again of water and the spirit). Peter's first harangue softens us by the human touch of its exordium, which was a quaint assurance to his hearers that they must believe him to be sober because it was too early in the day to get drunk; but of Jesus he had nothing to say except that he was the Christ foretold by the prophets as coming from the seed of David, and that they must believe this and be baptized. To this the other apostles added incessant denunciations of the Jews for having crucified him, and threats of the destruction that would overtake them if they did not repent: that is, if they did not join the sect which the apostles were now forming. A quite intolerable young speaker named Stephen delivered an oration to the council, in which he first inflicted on them a tedious sketch of the history of Israel, with which they were presumably as well acquainted as he, and then reviled them in the most insulting terms as "stiffnecked and uncircumcized." Finally, after boring and annoying them to the utmost bearable extremity, he looked up and declared that he saw the heavens open, and Christ standing on the right hand of God. This was too much: they threw him out of the city and stoned him to death. It was a severe way of suppressing a tactless and conceited bore; but it was pardonable and human in comparison to the slaughter of poor Ananias and Sapphira.

PAUL

Suddenly a man of genius, Paul, violently anti-Christian, enters on the scene, holding the clothes of the men who are stoning Stephen. He persecutes the Christians with great vigor, a sport which he combines with the business of a tentmaker. This temperamental hatred of Jesus, whom he has never seen, is a pathological symptom of that particular sort of conscience and nervous constitution which brings its victims under the tyranny of two delirious terrors: the terror of sin and the terror of death, which may be called also the terror of sex and the terror of life. Now Jesus, with his healthy conscience on his higher plane, was free from these terrors. He consorted freely with sinners, and was never concerned for a moment, as far as we know, about whether his conduct was sinful or not; so that he has forced us to accept him as the man without sin. Even if we reckon his last days as the days of his delusion, he none the less gave a fairly convincing exhibition of superiority to the fear of death. This must have both fascinated and horrified Paul, or Saul, as he was first called. The horror accounts for his fierce persecution of the Christians. The fascination accounts for the strangest of his fancies: the fancy for attaching the name of Jesus Christ to the great idea which flashed upon him on the road to Damascus, the idea that he could not only make a religion of his two terrors, but that the movement started by Jesus offered him the nucleus for his new Church. It was a monstrous idea; and the shock of it, as he afterwards declared, struck him blind for days. He heard Jesus calling to him from the clouds, "Why persecute me?" His natural hatred of the teacher for whom Sin and Death had no terrors turned into a wild personal worship of him which has the ghastliness of a beautiful thing seen in a false light.

The chronicler of the Acts of the Apostles sees nothing of the significance of this. The great danger of conversion in all ages has been that when the religion of the high mind is offered to the lower mind, the lower mind, feeling its fascination without understanding it, and being incapable of rising to it, drags it down to its level by degrading it. Years ago I said that the conversion of a savage to Christianity is the conversion of Christianity to savagery. The conversion of Paul was no conversion at all: it was Paul who converted the religion that had raised one man above sin and death into a religion that delivered millions of men so completely into their dominion that their own common nature became a horror to them, and the religious life became a denial of life. Paul had no intention of surrendering either his Judaism or his Roman citizenship to the new moral world (as Robert Owen called it) of Communism and Jesuism. Just as in our own time Karl Marx, not content to take political economy as he found it, insisted on rebuilding it from the bottom upwards in his own way, and thereby gave a new lease of life to the errors it was just outgrowing, so Paul reconstructed the old Salvationism from which Jesus had vainly tried to redeem him, and produced a fantastic theology which is still the most amazing thing of the kind known to us. Being intellectually an inveterate Roman Rationalist, always discarding the irrational real thing for the unreal but ratiocinable postulate, he began by discarding Man as he is, and substituted a postulate which he called Adam. And when he was asked, as he surely must have been in a world not wholly mad, what had become of the natural man, he replied "Adam *is* the natural man." This was confusing to simpletons, because according to tradition Adam was certainly the name of the natural man as created in the garden of Eden. It was as if a preacher of our own time had described as typically British Frankenstein's monster, and called him Smith, and somebody, on demanding what about the man in the street, had been told "Smith *is* the man in the street." The thing happens often enough; for indeed the world is full of these Adams and Smiths and men in the street and average sensual men and economic men and womanly women and what not, all of them imaginary Atlases carrying imaginary worlds on their unsubstantial shoulders.

The Eden story provided Adam with a sin: the "original sin" for which we are all damned. Baldly stated, this seems ridiculous; nevertheless it corresponds to something actually existent not only in Paul's consciousness but in our own. The original sin was not the eating of the forbidden fruit, but the consciousness of sin which the fruit produced. The moment Adam and Eve tasted the apple they found themselves ashamed of their sexual relation, which until then had seemed quite innocent to them; and there is no getting over the hard fact that this shame, or state of sin, has persisted to this day, and is one of the strongest of our instincts. Thus Paul's postulate of Adam as the natural man was pragmatically true: it worked. But the weakness of Pragmatism is that most theories will work if you put your back into making them work, provided they have some point of contact with human nature. Hedonism will pass the pragmatic test as well as Stoicism. Up to a certain point every social principle that is not absolutely idiotic works: Autocracy works in Russia and Democracy in America; Atheism works in France, Polytheism in India, Monotheism throughout Islam, and Pragmatism, or No-ism, in England. Paul's fantastic conception of the damned Adam, represented by Bunyan as a pilgrim with a great burden of sins on his back, corresponded to the fundamental condition of evolution, which is, that life, including human life, is continually evolving, and must therefore be continually ashamed of itself and its present and past. Bunyan's pilgrim wants to get rid of his bundle of sins; but he also wants to reach "yonder shining light"; and when at last his bundle falls off him into the sepulchre of Christ, his pilgrimage is still unfinished and his hardest trials still ahead of him.

His conscience remains uneasy; "original sin" still torments him; and his adventure with Giant Despair, who throws him into the dungeon of Doubting Castle, from which he escapes by the use of a skeleton key, is more terrible than any he met whilst the bundle was still on his back. Thus Bunyan's allegory of human nature breaks though the Pauline theology at a hundred points. His theological allegory, The Holy War, with its troops of Election Doubters, and its cavalry of "those that rode Reformadoes," is, as a whole, absurd, impossible, and, except in passages where the artistic old Adam momentarily got the better of the Salvationist theologian, hardly readable.

Paul's theory of original sin was to some extent idiosyncratic. He tells us definitely that he finds himself quite well able to avoid the sinfulness of sex by practising celibacy; but he recognizes, rather contemptuously, that in this respect he is not as other men are, and says that they had better marry than burn, thus admitting that though marriage may lead to placing the desire to please wife or husband before the desire to please God, yet preoccupation with unsatisfied desire may be even more ungodly than preoccupation with domestic affection. This view of the case inevitably led him to insist that a wife should be rather a slave than a partner, her real function being, not to engage a man's love and loyalty, but on the contrary to release them for God by relieving the man of all preoccupation with sex just as in her capacity of housekeeper and cook she relieves his preoccupation with hunger by the simple expedient of satisfying his appetite. This slavery also justifies itself pragmatically by working effectively; but it has made Paul the eternal enemy of Woman. Incidentally it has led to many foolish surmises about Paul's personal character and circumstances, by people so enslaved by sex that a celibate appears to them a sort of monster. They forget that not only whole priesthoods, official and unofficial, from Paul to Carlyle and Ruskin, have defied the tyranny of sex, but immense numbers of ordinary citizens of both sexes have, either voluntarily or under pressure of circumstances easily surmountable, saved their energies for less primitive activities.

Howbeit, Paul succeeded in stealing the image of Christ crucified for the figure-head of his Salvationist vessel, with its Adam posing as the natural man, its doctrine of original sin, and its damnation avoidable only by faith in the sacrifice of the cross. In fact, no sooner had Jesus knocked over the dragon of superstition than Paul boldly set it on its legs again in the name of Jesus.

THE CONFUSION OF CHRISTENDOM

Now it is evident that two religions having such contrary effects on mankind should not be confused as they are under a common name. There is not one word of Pauline Christianity in the characteristic utterances of Jesus. When Saul watched the clothes of the men who stoned Stephen, he was not acting upon beliefs which Paul renounced. There is no record of Christ's having ever said to any man: "Go and sin as much as you like: you can put it all on me." He said "Sin no more," and insisted that he was putting up the standard of conduct, not debasing it, and that the righteousness of the Christian must exceed that of the Scribe and Pharisee. The notion that he was shedding his blood in order that every petty cheat and adulterator and libertine might wallow in it and come out whiter than snow, cannot be imputed to him on his own authority. "I come as an infallible patent medicine for bad consciences" is not one of the sayings in the gospels. If Jesus could have been consulted on Bunyan's allegory as to that business of the burden of sin dropping from the pilgrim's back when he caught sight of the cross, we must infer from his teaching that he would have told Bunyan in forcible terms that he had never made a greater mistake in his life, and that the business of a Christ was to make self-satisfied sinners feel the burden of their sins and stop committing them instead of assuring them that they could not help it, as it was all Adam's fault, but that it did not matter as long as they were credulous and friendly about himself. Even when he believed himself to be a god, he did not regard himself as a scapegoat. He was to take away the sins of the world by good government, by justice and mercy, by setting the welfare of little children above the pride of princes, by casting all the quackeries and idolatries which now usurp and malversate the power of God into what our local authorities quaintly call the dust destructor, and by riding on the clouds of heaven in glory instead of in a thousand-guinea motor car. That was delirious, if you like; but it was the delirium of a free soul, not of a shamebound one like Paul's. There has really never been a more monstrous imposition perpetrated than the imposition of the limitations of Paul's soul upon the soul of Jesus.

THE SECRET OF PAUL'S SUCCESS

Paul must soon have found that his followers had gained peace of mind and victory over death and sin at the cost of all moral responsibility; for he did his best to reintroduce it by making good conduct the test of sincere belief, and insisting that sincere belief was necessary to salvation. But as his system was rooted in the plain fact that as what he called sin includes sex and is therefore an ineradicable part of human nature (why else should Christ have had to atone for the sin of all future generations?) it was impossible for him to declare that sin, even in its wickedest extremity, could forfeit the sinner's salvation if he repented and believed. And to this day Pauline Christianity is, and owes its enormous vogue to being, a premium on sin. Its consequences have had to be held in check by the worldlywise majority through a violently anti-Christian system of criminal law and stern morality. But of course the main restraint is human nature, which has good impulses as well as bad ones, and refrains from theft and murder and cruelty, even when it is taught that it can commit them all at the expense of Christ and go happily to heaven afterwards, simply because it does not always want to murder or rob or torture.

It is now easy to understand why the Christianity of Jesus failed completely to establish itself politically and socially, and was easily suppressed by the police and the Church, whilst Paulinism overran the whole western civilized world, which was at that time the Roman Empire, and was adopted by it as its official faith, the old avenging gods falling helplessly before the new Redeemer. It still retains, as we may see in Africa, its power of bringing to simple people a message of hope and consolation that no other religion offers. But this enchantment is produced by its spurious association with the personal charm of Jesus, and exists only for untrained minds. In the hands of a logical Frenchman like Calvin, pushing it to its utmost conclusions, and devising "institutes" for hardheaded adult Scots and literal Swiss, it becomes the most infernal of fatalisms; and the lives of civilized children are blighted by its logic whilst negro piccaninnies are rejoicing in its legends.

PAUL'S QUALITIES

Paul, however, did not get his great reputation by mere imposition and reaction. It is only in comparison with Jesus (to whom many prefer him) that he appears common and conceited. Though in The Acts he is only a vulgar revivalist, he comes out in his own epistles as a genuine poet, though by flashes only. He is no more a Christian than Jesus was a Baptist: he is a disciple of Jesus only as Jesus was a disciple of John. He does nothing that Jesus would have done, and says nothing that Jesus would have said, though much, like the famous ode to charity, that he would have admired. He is more Jewish than the Jews, more Roman than the Romans, proud both ways, full of startling confessions and self-revelations that would not surprise us if they were slipped into the pages of Nietzsche, tormented by an intellectual conscience that demanded an argued case even at the cost of sophistry, with all sorts of fine qualities and occasional illuminations, but always hopelessly in the toils of Sin, Death, and Logic, which had no power over Jesus. As we have seen, it was by introducing this bondage and terror of his into the Christian doctrine that he adapted it to the Church and State systems which Jesus transcended, and made it practicable by destroying the specifically Jesuit side of it. He would have been quite in his place in any modern Protestant State; and he, not Jesus, is the true head and founder of our Reformed Church, as Peter is of the Roman Church. The followers of Paul and Peter made Christendom, whilst the Nazarenes were wiped out.

THE ACTS OF THE APOSTLES

Here we may return to the narrative called The Acts of the Apostles, which we left at the point where the stoning of Stephen was followed by the introduction of Paul. The author of The Acts, though a good story-teller, like Luke, was (herein also like Luke) much weaker in power of thought than in imaginative literary art. Hence we find Luke credited with the authorship of The Acts by people who like stories and have no aptitude for theology, whilst the book itself is denounced as spurious by Pauline theologians because Paul, and indeed all the apostles, are represented in it as very commonplace revivalists, interesting us by their adventures more than by any qualities of mind or character. Indeed, but for the epistles, we should have a very poor opinion of the apostles. Paul in particular is described as setting a fashion which has remained in continual use to this day. Whenever he addresses an audience, he dwells with great zest on his misdeeds before his pseudo conversion, with the effect of throwing into stronger relief his present state of blessedness; and he tells the story of that conversion over and over again, ending with exhortations to the hearers to come and be saved, and threats of the wrath that will overtake them if they refuse. At any revival meeting today the same thing may be heard, followed by the same conversions. This is natural enough; but it is totally unlike the preaching of Jesus, who never talked about his personal history, and never "worked up" an audience to hysteria. It aims at a purely nervous effect; it brings no enlightenment; the most ignorant man has only to become intoxicated with his own vanity, and mistake his self-satisfaction for the Holy Ghost, to become qualified as an apostle; and it has absolutely nothing to do with the characteristic doctrines of Jesus. The Holy Ghost may be at work all round producing wonders of art and science, and strengthening men to endure all sorts of martyrdoms for the enlargement of knowledge, and the enrichment and intensification of life ("that ye may have life more abundantly"); but the apostles, as described in The Acts, take no part in the struggle except as persecutors and revilers. To this day, when their successors get the upper hand, as in Geneva (Knox's "perfect city of Christ") and in Scotland and Ulster, every spiritual activity but money-making and churchgoing is stamped out; heretics are ruthlessly persecuted; and such pleasures as money can purchase are suppressed so that its possessors are compelled to go on making money because there is nothing else to do. And the compensation for all this privation is partly an insane conceit of being the elect of God, with a reserved seat in heaven, and partly, since even the most infatuated idiot cannot spend his life admiring himself, the less innocent excitement of punishing other people for not admiring him, and the nosing out of the sins of the people who, being intelligent enough to be incapable of mere dull self-righteousness, and highly susceptible to the beauty and interest of the real workings of the Holy Ghost, try to live more rational and abundant lives. The abominable amusement of terrifying children with threats of hell is another of these diversions, and perhaps the vilest and most mischievous of them. The net result is that the imitators of the apostles, whether they are called Holy Willies or Stigginses in derision, or, in admiration, Puritans or saints, are, outside their own congregations, and to a considerable extent inside them, heartily detested. Now nobody detests Jesus, though many who have been tormented in their childhood in his name include him in their general loathing of everything connected with the word religion; whilst others, who know him only by misrepresentation as a sentimental pacifist and an ascetic, include him in their general dislike of that type of character. In the same way a student who has had to "get up" Shakespear as a college subject may hate Shakespear; and people who dislike the theatre may include Molière in that dislike without ever having read a line of his or witnessed one of his plays; but nobody with any knowledge of Shakespear or Molière could possibly detest them, or read without pity and horror a description of their being insulted, tortured, and killed. And the same is true of Jesus. But it requires the most strenuous effort of conscience to refrain from crying "Serve him right" when we read of the stoning of Stephen; and nobody has ever cared twopence about the martyrdom of Peter: many better men have died worse deaths: for example, honest Hugh Latimer, who was burned by us, was worth fifty Stephens and a dozen Peters. One feels at last that when Jesus called Peter from his boat, he spoiled an honest fisherman, and made nothing better out of the wreck than a salvation monger.

THE CONTROVERSIES ON BAPTISM AND TRANSUBSTANTIATION

Meanwhile the inevitable effect of dropping the peculiar doctrines of Jesus and going back to John the Baptist, was to make it much easier to convert Gentiles than Jews; and it was by following the line of least resistance that Paul became the apostle to the Gentiles. The Jews had their own rite of initiation: the rite of circumcision; and they were fiercely jealous for it, because it marked them as the chosen people of God, and set them apart from the Gentiles, who were simply the uncircumcized. When Paul, finding that baptism made way faster among the Gentiles than among the Jews, as it enabled them to plead that they too were sanctified by a rite of later and higher authority than the Mosaic rite, he was compelled to admit that circumcision did not matter; and this, to the Jews, was an intolerable blasphemy. To Gentiles like ourselves, a good deal of the Epistle to the Romans is now tedious to unreadableness because it consists of a hopeless attempt by Paul to evade the conclusion that if a man were baptized it did not matter a rap whether he was circumcized or not. Paul claims circumcision as an excellent thing in its way for a Jew; but if it has no efficacy towards salvation, and if salvation is the one thing needful—and Paul was committed to both propositions—his pleas in mitigation only made the Jews more determined to stone him.

Thus from the very beginning of apostolic Christianity, it was hampered by a dispute as to whether salvation was to be attained by a surgical operation or by a sprinkling of water: mere rites on which Jesus would not have wasted twenty words. Later on, when the new sect conquered the Gentile west, where the dispute had no practical application, the other ceremony—that of eating the god—produced a still more disastrous dispute, in which a difference of belief, not as to the obligation to perform the ceremony, but as to whether it was a symbolic or a real ingestion of divine substance, produced persecution, slaughter, hatred, and everything that Jesus loathed, on a monstrous scale.

But long before that, the superstitions which had fastened on the new faith made trouble. The parthenogenetic birth of Christ, simple enough at first as a popular miracle, was not left so simple by the theologians. They began to ask of what substance Christ was made in the womb of the virgin. When the Trinity was added to the faith the question arose, was the virgin the mother of God or only the mother of Jesus? Arian schisms and Nestorian schisms arose on these questions; and the leaders of the resultant agitations rancorously deposed one another and excommunicated one another according to their luck in enlisting the emperors on their side. In the IV century they began to burn one another for differences of opinion in such matters. In the VIII century Charlemagne made Christianity compulsory by killing those who refused to embrace it; and though this made an end of the voluntary character of conversion, Charlemagne may claim to be the first Christian who put men to death for any point of doctrine that really mattered. From his time onward the history of Christian controversy reeks with blood and fire, torture and warfare. The Crusades, the persecutions in Albi and elsewhere, the Inquisition, the "wars of religion" which followed the Reformation, all presented themselves as Christian phenomena; but who can doubt that they would have been repudiated with horror by Jesus? Our own notion that the massacre of St Bartholomew's was an outrage on Christianity, whilst the campaigns of Gustavus Adolphus, and even of Frederick the Great, were a defence of it, is as absurd as the opposite notion that Frederick was Antichrist and Torquemada and Ignatius Loyola men after the very heart of Jesus. Neither they nor their exploits had anything to do with him. It is probable that Archbishop Laud and John Wesley died equally persuaded that he in whose name they had made themselves famous on earth would receive them in Heaven with open arms. George Fox the Quaker would have had ten times their chance; and yet Fox made rather a miserable business of life.

Nevertheless all these perversions of the doctrine of Jesus derived their moral force from his credit, and so had to keep his gospel alive. When the Protestants translated the Bible into the vernacular and let it loose among the people, they did an extremely dangerous thing, as the mischief which followed proves; but they incidentally let loose the sayings of Jesus in open competition with the sayings of Paul and Koheleth and David and Solomon and the authors of Job and the Pentateuch; and, as we have seen, Jesus seems to be the winning name. The glaring contradiction between his teaching and the practice of all the States and all the Churches is no longer

hidden. And it may be that though nineteen centuries have
passed since Jesus was born (the date of his birth is now
quaintly given as 7 B.C., though some contend for 100 B.C.),
and though his Church has not yet been founded nor his political system tried, the bankruptcy of all the other systems when
audited by our vital statistics, which give us a final test for all
political systems, is driving us hard into accepting him, not as
a scapegoat, but as one who was much less of a fool in practical
matters than we have hitherto all thought him.

THE ALTERNATIVE CHRISTS

Let us now clear up the situation a little. The New Testament tells two stories for two different sorts of readers. One is
the old story of the achievement of our salvation by the sacrifice and atonement of a divine personage who was barbarously
slain and rose again on the third day: the story as it was accepted by the apostles. And in this story the political, economic,
and moral views of the Christ have no importance: the atonement is everything; and we are saved by our faith in it, and not
by works or opinions (other than that particular opinion) bearing on practical affairs.

The other is the story of a prophet who, after expressing several very interesting opinions as to practical conduct, both personal and political, which are now of pressing importance, and
instructing his disciples to carry them out in their daily life,
lost his head; believed himself to be a crude legendary form of
god; and under that delusion courted and suffered a cruel execution in the belief that he would rise from the dead and come
in glory to reign over a regenerated world. In this form, the
political, economic, and moral opinions of Jesus, as guides to
conduct, are interesting and important: the rest is mere psy-
chopathy and superstition. The accounts of the resurrection,
the parthenogenetic birth, and the more incredible miracles
are rejected as inventions; and such episodes as the conversa-

tion with the devil are classed with similar conversations re-
corded of St Dunstan, Luther, Bunyan, Swedenborg, and
Blake.

CREDULITY NO CRITERION

This arbitrary acceptance and rejection of parts of the gospel
is not peculiar to the Secularist view. We have seen Luke and
John reject Matthew's story of the massacre of the innocents
and the flight into Egypt without ceremony. The notion that
Matthew's manuscript is a literal and infallible record of facts,
not subject to the errors that beset all earthly chroniclers, would
have made John stare, being as it is a comparatively modern
fancy of intellectually untrained people who keep the Bible on
the same shelf with Napoleon's Book of Fate, Old Moore's
Almanack, and handbooks of therapeutic herbalism. You may
be a fanatical Salvationist and reject more miracle stories than
Huxley did; and you may utterly repudiate Jesus as the Savior
and yet cite him as a historical witness to the possession by men
of the most marvellous thaumaturgical powers. "Christ Scientist"
and Jesus the Mahatma are preached by people whom Peter
would have struck dead as worse infidels than Simon Magus;
and the Atonement is preached by Baptist and Congregation-
alist ministers whose views of the miracles are those of Ingersoll
and Bradlaugh. Luther, who made a clean sweep of all the
saints with their million miracles, and reduced the Blessed Virgin herself to the status of an idol, concentrated Salvationism
to a point at which the most execrable murderer who believes
in it when the rope is round his neck, flies straight to the arms
of Jesus, whilst Tom Paine and Shelley fall into the bottomless
pit to burn there to all eternity. And sceptical physicists like
Sir William Crookes demonstrate by laboratory experiments
that "mediums" like Dunglas Home can make the pointer of
a spring-balance go round without touching the weight sus-
pended from it.

BELIEF IN PERSONAL IMMORTALITY
NO CRITERION

Nor is belief in individual immortality any criterion. Theosophists, rejecting vicarious atonement so sternly that they insist that the smallest of our sins brings its Karma, also insist on
individual immortality and metempsychosis in order to provide
an unlimited field for Karma to be worked out by the unre-
deemed sinner. The belief in the prolongation of individual
life beyond the grave is far more real and vivid among table-
rapping Spiritualists than among conventional Christians. The
notion that those who reject the Christian (or any other)
scheme of salvation by atonement must reject also belief in personal immortality and in miracles is as baseless as the notion that
if a man is an atheist he will steal your watch.

I could multiply these instances to weariness. The main difference that set Gladstone and Huxley by the ears is not one between belief in supernatural persons of miraculous events and
the sternest view of such belief as a breach of intellectual integrity: it is the difference between belief in the efficacy of the
crucifixion as an infallible cure for guilt, and a congenital in-
capacity for believing this, or (the same thing) desiring to believe it.

THE SECULAR VIEW NATURAL, NOT
RATIONAL, THEREFORE INEVITABLE

It must therefore be taken as a flat fundamental modern fact,
whether we like it or not, that whilst many of us cannot believe that Jesus got his curious grip of our souls by mere sentimentality, neither can we believe that he was John Barleycorn.
The more our reason and study lead us to believe that Jesus was
talking the most penetrating good sense when he preached
Communism; when he declared that the reality behind the
popular belief in God was a creative spirit in ourselves called
by him the Heavenly Father and by us Evolution, Élan Vital,

Life Force and other names; when he protested against the
claims of marriage and the family to appropriate that high part
of our energy that was meant for the service of his Father,
the more impossible it becomes for us to believe that he was
talking equally good sense when he so suddenly announced
that he was himself a visible concrete God; that his flesh and
blood were miraculous food for us; that he must be tortured
and slain in the traditional manner and would rise from the
dead after three days; and that at his Second Coming the stars
would fall from heaven and he become king of an earthly
paradise. But it is easy and reasonable to believe that an overwrought preacher at last went mad as Swift and Ruskin and
Nietzsche went mad. Every asylum has in it a patient suffering
from the delusion that he is a god, yet otherwise sane enough.
These patients do not nowadays declare that they will be
barbarously slain and will rise from the dead, because they have
lost that tradition of the destiny of godhead; but they claim
everything appertaining to divinity that is within their knowledge.

Thus the gospels as memoirs and suggestive statements of
sociological and biological doctrine, highly relevant to modern
civilization, though ending in the history of a psychopathic delusion, are quite credible, intelligible, and interesting to modern thinkers. In any other light they are neither credible,
intelligible, nor interesting except to people upon whom the
delusion imposes.

"THE HIGHER CRITICISM"

Historical research and paleographic criticism will no doubt
continue their demonstrations that the New Testament, like the
Old, seldom tells a single story or expounds a single doctrine,
and gives us often an accretion and conglomeration of widely
discrete and even unrelated traditions and doctrines. But these
disintegrations, though technically interesting to scholars, and
gratifying or exasperating, as the case may be, to people who

are merely defending or attacking the paper fortifications of the
infallibility of the Bible, I have hardly anything to do with the
purpose of these pages. I have mentioned the fact that most of
the authorities are now agreed (for the moment) that the date
of the birth of Jesus may be placed at about 7 B.C.; but they
do not therefore date their letters 1923, nor, I presume, do
they expect me to do so. What I am engaged in is a criticism
(in the Kantian sense) of an established body of belief which
has become an actual part of the mental fabric of my readers;
and I should be the most exasperating of triflers and pedants if
I were to digress into a criticism of some other belief or nobelief
which my readers might conceivably profess if they were eru-
dite Scriptural paleographers and historians, in which case, by
the way, they would have to change their views so frequently
that the gospel they received in their childhood would dominate them after all by its superior persistency. The chaos of
mere facts in which the Sermon on the Mount and the Ode to
Charity suggest nothing but disputes as to whether they are
interpolations or not, in which Jesus becomes nothing but a
name suspected of belonging to ten different prophets or executed persons, in which Paul is only the man who could not
possibly have written the epistles attributed to him, in which
Chinese sages, Greek philosophers, Latin authors, and writers of
ancient anonymous inscriptions are thrown at our heads as the
sources of this or that scrap of the Bible, is neither a religion
nor a criticism of religion: one does not offer the fact that a
good deal of the medieval building in Peterborough Cathedral was found to be flagrant jerry-building as a criticism of the
Dean's sermons. For good or evil, we have made a synthesis out
of the literature we call the Bible; and though the discovery
that there is a good deal of jerry-building in the Bible is interesting in its way, because everything about the Bible is interesting, it does not alter the synthesis very materially even for the
paleographers, and does not alter it at all for those who know
no more about modern paleography than Archbishop Ussher

did. I have therefore indicated little more of the discoveries than Archbishop Ussher might have guessed for himself if he had read the Bible without prepossessions.

For the rest, I have taken the synthesis as it really lives and works in men. After all, a synthesis is what you want: it is the case you have to judge brought to an apprehensible issue for you. Even if you have little more respect for synthetic biography than for synthetic rubber, synthetic milk, and the still unachieved synthetic protoplasm which is to enable us to make different sorts of men as a pastrycook makes different sorts of tarts, the practical issue still lies as plainly before you as before the most credulous votaries of what pontificates as the Higher Criticism.

THE PERILS OF SALVATIONISM

The secular view of Jesus is powerfully reinforced by the increase in our day of the number of people who have had the means of educating and training themselves to the point at which they are not afraid to look facts in the face, even such terrifying facts as sin and death. The result is greater sternness in modern thought. The conviction is spreading that to encourage a man to believe that though his sins be as scarlet he can be made whiter than snow by an easy exercise of self-conceit, is to encourage him to be a rascal. It did not work so badly when you could also conscientiously assure him that if he let himself be caught napping in the matter of faith by death, a red-hot hell would roast him alive to all eternity. In those days a sudden death—the most enviable of all deaths—was regarded as the most frightful calamity. It was classed with plague, pestilence, and famine, battle and murder, in our prayers. But belief in that hell is fast vanishing. All the leaders of thought have lost it; and even for the rank and file it has fled to those parts of Ireland and Scotland which are still in the seventeenth century. Even there, it is tacitly reserved for the other fellow.

THE IMPORTANCE OF HELL IN THE
SALVATION SCHEME

The seriousness of throwing over hell whilst still clinging to the Atonement is obvious. If there is no punishment for sin there can be no self-forgiveness for it. If Christ paid our score, and if there is no hell and therefore no chance of our getting into trouble by forgetting the obligation, then we can be as wicked as we like with impunity inside the secular law, even from self-reproach, which becomes mere ingratitude to the Savior. On the other hand, if Christ did not pay our score, it still stands against us; and such debts make us extremely uncomfortable. The drive of evolution, which we call conscience and honor, seizes on such slips, and shames us to the dust for being so low in the scale as to be capable of them. The "saved" thief experiences an ecstatic happiness which can never come to the honest atheist: he is tempted to steal again to repeat the glorious sensation. But if the atheist steals he has no such happiness. He is a thief and knows that he is a thief. Nothing can rub that off him. He may try to soothe his shame by some sort of restitution or equivalent act of benevolence; but that does not alter the fact that he did steal; and his conscience will not be easy until he has conquered his will to steal and changed himself into an honest man by developing that divine spark within him which Jesus insisted on as the everyday reality of what the atheist denies.

Now though the state of the believers in the Atonement may thus be the happier, it is most certainly not more desirable from the point of view of the community. The fact that a believer is happier than a sceptic is no more to the point than the fact that a drunken man is happier than a sober one. The happiness of credulity is a cheap and dangerous quality of happiness, and by no means a necessity of life. Whether Socrates got as much happiness out of life as Wesley is an unanswerable question; but a nation of Socrateses would be much safer and happier than a nation of Wesleys; and its individuals would be higher in the evolutionary scale. At all events it is in the Socratic man and not in the Wesleyan that our hope lies now.

THE RIGHT TO REFUSE ATONEMENT

Consequently, even if it were mentally possible for all of us to believe in the Atonement, we should have to cry off it, as we evidently have a right to do. Every man to whom salvation is offered has an inalienable natural right to say "No, thank you: I prefer to retain my full moral responsibility: it is not good for me to be able to load a scapegoat with my sins: I should be less careful how I committed them if I knew they would cost me nothing." Then, too, there is the attitude of Ibsen: that iron moralist to whom the whole scheme of salvation was only an ignoble attempt to cheat God; to get into heaven without paying the price. To be let off, to beg for and accept eternal life as a present instead of earning it, would be mean enough even if we accepted the contempt of the Power on whose pity we were trading; but to bargain for a crown of glory as well! that was too much for Ibsen: it provoked him to exclaim, "Your God is an old man whom you cheat," and to lash the deadened conscience of the nineteenth century back to life with a whip of scorpions.

THE TEACHING OF CHRISTIANITY

And there I must leave the matter to such choice as your nature allows you. The honest teacher who has to make known to a novice the facts about Christianity cannot in any essential regard, I think, put the facts otherwise than as I have put them. If children are to be delivered from the proselytizing atheist on the one hand, and the proselytizing nun in the convent school on the other, with all the other proselytizers that lie between them, they must not be burdened with idle controversies as to whether there was ever such a person as Jesus or not. When Hume said that Joshua's campaigns were impossible, Whately did not wrangle about it: he proved, on the same lines, that the campaigns of Napoleon were impossible. Only fictitious characters will stand Hume's sort of examination: nothing will ever make Edward the Confessor and St Louis as real to us as Don Quixote and Mr Pickwick. We must cut the controversy short by declaring that there is the same evidence for the existence of Jesus as for that of any other person of his time; and the fact that you may not believe everything Matthew tells you no more disproves the existence of Jesus than the fact that you do not believe everything Macaulay tells you disproves the existence of William III. The gospel narratives in the main give you a biography which is quite credible and accountable on purely secular grounds when you have trimmed off everything that Hume or Grimm or Rousseau or Huxley or any modern bishop could reject as fanciful. Without going further than this, you can become a follower of Jesus just as you can become a follower of Confucius or Lao Tse, and may therefore call yourself a Jesuist, or even a Christian, if you hold, as the strictest Secularist quite legitimately may, that all prophets are inspired, and all men with a mission, Christs.

The teacher of Christianity has then to make known to the child, first the song of John Barleycorn, with the fields and seasons as witness to its eternal truth. Then, as the child's mind matures, it can learn, as historical and psychological phenomena, the tradition of the scapegoat, the Redeemer, the Atonement, the Resurrection, the Second Coming, and how, in a world saturated with this tradition, Jesus has been largely accepted as the long expected and often prophesied Redeemer, the Messiah, *the* Christ. It is open to the child also to accept him. If the child is built like Gladstone, he will accept Jesus as his Savior, and Peter and John the Baptist as the Savior's revealer and forerunner respectively. If he is built like Huxley, he will take the secular view, in spite of all that a pious family can do to prevent him. The important thing now is that the Gladstones and Huxleys should no longer waste their time irrelevantly and ridiculously wrangling about the Gadarene swine, and that they should make up their minds as to the soundness of the secular doctrines of Jesus; for it is about these that they may come to blows in our own time.

CHRISTIANITY AND THE EMPIRE

Finally, let us ask why it is that the old superstitions have so suddenly lost countenance that although, to the utter disgrace of the nation's leaders and rulers, the laws by which persecutors can destroy or gag all freedom of thought and speech in these matters are still unrepealed and ready to the hand of our bigots and fanatics (quite recently a respectable shopkeeper was convicted of "blasphemy" for saying that if a modern girl accounted for an illicit pregnancy by saying she had conceived of the Holy Ghost, we should know what to think: a remark which would never have occurred to him had he been properly taught how the story was grafted on the gospel), yet somehow they are used only against poor men, and that only in a half-hearted way. When we consider that from the time when the first scholar ventured to whisper as a professional secret that the Pentateuch could not possibly have been written by Moses to the time within my own recollection when Bishop Colenso, for saying the same thing openly, was inhibited from preaching and actually excommunicated, eight centuries elapsed (the point at issue, though technically interesting to paleographers and historians, having no more bearing on human welfare than the controversy as to whether uncial or cursive is the older form of writing); yet now, within fifty years of Colenso's heresy, there is not a Churchman of any authority living, or an educated layman, who could without ridicule declare that Moses wrote the Pentateuch as Pascal wrote his Thoughts or D'Aubigny his History of the Reformation, or that St Jerome wrote the passage about the three witnesses in the Vulgate, or that there are less than three different accounts of the creation jumbled together in the book of Genesis. Now the maddest Progressive will hardly contend that our growth in wisdom and liberality has been greater in the last half century than in the sixteen half centuries preceding: indeed it would be easier to sustain the thesis that the last fifty years have witnessed a distinct reaction from Victorian Liberalism to Collectivism which has perceptibly strengthened the State Churches. Yet the fact remains that whereas Byron's Cain, published a century ago, is a leading case on the point that there is no copyright in a blasphemous book, the Salvation Army might now include it among its publications without shocking anyone.

I suggest that the causes which have produced this sudden clearing of the air include the transformation of many modern States, notably the old self-contained French Republic and the tight little Island of Britain, into empires which overflow the frontiers of all the Churches. In India, for example, there are less than four million Christians out of a population of three hundred and sixteen and a half millions. The King of England is the defender of the faith; but what faith is now *the* faith? The inhabitants of this island would, within the memory of persons still living, have claimed that their faith is surely *the* faith of God, and that all others are heathen. But we islanders are only forty-five millions; and if we count ourselves all as Christians, there are still seventy-seven and a quarter million Mahometans in the Empire. Add to these the Hindoos and Buddhists, Sikhs and Jains, whom I was taught in my childhood, by way of religious instruction, to regard as gross idolaters consigned to eternal perdition, but whose faith I can now be punished for disparaging by a provocative word, and you have a total of over three hundred and forty-two and a quarter million heretics to swamp our forty-five million Britons, of whom, by the way, only six thousand call themselves distinctively "disciples of Christ," the rest being members of the Church of England and other denominations whose discipleship is less emphatically affirmed. In short, the Englishman of today, instead of being, like the forefathers whose ideas he clings to, a subject of a State practically wholly Christian, is now crowded, and indeed considerably overcrowded, into a corner of an Empire in which the Christians are a mere eleven per cent of the population; so that the Nonconformist who allows his umbrella stand to be sold up rather than pay rates towards the support of a Church of England school, finds himself paying taxes not only to endow the Church of Rome in Malta, but to send Christians to prison for the blasphemy of offering Bibles for sale in the streets of Khartoum.

Turn to France, a country ten times more insular in its preoccupation with its own language, its own history, its own character, than we, who have always been explorers and colonizers and grumblers. This once self-centred nation is forty millions strong. The total population of the French Republic is about one hundred and fourteen millions. The French are not in our hopeless Christian minority of eleven per cent; but they are in a minority of thirty-five per cent, which is fairly conclusive. And, being a more logical people than we, they have officially abandoned Christianity and declared that the French State has no specific religion.

Neither has the British State, though it does not say so. No doubt there are many innocent people in England who take Charlemagne's view, and would, as a matter of course, offer our eighty-nine per cent of "pagans, I regret to say" the alternative of death or Christianity but for a vague impression that these lost ones are all being converted gradually by the missionaries. But no statesman can entertain such ludicrously parochial delusions. No English king or French president can possibly govern on the assumption that the theology of Peter and Paul, Luther and Calvin, has any objective validity, or that the Christ is more than the Buddha or Jehovah more than Krishna, or Jesus more or less human than Mahomet or Zoroaster or Confucius. He is actually compelled, in so far as he makes laws against blasphemy at all, to treat all the religions, including Christianity, as blasphemous when paraded before people who are not accustomed to them and do not want them. And even that is a concession to a mischievous intolerance which an empire should use its control of education to eradicate.

On the other hand, Governments cannot really divest themselves of religion, or even of dogma. When Jesus said that people should not only live but live more abundantly, he was dogmatizing; and many Pessimist sages, including Shakespear, whose hero begged his friend to refrain from suicide in the words "Absent thee from felicity awhile," would say dogmatizing very perniciously. Indeed many preachers and saints declare, some of them in the name of Jesus himself, that this world is a vale of tears, and that our lives had better be passed in sorrow and even in torment, as a preparation for a better life to come. Make these sad people comfortable; and they baffle you by putting on hair shirts.

None the less, Governments must proceed on dogmatic assumptions, whether they call them dogmas or not; and they must clearly be assumptions common enough to stamp those who reject them as eccentrics or lunatics. And the greater and more heterogeneous the population the commoner the assumptions must be. A Trappist monastery can be conducted on assumptions which would in twenty-four hours provoke the village at its gates to insurrection. That is because the monastery selects its people; and if a Trappist does not like it he can leave it. But a subject of the British Empire or the French Republic is not selected; and if he does not like it he must lump it; for emigration is practicable only within narrow limits, and seldom provides an effective remedy, all civilizations being now much alike.

To anyone capable of comprehending government at all it must be evident without argument that the set of fundamental assumptions drawn up in the thirty-nine articles or in the Westminster Confession are wildly impossible as political constitutions for modern empires. A personal profession of them by any person disposed to take such professions seriously would practically disqualify him for high imperial office. A Calvinist Viceroy of India and a Particular Baptist Secretary of State for Foreign Affairs would wreck the empire. The Stuarts wrecked even the tight little island which was the nucleus of the empire by their Scottish logic and theological dogma; and it may be sustained very plausibly that the alleged aptitude of the English for self-government, which is contradicted by every chapter of their history, is really only an incurable inaptitude for theology, and indeed for co-ordinated thought in any direction, which makes them equally impatient of systematic despotism and systematic good government: their history being that of a badly governed and accidentally free people (comparatively). Thus our success in colonizing, as far as it has not been produced by exterminating the natives, has been due to our indifference to the salvation of our subjects. Ireland is the exception which proves the rule; for Ireland, the standing instance of the inability of the English to colonize without extermination of natives, is also the one country under British rule in which the conquerors and colonizers proceeded on the assumption that their business was to establish Protestantism as well as to make money and thereby secure at least the lives of the unfortunate inhabitants out of whose labor it could be made. At this moment Ulster is refusing to accept fellow-citizenship with the other Irish provinces because the south believes in St Peter and Bossuet, and the north in St Paul and Calvin. Imagine the effect of trying to govern India or Egypt from Belfast or from the Vatican!

The position is perhaps graver for France than for England, because the sixty-five per cent of French subjects who are neither French nor Christian nor Modernist includes some thirty millions of negroes who are susceptible, and indeed highly susceptible, of conversion to those salvationist forms of pseudo-Christianity which have produced all the persecutions and religious wars of the last fifteen hundred years. When the late explorer Sir Henry Stanley told me of the emotional grip

which Christianity had over the Baganda tribes, and read me
their letters, which were exactly like medieval letters in their
literal faith and ever-present piety, I said "Can these men
handle a rifle?" To which Stanley replied with some scorn "Of
course they can, as well as any white man." Now at this moment
(1915) a vast European war is being waged, in which the French
are using Senegalese soldiers. I ask the French Government,
which, like our own Government, is deliberately leaving the
religious instruction of these negroes in the hands of missions
of Petrine Catholics and Pauline Calvinists, whether they have
considered the possibility of a new series of crusades, by ardent
African Salvationists, to rescue Paris from the grip of the modern scientific "infidel," and to raise the cry of "Back to the Apostles: back to Charlemagne!"

We are more fortunate in that an overwhelming majority of
our subjects are Hindoos, Mahometans, and Buddhists: that is,
they have, as a prophylactic against salvationist Christianity,
highly civilized religions of their own. Mahometanism, which
Napoleon at the end of his career classed as perhaps the best
popular religion for modern political use, might in some respects
have arisen as a reformed Christianity if Mahomet had had to
deal with a population of seventeenth-century Christians instead of Arabs who worshipped stones. As it is, men do not reject Mahomet for Calvin; and to offer a Hindoo so crude a
theology as ours in exchange for his own, or our Jewish canoni-
cal literature as an improvement on Hindoo scripture, is to offer
old lamps for older ones in a market where the oldest lamps,
like old furniture in England, are the most highly valued.

Yet, I repeat, government is impossible without a religion:
that is, without a body of common assumptions. The open mind
never acts: when we have done our utmost to arrive at a reasonable conclusion, we still, when we can reason and investigate
no more, must close our minds for the moment with a snap,
and act dogmatically on our conclusions. The man who waits
to make an entirely reasonable will dies intestate. A man so rea-

sonable as to have an open mind about theft and murder, or about the need for food and reproduction, might just as well be a fool and a scoundrel for any use he could be as a legislator or a State official. The modern pseudo-democratic statesman, who says that he is only in power to carry out the will of the people, and moves only as the cat jumps, is clearly a political and intellectual brigand. The rule of the negative man who has no convictions means in practice the rule of the positive mob. Freedom of conscience as Cromwell used the phrase is an excellent thing; nevertheless if any man had proposed to give effect to freedom of conscience as to cannibalism in England, Cromwell would have laid him by the heels almost as promptly as he would have laid a Roman Catholic, though in Fiji at the same moment he would have supported heartily the freedom of conscience of a vegetarian who disparaged the sacred diet of Long Pig.

Here then comes in the importance of the repudiation by Jesus of proselytism. His rule "Dont pull up the tares: sow the wheat: if you try to pull up the tares you will pull up the wheat with it" is the only possible rule for a statesman governing a modern empire, or a voter supporting such a statesman. There is nothing in the teaching of Jesus that cannot be assented to by a Brahman, a Mahometan, a Buddhist or a Jew, without any question of their conversion to Christianity. In some ways it is easier to reconcile a Mahometan to Jesus than a British parson, because the idea of a professional priest is unfamiliar and even monstrous to a Mahometan (the tourist who persists in asking who is the dean of St Sophia puzzles beyond words the sacristan who lends him a huge pair of slippers); and Jesus never suggested that his disciples should separate themselves from the laity: he picked them up by the wayside, where any man or woman might follow him. For priests he had not a civil word; and they showed their sense of his hostility by getting him killed as soon as possible. He was, in short, a thorough-going anti-Clerical. And though, as we have seen, it is only by political means that his doctrine can be put into practice, he not only never suggested a sectarian theocracy as a form of government, and would certainly have prophesied the downfall of the late President Kruger if he had survived to his time, but, when challenged, he refused to teach his disciples not to pay tribute to Caesar, admitting that Caesar, who presumably had the kingdom of heaven within him as much as any disciple, had his place in the scheme of things. Indeed the apostles made this an excuse for carrying subservience to the State to a pitch of idolatry that ended in the theory of the divine right of kings, and provoked men to cut kings' heads off to restore some sense of proportion in the matter. Jesus certainly did not consider the overthrow of the Roman empire or the substitution of a new ecclesiastical organization for the Jewish Church or for the priesthood of the Roman gods as part of his program. He said that God was better than Mammon; but he never said that Tweedledum was better than Tweedledee; and that is why it is now possible for British citizens and statesmen to follow Jesus, though they cannot possibly follow either Tweedledum or Tweedledee without bringing the empire down with a crash on their heads. And at that I must leave it.

LONDON, *December* 1915.

PROLOGUE

OVERTURE: forest sounds, roaring of lions, Christian hymn faintly.

A jungle path. A lion's roar, a melancholy suffering roar, comes from the jungle. It is repeated nearer. The lion limps from the jungle on three legs, holding up his right forepaw, in which a huge thorn sticks. He sits down and contemplates it. He licks it. He shakes it. He tries to extract it by scraping it along the ground, and hurts himself worse. He roars piteously. He licks it again. Tears drop from his eyes. He limps painfully off the path and lies down under the trees, exhausted with pain. Heaving a long sigh, like wind in a trombone, he goes to sleep.

Androcles and his wife Megaera come along the path. He is a small, thin, ridiculous little man who might be any age from thirty to fifty-five. He has sandy hair, watery compassionate blue eyes, sensitive nostrils, and a very presentable forehead; but his good points go no further: his arms and legs and back, though wiry of their kind, look shrivelled and starved. He carries a big bundle, is very poorly clad, and seems tired and hungry.

His wife is a rather handsome pampered slattern, well fed and in the prime of life. She has nothing to carry, and has a stout stick to help her along.

MEGAERA (*suddenly throwing down her stick*) I wont go another step.

ANDROCLES (*pleading wearily*) Oh, not again, dear. Whats the good of stopping every two miles and saying you wont go another step? We must get on to the next village before night. There are wild beasts in this wood: lions, they say.

MEGAERA. I dont believe a word of it. You are always threat-

429

ening me with wild beasts to make me walk the very soul out
of my body when I can hardly drag one foot before another.
We havnt seen a single lion yet.

ANDROCLES. Well, dear, do you want to see one?

MEGAERA (*tearing the bundle from his back*) You cruel
brute, you dont care how tired I am, or what becomes of me
(*she throws the bundle on the ground*): always thinking of
yourself. Self! self! self! always yourself! (*She sits down on the
bundle*).

ANDROCLES (*sitting down sadly on the ground with his elbows on his knees and his head in his hands*) We all have to
think of ourselves occasionally, dear.

MEGAERA. A man ought to think of his wife sometimes.

ANDROCLES. He cant always help it, dear. You make me think
of you a good deal. Not that I blame you.

MEGAERA. Blame me! I should think not indeed. Is it my
fault that I'm married to you?

ANDROCLES. No, dear: that is my fault.

MEGAERA. Thats a nice thing to say to me. Arnt you happy
with me?

ANDROCLES. I dont complain, my love.

MEGAERA. You ought to be ashamed of yourself.

ANDROCLES. I am, my dear.

MEGAERA. Youre not: you glory in it.

ANDROCLES. In what, darling?

MEGAERA. In everything. In making me a slave, and making
yourself a laughing-stock. It's not fair. You get me the name
of being a shrew with your meek ways, always talking as if
butter wouldnt melt in your mouth. And just because I look a
big strong woman, and because I'm goodhearted and a bit
hasty, and because youre always driving me to do things I'm
sorry for afterwards, people say "Poor man: what a life his wife
leads him!" Oh, if they only knew! And you think I dont know.
But I do, I do, (*screaming*) I do.

ANDROCLES. Yes, my dear: I know you do.

MEGAERA. Then why dont you treat me properly and be a good husband to me?

ANDROCLES. What can I do, my dear?

MEGAERA. What can you do! You can return to your duty, and come back to your home and your friends, and sacrifice to the gods as all respectable people do, instead of having us hunted out of house and home for being dirty disreputable blaspheming atheists.

ANDROCLES. I'm not an atheist, dear: I am a Christian.

MEGAERA. Well, isnt that the same thing, only ten times worse? Everybody knows that the Christians are the very lowest of the low.

ANDROCLES. Just like us, dear.

MEGAERA. Speak for yourself. Dont you dare to compare me to common people. My father owned his own public-house; and sorrowful was the day for me when you first came drinking in our bar.

ANDROCLES. I confess I was addicted to it, dear. But I gave it up when I became a Christian.

MEGAERA. Youd much better have remained a drunkard. I can forgive a man being addicted to drink: it's only natural; and I dont deny I like a drop myself sometimes. What I cant stand is your being addicted to Christianity. And whats worse again, your being addicted to animals. How is any woman to keep her house clean when you bring in every stray cat and lost cur and lame duck in the whole countryside? You took the bread out of my mouth to feed them: you know you did: dont attempt to deny it.

ANDROCLES. Only when they were hungry and you were getting too stout, dearie.

MEGAERA. Yes: insult me, do. (*Rising*) Oh! I wont bear it another moment. You used to sit and talk to those dumb brute beasts for hours, when you hadnt a word for me.

ANDROCLES. They never answered back, darling. (*He rises and again shoulders the bundle*).

MEGAERA. Well, if youre fonder of animals than of your own wife, you can live with them here in the jungle. Ive had enough of you. I'm going back. I'm going home.

ANDROCLES (*barring the way back*) No, dearie: dont take on like that. We cant go back. Weve sold everything: we should starve; and I should be sent to Rome and thrown to the lions—

MEGAERA. Serve you right! I wish the lions joy of you. (*Screaming*) Are you going to get out of my way and let me go home?

ANDROCLES. No, dear—

MEGAERA. Then I'll make my way through the forest; and when I'm eaten by the wild beasts youll know what a wife youve lost. (*She dashes into the jungle and nearly falls over the sleeping lion*). Oh! oh! Andy! Andy! (*She totters back and collapses into the arms of Androcles, who, crushed by her weight, falls on his bundle*).

ANDROCLES (*extracting himself from beneath her and slapping her hands in great anxiety*) What is it, my precious, my pet? Whats the matter? (*He raises her head. Speechless with terror, she points in the direction of the sleeping lion. He steals cautiously towards the spot indicated by Megaera. She rises with an effort and totters after him*).

MEGAERA. No, Andy: youll be killed. Come back.

The lion utters a long snoring sigh. Androcles sees the lion, and recoils fainting into the arms of Megaera, who falls back on the bundle. They roll apart and lie staring in terror at one another. The lion is heard groaning heavily in the jungle.

ANDROCLES (*whispering*) Did you see? A lion.

MEGAERA (*despairing*) The gods have sent him to punish us because youre a Christian. Take me away, Andy. Save me.

ANDROCLES (*rising*) Meggy: theres one chance for you. Itll take him pretty nigh twenty minutes to eat me (I'm rather stringy and tough) and you can escape in less time than that.

MEGAERA. Oh, dont talk about eating. (*The lion rises with a great groan and limps towards them*). Oh! (*She faints*).

ANDROCLES (*quaking, but keeping between the lion and Megaera*) Dont you come near my wife, do you hear? (*The lion groans. Androcles can hardly stand for trembling*). Meggy: run. Run for your life. If I take my eye off him, it's all up. (*The lion holds up his wounded paw and flaps it piteously before Androcles*). Oh, he's lame, poor old chap! He's got a thorn in his paw. A frightfully big thorn. (*Full of sympathy*) Oh, poor old man! Did um get an awful thorn into um's tootsums wootsums? Has it made um too sick to eat a nice little Christian man for um's breakfast? Oh, a nice little Christian man will get um's thorn out for um; and then um shall eat the nice Christian man and the nice Christian man's nice big tender wifey pifey. (*The lion responds by moans of self-pity*). Yes, yes, yes, yes, yes. Now, now (*taking the paw in his hand*), um is not to bite and not to scratch, not even if it hurts a very very little. Now make velvet paws. Thats right. (*He pulls gingerly at the thorn. The lion, with an angry yell of pain, jerks back his paw so abruptly that Androcles is thrown on his back*). Steadeee! Oh, did the nasty cruel little Christian man hurt the sore paw? (*The lion moans assentingly but apologetically*). Well, one more little pull and it will be all over. Just one little, little, leetle pull; and then um will live happily ever after. (*He gives the thorn another pull. The lion roars and snaps his jaws with a terrifying clash*). Oh, mustnt frighten um's good kind doctor, um's affectionate nursey. That didnt hurt at all: not a bit. Just one more. Just to shew how the brave big lion can bear pain, not like the little crybaby Christian man. Oopsh! (*The thorn comes out. The lion yells with pain, and shakes his paw wildly*). Thats it! (*Holding up the thorn*). Now it's out. Now lick um's paw to take away the nasty inflammation. See? (*He licks his own hand. The lion nods intelligently and licks his paw industriously*). Clever little lionypiony! Understands um's dear old friend Andy Wandy. (*The lion licks his face*). Yes, kissums Andy Wandy. (*The lion, wagging his tail violently, rises on his hind legs, and embraces*

Androcles, who makes a wry face and cries) Velvet paws! Velvet paws! (*The lion draws in his claws*). Thats right. (*He embraces the lion, who finally takes the end of his tail in one paw, places that tight round Androcles' waist, resting it on his hip. Androcles takes the other paw in his hand, stretches out his arm, and the two waltz rapturously round and round and finally away through the jungle*).

MEGAERA (*who has revived during the waltz*) Oh, you coward, you havnt danced with me for years; and now you go off dancing with a great brute beast that you havnt known for ten minutes and that wants to eat your own wife. Coward! Coward! Coward (*She rushes off after them into the jungle*).

ACT I

EVENING. The end of three converging roads to Rome. Three triumphal arches span them where they debouch on a square at the gate of the city. Looking north through the arches one can see the campagna threaded by the three long dusty tracks. On the east and west sides of the square are long stone benches. An old beggar sits on the east side, his bowl at his feet.

Through the eastern arch a squad of Roman soldiers tramps along escorting a batch of Christian prisoners of both sexes and all ages, among them one Lavinia, a good-looking resolute young woman, apparently of higher social standing than her fellow-prisoners. A centurion, carrying his vinewood cudgel, trudges alongside the squad, on its right, in command of it. All are tired and dusty; but the soldiers are dogged and indifferent, the Christians lighthearted and determined to treat their hardships as a joke and encourage one another.

A bugle is heard far behind on the road, where the rest of the cohort is following.

CENTURION (*stopping*) Halt! Orders from the Captain. (*They halt and wait*). Now then, you Christians, none of your larks. The Captain's coming. Mind you behave yourselves. No singing. Look respectful. Look serious, if youre capable of it. See that big building over there! Thats the Coliseum. Thats where youll be thrown to the lions or set to fight the gladiators presently. Think of that; and itll help you to behave properly before the Captain. (*The Captain arrives*). Attention! Salute! (*The soldiers salute*).

A CHRISTIAN (*cheerfully*) God bless you, Captain!

THE CENTURION (*scandalized*) Silence!

The Captain, a patrician, handsome, about thirty-five, very cold and distinguished, very superior and authoritative, steps up on a stone seat at the west side of the square, behind the centurion, so as to dominate the others more effectually.

THE CAPTAIN. Centurion.

THE CENTURION (*standing at attention and saluting*) Sir?

THE CAPTAIN (*speaking stiffly and officially*) You will remind your men, Centurion, that we are now entering Rome. You will instruct them that once inside the gates of Rome they are in the presence of the Emperor. You will make them understand that the lax discipline of the march cannot be permitted here. You will instruct them to shave every day, not every week. You will impress on them particularly that there must be an end to the profanity and blasphemy of singing Christian hymns on the march. I have to reprimand you, Centurion, for not only allowing this, but actually doing it yourself.

THE CENTURION (*apologetic*) The men march better, Captain.

THE CAPTAIN. No doubt. For that reason an exception is made in the case of the march called Onward Christian Soldiers. This may be sung, except when marching through the forum or within hearing of the Emperor's palace; but the words must be altered to "Throw them to the Lions."

The Christians burst into shrieks of uncontrollable laughter, to the great scandal of the Centurion.

CENTURION. Silence! Silen-n-n-n-nce! Wheres your behavior? Is that the way to listen to an officer? (*To the Captain*) Thats what we have to put up with from these Christians every day, sir. Theyre always laughing and joking something scandalous. Theyve no religion: thats how it is.

LAVINIA. But I think the Captain meant us to laugh, Centurion. It was so funny.

CENTURION. Youll find out how funny it is when youre thrown to the lions tomorrow. (*To the Captain, who looks displeased*) Beg pardon, Sir. (*To the Christians*) Silennnnce!

THE CAPTAIN. You are to instruct your men that all intimacy with Christian prisoners must now cease. The men have fallen into habits of dependence upon the prisoners, especially the female prisoners, for cooking, repairs to uniforms, writing letters, and advice in their private affairs. In a Roman soldier such dependence is inadmissible. Let me see no more of it whilst we are in the city. Further, your orders are that in addressing Christian prisoners, the manners and tone of your men must express abhorrence and contempt. Any shortcoming in this respect will be regarded as a breach of discipline. (*He turns to the prisoners*) Prisoners.

CENTURION (*fiercely*) Prisonerrrrrs! Tention! Silence!

THE CAPTAIN. I call your attention, prisoners, to the fact that you may be called on to appear in the Imperial Circus at any time from tomorrow onwards according to the requirements of the managers. I may inform you that as there is a shortage of Christians just now, you may expect to be called on very soon.

LAVINIA. What will they do to us, Captain?

CENTURION. Silence!

THE CAPTAIN. The women will be conducted into the arena with the wild beasts of the Imperial Menagerie, and will suffer the consequences. The men, if of an age to bear arms, will be given weapons to defend themselves, if they choose, against the Imperial Gladiators.

LAVINIA. Captain: is there no hope that this cruel persecution—

CENTURION (*shocked*) Silence! Hold your tongue, there. Persecution, indeed!

THE CAPTAIN (*unmoved and somewhat sardonic*) Persecution is not a term applicable to the acts of the Emperor. The Emperor is the Defender of the Faith. In throwing you to the lions he will be upholding the interests of religion in Rome. If you were to throw him to the lions, that would no doubt be persecution.

The Christians again laugh heartily.

CENTURION (*horrified*) Silence, I tell you! Keep silence there. Did anyone ever hear the like of this?

LAVINIA. Captain: there will be nobody to appreciate your jokes when we are gone.

THE CAPTAIN (*unshaken in his official delivery*) I call the attention of the female prisoner Lavinia to the fact that as the Emperor is a divine personage, her imputation of cruelty is not only treason, but sacrilege. I point out to her further that there is no foundation for the charge, as the Emperor does not desire that any prisoner should suffer; nor can any Christian be harmed save through his or her own obstinacy. All that is necessary is to sacrifice to the gods: a simple and convenient ceremony effected by dropping a pinch of incense on the altar, after which the prisoner is at once set free. Under such circumstances you have only your own perverse folly to blame if you suffer. I suggest to you that if you cannot burn a morsel of incense as a matter of conviction, you might at least do so as a matter of good taste, to avoid shocking the religious convictions of your fellow citizens. I am aware that these considerations do not weigh with Christians; but it is my duty to call your attention to them in order that you may have no ground for complaining of your treatment, or of accusing the Emperor of cruelty when he is shewing you the most signal clemency. Looked at from this point of view, every Christian who has perished in the arena has really committed suicide.

LAVINIA. Captain: your jokes are too grim. Do not think it is easy for us to die. Our faith makes life far stronger and more wonderful in us than when we walked in darkness and had nothing to live for. Death is harder for us than for you: the martyr's agony is as bitter as his triumph is glorious.

THE CAPTAIN (*rather troubled, addressing her personally and gravely*) A martyr, Lavinia, is a fool. Your death will prove nothing.

LAVINIA. Then why kill me?

THE CAPTAIN. I mean that truth, if there be any truth, needs no martyrs.

LAVINIA. No; but my faith, like your sword, needs testing. Can you test your sword except by staking your life on it?

THE CAPTAIN (*suddenly resuming his official tone*) I call the attention of the female prisoner to the fact that Christians are not allowed to draw the Emperor's officers into arguments and put questions to them for which the military regulations provide no answer. (*The Christians titter*).

LAVINIA. Captain: how c a n you?

THE CAPTAIN. I call the female prisoner's attention specially to the fact that four comfortable homes have been offered her by officers of this regiment, of which she can have her choice the moment she chooses to sacrifice as all wellbred Roman ladies do. I have no more to say to the prisoners.

CENTURION. Dismiss! But stay where you are.

THE CAPTAIN. Centurion: you will remain here with your men in charge of the prisoners until the arrival of three Christian prisoners in the custody of a cohort of the tenth legion. Among these prisoners you will particularly identify an armorer named Ferrovius, of dangerous character and great personal strength, and a Greek tailor reputed to be a sorcerer, by name Androcles. You will add the three to your charge here and march them all to the Coliseum, where you will deliver them into the custody of the master of the gladiators and take his receipt, countersigned by the keeper of the beasts and the acting manager. You understand your instructions?

CENTURION. Yes, sir.

THE CAPTAIN. Dismiss. (*He throws off his air of parade, and descends from his perch. The Centurion seats himself on it and prepares for a nap, whilst his men stand at ease. The Christians sit down on the west side of the square, glad to rest. Lavinia alone remains standing to speak to the Captain*).

LAVINIA. Captain: is this man who is to join us the famous

Ferrovius, who has made such wonderful conversions in the northern cities?

THE CAPTAIN. Yes. We are warned that he has the strength of an elephant and the temper of a mad bull. Also that he is stark mad. Not a model Christian, it would seem.

LAVINIA. You need not fear him if he is a Christian, Captain.

THE CAPTAIN (*coldly*) I shall not fear him in any case, Lavinia.

LAVINIA (*her eyes dancing*) How brave of you, Captain!

THE CAPTAIN. You are right: it was a silly thing to say. (*In a lower tone, humane and urgent*) Lavinia: do Christians know how to love?

LAVINIA (*composedly*) Yes, Captain: they love even their enemies.

THE CAPTAIN. Is that easy?

LAVINIA. Very easy, Captain, when their enemies are as handsome as you.

THE CAPTAIN. Lavinia: you are laughing at me.

LAVINIA. At you, Captain! Impossible.

THE CAPTAIN. Then you are flirting with me, which is worse. Dont be foolish.

LAVINIA. But such a very handsome captain.

THE CAPTAIN. Incorrigible! (*Urgently*) Listen to me. The men in that audience tomorrow will be the vilest of voluptuaries: men in whom the only passion excited by a beautiful woman is a lust to see her tortured and torn shieking limb from limb. It is a crime to gratify that passion. It is offering yourself for violation by the whole rabble of the streets and the riff-raff of the court at the same time. Why will you not choose rather a kindly love and an honorable alliance?

LAVINIA. They cannot violate my soul. I alone can do that by sacrificing to false gods.

THE CAPTAIN. Sacrifice then to the true God. What does his name matter? We call him Jupiter. The Greeks call him Zeus.

Call him what you will as you drop the incense on the altar flame: He will understand.

LAVINIA. No. I couldn't. That is the strange thing, Captain, that a little pinch of incense should make all that difference. Religion is such a great thing that when I meet really religious people we are friends at once, no matter what name we give to the divine will that made us and moves us. Oh, do you think that I, a woman, would quarrel with you for sacrificing to a woman god like Diana, if Diana meant to you what Christ means to me? No: we should kneel side by side before her altar like two children. But when men who believe neither in my god nor in their own—men who do not know the meaning of the word religion—when these men drag me to the foot of an iron statue that has become the symbol of the terror and darkness through which they walk, of their cruelty and greed, of their hatred of God and their oppression of man—when they ask me to pledge my soul before the people that this hideous idol is God, and that all this wickedness and falsehood is divine truth, I cannot do it, not if they could put a thousand cruel deaths on me. I tell you, it is physically impossible. Listen, Captain: did you ever try to catch a mouse in your hand? Once there was a dear little mouse that used to come out and play on my table as I was reading. I wanted to take him in my hand and caress him; and sometimes he got among my books so that he could not escape me when I stretched out my hand. And I did stretch out my hand; but it always came back in spite of me. I was not afraid of him in my heart; but my hand refused: it is not in the nature of my hand to touch a mouse. Well, Captain, if I took a pinch of incense in my hand and stretched it out over the altar fire, my hand would come back. My body would be true to my faith even if you could corrupt my mind. And all the time I should believe more in Diana than my persecutors have ever believed in anything. Can you understand that?

THE CAPTAIN (*simply*) Yes: I understand that. But my hand would not come back. The hand that holds the sword has been trained not to come back from anything but victory.

LAVINIA. Not even from death?

THE CAPTAIN. Least of all from death.

LAVINIA. Then I must not come back from death either. A woman has to be braver than a soldier.

THE CAPTAIN. Prouder, you mean.

LAVINIA (*startled*) Prouder! You call our courage pride!

THE CAPTAIN. There is no such thing as courage: there is only pride. You Christians are the proudest devils on earth.

LAVINIA (*hurt*) Pray God then my pride may never become a false pride. (*She turns away as if she did not wish to continue the conversation, but softens and says to him with a smile*) Thank you for trying to save me.

THE CAPTAIN. I knew it was no use; but one tries in spite of one's knowledge.

LAVINIA. Something stirs, even in the iron breast of a Roman soldier?

THE CAPTAIN. It will soon be iron again. I have seen many women die, and forgotten them in a week.

LAVINIA. Remember me for a fortnight, handsome Captain. I shall be watching you, perhaps.

THE CAPTAIN. From the skies? Do not deceive yourself, Lavinia. There is no future for you beyond the grave.

LAVINIA. What does that matter? Do you think I am only running away from the terrors of life into the comfort of heaven? If there were no future, or if the future were one of torment, I should have to go just the same. The hand of God is upon me.

THE CAPTAIN. Yes: when all is said, we are both patricians, Lavinia, and must die for our beliefs. Farewell. (*He offers her his hand. She takes it and presses it. He walks away, trim and calm. She looks after him for a moment, and cries a little as he disappears through the eastern arch. A trumpet-call is heard from the road through the western arch).*

CENTURION *(waking up and rising)* Cohort of the tenth with prisoners. Two file out with me to receive them. *(He goes out through the western arch, followed by four soldiers in two files).*

Lentulus and Metellus come into the square from the west side with a little retinue of servants. Both are young courtiers, dressed in the extremity of fashion. Lentulus is slender, fair-haired, epicene. Metellus is manly, compactly built, olive skinned, not a talker.

LENTULUS. Christians, by Jove! Lets chaff them.

METELLUS. Awful brutes. If you knew as much about them as I do you wouldnt want to chaff them. Leave them to the lions.

LENTULUS *(indicating Lavinia, who is still looking towards the arches after the Captain)* That woman's got a figure. *(He walks past her, staring at her invitingly; but she is preoccupied and is not conscious of him).* Do you turn the other cheek when they kiss you?

LAVINIA *(starting)* What?

LENTULUS. Do you turn the other cheek when they kiss you, fascinating Christian?

LAVINIA. Dont be foolish. *(To Metellus, who has remained on her right, so that she is between them)* Please dont let your friend behave like a cad before the soldiers. How are they to respect and obey patricians if they see them behaving like street boys? *(Sharply to Lentulus)* Pull yourself together, man. Hold your head up. Keep the corners of your mouth firm; and treat me respectfully. What do you take me for?

LENTULUS *(irresolutely)* Look here, you know: I—you—I—

LAVINIA. Stuff! Go about your business. *(She turns decisively away and sits down with her comrades, leaving him disconcerted).*

METELLUS. You didnt get much out of that. I told you they were brutes.

LENTULUS. Plucky little filly! I suppose she thinks I care. (*With an air of indifference he strolls with Metellus to the east side of the square, where they stand watching the return of the Centurion through the western arch with his men, escorting three prisoners: Ferrovius, Androcles, and Spintho. Ferrovius is a powerful, choleric man in the prime of life, with large nostrils, staring eyes, and a thick neck: a man whose sensibilities are keen and violent to the verge of madness. Spintho is a debauchee, the wreck of a good-looking man gone hopelessly to the bad. Androcles is overwhelmed with grief, and is restraining his tears with great difficulty*).

THE CENTURION (*to Lavinia*) Here are some pals for you. This little bit is Ferrovius that you talk so much about. (*Ferrovius turns on him threateningly. The Centurion holds up his left forefinger in admonition*). Now remember that youre a Christian, and that youve got to return good for evil. (*Ferrovius controls himself convulsively; moves away from temptation to the east side near Lentulus; clasps his hands in silent prayer; and throws himself on his knees*). Thats the way to manage them, eh! This fine fellow (*indicating Androcles, who comes to his left, and makes Lavinia a heart-broken salutation*) is a sorcerer. A Greek tailor, he is. A real sorcerer, too: no mistake about it. The tenth marches with a leopard at the head of the column. He made a pet of the leopard; and now he's crying at being parted from it. (*Androcles sniffs lamentably*). Aint you, old chap? Well, cheer up, we march with a Billy goat (*Androcles brightens up*) thats killed two leopards and ate a turkey-cock. You can have him for a pet if you like. (*Androcles, quite consoled, goes past the Centurion to Lavinia, and sits down contentedly on the ground on her left*). This dirty dog (*collaring Spintho*) is a real Christian. He mobs the temples, he does (*at each accusation he gives the neck of Spintho's tunic a twist*); he goes smashing things mad drunk, he does; he steals the gold vessels, he does; he assaults the priestesses, he does—yah! (*He flings Spintho into the middle of the group of prisoners*). Youre the sort that makes duty a pleasure, you are.

SPINTHO (*gasping*) Thats it: strangle me. Kick me. Beat me. Revile me. Our Lord was beaten and reviled. Thats my way to heaven. Every martyr goes to heaven, no matter what he's done. That is so, isnt it, brother?

CENTURION. Well, if youre going to heaven, I dont want to go there. I wouldnt be seen with you.

LENTULUS. Haw! Good! (*Indicating the kneeling Ferrovius*). Is this one of the turn-the-other-cheek gentlemen, Centurion?

CENTURION. Yes, sir. Lucky for you too, sir, if you want to take any liberties with him.

LENTULUS (*to Ferrovius*) You turn the other cheek when youre struck, I'm told.

FERROVIUS (*slowly turning his great eyes on him*) Yes, by the grace of God, I do, now.

LENTULUS. Not that youre a coward, of course; but out of pure piety.

FERROVIUS. I fear God more than man; at least I try to.

LENTULUS. Lets see. (*He strikes him on the cheek. Androcles makes a wild movement to rise and interfere; but Lavinia holds him down, watching Ferrovius intently. Ferrovius, without flinching, turns the other cheek. Lentulus, rather out of countenance, titters foolishly, and strikes him again feebly*). You know, I should feel ashamed if I let myself be struck like that, and took it lying down. But then I'm not a Christian: I'm a man. (*Ferrovius rises impressively and towers over him. Lentulus becomes white with terror; and a shade of green flickers in his cheek for a moment*).

FERROVIUS (*with the calm of a steam hammer*) I have not always been faithful. The first man who struck me as you have just struck me was a stronger man than you: he hit me harder than I expected. I was tempted and fell; and it was then that I first tasted bitter shame. I never had a happy moment after that until I had knelt and asked his forgiveness by his bedside in the hospital. (*Putting his hands on Lentulus's shoulders with paternal weight*). But now I have learnt to resist with a strength that is not my own. I am not ashamed now, nor angry.

LENTULUS (*uneasily*) Er—good evening. (*He tries to move away*).

FERROVIUS (*gripping his shoulders*) Oh, do not harden your heart, young man. Come: try for yourself whether our way is not better than yours. I will now strike you on one cheek; and you will turn the other and learn how much better you will feel than if you gave way to the promptings of anger. (*He holds him with one hand and clenches the other fist*).

LENTULUS. Centurion: I call on you to protect me.

CENTURION. You asked for it, sir. It's no business of ours. Youve had two whacks at him. Better pay him a trifle and square it that way.

LENTULUS. Yes, of course. (*To Ferrovius*) It was only a bit of fun, I assure you: I meant no harm. Here. (*He proffers a gold coin*).

FERROVIUS (*taking it and throwing it to the old beggar, who snatches it up eagerly, and hobbles off to spend it*) Give all thou hast to the poor. Come, friend: courage! I may hurt your body for a moment; but your soul will rejoice in the victory of the spirit over the flesh. (*He prepares to strike*).

ANDROCLES. Easy, Ferrovius, easy: you broke the last man's jaw.

Lentulus, with a moan of terror, attempts to fly; but Ferrovius holds him ruthlessly.

FERROVIUS. Yes; but I saved his soul. What matters a broken jaw?

LENTULUS. Dont touch me, do you hear? The law—

FERROVIUS. The law will throw me to the lions tomorrow: what worse could it do were I to slay you? Pray for strength; and it shall be given to you.

LENTULUS. Let me go. Your religion forbids you to strike me.

FERROVIUS. On the contrary, it commands me to strike you. How can you turn the other cheek, if you are not first struck on the one cheek?

LENTULUS (*almost in tears*) But I'm convinced already that what you said is quite right. I apologize for striking you.

FERROVIUS (*greatly pleased*) My son: have I softened your heart? Has the good seed fallen in a fruitful place? Are your feet turning towards a better path?

LENTULUS (*abjectly*) Yes, yes. Theres a great deal in what you say.

FERROVIUS (*radiant*) Join us. Come to the lions. Come to suffering and death.

LENTULUS (*falling on his knees and bursting into tears*) Oh, help me. Mother! mother!

FERROVIUS. These tears will water your soul and make it bring forth good fruit, my son. God has greatly blessed my efforts at conversion. Shall I tell you a miracle—yes, a miracle —wrought by me in Cappadocia? A young man—just such a one as you, with golden hair like yours—scoffed at and struck me as you scoffed at and struck me. I sat up all night with that youth wrestling for his soul; and in the morning not only was he a Christian, but his hair was as white as snow. (*Lentulus falls in a dead faint*). There, there: take him away. The spirit has overwrought him, poor lad. Carry him gently to his house; and leave the rest to heaven.

CENTURION. Take him home. (*The servants, intimidated, hastily carry him out. Metellus is about to follow when Ferrovius lays his hand on his shoulder*).

FERROVIUS. You are his friend, young man. You will see that he is taken safely home.

METELLUS (*with awestruck civility*) Certainly, sir. I shall do whatever you think best. Most happy to have made your acquaintance, I'm sure. You may depend on me. Good evening, sir.

FERROVIUS (*with unction*) The blessing of heaven upon you and him.

Metellus follows Lentulus. The Centurion returns to his seat to resume his interrupted nap. The deepest awe has settled on the spectators. Ferrovius, with a long sigh of happiness, goes to Lavinia, and offers her his hand.

LAVINIA (*taking it*) So that is how you convert people, Ferrovius.

FERROVIUS. Yes: there has been a blessing on my work in spite of my unworthiness and my backslidings—all through my wicked, devilish temper. This man—

ANDROCLES (*hastily*) Dont slap me on the back, brother. She knows you mean me.

FERROVIUS. How I wish I were weak like our brother here! for then I should perhaps be meek and gentle like him. And yet there seems to be a special providence that makes my trials less than his. I hear tales of the crowd scoffing and casting stones and reviling the brethren; but when I come, all this stops: my influence calms the passions of the mob: they listen to me in silence; and infidels are often converted by a straight heart-to-heart talk with me. Every day I feel happier, more confident. Every day lightens the load of the great terror.

LAVINIA. The great terror? What is that?

Ferrovius shakes his head and does not answer. He sits down beside her on her left, and buries his face in his hands in gloomy meditation.

ANDROCLES. Well, you see, sister, he's never quite sure of himself. Suppose at the last moment in the arena, with the gladiators there to fight him, one of them was to say anything to annoy him, he might forget himself and lay that gladiator out.

LAVINIA. That would be splendid.

FERROVIUS (*springing up in horror*) What!

ANDROCLES. Oh, sister!

FERROVIUS. Splendid to betray my master, like Peter! Splendid to act like any common blackguard in the day of my proving! Woman: you are no Christian. (*He moves away from her to the middle of the square, as if her neighborhood contaminated him*).

LAVINIA (*laughing*) You know, Ferrovius, I am not always a Christian. I dont think anybody is. There are moments when I forget all about it, and something comes out quite naturally, as it did then.

SPINTHO. What does it matter? If you die in the arena, youll be a martyr; and all martyrs go to haven, no matter what they have done. Thats so, isnt it, Ferrovius?

FERROVIUS. Yes: that is so, if we are faithful to the end.

LAVINIA. I'm not so sure.

SPINTHO. Dont say that. Thats blasphemy. Dont say that, I tell you. We shall be saved, no matter WHAT we do.

LAVINIA. Perhaps you men will all go into heaven bravely and in triumph, with your heads erect and golden trumpets sounding for you. But I am sure I shall only be allowed to squeeze myself in through a little crack in the gate after a great deal of begging. I am not good always: I have moments only.

SPINTHO. Youre talking nonsense, woman. I tell you, martyrdom pays all scores.

ANDROCLES. Well, let us hope so, brother, for your sake. Youve had a gay time, havnt you? with your raids on the temples. I cant help thinking that heaven will be very dull for a man of your temperament. (*Spintho snarls*). Dont be angry: I say it only to console you in case you should die in your bed tonight in the natural way. Theres a lot of plague about.

SPINTHO (*rising and running about in abject terror*) I never thought of that. Oh Lord, spare me to be martyred. Oh, what a thought to put into the mind of a brother! Oh, let me be martyred today, now. I shall die in the night and go to hell. Youre a sorcerer: youve put death into my mind. Oh, curse you, curse you! (*He tries to seize Androcles by the throat*).

FERROVIUS (*holding him in a grasp of iron*) Whats this, brother? Anger! Violence! Raising your hand to a brother Christian!

SPINTHO. It's easy for you. Youre strong. Your nerves are all right. But I'm full of disease. (*Ferrovius takes his hand from him with instinctive disgust*). Ive drunk all my nerves away. I shall have the horrors all night.

ANDROCLES (*sympathetic*) Oh, dont take on so, brother. We're all sinners.

SPINTHO (*snivelling, trying to feel consoled*) Yes: I daresay if the truth were known, youre all as bad as I am.

LAVINIA (*contemptuously*) Does that comfort you?

FERROVIUS (*sternly*) Pray, man, pray.

SPINTHO. Whats the good of praying? If we're martyred we shall go to heaven, shant we, whether we pray or not?

FERROVIUS. Whats that? Not pray! (*Seizing him again*) Pray this instant, you dog, you rotten hound, you slimy snake, you beastly goat, or—

SPINTHO. Yes: beat me: kick me. I forgive you: mind that.

FERROVIUS (*spurning him with loathing*) Yah! (*Spintho reels away and falls in front of Ferrovius*).

ANDROCLES (*reaching out and catching the skirt of Ferrovius's tunic*) Dear brother: if you wouldnt mind—just for my sake—

FERROVIUS. Well?

ANDROCLES. Dont call him by the names of the animals. Weve no right to. Ive had such friends in dogs. A pet snake is the best of company. I was nursed on goat's milk. Is it fair to them to call the like of him a dog or a snake or a goat?

FERROVIUS. I only meant that they have no souls.

ANDROCLES (*anxiously protesting*) Oh, believe me, they have. Just the same as you and me. I really dont think I could consent to go to heaven if I thought there were to be no animals there. Think of what they suffer here.

FERROVIUS. Thats true. Yes: that is just. They will have their share in heaven.

SPINTHO (*who has picked himself up and is sneaking past Ferrovius on his left, sneers derisively*)!!

FERROVIUS (*turning on him fiercely*) Whats that you say?

SPINTHO (*cowering*) Nothing.

FERROVIUS (*clenching his fist*) Do animals go to heaven or not?

SPINTHO. I never said they didnt.

FERROVIUS (*implacable*) Do they or do they not?

SPINTHO. They do: they do. (*Scrambling out of Ferrovius's reach*). Oh, curse you for frightening me!

A bugle call is heard.

CENTURION (*waking up*) Tention! Form as before. Now then, prisoners: up with you and trot along spry. (*The soldiers fall in. The Christians rise*).

A man with an ox goad comes running through the central arch.

THE OX DRIVER. Here, you soldiers! clear out of the way for the Emperor.

THE CENTURION. Emperor! Wheres the Emperor? You aint the Emperor, are you?

THE OX DRIVER. It's the menagerie service. My team of oxen is drawing the new lion to the Coliseum. You clear the road.

CENTURION. What! Go in after you in your dust, with half the town at the heels of you and your lion! Not likely. We go first.

THE OX DRIVER. The menagerie service is the Emperor's personal retinue. You clear out, I tell you.

CENTURION. You tell me, do you? Well, I'll tell you something. If the lion is menagerie service, the lion's dinner is menagerie service too. This (*pointing to the Christians*) is the lion's dinner. So back with you to your bullocks double quick; and learn your place. March. (*The soldiers start*). Now then, you Christians: step out there.

LAVINIA (*marching*) Come along, the rest of the dinner. I shall be the olives and anchovies.

ANOTHER CHRISTIAN (*laughing*) I shall be the soup.

ANOTHER. I shall be the fish.

ANOTHER. Ferrovius shall be the roast boar.

FERROVIUS (*heavily*) I see the joke. Yes, yes: I shall be the roast boar. Ha! ha! (*He laughs conscientiously and marches out with them*).

ANDROCLES (*following*) I shall be the mince pie. (*Each announcement is received with a louder laugh by all the rest as the joke catches on*).

CENTURION (*scandalized*) Silence! Have some sense of your situation. Is this the way for martyrs to behave? (*To Spintho, who is quaking and loitering*) I know what youll be at that dinner. Youll be the emetic. (*He shoves him rudely along*).

SPINTHO. It's too dreadful: I'm not fit to die.

CENTURION. Fitter than you are to live, you swine.

They pass from the square westward. The oxen, drawing a waggon with a great wooden cage and the lion in it, arrive through the central arch.

ACT II

BEHIND the Emperor's box at the Coliseum, where the performers assemble before entering the arena. In the middle a wide passage leading to the arena descends from the floor level under the imperial box. On both sides of this passage steps ascend to a landing at the back entrance to the box. The landing forms a bridge across the passage. At the entrance to the passage are two bronze mirrors, one on each side.

On the west side of this passage, on the right hand of anyone coming from the box and standing on the bridge, the martyrs are sitting on the steps. Lavinia is seated half-way up, thoughtful, trying to look death in the face. On her left Androcles consoles himself by nursing a cat. Ferrovius stands behind them, his eyes blazing, his figure stiff with intense resolution. At the foot of the steps crouches Spintho, with his head clutched in his hands, full of horror at the approach of martyrdom.

On the east side of the passage the gladiators are standing and sitting at ease, waiting, like the Christians, for their turn in the arena. One (Retiarius) is a nearly naked man with a net and a trident. Another (Secutor) is in armor with a sword. He carries a helmet with a barred visor. The editor of the gladiators sits on a chair a little apart from them.

The Call Boy enters from the passage.

THE CALL BOY. Number six. Retiarius versus Secutor.

The gladiator with the net picks it up. The gladiator with the helmet puts it on; and the two go into the arena, the net thrower taking out a little brush and arranging his hair as he goes, the other tightening his straps and shaking his shoulders loose. Both look at themselves in the mirrors before they enter the passage.

LAVINIA. Will they really kill one another?

SPINTHO. Yes, if the people turn down their thumbs.

THE EDITOR. You know nothing about it. The people indeed! Do you suppose we would kill a man worth perhaps fifty talents to please the riffraff? I should like to catch any of my men at it.

SPINTHO. I thought—

THE EDITOR (*contemptuously*) You thought! Who cares what you think? You u l l be killed all right enough.

SPINTHO (*groans and again hides his face*)!!!

LAVINIA. Then is nobody ever killed except us poor Christians?

THE EDITOR. If the vestal virgins turn down their thumbs, thats another matter. Theyre ladies of rank.

LAVINIA. Does the Emperor ever interfere?

THE EDITOR. Oh, yes: he turns his thumb up fast enough if the vestal virgins want to have one of his pet fighting men killed.

ANDROCLES. But dont they ever just only pretend to kill one another? Why shouldn't you pretend to die, and get dragged out as if you were dead; and then get up and go home, like an actor?

THE EDITOR. See here: you want to know too much. There will be no pretending about the new lion: let that be enough for you. He's hungry.

SPINTHO (*groaning with horror*) Oh, Lord! cant you stop talking about it? Isnt it bad enough for us without that?

ANDROCLES. I'm glad he's hungry. Not that I want him to suffer, poor chap! but then he'll enjoy eating me so much more. Theres a cheerful side to everything.

THE EDITOR (*rising and striding over to Androcles*) Here: dont you be obstinate. Come with me and drop the pinch of incense on the altar. Thats all you need do to be let off.

ANDROCLES. No: thank you very much indeed; but I really mustnt.

THE EDITOR. What! Not to save your life?

ANDROCLES. I'd rather not. I couldnt sacrifice to Diana: she's a huntress, you know, and kills things.

THE EDITOR. That dont matter. You can choose your own altar. Sacrifice to Jupiter: he likes animals: he turns himself into an animal when he goes off duty.

ANDROCLES. No: it's very kind of you; but I feel I cant save myself that way.

THE EDITOR. But I dont ask you to do it to save yourself: I ask you to do it to oblige me personally.

ANDROCLES (scrambling up in the greatest agitation) Oh, please dont say that. This is dreadful. You mean so kindly by me that it seems quite horrible to disoblige you. If you could arrange for me to sacrifice when theres nobody looking, I shouldnt mind. But I must go into the arena with the rest. My honor, you know.

THE EDITOR. Honor! The honor of a tailor?

ANDROCLES (apologetically) Well, perhaps honor is too strong an expression. Still, you know, I couldn't allow the tailors to get a bad name through me.

THE EDITOR. How much will you remember of all that when you smell the beast's breath and see his jaws opening to tear out your throat?

SPINTHO (rising with a yell of terror) I cant bear it. Wheres the altar? I'll sacrifice.

FERROVIUS. Dog of an apostate. Iscariot!

SPINTHO. I'll repent afterwards. I fully mean to die in the arena: I'll die a martyr and go to heaven; but not this time, not now, not until my nerves are better. Besides, I'm too young: I want to have just one more good time. (The gladiators laugh at him). Oh, will no one tell me where the altar is? (He dashes into the passage and vanishes).

ANDROCLES (to the Editor, pointing after Spintho) Brother: I cant do that, not even to oblige you. Dont ask me.

THE EDITOR. Well, if youre determined to die, I cant help you. But I wouldnt be put off by a swine like that.

FERROVIUS. Peace, peace: tempt him not. Get thee behind him, Satan.

THE EDITOR (*flushing with rage*) For two pins I'd take a turn in the arena myself today, and pay you out for daring to talk to me like that.

Ferrovius springs forward.

LAVINIA (*rising quickly and interposing*) Brother, brother: you forget.

FERROVIUS (*curbing himself by a mighty effort*) Oh, my temper, my wicked temper! (*To the Editor, as Lavinia sits down again, reassured*) Forgive me, brother. My heart was full of wrath: I should have been thinking of your dear precious soul.

THE EDITOR. Yah! (*He turns his back on Ferrovius contemptuously, and goes back to his seat*).

FERROVIUS (*continuing*) And I forgot it all: I thought of nothing but offering to fight you with one hand tied behind me.

THE EDITOR (*turning pugnaciously*) What!

FERROVIUS (*on the border line between zeal and ferocity*) Oh, dont give way to pride and wrath, brother. I could do it so easily. I could—

They are separated by the Menagerie Keeper, who rushes in from the passage, furious.

THE KEEPER. Heres a nice business! Who let that Christian out of here down to the dens when we were changing the lion into the cage next the arena?

THE EDITOR. Nobody let him. He let himself.

THE KEEPER. Well, the lion's ate him.

Consternation. The Christians rise, greatly agitated. The gladiators sit callously, but are highly amused. All speak or cry out or laugh at once. Tumult.

LAVINIA. Oh, poor wretch! FERROVIUS. The apostate has perished. Praise be to God's justice! ANDROCLES. The poor beast was starving. It couldn't help itself. THE CHRISTIANS. What! Ate him! How frightful! How terrible! Without a moment to repent! God be merciful to him, a sinner! Oh, I cant bear to think of it! In the midst of his sin! Horrible, horrible! THE EDITOR. Serve the rotter right! THE GLADIATORS. Just walked into it, he did. He's martyred all right enough. Good old lion! Old Jock doesnt like that: look at his face. Devil a better! The Emperor will laugh when he hears of it. I cant help smiling. Ha ha ha!!!!!

THE KEEPER. Now his appetite's taken off, he wont as much as look at another Christian for a week.

ANDROCLES. Couldnt you have saved him, brother?

THE KEEPER. Saved him! Saved him from a lion that I'd just got mad with hunger! a wild one that came out of the forest not four weeks ago! He bolted him before you could say Balbus.

LAVINIA (sitting down again) Poor Spintho! And it wont even count as martyrdom!

THE KEEPER. Serve him right! What call had he to walk down the throat of one of my lions before he was asked?

ANDROCLES. Perhaps the lion wont eat me now.

THE KEEPER. Yes: thats just like a Christian: think only of yourself! What am I to do? What am I to say to the Emperor when he sees one of my lions coming into the arena half asleep?

THE EDITOR. Say nothing. Give your old lion some bitters and a morsel of fried fish to wake up his appetite. (Laughter).

THE KEEPER. Yes: it's easy for you to talk; but—

THE EDITOR (scrambling to his feet) Sh! Attention there! The Emperor. (The Keeper bolts precipitately into the passage. The gladiators rise smartly and form into line).

The Emperor enters on the Christians' side, conversing with Metellus, and followed by his suite.

THE GLADIATORS. Hail, Caesar! those about to die salute thee.

CAESAR. Good morrow, friends.

Metellus shakes hands with the Editor, who accepts his condescension with bluff respect.

LAVINIA. Blessing, Caesar, and forgiveness!

CAESAR (*turning in some surprise at the salutation*) There is no forgiveness for Christianity.

LAVINIA. I did not mean that, Caesar. I mean that we forgive you.

METELLUS. An inconceivable liberty! Do you not know, woman, that the Emperor can do no wrong and therefore cannot be forgiven?

LAVINIA. I expect the Emperor knows better. Anyhow, we forgive him.

THE CHRISTIANS. Amen!

CAESAR. Metellus: you see now the disadvantage of too much severity. These people have no hope; therefore they have nothing to restrain them from saying what they like to me. They are almost as impertinent as the gladiators. Which is the Greek sorcerer?

ANDROCLES (*humbly touching his forelock*) Me, your Worship.

CAESAR. My Worship! Good! A new title. Well: what miracles can you perform?

ANDROCLES. I can cure warts by rubbing them with my tailor's chalk; and I can live with my wife without beating her.

CAESAR. Is that all?

ANDROCLES. You dont know her, Caesar, or you wouldnt say that.

CAESAR. Ah, well, my friend, we shall no doubt contrive a happy release for you. Which is Ferrovius?

FERROVIUS. I am he.

CAESAR. They tell me you can fight.

FERROVIUS. It is easy to fight. *I* can die, Caesar.

CAESAR. That is still easier, is it not?

FERROVIUS. Not to me, Caesar. Death comes hard to my flesh; and fighting comes very easily to my spirit (*beating his breast and lamenting*) Oh, sinner that I am! (*He throws himself down on the steps, deeply discouraged*).

CAESAR. Metellus: I should like to have this man in the Pretorian Guard.

METELLUS. I should not, Caesar. He looks a spoilsport. There are men in whose presence it is impossible to have any fun: men who are a sort of walking conscience. He would make us all uncomfortable.

CAESAR. For that reason, perhaps, it might be well to have him. An Emperor can hardly have too many consciences. (*To Ferrovius*) Listen, Ferrovius. (*Ferrovius shakes his head and will not look up*). You and your friends shall not be outnumbered today in the arena. You shall have arms; and there will be no more than one gladiator to each Christian. If you come out of the arena alive, I will consider favorably any request of yours, and give you a place in the Pretorian Guard. Even if the request be that no questions be asked about your faith I shall perhaps not refuse it.

FERROVIUS. I will not fight. I will die. Better stand with the archangels than with the Pretorian Guard.

CAESAR. I cannot believe that the archangels—whoever they may be—would not prefer to be recruited from the Pretorian Guard. However, as you please. Come: let us see the show.

As the Court ascends the steps, Secutor and Retiarius return from the arena through the passage: Secutor covered with dust and very angry: Retiarius grinning.

SECUTOR. Ha, the Emperor. Now we shall see. Caesar: I ask you whether it is fair for the Retiarius, instead of making a fair throw of his net at me, to swish it along the ground and throw the dust in my eyes, and then catch me when I'm blinded. If the vestals had not turned up their thumbs I should have been a dead man.

CAESAR (*halting on the stair*) There is nothing in the rules against it.

SECUTOR (*indignantly*) Caesar: is it a dirty trick or is it not?

CAESAR. It is a dusty one, my friend. (*Obsequious laughter*) Be on your guard next time.

SECUTOR. Let h i m be on his guard. Next time I'll throw my sword at his heels and strangle him with his own net before he can hop off. (*To the Retiarius*) You see if I dont. (*He goes out past the gladiators, sulky and furious*).

CAESAR (*to the chuckling Retiarius*). These tricks are not wise, my friend. The audience likes to see a dead man in all his beauty and splendor. If you smudge his face and spoil his armor they will shew their displeasure by not letting you kill him. And when your turn comes, they will remember it against you and turn their thumbs down.

THE RETIARIUS. Perhaps that is why I did it, Caesar. He bet me ten sesterces that he would vanquish me. If I had had to kill him I should not have had the money.

CAESAR (*indulgent, laughing*) You rogues: there is no end to your tricks. I'll dismiss you all and have elephants to fight. T h e y fight fairly. (*He goes up to his box, and knocks at it. It is opened from within by the Captain, who stands as on parade to let him pass*).

The Call Boy comes from the passage, followed by three attendants carrying respectively a bundle of swords, some helmets, and some breastplates and pieces of armor which they throw down in a heap.

THE CALL BOY. By your leave, Caesar. Number eleven! Gladiators and Christians!

Ferrovius springs up, ready for martyrdom. The other Christians take the summons as best they can, some joyful and brave, some patient and dignified, some tearful and helpless, some embracing one another with emotion. The Call Boy goes back into the passage.

CAESAR (*turning at the door of the box*) The hour has come, Ferrovius. I shall go into my box and see you killed, since you scorn the Pretorian Guard. (*He goes into the box. The Captains shuts the door, remaining inside with the Emperor. Metellus and the rest of the suite disperse to their seats. The Christians, led by Ferrovius, move towards the passage*).

LAVINIA (*to Ferrovius*) Farewell.

THE EDITOR. Steady there. You Christians have got to fight. Here! arm yourselves.

FERROVIUS (*picking up a sword*) I'll die sword in hand to shew people that I could fight if it were my Master's will, and that I could kill the man who kills me if I chose.

THE EDITOR. Put on that armor.

FERROVIUS. No armor.

THE EDITOR (*bullying him*) Do what youre told. Put on that armor.

FERROVIUS (*gripping the sword and looking dangerous*) I said, No armor.

THE EDITOR. And what am I to say when I am accused of sending a naked man in to fight my men in armor?

FERROVIUS. Say your prayers, brother; and have no fear of the princes of this world.

THE EDITOR. Tsha! You obstinate fool! (*He bites his lips irresolutely, not knowing exactly what to do*).

ANDROCLES (*to Ferrovius*) Farewell, brother, till we meet in the sweet by-and-by.

THE EDITOR (*to Androcles*) You are going too. Take a sword there; and put on any armor you can find to fit you.

ANDROCLES. No, really: I cant fight: I never could: I cant bring myself to dislike anyone enough. I'm to be thrown to the lions with the lady.

THE EDITOR. Then get out of the way and hold your noise. (*Androcles steps aside with cheerful docility*). Now then! Are you all ready there?

A trumpet is heard from the arena.

FERROVIUS (*starting convulsively*) Heaven give me strength!

THE EDITOR. Aha! That frightens you, does it?

FERROVIUS. Man: there is no terror like the terror of that sound to me. When I hear a trumpet or a drum or the clash of steel or the hum of the catapult as the great stone flies, fire runs through my veins: I feel my blood surge up hot behind my eyes: I must charge: I must strike: I must conquer: Caesar himself will not be safe in his imperial seat if once that spirit gets loose in me. Oh, brothers, pray! exhort me! remind me that if I raise my sword my honor falls and my Master is crucified afresh.

ANDROCLES. Just keep thinking how cruelly you might hurt the poor gladiators.

FERROVIUS. It does not hurt a man to kill him.

LAVINIA. Nothing but faith can save you.

FERROVIUS. Faith! Which faith? There are two faiths. There is our faith. And there is the warrior's faith, the faith in fighting, the faith that sees God in the sword. How if that faith should overwhelm me?

LAVINIA. You will find your real faith in the hour of trial.

FERROVIUS. That is what I fear. I know that I am a fighter. How can I feel sure that I am a Christian?

ANDROCLES. Throw away the sword, brother.

FERROVIUS. I cannot. It cleaves to my hand. I could as easily throw a woman I loved from my arms. (*Starting*) Who spoke that blasphemy? Not I.

LAVINIA. I cant help you, friend. I cant tell you not to save your own life. Something wilful in me wants to see you fight your way into heaven.

FERROVIUS. Ha!

ANDROCLES. But if you are going to give up our faith, brother, why not do it without hurting anybody? Dont fight them. Burn the incense.

FERROVIUS. Burn the incense! Never.

LAVINIA. This is only pride, Ferrovius.

FERROVIUS. O n l y pride! What is nobler than pride? (*Conscience stricken*) Oh, I'm steeped in sin. I'm proud of my pride.

LAVINIA. They say we Christians are the proudest devils on earth—that only the weak are meek. Oh, I am worse than you. I ought to send you to death; and I am tempting you.

ANDROCLES. Brother, brother: let t h e m rage and kill: let u s be brave and suffer. You must go as a lamb to the slaughter.

FERROVIUS. Aye, aye: that is right. Not as a lamb is slain by the butcher; but as a butcher might let himself be slain by a (*looking at the Editor*) by a silly ram whose head he could fetch off in one twist.

Before the Editor can retort, the Call Boy rushes up through the passage, and the Captain comes from the Emperor's box and descends the steps.

THE CALL BOY. In with you: into the arena. The stage is waiting.

THE CAPTAIN. The Emperor is waiting. (*To the Editor*) What are you dreaming of, man? Send your men in at once.

THE EDITOR. Yes, sir: it's these Christians hanging back.

FERROVIUS (*in a voice of thunder*) Liar!

THE EDITOR (*not heeding him*) March. (*The gladiators told off to fight with the Christians march down the passage*) Follow up there, you.

THE CHRISTIAN MEN AND WOMEN (*as they part*) Be steadfast, brother. Farewell. Hold up the faith, brother. Farewell. Go to glory, dearest. Farewell. Remember: we are praying for you. Farewell. Be strong, brother. Farewell. Dont forget that the divine love and our love surround you. Farewell. Nothing can hurt you: remember that, brother. Farewell. Eternal glory, dearest. Farewell.

THE EDITOR (*out of patience*) Shove them in, there.

The remaining gladiators and the Call Boy make a movement towards them.

FERROVIUS (*interposing*) Touch them, dogs; and we die here, and cheat the heathen of their spectacle. (*To his fellow Christians*) Brothers: the great moment has come. That passage is your hill to Calvary. Mount it bravely, but meekly; and remember! not a word of reproach, not a blow nor a struggle. Go. (*They go out through the passage. He turns to Lavinia*) Farewell.

LAVINIA. You forget: I must follow before you are cold.

FERROVIUS. It is true. Do not envy me because I pass before you to glory. (*He goes through the passage*).

THE EDITOR (*to the Call Boy*) Sickening work, this. Why cant they all be thrown to the lions? It's not a man's job. (*He throws himself moodily into his chair*).

The remaining gladiators go back to their former places indifferently. The Call Boy shrugs his shoulders and squats down at the entrance to the passage, near the Editor.

Lavinia and the Christian women sit down again, wrung with grief, some weeping silently, some praying, some calm and steadfast. Androcles sits down at Lavinia's feet. The Captain stands on the stairs, watching her curiously.

ANDROCLES. I'm glad I havnt to fight. That would really be an awful martyrdom. I a m lucky.

LAVINIA (*looking at him with a pang of remorse*) Androcles: burn the incense: youll be forgiven. Let my death atone for both. I feel as if I were killing you.

ANDROCLES. Dont think of me, sister. Think of yourself. That will keep your heart up.

The Captain laughs sardonically.

LAVINIA (*startled: she had forgotten his presence*) Are you there, handsome Captain? Have you come to see me die?

THE CAPTAIN (*coming to her side*) I am on duty with the Emperor, Lavinia.

LAVINIA. Is it part of your duty to laugh at us?

THE CAPTAIN. No: that is part of my private pleasure. Your friend here is a humorist. I laughed at his telling you to think of yourself to keep up your heart. *I* say, think of yourself and burn the incense.

LAVINIA. He is not a humorist: he was right. You ought to know that, Captain: you have been face to face with death.

THE CAPTAIN. Not with certain death, Lavinia. Only death in battle, which spares more men than death in bed. What you are facing is certain death. You have nothing left now but your faith in this craze of yours: this Christianity. Are your Christian fairy stories any truer than our stories about Jupiter and Diana, in which, I may tell you, I believe no more than the Emperor does, or any educated man in Rome?

LAVINIA. Captain: all that seems nothing to me now. I'll not say that death is a terrible thing; but I will say that it is so real a thing that when it comes close, all the imaginary things—all the stories, as you call them—fade into mere dreams beside that inexorable reality. I know now that I am not dying for stories or dreams. Did you hear of the dreadful thing that happened here while we were waiting?

THE CAPTAIN. I heard that one of your fellows bolted, and ran right into the jaws of the lion. I laughed. I still laugh.

LAVINIA. Then you dont understand what that meant?

THE CAPTAIN. It meant that the lion had a cur for his breakfast.

LAVINIA. It meant more than that, Captain. It meant that a man cannot die for a story and a dream. None of us believed the stories and the dreams more devoutly than poor Spintho; but he could not face the great reality. What he would have called my faith has been oozing away minute by minute whilst Ive been sitting here, with death coming nearer and nearer, with reality become realler and realler, with stories and dreams fading away into nothing.

THE CAPTAIN. Are you then going to die for nothing?

LAVINIA. Yes: that is the wonderful thing. It is since all the stories and dreams have gone that I have now no doubt at all that I must die for something greater than dreams or stories.

THE CAPTAIN. But for what?

LAVINIA. I dont know. If it were for anything small enough to know, it would be too small to die for. I think I'm going to die for God. Nothing else is real enough to die for.

THE CAPTAIN. What is God?

LAVINIA. When we know that, Captain, we shall be gods ourselves.

THE CAPTAIN. Lavinia: come down to earth. Burn the incense and marry me.

LAVINIA. Handsome Captain: would you marry me if I hauled down the flag in the day of battle and burnt the incense? Sons take after their mothers, you know. Do you want your son to be a coward?

THE CAPTAIN (*strongly moved*) By great Diana, I think I would strangle you if you gave in now.

LAVINIA (*putting her hand on the head of Androcles*) The hand of God is on us three, Captain.

THE CAPTAIN. What nonsense it all is! And what a monstrous thing that you should die for such nonsense, and that I should look on helplessly when my whole soul cries out against it! Die then if you must; but at least I can cut the Emperor's throat and then my own when I see your blood.

The Emperor throws open the door of his box angrily, and appears in wrath on the threshold. The Editor, the Call Boy, and the gladiators spring to their feet.

THE EMPEROR. The Christians will not fight; and your curs cannot get their blood up to attack them. It's all that fellow with the blazing eyes. Send for the whip. (*The Call Boy rushes out on the east side for the whip*). If that will not move them, bring the hot irons. The man is like a mountain. (*He returns angrily into the box and slams the door*).

The Call Boy returns with a man in a hideous Etruscan mask, carrying a whip. They both rush down the passage into the arena.

LAVINIA (*rising*) Oh, that is unworthy. Can they not kill him without dishonoring him?

ANDROCLES (*scrambling to his feet and running into the middle of the space between the staircase*) It's dreadful. Now I want to fight. I cant bear the sight of a whip. The only time I ever hit a man was when he lashed an old horse with a whip. It was terrible: I danced on his face when he was on the ground. He mustnt strike Ferrovius: I'll go into the arena and kill him first. (*He makes a wild dash into the passage. As he does so a great clamor is heard from the arena, ending in wild applause. The gladiators listen and look inquiringly at one another*).

THE EDITOR. Whats up now?

LAVINIA (*to the Captain*) What has happened, do you think?

THE CAPTAIN. What can happen? They are killing them, I suppose.

ANDROCLES (*running in through the passage, screaming with horror and hiding his eyes*)!!!

LAVINIA. Androcles, Androcles: whats the matter?

ANDROCLES. Oh dont ask me, dont ask me. Something too dreadful. Oh! (*He crouches by her and hides his face in her robe, sobbing*).

THE CALL BOY (*rushing through from the passage as before*) Ropes and hooks there! Ropes and hooks!

THE EDITOR. Well, need you excite yourself about it? (*Another burst of applause*).

Two slaves in Etruscan masks, with ropes and drag hooks, hurry in.

ONE OF THE SLAVES. How many dead?

THE CALL BOY. Six. (*The slave blows a whistle twice; and four more masked slaves rush through into the arena with the same apparatus*) And the basket. Bring the baskets (*The slave whistles three times, and runs through the passage with his companion*).

THE CAPTAIN. Who are the baskets for?

THE CALL BOY. For the whip. He's in pieces. Theyre all in pieces, more or less. (*Lavinia hides her face*).

Two more masked slaves come in with a basket and follow the others into the arena, as the Call Boy turns to the gladiators and exclaims, exhausted) Boys: he's killed the lot.

THE EMPEROR (*again bursting from his box, this time in an ecstasy of delight*) Where is he? Magnificent! He shall have a laurel crown.

Ferrovius, madly waving his bloodstained sword, rushes through the passage in despair, followed by his co-religionists, and by the menagerie keeper, who goes to the gladiators. The gladiators draw their swords nervously).

FERROVIUS. Lost! lost for ever! I have betrayed my Master. Cut off this right hand: it has offended. Ye have swords, my brethren: strike.

LAVINIA. No, no. What have you done, Ferrovius?

FERROVIUS. I know not; but there was blood behind my eyes; and theres blood on my sword. What does that mean?

THE EMPEROR (*enthusiastically, on the landing outside his box*) What does it mean? It means that you are the greatest man in Rome. It means that you shall have a laurel crown of gold. Superb fighter: I could almost yield you my throne. It is a record for my reign: I shall live in history. Once, in Domitian's time, a Gaul slew three men in the arena and gained his freedom. But when before has one naked man slain six armed men of the bravest and best? The persecution shall cease: if Christians can fight like this, I shall have none but Christians to fight for me. (*To the gladiators*) You are ordered to become Christians, you there: do you hear?

RETIARIUS. It is all one to us, Caesar. Had I been there with my net, the story would have been different.

THE CAPTAIN (*suddenly seizing Lavinia by the wrist and dragging her up the steps to the Emperor*) Caesar: this woman is the sister of Ferrovius. If she is thrown to the lions he will fret. He will lose weight; get out of condition—

THE EMPEROR. The lions? Nonsense! (*To Lavinia*) Madam: I am proud to have the honor of making your acquaintance. Your brother is the glory of Rome.

LAVINIA. But my friends here. Must they die?

THE EMPEROR. Die! Certainly not. There has never been the slightest idea of harming them. Ladies and gentlemen: you are all free. Pray go into the front of the house and enjoy the spectacle to which your brother has so splendidly contributed. Captain: oblige me by conducting them to the seats reserved for my personal friends.

THE MENAGERIE KEEPER. Caesar: I must have one Christian for the lion. The people have been promised it; and they will tear the decorations to bits if they are disappointed.

THE EMPEROR. True, true: we must have somebody for the new lion.

FERROVIUS. Throw me to him. Let the apostate perish.

THE EMPEROR. No, no: you would tear him in pieces, my friend; and we cannot afford to throw away lions as if they were mere slaves. But we must have somebody. This is really extremely awkward.

THE MENAGERIE KEEPER. Why not that little Greek chap? He's not a Christian: he's a sorcerer.

THE EMPEROR. The very thing: he will do very well.

THE CALL BOY (*issuing from the passage*) Number twelve. The Christian for the new lion.

ANDROCLES (*rising, and pulling himself sadly together*) Well, it was to be, after all.

LAVINIA. I'll go in his place, Caesar. Ask the Captain whether they do not like best to see a woman torn to pieces. He told me so yesterday.

THE EMPEROR. There is something in that: there is certainly something in that—if only I could feel sure that your brother would not fret.

ANDROCLES. No: I should never have another happy hour. No: on the faith of a Christian and the honor of a tailor, I accept the lot that has fallen on me. If my wife turns up, give her my love and say that my wish was that she should be happy with her next, poor fellow! Caesar: go to your box and see how a tailor can die. Make way for number twelve there. (*He marches out along the passage*).

The vast audience in the amphitheatre now sees the Emperor re-enter his box and take his place as Androcles, desperately frightened, but still marching with piteous devotion, emerges

*from the other end of the passage, and finds himself at the
focus of thousands of eager eyes. The lion's cage, with a heavy
portcullis grating, is on his left. The Emperor gives a signal.
A gong sounds. Androcles shivers at the sound; then falls on his
knees and prays. The grating rises with a clash. The lion
bounds into the arena. He rushes round frisking in his freedom. He sees Androcles. He stops; rises stiffly by straightening
his legs; stretches out his nose forward and his tail in a hori-
zontal line behind, like a pointer, and utters an appalling roar.
Androcles crouches and hides his face in his hands. The lion
gathers himself for a spring, swishing his tail to and fro through
the dust in an ecstasy of anticipation. Androcles throws up his
hands in supplication to heaven. The lion checks at the sight
of Androcles's face. He then steals towards him; smells him;
arches his back; purrs like a motor car; finally rubs himself
against Androcles, knocking him over. Androcles, supporting
himself on his wrist, looks affrightedly at the lion. The lion
limps on three paws, holding up the other as if it was wounded.
A flash of recognition lights up the face of Androcles. He flaps
his hand as if it had a thorn in it, and pretends to pull the
thorn out and to hurt himself. The lion nods repeatedly. Androcles holds out his hands to the lion, who gives him both
paws, which he shakes with enthusiasm. They embrace rapturously, finally waltz round the arena amid a sudden burst of
deafening applause, and out through the passage, the Emperor
watching them in breathless astonishment until they disappear,
when he rushes from his box and descends the steps in frantic
excitement.*

THE EMPEROR. My friends, an incredible! an amazing thing!
has happened. I can no longer doubt the truth of Christianity.
(*The Christians press to him joyfully*). This Christian sorcerer
—(*with a yell, he breaks off as he sees Androcles and the lion
emerge from the passage, waltzing. He bolts wildly up the
steps into his box, and slams the door. All, Christians and
gladiators alike, fly for their lives, the gladiators bolting into the*

arena, the others in all directions. The place is emptied with magical suddenness).

ANDROCLES (*naïvely*) Now I wonder why they all run away from us like that. (*The lion, combining a series of yawns, purrs, and roars, achieves something very like a laugh.*)

THE EMPEROR (*standing on a chair inside his box and looking over the wall*) Sorcerer: I command you to put that lion to death instantly. It is guilty of high treason. Your conduct is most disgra—(*the lion charges at him up the stairs*) Help! (*He disappears. The lion rears against the box; looks over the partition at him; and roars. The Emperor darts out through the door and down to Androcles, pursued by the lion.*)

ANDROCLES. Dont run away, sir: he cant help springing if you run. (*He seizes the Emperor and gets between him and the lion, who stops at once*). Dont be afraid of him.

THE EMPEROR. I am n o t afraid of him. (*The lion crouches, growling. The Emperor clutches Androcles*). Keep between us.

ANDROCLES. Never be afraid of animals, your worship: thats the great secret. He'll be as gentle as a lamb when he knows that you are his friend. Stand quite still; and smile; and let him smell you all over just to reassure him; for, you see, he's afraid of you; and he must examine you thoroughly before he gives you his confidence. (*To the lion*) Come now, Tommy; and speak nicely to the Emperor, the great good Emperor who has power to have all our heads cut off if we dont behave very v e r y respectfully to him.

The lion utters a fearful roar. The Emperor dashes madly up the steps, across the landing, and down again on the other side, with the lion in hot pursuit. Androcles rushes after the lion; overtakes him as he is descending; and throws himself on his back, trying to use his toes as a brake. Before he can stop him the lion gets hold of the trailing end of the Emperor's robe.

ANDROCLES. Oh bad wicked Tommy, to chase the Emperor like that! Let go the Emperor's robe at once, sir: wheres your manners? (*The lion growls and worries the robe*). Dont pull it away from him, your worship. He's only playing. Now I shall be really angry with you, Tommy, if you dont let go. (*The lion growls again*). I'll tell you what it is, sir: he thinks you and I are not friends.

THE EMPEROR (*trying to undo the clasp of his brooch*) Friends! You infernal scoundrel (*the lion growls*)—dont let him go. Curse this brooch! I cant get it loose.

ANDROCLES. We mustnt let him lash himself into a rage. You must shew him that you are my particular friend—if you will have the condescension. (*He seizes the Emperor's hands and shakes them cordially*). Look, Tommy: the nice Emperor is the dearest friend Andy Wandy has in the whole world: he loves him like a brother.

THE EMPEROR. You little brute, you damned filthy little dog of a Greek tailor: I'll have you burnt alive for daring to touch the divine person of the Emperor. (*The lion growls*).

ANDROCLES. Oh dont talk like that, sir. He understands every word you say: all animals do: they take it from the tone of your voice. (*The lion growls and lashes his tail*). I think he's going to spring at your worship. If you wouldnt mind saying something affectionate. (*The lion roars*).

THE EMPEROR (*shaking Androcles's hands frantically*) My dearest Mr Androcles, my sweetest friend, my long lost brother, come to my arms. (*He embraces Androcles*). Oh, what an abominable smell of garlic!

The lion lets go the robe and rolls over on his back, clasping his forepaws over one another coquettishly above his nose.

ANDROCLES. There! You see, your worship, a child might play with him now. See! (*He tickles the lion's belly. The lion wriggles ecstatically*). Come and pet him.

THE EMPEROR. I must conquer these unkingly terrors. Mind you dont go away from him, though. (*He pats the lion's chest*).

ANDROCLES. Oh, sir, how few men would have the courage to do that!

THE EMPEROR. Yes: it takes a bit of nerve. Let us have the Court in and frighten them. Is he safe, do you think?

ANDROCLES. Quite safe now, sir.

THE EMPEROR (*majestically*) What ho, there! All who are within hearing, return without fear. Caesar has tamed the lion. (*All the fugitives steal cautiously in. The menagerie keeper comes from the passage with other keepers armed with iron bars and tridents*). Take those things away. I have subdued the beast. (*He places his foot on it*).

FERROVIUS (*timidly approaching the Emperor and looking down with awe on the lion*) It is strange that I, who fear no man, should fear a lion.

THE CAPTAIN. Every man fears something, Ferrovius.

THE EMPEROR. How about the Pretorian Guard now?

FERROVIUS. In my youth I worshipped Mars, the God of War. I turned from him to serve the Christian god; but today the Christian god forsook me; and Mars overcame me and took back his own. The Christian god is not yet. He will come when Mars and I are dust; but meanwhile I must serve the gods that are, not the God that will be. Until then I accept service in the Guard, Caesar.

THE EMPEROR. Very wisely said. All really sensible men agree that the prudent course is to be neither bigoted in our attachment to the old nor rash and unpractical in keeping an open mind for the new, but to make the best of both dispensations.

THE CAPTAIN. What do you say, Lavinia? Will you too be prudent?

LAVINIA (*on the stairs*) No: I'll strive for the coming of the God who is not yet.

THE CAPTAIN. May I come and argue with you occasionally?

LAVINIA. Yes, handsome Captain: you may. (*He kisses her hand*).

THE EMPEROR. And now, my friends, though I do not, as you see, fear this lion, yet the strain of his presence is considerable; for none of us can feel quite sure what he will do next.

THE MENAGERIE KEEPER. Caesar: give us this Greek sorcerer to be a slave in the menagerie. He has a way with the beasts.

ANDROCLES (*distressed*) Not if they are in cages. They should not be kept in cages. They must be all let out.

THE EMPEROR. I give this sorcerer to be a slave to the first man who lays hands on him. (*The menagerie keepers and the gladiators rush for Androcles. The lion starts up and faces them. They surge back*). You see how magnanimous we Romans are, Androcles. We suffer you to go in peace.

ANDROCLES. I thank your worship. I thank you all, ladies and gentlemen. Come, Tommy. Whilst we stand together, no cage for you: no slavery for me. (*He goes out with the lion, everybody crowding away to give him as wide a berth as possible*).

*   *   *

In this play I have presented one of the Roman persecutions of the early Christians, not as the conflict of a false theology with a true, but as what all such persecutions essentially are: an attempt to suppress a propaganda that seemed to threaten the interests involved in the established law and order, organized and maintained in the name of religion and justice by politicians who are pure opportunist Have-and-Holders. People who are shewn by their inner light the possibility of a better world based on the demand of the spirit for a nobler and more abundant life, not for themselves at the expense of others, but for everybody, are naturally dreaded and therefore hated by the Have-and-Holders, who keep always in reserve two sure weapons against them. The first is a persecution effected by the provocation, organization, and arming of that herd instinct which makes men abhor all departures from custom, and, by the most cruel punishments and the wildest calumnies, force eccentric people to behave and profess exactly as other people do. The second is by leading the herd to war, which immediately and infallibly makes them forget everything, even their most cherished and hard won public liberties and private interests, in the irresistible surge of their pugnacity and the tense preoccupation of their terror.

There is no reason to believe that there was anything more in the Roman persecutions than this. The attitude of the Roman Emperor and the officers of his staff towards the opinions at issue were much the same as those of a modern British Home Secretary towards members of the lower middle classes when some pious policeman charges them with Bad Taste, technically called blasphemy: Bad Taste being a violation of Good Taste, which in such matters practically means Hypocrisy. The Home Secretary and the judges who try the case are usually far more sceptical and blasphemous than the poor men whom they persecute; and their professions of horror at the blunt utterance of their own opinions are revolting to those behind the scenes who have any genuine religious sensibility; but the thing is done because the governing classes, provided only the law against blasphemy is not applied to themselves, strongly approve of such persecution because it enables them to represent their own privileges as part of the religion of the country.

Therefore my martyrs are the martyrs of all time, and my persecutors the persecutors of all time. My Emperor, who has no sense of the value of common people's lives, and amuses himself with killing as carelessly as with sparing, is the sort of monster you can make of any silly-clever gentleman by idolizing him. We are still so easily imposed on by such idols that one of the leading pastors of the Free Churches in London denounced my play on the ground that my persecuting Emperor is a very fine fellow, and the persecuted Christians ridiculous. From which I conclude that a popular pulpit may be as perilous to a man's soul as an imperial throne.

All my articulate Christians, the reader will notice, have different enthusiasms, which they accept as the same religion only because it involves them in a common opposition to the official religion and consequently in a common doom. Androcles is a humanitarian naturalist, whose views surprise everybody. Lavinia, a clever and fearless freethinker, shocks the Pauline Ferrovius, who is comparatively stupid and conscience ridden. Spintho, the blackguardly debauchee, is presented as one of the typical Christians of that period on the authority of St Augustine, who seems to have come to the conclusion at one period of his development that most Christians were what we call wrong uns. No doubt he was to some extent right: I have had occasion often to point out that revolutionary movements attract those who are not good enough for established institutions as well as those who are too good for them.

But the most striking aspect of the play at this moment is the terrible topicality given it by the war. We were at peace when I pointed out, by the mouth of Ferrovius, the path of an honest man who finds out, when the trumpet sounds, that he cannot follow Jesus. Many years earlier, in The Devil's Disciple, I touched the same theme even more definitely, and shewed the minister throwing off his black coat for ever when he discovered, amid the thunder of the captains and the shouting, that he was a born fighter. Great numbers of our clergy have found themselves of late in the position of Ferrovius and Anthony Anderson. They have discovered that they hate not only their enemies but everyone who does not share their hatred, and that they want to fight and to force other people to fight. They have turned their churches into recruiting stations and their vestries into munition workshops. But it has never occurred to them to take off their black coats and say quite simply, "I find in the hour of trial that the Sermon on the Mount is tosh, and that I am not a Christian. I apologize for all the unpatriotic nonsense I have been preaching all these years. Have the goodness to give me a revolver and a commission in a regiment which has for its chaplain a priest of the god Mars: *my* God." Not a bit of it. They have stuck to their livings and served Mars in the name of Christ, to the scandal of all religious mankind. When the Archbishop of York behaved like a gentleman and the Head Master of Eton preached a Christian sermon, and were reviled by the rabble, the Martian parsons encouraged the rabble. For this they made no apologies or excuses, good or bad. They simply indulged their passions, just as they had always indulged their class prejudices and commercial interests, without troubling themselves for a moment as to whether they were Christians or not. They did not protest even when a body calling itself the Anti-German League (not having noticed, apparently, that it had been anticipated by the British Empire, the French Republic, and the Kingdoms of Italy, Japan, and Serbia) actually succeeded in closing a church at Forest Hill in which God was worshipped in the German language. One would have supposed that this grotesque outrage on the commonest decencies of religion would have provoked a remonstrance from even the worldliest bench of bishops. But no: apparently it seemed to the bishops as natural that the House of God should be looted when He allowed German to be spoken in it as that a baker's shop with a German name over the door should be pillaged. Their verdict was, in effect, "Serve God right, for creating the Germans!" The incident would have been impossible in a country where the Church was as powerful as the Church of England, had it had at the same time a spark of catholic as distinguished from tribal religion in it. As it is, the thing occurred; and as far as I have observed, the only people who gasped were the Freethinkers.

Thus we see that even among men who make a profession of religion the great majority are as Martian as the majority of their congregations. The average clergyman is an official who makes his living by christening babies, marrying adults, conducting a ritual, and making the best he can (when he has any conscience about it) of a certain routine of school superintendence, district visiting, and organization of almsgiving, which does not necessarily touch Christianity at any point except the point of the tongue. The exceptional or religious clergyman may

be an ardent Pauline salvationist, in which case his more cultivated parishioners dislike him, and say that he ought to have
joined the Methodists. Or he may be an artist expressing religious emotion without intellectual definition by means of poetry,
music, vestments, and architecture, also producing religious
ecstasy by physical expedients, such as fasts and vigils, in
which case he is denounced as a Ritualist. Or he may be either
a Unitarian Deist like Voltaire or Tom Paine, or the more modern sort of Anglican Theosophist to whom the Holy Ghost is
the Élan Vital of Bergson, and the Father and Son are an expression of the fact that our functions and aspects are manifold,
and that we are all sons and all either potential or actual parents, in which case he is strongly suspected by the straiter Salvationists of being little better than an Atheist. All these va-
rieties, you see, excite remark. They may be very popular with
their congregations; but they are regarded by the average man
as the freaks of the Church. The Church, like the society of
which it is an organ, is balanced and steadied by the great
Philistine mass above whom theology looms as a highly spoken
of and doubtless most important thing, like Greek Tragedy, or
classical music, or the higher mathematics, but who are very
glad when church is over and they can go home to lunch or
dinner, having in fact, for all practical purposes, no reasoned
convictions at all, and being equally ready to persecute a poor
Freethinker for saying that St James was not infallible, and to
send one of the Peculiar People to prison for being so very
peculiar as to take St James seriously.

In short, a Christian martyr was thrown to the lions not
because he was a Christian, but because he was a crank: that
is, an unusual sort of person. And multitudes of people, quite
as civilized and amiable as we, crowded to see the lions eat him
just as they now crowd the lion-house in the Zoo at feeding-
time, not because they really cared twopence about Diana or
Christ, or could have given you any intelligent or correct account of the things Diana and Christ stood against one another

for, but simply because they wanted to see a curious and exciting spectacle. You, dear reader, have probably run to see a fire; and if somebody came in now and told you that a lion was chasing a man down the street you would rush to the window. And if anyone were to say that you were as cruel as the people who let the lion loose on the man, you would be justly indignant. Now that we may no longer see a man hanged, we assemble outside the jail to see the black flag run up. That is our duller method of enjoying ourselves in the old Roman spirit. And if the Government decided to throw persons of unpopular or eccentric views to the lions in the Albert Hall or the Earl's Court stadium tomorrow, can you doubt that all the seats would be crammed, mostly by people who could not give you the most superficial account of the views in question. Much less unlikely things have happened. It is true that if such a revival does take place soon, the martyrs will not be members of heretical religious sects: they will be Peculiars, Anti-Vivisectionists, Flat-Earth men, scoffers at the laboratories, or infidels who refuse to kneel down when a procession of doctors goes by. But the lions will hurt them just as much, and the spectators will enjoy themselves just as much, as the Roman lions and spectators used to do.

It was currently reported in the Berlin newspapers that when Androcles was first performed in Berlin, the Crown Prince rose and left the house, unable to endure the (I hope) very clear and fair exposition of autocratic Imperialism given by the Roman captain to his Christian prisoners. No English Imperialist was intelligent and earnest enough to do the same in London. If the report is correct, I confirm the logic of the Crown Prince, and am glad to find myself so well understood. But I can assure him that the Empire which served for my model when I wrote Androcles was, as he is now finding to his cost, much nearer my home than the German one.